Advanced Smalltalk

JONATHAN PLETZKE

Wiley Computer Publishing

John Wiley & Sons, Inc.
New York • Chichester • Brisbane • Toronto • Singapore • Weinheim

Publisher: Katherine Schowalter
Editor: Theresa Hudson
Managing Editor: Micheline Frederick
Electronic Products, Associate Editor: Mike Green
Text Design & Composition: North Market Street Graphics

Designations used by companies to distinguish their products are often claimed as trademarks. In all instances where John Wiley & Sons, Inc., is aware of a claim, the product names appear in initial capital or ALL CAPITAL LETTERS. Readers, however, should contact the appropriate companies for more complete information regarding trademarks and registration.

The VisualAge logo is a trademark of the IBM Corporation; reproduced by permission. Reprinted by permission from VisualAge Smalltalk copyright 1996 by International Business Machines Corporation.
Tensegrity is copyright © 1993–1996, Polymorphic Software Inc.
Copyright ParcPlace-Digitalk, Inc. All Rights Reserved
Copyright 1996 Rational Software Corporation

This text is printed on acid-free paper.

This publication is designed to provide accurate and authoritative information in regard to the subject matter covered. It is sold with the understanding that the publisher is not engaged in rendering legal, accounting, or other professional service. If legal advice or other expert assistance is required, the services of a competent professional person should be sought.

Library of Congress Cataloging-in-Publication Data:
Pletzke, Jonathan.
    Advanced Smalltalk / Jonathan Pletzke.
      p.   cm.
    Includes index.
    ISBN 0-471-16350-3 (pbk. : alk. paper)
    1. Smalltalk (Computer program language)   I. Title.
QA76.73.S59P54   1996   96-28542
005.13'3—dc20   CIP

Printed in the United States of America
10 9 8 7 6 5 4 3 2 1

To Victoria

Acknowledgments

I am grateful to those who came before me and hope to be an inspiration to those that follow.

Thanks to:

Victoria Pletzke for all the graphics, reviewing, questioning, and patience. Chester, Linda, Adrienne, and Edith for putting up with me all these years.

Frank Cecere, Peter Coates, Paul Jasek, Dennis Kornbluh, Anthony Lander, Mike Mozeika, Joe Rosenholz, Dave Simmons for reviewing portions of the manuscript.

Eric Clayberg (ObjectShare), Steve Harris and Hal Hildebrand (Polymorphic), Nobuko Isomata (QKS), Craig Latta (Synopsis), Robert Reid, Doug Shaker (Smalltalk Store), Dave Simmons (QKS), Tom Thornbury (Dun & Bradstreet), First Class Software, Gemstone, IBM, ObjectPeople, ParcPlace-Digitalk, QKS, and VMark for products, ideas, and other good stuff.

Alan Kay, Dan Ingalls, Adele Goldberg, Kent Beck, Ward Cunningham, Ralph Johnson, Wilf LaLonde, John Pugh, David Robson, Jan Steinman, Paul White for contributions to the Smalltalk language, learning, and concepts.

Special thanks to contributors to the Smalltalk Archives (st.cs.uiuc.edu), and Ralph Johnson for hosting the site and allowing it to be included on the CD-ROM.

About the Author

Jonathan Pletzke is the president of the Technical Expertise Corporation, a small consulting and software company located in Morristown, NJ. He has worked extensively with all the major versions of Smalltalk, as well as C++, C, BASIC, Pascal, Assembly, and FORTRAN. Jonathan holds a degree in Electrical Engineering from the University of Maryland. He can be reached via email: jpletzke@sprynet.com, or 72603.563@compuserve.com.

C O N T E N T S

V

F O R E W O R D

I am honored to have been asked by Jon to write the foreword to this book. Jon and I met almost 15 years ago as members of an Atari-800 user group. We became friends and had frequent discussions on the computer industry and its evolution.

When I set out to build QKS' SmalltalkAgents as a next-generation Smalltalk, Jon and I had many discussions. This foreword is a brief attempt to capture some of the ideas and opinions we discussed, which are also represented in the goals for the QKS Smalltalk product, SmalltalkAgents. The goals and the resultant QKS product implementation were impacted in a number of areas by the discussions with Jon. Those conversations were also a key turning point in Jon's career because they were his introduction to the Smalltalk language and the business of using Smalltalk. Since then he has become an active player in the Smalltalk industry. He lives and breathes in the Smalltalk corporate consulting world.

The Smalltalk Jon saw when I first set out to build SmalltalkAgents was a far cry from the Smalltalk systems we see offered today. The requirements and expectations in the industry have changed, and Smalltalk has evolved into a right solution at the right time. As a language and an object system, it has come of age in the sense that the hardware and related software technologies have caught up and come into synch with the design and capabilities of Smalltalk. Smalltalk needed more resources than machines had in the '80s, but machines and operating systems have long since overcome these limitations, and now have room and power to spare.

When I first began working with Smalltalk, the commonly available computer CPU was too slow, had insufficient RAM, and the world was treating applications larger than a 320KB floppy as unrealistic. Five years of dramatic change leave me wondering where we will be in the next five years.

We now see common C/C++ applications running in 3 to 7MB of RAM and hoarding tens of megabytes of diskspace. The common CPU runs so fast that most software is bottlenecked by the speed of graphics and the system bus, not a program's logic or algorithmic calculations. The cost of disk drives has plummeted to make them unbelievably inexpensive. The standard RAM in a machine is 16MB, which, when combined with modern operating systems technology for virtual memory, means that memory is not the issue of a few years ago.

The Internet and the Future of Software Engineering

Recent years have seen the massive rise of the Internet phenomenon, and with its cresting wave the Java language has captured tremendous media attention and is often touted as the future for all software engineering. I often hear the mainstream pundits who took issue with Smalltalk's size and speed now rally around a new language with similar characteristics but with a C++ flavor to its mode of use in the development process.

What I think has been obscured by the media attention is that in the last five years there has been an important change in focus for software engineering. Most software production is now expected to be carried out in tool environments, such as Smalltalk, that deliver a smooth collective integration of a language or languages, a framework or suite of libraries and components, and a visual environment for fabricating the software. In this latter view of software development, the specific language is not center stage, only its characteristics as they enhance the "collective" tool environment.

It is not clear whether Java, which does not have an established development environment but rather stands on its own as a new language and a young evolving set of competing frameworks, has the same elements that make Smalltalk such a good language for scaleable client/server middleware and custom software solutions. Here are a few of my thoughts: Ease of use in any tool increases the accessibility to a broad audience; productivity plays to business concerns; robustness and the ability to evolve existing software is often considered essential; and componentization often eliminates the vast majority of the programming tasks of yesteryear.

There are clearly challenges facing developers today, and my comparison to the tools available has Smalltalk standing out as a successful solution to the engineering and business challenges of today's software industry.

Tools and Focusing on a Problem

Programmers want to focus on solving their specific programming problem. Tools should help. Ideally, they should work so well that they become an extension of the programmer, and not even register at the conscious level. Where they don't, the programmer should be empowered to make or obtain the necessary changes. In this regard, Smalltalk extends object-oriented philosophy to the entire development problem by making the development system and the application one integrated environment.

Smalltalk is a development environment where the moment the pre-fabricated application starts up it is "live" with objects that persist from the last time the environment was run. Smalltalk provides not only a prebuilt framework of classes and methods but also a live application composed of prebuilt objects. The development process becomes an interactive one of modification where cause-effect can be fluidly explored, and questions of design and use can be rapidly experimented with. This interactivity offers simplicity and consistency throughout the programming experience.

In the area of programmer effort and the expression of intent, the Smalltalk language is an excellent balance of expressiveness versus computer-aided support because the programmer is not burdened with the concerns of defining types for variables. This traditionally accepted bookkeeping requirement costs programmers much of their effort, yet serves little purpose in a fully object-oriented arena.

Construction and Wiring of Systems

The area where work is needed for every development system today is that of helping the developer manage the complexity of large frameworks and having the required knowledge to use them effectively and efficiently. This is perhaps the single most important challenge today, and I believe it is the reason we have seen such an emphasis on components and systems for wiring or scripting of components.

Smalltalk has taken on this challenge through tools for navigating and presenting frameworks and the contractual rules for using them. It has also embraced component technology by allowing the duality of component solutions and scaleable systems with complex interaction. Today we commonly see components built in Smalltalk, and we see Smalltalk applications making use of components built in languages such as C and C++.

Expertise

The pattern of "temporal knowledge" I see is that of an engineer needing to make short-term expert use of a specific subset of the object system. The measure of a good framework is how well the framework and its tools are organized to help engineers learn it or refresh their prior knowledge of it. Being able to become an expert in hours on a subsystem and then forget about it a day or so later is essential to the building and evolution of complex systems. This is the often forgotten portion of scaleability, and it is an area where I believe Smalltalk environments and methodologies succeed more often than other languages.

I use the label of "temporal expertise" to describe the problem of learning or knowing enough about some aspect "framework" to make effective use of it for developing a software solution and sharing that solution with a team of developers. I believe that leveraging Smalltalk's advantage of being able to trivially extend its development environment by integrating documentation tools and hypermedia into the environment is central to meeting the challenge capturing and recovering "temporal" design knowledge for frameworks and component interaction relationships.

Patterns

One of the other areas that has seen increased attention in the last few years is the emphasis on patterns in code design as a means of addressing the temporal expertise challenge and promoting reusable design. The undertone in each of these areas is the emphasis on design and the ease with which software engineers can learn a design, refresh their expertise on a design, or extend and modify a design for evolution and reuse.

Learning Smalltalk and Design Skills

Learning Smalltalk is often expressed as consisting of three phases. The first phase is learning to read and understand the statements in an arbitrary piece of Smalltalk source code. This phase begins within a few hours and with applied effort is typically well understood within a week.

The second phase is learning the standard classes and the basic concepts of object-oriented design within the context of the standard Smalltalk framework elements. This phase typically takes three to six months of applied effort to build a comfortable working base.

The third phase is much harder to measure or define. I like to express it as the point at which an engineer has acquired an instinctual level of understanding about Smalltalk development. This requires experience with a wide range of coding techniques, expertise in the implementation of a number of different solutions, as well as crossing over the hump of being able to lay out an entire design before coding.

The design issue is often religious, and there are different schools of thought with regard to methodologies, mentoring, and use of patterns. But whichever school of thought one adopts, the net result is that those Smalltalk developers who have mastered the third phase are among the most prolific and efficient developers of quality, reliable code available in the software engineering industry. This third phase takes one to two years to really master.

Interoperability: Enhancing Other Services and Being a Team Player

Perhaps the last and most important of the items on my list of issues for Smalltalk today is that of interoperability with other languages. This area not only includes the ability for Smalltalk to be user-interchangeable in an application or subsystem with C and C++ code, but, more important, that learning to use Smalltalk by those familiar with C and C++ programming be addressed. If Smalltalk is to succeed as a mainstream language, it is essential that the large base of existing developers have a measure of comfort that their skill set can be carried over when they make use of Smalltalk, or they simply will not adopt it as a language for development. If they don't adopt it, then they will denigrate it when they feel threatened with having to use it.

It is for this reason that during much of the evolution of Smalltalk it has had to tread the thin line between language cleanliness and the pragmatics of common use. Like the English language, computer languages (and their related tools and frameworks) are living languages, and they must evolve or they become dead languages.

I applaud the work presented in *Advanced Smalltalk* because I believe it to be one of the first books on Smalltalk that was designed with the experienced programmer in mind. It presents Smalltalk and how it can be used effectively for performing tasks that developers in the middleware world and the hardcore C/C++ worlds expect to carry out. It does so by comparing and contrasting the solutions provided by the various Smalltalk vendors, enabling the developer to make informed design decisions and helping the developer to reassure management and clients that Smalltalk code is cross-vendor portable when designed properly, while making clear that differentiation among the vendors also bears meaningful fruit for many solutions.

Dave Simmons

President and Chief Technical Officer,

Quasar Knowledge Systems, Inc.

P R E F A C E

This is the book I would have liked to buy a few years ago. There has been little available that answers many of the questions I've had about exploiting the
full functionality of Smalltalk. This book covers both applications programming and systems-level programming with examples, working programs,
and snippets of useful code. I am familiar with this area and have a set of my
own most useful routines that I have created over the past few years.

The purpose of this book is to take Smalltalkers beyond the basics.
Many Smalltalkers are familiar with one vendor's class library, including the
GUI and some SQL, but few know several vendors' offerings and the details
of the differences among vendors. In the book I cover:

- areas that result in the most frequently asked questions
- ways to work smarter and better
- some extremely useful areas that will improve office work
- some fun topics that are more advanced and seem to have a common
  thread among Smalltalkers.

I put the more conceptual and basic pieces at the beginning so that
you will be able to relate to the issues early and reap immediate benefits.
You will also be able to get started with the book away from the computer. Later, when at the computer, you can turn to the most useful chapters and pick among topics of the most interest personally. The fun stuff
is at the end because it tends to involve many concepts from the earlier
chapters, and is also the most advanced or difficult material. This should
indicate to you that you may wish to attempt examples in the previous
chapters before these final chapters, especially if you have trouble with
the code.

Each chapter has an introduction outlining its contents. The last item
is a summary providing a review of the chapter's contents. Hints and pro-

gramming examples are integrated into every possible place since these give the most direct value to you, the reader, and clearly represent concepts within Smalltalk. Code samples in Smalltalk are easily entered, expanded, and used without a complex compile cycle. This makes it easy to provide many diverse examples. Hints as to how to provide a better program, work better programming, and more are incorporated wherever possible, though these are fewer in number than the code samples.

Since this is an intermediate/advanced book, I assume that you have either gone through tutorials and written some basic programs in Smalltalk (without necessarily any other programming experience), or that you are familiar with the Smalltalk environment but do not know it well. You may be familiar with another object-oriented system with similar characteristics of Smalltalk like Lisp, Oberon, Dylan, or even C++, so I draw analogies wherever possible.

Every Smalltalk programmer needs as much good information as possible. You need routines for your personal toolbox, guidance to work smarter, and explanations and examples of how to create various types of applications. This is not intended to be a book that deals with Smalltalk in the same manner as Visual Basic. Although this is a popular comparison and may share part of the same market, there are significant differences that steer this book away from the same simplistic applications that Visual Basic addresses.

This book deals with many versions of the Smalltalk language, in both a general and specific manner. It is chocked full of useful code samples, good techniques, personal opinions, general advice, and accumulated knowledge from my personal programming experience. The depth and breadth of coverage for any particular version of Smalltalk may vary from one chapter to the next, as both features and my familiarity with them vary from vendor to vendor.

This book has been prepared as both a reference and an instructional manual. The approach is to cover the common coding issues between the major commercially available Smalltalk versions at the time of writing. Each version is offset by an icon which later appears at version-specific sections in the text. The Smalltalk environments covered are:

ParcPlace

VisualWorks for OS/2 V2.5
VisualWorks for Windows V2.5

Digitalk

Visual Smalltalk Enterprise for Windows V3.10

Visual Smalltalk Enterprise for OS/2 V3.10

VMARK

ObjectStudio for Windows V4.1

Synchrony for Windows V2.0

IBM

VisualAge Team for Windows V3.0

QKS

SmalltalkAgents for Macintosh 2.0.3

Other Smalltalk Environments Indirectly Covered

Smalltalk/X

Little Smalltalk

GNU Smalltalk

VisualWorks for Mac, UNIX/X/Motif

IBM Smalltalk for IBM Mainframes

Digitalk Smalltalk/V 2.0 for Windows, Mac, OS/2

Easel ObjectStudio(Enfin) for UNIX

OTI Smalltalk for embedded Applications (68K CPUs)

Overview of Chapters

Chapter 1, Smalltalk History and Concepts: A brief history of Smalltalk is presented, from origin to commercialization to the present day. Some of the key concepts of Smalltalk are summarized here.

Chapter 2, Style: This chapter covers many of the elements that contribute to a quality Smalltalk program. Topics include method style, class inheritance, system class changes, dynamic messaging, and documentation.

Chapter 3, Dependencies: The dependency mechanism allows one object to be notified when another object changes. This topic is covered with a description of how it works, how to use it, why to use it, and a reference to its use.

Chapter 4, Processes and Threads: A brief overview of the concepts of processes and threads and how they apply to parallel processing in Smalltalk is presented, followed by synchronization concepts, examples, and a reference to the thread-related classes.

Chapter 5, Exceptions: An exception handling system is provided in Smalltalk. This allows programs to handle exceptional events or data without producing an error or crashing. An overview of the concepts is presented, followed by in-depth analysis of each of the Smalltalk mechanisms, how to use them, and a reference.

Chapter 6, Methodology and Project Management: These days everyone is selling a methodology. They are all slightly different, take a long time to learn, and may not help you to be more productive immediately. A simple, get-it-done methodology is presented here, with references and comparisons to using a standard methodology. The entire project life cycle is discussed, with an emphasis throughout the chapter on the engineering of a system from "cradle to grave."

Chapter 7, Methodology Applied: A Personal Information Manager (PIM): An end-to-end example of designing and building an application in Smalltalk is presented here in brief form. A Personal Information Manager (PIM) is the target program, and the steps to deliver the application are discussed. The code for the PIM is also presented.

Chapter 8, Frameworks: Just what is a framework? And how is it different from a pattern? Answers to these questions and a few resources for learning more are presented here.

Chapter 9, Patterns: What is a pattern? How do you write one? Where can you find more? And where can you learn more? These questions are answered here.

Chapter 10, Smalltalk Bugs: Some of the biggest gotchas of Smalltalk programming are presented here, with some tips on avoiding them.

Chapter 11, Development Tricks: Here is a compilation of the most useful pieces of Smalltalk trickery that I have accumulated. It covers items like bookmarks, safe halting, and printing.

Chapter 12, Message Frequency: Ever wonder which methods are written the most when writing Smalltalk code? A statistics gathering program is written for five versions of Smalltalk, and the programs and the results are presented here.

Chapter 13, The Most Useful Methods: These are the most useful methods that could be gleaned from the vast set of hundreds of classes and thousands of methods. This is the short version and cheat-sheet for the class encyclopedia. See how many you use regularly, and those that you may have missed.

Chapter 14, Team Work: Nothing is more challenging than organizing a group of people to accomplish one task. Sometimes it may seem easier to part oceans or make the earth move, but here are some tips on how to work together using Smalltalk as the development language. Low-budget techniques are discussed, as well as the use of two of the leading team development tools: Team/V and ENVY.

Chapter 15, Profiling/Tuning: Ever wonder why you agree with non-Smalltalkers when they say Smalltalk is slow? Now you won't have to hide your face in shame once your programs have been souped up with some tuning tips. The steps necessary to identify program bottlenecks, with solutions to many problems are presented here. Many good techniques to write faster code the first time around are also presented.

Chapter 16, Application Delivery: One of the most puzzling concepts to new Smalltalk programmers is how to deliver a program once it is written. Many people are familiar with a "compile-link-deliver" cycle, so the switch to a "customize the running application" approach is uncertain. Issues and techniques to deliver your Smalltalk application to your customers are discussed, along with the process to do so in each of the Smalltalk versions.

Chapter 17, Primitives and External Code: It is nearly impossible to deliver a fully functional Smalltalk application without writing code outside the Smalltalk environment. Whether it is C or Assembly primitives or COBOL external code, integrating non-Smalltalk legacy code with your Smalltalk application is a common challenge with many pitfalls. Examples are provided for versions of Smalltalk for both primitives and external code calls, with a template file so that you can create your own code right away.

Chapter 18, SQL Databases: The majority of enterprise information is stored in databases, and whether they be flat files, hierarchical databases, or SQL databases, you need to be able to access this information in Smalltalk. Some of the approaches to storage and retrieval of database information are discussed, with relevant issues and a survey of available options. Also covered are data migration strategy, data security issues, and examples of accessing SQL databases from Smalltalk.

Chapter 19, External Storage and Persistent Objects: What happens when you need to store and retrieve data, but don't need to keep a legacy database (or can migrate the data), or have a new application that will be totally object-oriented? You can't expect each user to have a development license and save the image in order to store objects, so you make the objects persistent. Persistent objects are usually binary files or databases that keep objects alive when the application is not running. They take the form of source code that re-creates binary objects, file-based object storage (ObjectFiler, BOSS, PIPO, SOM), or object databases like Tensegrity, Gemstone, Versant, and so on. This chapter covers the strategies, products, and examples of how to effectively make your objects persistent.

Chapter 20, Internet and Web Applications: With all the hype and the ensuing product frenzy, Smalltalk is fast becoming a solution for complex Internet/Web-based applications. Transmission Control Protocol/Internet Protocol (TCP/IP) are the network protocols for communications, essential to working on the Internet. This chapter includes an overview of resources, the TCP/IP protocol, HyperText Transfer Protocol (HTTP), HyperText Markup Language (HTML), and examples of communications code, including sockets and an Internet Web server that will allow you to create Web aware applications today.

Chapter 21, Neural Networks: The notion of an artificial brain is very appealing. Neural networks are a step in this direction in that they "learn" the appropriate response to a stimulus through training, and then respond to the same and similar stimuli with the learned response. You will learn about neural networks, their uses, and the application of neural networks to Smalltalk applications. A functioning neural network program is included, and the details of its functionality are discussed.

Appendix A, Smalltalk Resources: Who, what, where, including: books, software, training, and user Groups.

Appendix B, Smalltalk Interview Questions: How do you qualify the Smalltalk developers on your project, especially when you are new to Smalltalk? Here are questions designed to promote an exchange of information relevant to Smalltalk development.

Appendix C, Class Hierarchy Comparisons: A class hierarchy listing for each of the major versions of Smalltalk serves as a quick reference when programming in the language.

Appendix D, ANSI Smalltalk Standard: The latest unofficial information for the ANSI Smalltalk standard is included here for your reference.

Appendix E, On the CD-ROM: A listing of the contents on the CD and how to get started with it.

Smalltalk History and Concepts

Introduction

In this chapter we will take a brief trip back in time to the origins of the Smalltalk programming language and environment. We will see where Smalltalk came from, who was involved, see some of the sights along the way, the birth of commercially available Smalltalk implementations, and end up with the current state of Smalltalk. A few programming terms that emerged from Smalltalk will be reviewed at the end of the chapter.

History

Predecessors

Smalltalk did not mysteriously appear on the scene out of thin air. The concepts and origins of Smalltalk were first seen in the late 1960s in the mind of Alan Kay. Alan had worked with a peculiar implementation of ALGOL, called Simula. This experience, along with Alan's work on other programming projects, led him to a new organization within Xerox: the Palo Alto Research Center (PARC). At PARC, Alan worked on concepts for programming that were directed toward enabling more people to create complex applications. This involved the vision of an iconic programming language that would be simple enough for children to program.

Smalltalk was the operating system on the Xerox Dynabook later known as the ALTO. The Dynabook was to be the computer for everyone: lightweight, portable, and easy to use. Alan finally realized much of this with the Macintosh and the Powerbook at Apple Computer when he left PARC to join Apple. Of course, Alan did not work alone. Dan Ingalls wrote approximately 80 major releases of Smalltalk from the '70s through the early '80s. Adele Goldberg, recently an executive at ParcPlace, was brought onto the Smalltalk project because of her work with children as users. The team was large, and contributions by others were many: music systems, overlapping windows, turtle graphics, even the development tools that we see in Smalltalk today. There were many releases of Smalltalk from PARC, but the most notable were Smalltalk-71, Smalltalk-72, Smalltalk-74 (Fast-Talk), and Smalltalk-76.

As work went on, it was apparent that learning the syntax of Smalltalk, a one-page or so description, was no problem. It was learning the design of systems in Smalltalk and the learning of the reuseable classes that took time. Today, the syntax is still easy, and the problem is with the complexity and richness of the solutions available. When comparing Smalltalk with C++, many people believe that learning Smalltalk is more difficult than C++. But they are comparing apples to oranges. Learning the Smalltalk syntax takes one day; learning the C++ syntax takes weeks. Learning the Smalltalk class library takes a lifetime; learning the C++ class library takes even longer.

In August 1981, an entire issue of *Byte* magazine was devoted to Smalltalk. These articles were the first major public showing of the Smalltalk system, and were received incredibly well. People are still in awe of Smalltalk today. This issue was followed by more details of the Smalltalk language in a series of books by Adele Goldberg and Dave Robson in 1983.

Commercialization

In order for mere mortals like myself to use Smalltalk, we did not study the available literature and build our own virtual machine. We looked to the marketplace for an available product that would provide Smalltalk for our personal computers. The first commercially available release of Smalltalk was from a company called Digitalk. It ran under MS-DOS on an IBM PC, and used character graphics to create a GUI-like environment. This product was called Methods (later Smalltalk/V-286 and Smalltalk/V-386) and has since been superseded by Smalltalk/V-Mac (now discontinued), Smalltalk/V Windows, and Smalltalk/V OS/2 (both now called Visual Smalltalk).

Adele Goldberg led the Xerox spinoff called ParcPlace Systems, followed with the release of Smalltalk-80, renamed to Objectworks/Smalltalk (when they added C++ to the product line), and finally renamed to Visual-Works (after dropping C++). ParcPlace and Digitalk have now merged, and will have a combined product, yet to be named in the near future.

The United States wasn't the only place that Smalltalk was being created. In Canada, a company called Object Technology International (purchased by IBM in 1996), was creating its own version of Smalltalk. This product was made available on Motorola-embedded systems including real-time operating systems like VX-Works (on a VME-BUS).

Enfin Smalltalk was created as a quasi-Smalltalk environment that would be easier to learn and more familiar to C programmers. It originally had a language syntax called Arago that was essentially Smalltalk syntax in reverse. It has grown and is now available as ObjectStudio on Windows, OS/2, and Unix platforms, from a company called VMARK, after they bought Easel, who purchased Enfin.

In Washington, DC, Smalltalk was also underway. Quasar Knowledge Systems (QKS) created a version of Smalltalk that would provide all of the native capability of the Macintosh within a Smalltalk development environment. Apple Smalltalk had been discontinued, and the Digitalk Smalltalk/V for the Mac did not support many of the native Macintosh features.

The most recent commercialization of Smalltalk is the variety of Smalltalk products from IBM. These products are enhancements of the OTI Smalltalk and the PARTS technology for visual application building. IBM Smalltalk comes with or without its VisualAge visual programming environment, and is available for OS/2, Windows, and AIX. With the recent availability of Smalltalk/MVS, Smalltalk is now available to run on a mainframe system.

Noncommercial Versions

There are a few versions of Smalltalk that are available at no charge. These are currently limited in scope and support, and are not recommended for beginners, unless they are seasoned C programmers, as they are available in C source code form. These versions include Little-Smalltalk, Smalltalk-X, and GNU Smalltalk, which can all be found on Internet archives and the CD-ROM included with this book.

Smalltalk in a Nutshell

Syntax

The original syntax of Smalltalk fit on a single page, and it still does today. The syntax for all versions of Smalltalk is very similar, but not exactly the same. One of the goals of the ANSI Smalltalk committee (X3J20) was to provide a standard syntax for all versions of Smalltalk. This goal has been realized, and the syntax is presented in the beginning of the ANSI Smalltalk Appendix.

Libraries

The libraries of the Smalltalk language are numerous and varied. Some standardization of the libraries is being addressed by the ANSI Smalltalk committee, but major differences will exist in the foreseeable future. There are some methods that are essential to understand well, and these can be found in the chapter entitled Most Useful Methods.

Concepts

Many of the terms in Smalltalk are simply new words for concepts that you already know. An **object-oriented pointer** (OOP) points to an **object.** The object is a data structure that has additional properties. These properties include a set of functions and procedures that operate on the object's data space, known as **methods.** The definition of the object and its associated methods is contained in a **class,** the cookie cutter for creating **instances** of the object. The class executes a method when it is sent a **message** by the same name. The sender of the message can be the class or any other object or class in the system. The class creates an instance of itself (an object) when it is sent the message *new.* The class itself is an instance of another class, called **metaclass.** This is how everything in Smalltalk is an object.

Different objects (which have their methods defined in a class) that respond to the same message but are of different classes exhibit **polymorphism.** Objects can respond to a message that is not defined in their class, but in an associated class, called a **superclass,** from which it **inherits** these methods. Variables declared in a class are accessible only to methods defined for the class and to no others and provide **encapsulation.**

Smalltalk automatically allocates and frees memory for your application and uses a **garbage collector** to do this. It is not an interpreted language, but is compiled into a combination of **byte-codes** that are executed by the **virtual machine,** and native machine language. Smalltalk is a weakly typed language that does not allow the definition of a variable to only contain a **string** or an **integer,** but allows any object (via its object-oriented pointer) to be stored in a variable. Smalltalk has **dynamic binding** that selects the appropriate method to be called at runtime instead of when compiling. Each method is compiled when it is saved and not recompiled after that, in a process known as **incremental compilation.** All compiled code and data objects are stored in memory in an **image,** which is then written to disk to save the development environment.

2

Style

The subject of style is not absolute. Instead, it is a creative area that allows for many diverse approaches, many of which are good at solving the problem of creating good Smalltalk applications. In this chapter, you will learn about some approaches to Smalltalk style. This chapter is not meant to dictate the way to write Smalltalk code, but to point out Smalltalk coding issues and possible solutions. You will learn about:

- good ways to write Smalltalk methods
- good ways to organize classes
- how to subclass and partition a growing class
- how to aggregate functionality into a superclass
- issues involved in making system class changes
- how to create dynamic messages
- ways to document methods and classes

Let this chapter serve as a springboard for creating your ideas on how best to create your Smalltalk applications with style and quality. You have already found that Smalltalk is superior in many ways to other languages, but don't forget that it is still possible to make the same mistakes in Smalltalk as with other languages (and sometimes make them far worse!). It is only through understanding and exploration that you will discover how best to program in Smalltalk.

Elements of a Good Smalltalk Method

Why Are Good Methods Important in Smalltalk Programming?

Good methods are the essential brickwork of a good Smalltalk program. The design may be the blueprint, and the base class hierarchy the foundation on which it is built, but the methods for the application are essential to an application that will withstand the test of time (and a demanding user community).

Quality is a signpost of the world, and the computer industry is no exception. Many major projects have failed or succeeded based on the quality of the effort and the product. Strong method quality is equally essential to a successful application as the design of the application. Cost savings can be measured in a reduced number of fixes, ease of fixing or evolving the system based on shifting user requirements, and long-term reusability and extensibility of the system. Keeping these factors in mind, a good-quality Smalltalk method can be considered an investment, not a cost, and should be treated as such.

The elements of a good method are discussed here, and you should apply these criteria, and others that you may discover along the way, to the methods generated for your Smalltalk application.

Use an Appropriate Method Name

The method name within a class should indicate clearly the functionality and use of the method. Sometimes this is not possible, but in most cases it is. Stick to a consistent capitalization method that agrees with Smalltalk.

A common convention is to use lowercase for instance methods, with the first letter of following words capitalized. Examples of this are `doTheWindows`, `tryHarder`. The first method should do the windows, as the name indicates, and would probably exist as a high-level method within a class that interfaces to a window-washing robot. The second method might adjust several parameters in order to increase the effort at which an algorithm or machine would solve a problem or initiate an action.

Methods with arguments should have the identifiers for the arguments starting with a lowercase letter, and follow the switch case rule for the words following the first. Examples of this are `doTheWindows:with:` and `tryHarder:usingRule:`.

Class methods typically also start with a lowercase letter, although the class variables are capitalized. Examples include `defaultFilePath` and `currentDatabaseConnection`. These methods are useful to all instances of the class and the subclasses. Class instance methods have a similar capitalization and only differ from class methods in storage: class instance methods do not share the same value with the superclass, but only the variable name.

Use the Appropriate Type of Variable

There are many different types of variables found in Smalltalk. These include **temporaries, block temporaries, class, class instance, instance, pool,** and **global.** The scope of each variable, along with an example of its use is shown in Table 2.1.

Use an Appropriate Variable Name

There are rules of thumb for the naming of the different types of variables found in Smalltalk programming.

Class variables are usually capitalized and named for the piece of data that they hold in common for all instances of the class and its subclasses. They are often useful in place of a global when data needs to be shared among instances of a class and instances of subclasses. Many times, class variables are named the same as the class method that returns the value. Examples include `CurrentFilePath` and `LogoPictureHandle`.

Instance variables are usually lowercase. They are descriptive of the content of the data held, and may indicate the type of data held. It is not recommended to name the type of data because it can change, and is not entirely predictable at coding time. Rather, a group of variable comments should be included as stated in a separate section later. Examples: `person`, `people` (indicating an instance of a `Collection`), `cityState`, and `value` (perhaps a subclass of `Magnitude`).

TABLE 2.1 The Smalltalk Variable Types, Scopes, and Examples

Variable Type	Scope	Example
block temporary*	a block	[:arg		blockTemp	]
temporary	a method		temporary	
instance	all instance methods for class	myInstanceVariable
class instance*	class methods for class, uniquely for each subclass	ClassInstanceVariable
class	class methods for class, common for each subclass	ClassVariable
pool	class and instance methods for a class that includes pool in definition	WindowConstants
global	workspaces, class and instance methods	Smalltalk

*not available in all versions

Class instance variables are not available in all versions of Smalltalk. They provide a space for common class data storage that only extends to instances of the class, with subclasses possessing a different space for storage. Capitalization follows the convention of class variables: they are capitalized.

Temporary variables don't have a standard approach. Usually they follow capitalization rules for instance variables. Some programmers like to use simple grammar to discern these variables, opting for names like: `myCollection`, `aString`, `theValue`. These are good choices if the type is known, otherwise `thePerson`, or `thePeople` might be better.

Block temporary variables follow the same rules as temporaries, and do not appear in all versions of Smalltalk. These variables are scoped to the block context and perform much the same function as temporaries that are used inside the block.

Class names and **global items** (heaven forbid!) should start with a capital letter. Some people prefer to preface a global with a "G" to identify what scope the variable is, and as a mark of shame. Examples of this are `Object`, `Smalltalk`, and `GMyGlobal`. `Object` is a class, `Smalltalk` is a global (but it can't be renamed!) and `GMyGlobal` is a global. `GMyGlobal` and `Object` will appear in the instance of `SystemDictionary` (see, here's another class!) called `Smalltalk` in most environments (`System` in ObjectStudio).

Use Identifiable Argument Names

The names of the arguments in the method should be useful as a hint as to the functionality of the method and the types of arguments expected. Names like `arg1` and `arg2` are not helpful, because the expected content of `arg1` and `arg2` is not known to the reader of the method. Names like `theTitleString` and `descriptionCollection` are much more helpful because they not only give information as to the content of the data, but also to the type of data passed in as the argument. Names should also indicate the role of the variable, like `descriptionCollection` instead of `aCollection` or `theTitleString` instead of `theString`.

Use Comments

Comments appearing at the top of each method are essential to a good method. They help other programmers to understand your code, they help you to remember what you did in this method, and serve as a repository for any additional interesting information. More detail on comments appears later in this chapter and is essential reading for any Smalltalk programmer.

An example of a good comment that describes the action in plain English as well as the use of the method:

```
myMethod
"Public - Answers the current location of self.as a Point"
^self asPoint
```

LISTING 2.1   A good comment for a method.

An example of a bad comment that doesn't tell the usage of the method and reads exactly as the source code.

```
myMethod
"calls asPoint and returns it"
^self asPoint
```

LISTING 2.2   A poor comment for a method.

Pick One: Public, Private, or Friend

The definition of the method should include some indication as to whether the method is supported as a public function and is a part of the public application programming interface (API) of the class. If the method is not intended for general public use, it may be either a private method, not to be used outside of the class, or a friend method, to be used only by classes that closely cooperate with the class in which the method is implemented.

A **public method** is one that is available to all users of the class. Though some classes may not be public themselves, the notion of whether any particular method is available to the outside users of the class is conveyed through the notation in the comment of the method that the method is public. Public methods should be defined early in the design of the class and remain available and nearly consistent throughout the development life cycle for the class.

```
asString
"Public - Answer self as an instance of String"
^self contents asString
```

LISTING 2.3   A public method.

A **private method** is available to methods within the class. This means that another class using the class with the defined private method should not use the method, but stick to the defined public interface. Subclasses of the class will also be able to use any private method defined by a parent class.

```
calculate
"Private - Only recalculate when set to automatic or menu option picked"
^self contents: (self newValue)
```

LISTING 2.4   A private method.

A **friend method** sits on the fence between public and private. It is available to the class itself as a private method, and is available to a limited audience of users of the class like a public method. The use of friends is controversial, so it is best to limit their use. The primary argument against using friends is that they violate the encapsulation of a class, so use them only when necessary, which means when a "quick and dirty" solution is needed, or the cost to rework the class is much higher than using the friend. Since there is nothing disallowing the use of any method by another class in Smalltalk, the violation can occur with friend or private, and it is up to the individual programmer to enforce. Friend methods also provide a collaborating set of classes a way to work more closely together, using these semiprivate methods.

```
currentRectangle
"Friend - Answer current bounds as aRectangle"
^self rectangle
```

LISTING 2.5   A friend method.

Don't Violate Another Class' API

The method should not violate another class' public API by calling private functions. If the design is adequate, there should be no need to violate the API. Many times, violations of an API are committed because the necessary information to use a class is not available, and a private method seems to be exactly what the programmer needs. Take the time to understand the class and the public interface, and obey the rules that you set up for yourself when programming in Smalltalk.

Keep Methods to a Moderate Length

It is hard to define how long is too long, and how short is too short, but a method that is an entire application and takes several pages is too long. An accessor method may do nothing but simply return itself, and occasionally a method may simply call another for redirection or compatibility with a changing class, but the number of message sends slows down the application, and functioning units should do something besides just call another method.

Each Method Should Have Only One Purpose

Each method should have a single purpose, documented in the method comment at the beginning of a method. Multipurpose methods may be confusing and are hard to modify in one way without affecting the other functionality of the method. Multipurpose methods are the equivalent of multipersonality people, and are very hard to understand and work with in a normal manner.

A Method Should Have No Side Effects

When a method has a purpose, and it accomplishes that purpose, there should be no other action that occurs to other parts of the system.

Dependencies Should Be Set to Announce Changes

Instead of explicitly changing dependent instance variables, code should use the dependency mechanism. When a data member changes, and that data member may have a dependent, the code should announce "I've changed" using the dependency mechanism, instead of directly manipulating code. The use of the dependency mechanism and the reasons for using it are discussed in Chapter 3.

Errors Should Be Handled Using Exception Mechanisms

This really is an issue of style. Programming the way most have learned does not account for errors or exceptional events. The code typically goes through and solves the problem, but breaks down when error conditions occur, primarily because no strategy exists to handle the errors. Exception-handling mechanisms are available in most versions of Smalltalk and provide the functionality required to handle an error condition, but the style of the code should take into account the use of the exception-handling mechanism. Exception handling is discussed further in Chapter 5.

Spacing within the Method Should Be Consistent

A convention needs to be established for how the code will be spaced. For VisualWorks users, the convention may be the default configuration for the autoformatter that formats code when it is saved. For other users, the spacing between braces and brackets and the points at which the line breaks needs to be consistent within a method, if not for all methods. This does not mean the method will run better or faster, but that the code may be more organized, better written, and much more maintainable. Many times a programmer will completely reformat a method in order to understand it if it does not have any conventions. Another option is to create your own autoformatter that uses your own rules for saved methods.

All Variables Should Be Described

Since Smalltalk is not a strongly typed language, the type of a variable may not be known, but that does not mean the Smalltalk code should be weakly documented. The type of data in a variable may not be known at the time of writing a method, but the general content of the variable should be describable in some terms and included in the method. Comments should include an indication of type of content if it is known at the time the code is written. One way to do this is to include a class method called NOTES or COMMENT. This method should simply return a string that contains descriptive content. This string can then be used for documentation of the system. An example of this is:

```
NOTES
"Public - Answer a string containing a description of the variables defined
for the class and its instances"

^'
Comment:
--------
MyClass - generates a PARTS view for an domain object.
---------
VARIABLES
---------

Instance Variables
------------------
domainObject - a single instance of a domainObject subclass
partsApplication - a single instance of PARTSApplication
partsWidgets - an OrderedCollection of the GUI widgets

Class Instance Variables
------------------------
None

Class Variables
---------------
None


--------------
PUBLIC METHODS
--------------

Accessors
---------
domainObject: anObject
domainObject

Generation
----------
partsView - Answers the PART view for a domainObject
'
```

LISTING 2.6 A sample comment method for a class.

Tricky Portions of Code Should Be Commented

Whenever something is really neat or tricky, comment it. It may be obvious, simple, and elegant to you, but the next person to read the code may not understand it. For that matter, you may not understand it the next day, week, or a year later. This is standard computer science stuff, but it is a component of a good Smalltalk method.

```
doesNotUnderstand: aMessage
"Private - Handle messages not understood. Try to pass the message to
domainObject."

"See if domainObject can perform aMessage"
(domainObject respondsTo: aMessage)
    "domainObject can perform aMessage, so do it!"
    ifTrue: [ ^domainObject perform: aMessage ]
    "domainObject doesn't understand, so pass to superclass"
    ifFalse: [ ^super doesNotUnderstand: aMessage ].
```

LISTING 2.7   A comment for a tricky piece of code.

The Why of Code Should Be Commented

Ever wonder why you wrote the code a certain way after coming back to it? If you use an `IdentityDictionary` instead of a `Dictionary` for speed reasons and converted `Symbols` to `Strings`, document it in the code for future reference. A sentence or two should serve to jog the memory or give a starting point for understanding to another programmer reading the code.

Make the Method Testable

This one seems to escape almost every programmer. Most programmers never spend much time in the test lab, so understanding how to test code is poor. A good rule of thumb for making a method testable is to treat it like a mini science experiment. The input criteria should be known, and the expected output should match the real output. Other methods within the class can be saved to retest the methods as they evolve over time. This can be a real quality boost, especially if the test methods are written in conjunction with the application code, and are reused over the life cycle of the application.

Use No Absolute References

When referencing a method within the class, it is better to use a nonabsolute reference, so that inherited code has a better chance of working correctly. If we define a class method called `hello` in the class `MyClass` and refer to it in an instance method, we could use either `self class hello` or `MyClass hello`. The former is the preferred approach, since subclasses of

`MyClass` will then look to the subclass first, instead of always going to the superclass. The latter example can be difficult to debug since it works properly for the superclass, but may break down when used for a subclass that may attempt to override the `hello` method.

Use Local Accessors for Instance Variables

A great deal of benefit can be realized by using local accessors for instance variable access. They isolate the variable from the program and enhance encapsulation. A good rule of thumb is to create accessors (setters/getters) for each instance variable, and to label them as either public or private. If the methods consistently use the accessors, changes to the instance variables can be made more quickly. Some examples of the types of changes that can occur include separation of the instance variable into a separate class, a change in the expected object of the instance variable, and most important, the tracking of changes to the instance variable and the effects on other objects in the system.

Elements of Good Class Organization

Organizing your classes correctly is an effective way to improve the quality and reuse of code. There are various techniques available to improve the organization of code in Smalltalk classes. These techniques are easy to implement if they are understood, and can add value to almost any set of Smalltalk classes. The various benefits of good class organization and approaches to achieving these benefits are covered in this section.

The first benefit of good class organization is that reusable classes cost less to maintain. This means that if a class is reusable, the cost of maintaining a second code set is eliminated. The number of times that this class is reused increases the savings in maintenance, and the number of classes being reused also increases the maintenance cost savings. The up-front development cost may be less, but can only be arrived at after an increased level of analysis and design; so, for the worst case of analysis and design, the cost would match an average effort in coding the pieces separately.

The second benefit of good class organization is that general classes are more easily reusable. If we design a class called `Customer` to contain generic data for any customer, as opposed to a specific subset or superset for a business, the class can be reused for another client, to add a new type of customer to the application, or to merge with another organization that has a different view of the customer. Having several different `Customer` classes for each type does not lead to good organization and is not very reusable. If, instead, each type of `Customer` is either a subclass (least favorite choice), or an instance of the standard `Customer` class with additional data contained as instance variables, then the class is organized well, can be reused, is generic, and not redundant.

The third benefit of good class organization is that a clearly defined API insulates users of the class from implementation changes within the class. This means that if you create a class and provide it to other programmers to use, you can then feel free to improve the implementation of the functionality at your discretion. It also provides for an interface with which to code against the class without having written the class. Thus, programmers using the class can begin without you having written the class. It can also hide any additional usage or evolutionary changes that occur. This assumes, of course, that the programmers using your class stick to the public API and do not use the private or friend methods for their code.

With these benefits, part of the task at hand is to keep good encapsulation alive within the programming effort. Good encapsulation can exist within Smalltalk only if the programmers agree to obey the rules of encapsulation and keep in mind that certain programming activities provide for good encapsulation and others provide for poor encapsulation or none at all.

The first step toward achieving good encapsulation is to keep methods from poking around inside other classes. This means that the programmers using a class do not violate the public API of the class. If they do, then they may need to rewrite portions of the code that are affected by the revision or elimination of nonpublic methods. When a programmer signs up to do object-oriented programming, the programmer should say the object-oriented pledge, which includes a section on "ensuring good encapsulation at all times." For C++ programmers, the interface is explicitly specified in the definition of the class, and private methods are not in scope for methods outside the class and are not resolved. This mechanism is not implemented in Smalltalk, and so it requires diligence on the programmer's side to think before coding.

The second step toward achieving good encapsulation is to make a public interface and stick to it. Sure, APIs need to evolve with the system, but if the original API is so far off, then perhaps the entire design is wrong, and some serious redefinitions need to occur. More likely, the implementor of the class will realize that there is a more elegant way for the class to communicate with the outside world and attempt to provide this interface to the world without concern for others coding to the public API. This happens when there is only one programmer, and code has to be rewritten as a result. The best solution is to spend enough time understanding the class to get a reasonable API, and then to support that API, not because it's the best, but because it is the contract that has been made between programmers.

The third step toward achieving good encapsulation is to use friends only when absolutely necessary. Friends is a useful concept from C++ that allows a few classes, closely related, to poke and prod within each other to achieve a programming task. This is not a good way to do business, but is the equivalent of letting some people do business in the normal way—a few special friends come in and do as they please with few controls on how they do their thing. Sometimes, friends are the solution because this method solves a problem quickly when the resolution by other means requires a huge rework effort.

The following techniques, **subclassing, aggregation, system class changes,** and **dynamic messages,** are tools in the Smalltalk programmers toolbox that help to provide a better class organization for the application. Sometimes, all techniques can be applied, other times one or none is applicable, but there is value in each of these techniques.

Subclassing

The technique of subclassing allows you to create classes that separate functionality from a growing class into more appropriate pieces. Since the pieces probably have grown together in one class and do not seem to match well anymore, it is best to split this compound class into two or more classes, as shown in Figure 2.1, and to keep their common base functionality within the existing superclass.

It is better to create several classes to hold the data and functionality than to put all methods and variables into one "megaclass." If all data and functions are put into only one class, then the benefits of reuse and encapsulation are lost. All data accesses within the class are at the same scope and

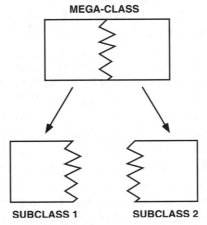

FIGURE 2.1 Split a large "megaclass" into subclasses.

no hiding of data is possible. The class is probably so large and specific that the reuse of it, or even a part of it, is not possible unless the pieces are split off and rewritten. A much better approach is to split a growing megaclass into pieces based on common data and functionality.

The first approach to splitting a megaclass into pieces is to split the class into subclasses based on variables and data abstraction. If the megaclass contains information for a customer and an order, then the division into separate subclasses, one `Customer`, the other `Order` is simple. Variables specific to `Customer`, like `customerName` and `customerAddress`, should go into the `Customer` class, and data specific to the `Order`, like `orderNumber` and `shipDate`, should appear in the `Order` class. Common variables, such as `operatorInitials` and `lastModificationDate`, can remain in the megaclass to be inherited by each of the subclasses.

The second approach to splitting a megaclass into pieces is to split the class based on organization of functionality. If there is no specific split based on data, then the functionality may suggest a particular subclassing strategy. If the megaclass contains both functionality for a serial communications connection and a parallel communications connection, and routines are common, then two subclasses, `SerialComm` and `ParallelComm` may be useful to organize the functionality. Common functionality should still remain in the parent class, but the specific functionality for parallel and serial connections should go into `SerialComm` and `ParallelComm`, respectively. These classes will inherit the common functionality from the parent, have specific functionality not defined in the parent, and override anything that is not shared by the classes.

The third approach to splitting a megaclass into pieces is to split the class for modularity and encapsulation. The modularity may not fall across functional lines, but serve as a means for dividing work among team members, separate a public portion of a subsystem from the private portion or other criteria on an ad hoc basis.

While this splitting and reorganizing of code is occurring, it is a good idea to generalize common methods. If the common methods (those that will remain in the parent class) are general enough to be shared by the two or more children that you are creating, then the common methods are probably general and useful enough to reuse with other subclasses. Generalizing them at this point will improve the chances that another subclass can be created as needed in the future.

Advantages/Disadvantages of Subclassing

Advantage: reduces storage size and memory requirements

Advantage: partitions code for division of work/testing/maintenance

Disadvantage: thinking required

Disadvantage: places where class were previously used may need to change to new class

Aggregation

The process of aggregation is the gathering together of similar data and methods from a group of classes into a common superclass. This means that for a group of classes that have a common ancestry, data members and methods that are held in common are moved from each class into a common superclass from which each class will inherit these data members and methods, as shown in Figure 2.2.

In order to aggregate classes, the classes must have common ancestry. This is because, within Smalltalk, there is no multiple inheritance, so that the class may have only one parent. There are ways to fake multiple inheritance, but those do not lend themselves easily to most applications. The classes must share a common ancestry because during the process of aggregating the common data and functionality, the classes will be reparented to the new superclass.

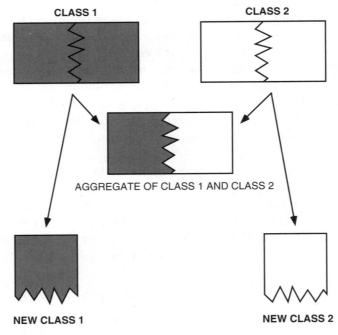

FIGURE 2.2   Aggregate common functionality into a common superclass.

The classes to be aggregated should also have some level of redundant functionality. There is no point in joining several classes that have no common functionality. If data is shared in common and there is no redundant functionality, then the design of the classes may be questioned, and a separate class with functionality may be created to hold that data and functionality, but not necessarily as a superclass for the classes.

If the classes share common data elements, then they should be aggregated. The premise behind object-oriented programming and design is that functionality is contained with data items, so that the data items are the drivers for the organization within the system. If common data items are identified in a group of classes, then these common data items may be pulled from the classes and put into a superclass from which these classes may inherit the data members and the functionality held in common.

So, the process of aggregating classes involves analyzing a group of classes that have a common base of data and functionality to create a new superclass in which common data members and methods will be stored. Each subclass will then be reparented to the new superclass, and the functionality will be in one common place, to be maintained only once, and grouped based on the common data and functionality.

In the process of aggregating the classes into a superclass, the need often arises to take one or more specific methods and generalize them for the set of classes. This most often happens when the classes have grown through an iterative development process, and the realization that the classes are truly of the same type does not occur until the code has been written in at least two different forms. The generalizing of a specific method is a good activity because it forces the rethinking of the functionality in more general terms, and usually leads to a more understandable, efficient, and simple method.

The Ten Steps of Aggregation

1. Determine common data elements.
2. Determine common functionality.
3. Create a new class to become the superclass. Use the same parent as the other classes.
4. Insert common data elements into new class.
5. Insert common methods into new class.
6. Generalize and rewrite methods in new class.
7. Reparent other classes to the new class.
8. Remove data elements from other classes.
9. Remove methods from other classes.
10. Override methods where necessary in other classes.

Advantages/Disadvantages of Aggregation

Advantage: maintain only one code set

Advantage: further reuse possible

Disadvantage: must reparent classes

Disadvantage: must generalize methods

Disadvantage: thinking required

System Class Changes

What are **system classes?** What are **base classes?** Are they the same? Yes and no. System classes and base classes are those classes that are part of the Smalltalk image that ships with the Smalltalk environment; but depending on whose definition you use, there are differences between the two definitions. System classes can be thought of as a subset of the base classes and consists of those classes that are necessary to run the system. Base classes form the basis for an application, but may not be required to run the Smalltalk system unless they are also system classes. So, simply put, all system classes are also base classes, but not all base classes are system classes. Why make the distinction? System classes tend to ship in the Smalltalk image with instances already in existence, and sometimes the instances cannot be mutated from within the Smalltalk environment, posing the problem of how to change them when needed.

Reasons to change system classes include additional GUI behavior, operating system-dependent behavior, or global changes to objects within the environment. The need to change the system class, with its existing instances, is tied into the fact that the Smalltalk environment cannot simply dump all operating system and Smalltalk memory and processes to replace them with another set. They must be modified on the fly to include new behavior such as drag-and-drop functionality.

An obvious question to the changing of a system class is: Why not subclass the system class? It is sometimes possible to do so, if the point at which the instance comes into existence is known, but many times the instances are part of the image, not subject to garbage collection; or the source code that creates instances is unavailable or far too complex to modify simply.

The problem with changing system classes occurs when a new version of the Smalltalk environment arrives, the code must be shared with another programmer's workstation, the code must be moved to another operating system platform, or the operating system changes underneath Smalltalk. The problem with a new version of Smalltalk occurs when the system classes have changed from one version to the next and the functionality must be restored and probably recoded. The problem with sharing with another user is that all changes must be tracked and tested against all machine configurations. When the program is moved to another operating system or the operating system version changes underneath Smalltalk, the changes may not solve the problem or fit the operating system.

Changes to system classes have problems, but they are not forbidden. Why do people change the system classes? Because it may be the only way to get certain functionality, and it may be much more cost-effective than other solutions. Certain operating system-specific features, such as the main graphical user interface (GUI) window, are created when the Smalltalk environment is started. It is very difficult to take down that main window and reinstantiate it with a different class of window. Additional functionality may be much more easily added to the GUI by modifying a system class, and the cost may be much less to do it for a few platforms than to attempt a different architecture that does not closely work with the Smalltalk environment.

Although the functionality of a system class change may be available through some other means, the modification of a system class may be necessary, and, if not necessary, it is a "quick and dirty" approach to getting the job done.

An additional way to work with system class changes is to redirect messages sent to a system class to another class created as an auxiliary to the system class. In this way, the code can be placed in one class (except for the redirecting methods), and behavior for the system class can be enhanced by the auxiliary class. If methods in the system class are modified or overridden, code can be placed in the system class, or the message redirected to the auxiliary class.

One trick to passing messages from a system class to an auxiliary class is to override the doesNotUnderstand: message defined in Object. The standard behavior is to cause an exception to occur, typically with an error message and a debugger session when developing code. Overriding this method and passing the messages to the auxiliary class would allow the auxiliary class to attempt to process the messages before invoking its own doesNotUnderstand: method. It is important to note that if the auxiliary class is a subclass of the system class, then doesNotUnderstand: must be redefined in the auxiliary class to be the same as the method in Object. Here's an example of a doesNotUnderstand: method that will send messages to an instance of a class called AuxiliaryClass:

```
doesNotUnderstand: aMessage
"Public - override default behavior to re-direct to AuxiliaryClass"
^myAuxiliaryClassInstance perform: aMessage
```

LISTING 2.8 Redirecting a message to another receiver.

NOTE: It is not good practice to do this frequently. Code is harder to follow when a message sent to a class is redirected in this fashion. Execution speed is very slow, so use it sparingly, carefully, and document it well!

Dynamic Messages

The concept of a dynamically computed message is a neat concept available to the programmer in Smalltalk. The exact nature of the message to be sent is not known at the time of coding, but an algorithm detailing possibilities is known, and used to cause message sends to occur. A conceptual diagram of the dynamic message process is shown in Figure 2.3.

The approach to calculating the message to be sent can use an algorithm, look up a key in a dictionary, or append arguments to a base message, depending on data available. An algorithm to calculate a message to send can be based upon the result of another message send or a piece of data. Another approach is to map a set of data onto a set of messages using a dictionary. If the keys in the dictionary are the set of data, and the values in the dictionary are the set of messages, the mapping can be as simple as a lookup. Arguments can be appended to any message based on any criteria including the number of elements in an array. For example, if the program has an array for address data, and the data must be passed into a method as individual strings, then the data elements in the array may be presented to the message-sending algorithm with the appropriate number of `with:` arguments appended to the message string. The syntax for sending messages in Smalltalk is as follows:

```
perform: aSymbol
perform: aSymbol with: anObject
perform: aSymbol with: firstObject with: secondObject
perform: aSymbol with: firstObject with: secondObject with: thirdObject
```

LISTING 2.9 The syntax for performing messages in Smalltalk.

These methods are defined in the `Object` class. The argument `aSymbol` is sent to the receiver and is an instance of `Symbol`. The number of arguments can range from none to three or more. Examples of this are:

```
self perform: #close.
self perform: #print: with: 'My String'.
self perform: #add:to: with: 1 with: 2.
self perform: #first:middle:last: with: 'one' with: #two with: 3.
```

LISTING 2.10 A few examples of sending the perform message.

The method in Listing 2.11 differs from the previous in that the arguments are contained in an array that is passed as one argument to the per-

FIGURE 2.3 Smalltalk allows messages to be created dynamically, on the fly, by using data to determine the message sent.

`form` method, which then unpackages the arguments from `anArray` and places them on the stack for the message send. This allows methods with any number of arguments, including those with more than three arguments, to be sent using the `perform` mechanism.

```
perform: aSymbol withArguments: anArray
```

LISTING 2.11 A general form of the `Perform` message.

In addition to calculating a message, Smalltalk can check if the receiver will understand the message before sending it. The following code checks the receiver to see if it understands the message before sending it:

```
(receiver respondsTo: aSymbol)
ifTrue:
    [
    receiver perform: aSymbol.
    ]
ifFalse:
    [
    self doAlternateThing.
    ].
```

LISTING 2.12 Checking if the receiver understands the message before performing it.

Advantages/Disadvantages of Dynamic Messages

Advantage: centrally locate code

Advantage: keep code out of system classes

Disadvantage: may break encapsulation (messages not contained in receiver)

Documenting Methods and Classes

Documentation for Smalltalk programs currently has no defined standard format, but it is closer to achieving a de facto standard due to the uniformity in the Smalltalk environment and the examples provided by the Smalltalk vendors. Documentation is an important part of any software development effort. In this section, the various needs of Smalltalk documentation will be discussed, along with the components of the documentation, some ideas on how to provide the documentation, and an overview of Class Publisher, a commercially available documentation product.

Documentation Needs

The needs of Smalltalk programmers for documentation are similar to those of other programmers, but the exact nature differs because of the nature of the class libraries and the development environment. Since the Smalltalk programmer is used to working with a rapid development tool, the documentation should be easily available and usable with the environment, yet not interfere with the programming task. Some on-line documentation browsers can cause the programmer to do a lot of extra work to view a page and enter code at the same time, while the printed version has a slower access time, but is more pleasant to read and travels better. The variety of the documentation media aside, the needs of the Smalltalk programmer for documentation follow.

Class

Each class needs to have a description of its purpose, ancestry, and relationship to other classes in the system.

Methods

Methods include class and instance methods. Each method needs to have a comment at the top that contains information on the purpose of the method, the return value, and whether it is public, private, or friend.

Data Items

Data items include instance variables, class variables, class instance variables, and method arguments. The scope, lifetime, typical content, expected type, state, and purpose of each data item should be documented.

Code Samples

One of the best aspects of Smalltalk is the way that you can browse code samples that use a particular method or class of interest. In addition to using the browsing tools to identify uses of the method or class, sample code included in the documentation of the class or method helps to understand

and use the code. Sample code that includes the test methods that verify the class and method functionality is particularly helpful, so that the correct behavior can be observed.

Solutions

There are many ways to serve the documentation needs in the Smalltalk environment. Possibilities include complete manual tracking of all information, use of additional methods to store data, automated tools to generate information about Smalltalk code, and use of commercially available documentation tools.

Tracking all information about a rapidly evolving class in a separate application can be a tedious task. Instead, placing documentation for the class and methods in the Smalltalk environment provides easy access to update or browse the documentation. One possible way to increase the likelihood of quality documentation is to create a method or set of methods specifically to hold documentation for the class. For example, if you wish to store general information about the use of a class, you can create a class method in each of your classes called NOTES and use it to store textual information about the class. The NOTES method can be in the format to return a string as its value for direct access to the information; or the content can consist of comments that must be parsed out using the class reading functionality of Smalltalk. An example NOTES method is:

```
NOTES
    "Public - Answer the documentation for this class"
    ^'My class is the best and it does everything.'
```

Expanding on this principle, the content for much of the class documentation can be stored in comments at the top of each method. Using this approach, the example program in Listing 2.13 can produce a nice class encyclopedia from the information contained in each method comment. This listing is for VisualSmalltalk; other implementations for the other major Smalltalks can be found on the CD-ROM.

```
Object
    subclass: #DocumentationGenerator
    instanceVariableNames: 'isRTF'
    classVariableNames: ''
    poolDictionaries: ''
    category: 'DocumentationGenerator'!

ReadWriteStream
    subclass: #RTFStream
    instanceVariableNames: ''
```

Continued

```
        classVariableNames: ''
        poolDictionaries: ''
        category: 'DocumentationGenerator'!


!DocumentationGenerator methodsFor: 'text generators' !

classAnnotationsOn: myStream
forHandle: myClassHandle
    "Private - Place myClassHandle annotation on myStream"

    (((myClassHandle annotationNamed: 'Comment') isNil) or: [(myClassHandle
annotationNamed: 'Comment') size < 2])
        ifFalse:
            [myStream
                nextPutAll: (myClassHandle annotationNamed: 'Comment');
                cr.
            ]!

classDescriptionOn: myStream
for: myClass
    "Private - Place myClass description on myStream"

    (myClass class methodDictionary select: [ :each | each selector = #COMMENT
    isEmpty
        ifFalse:
            [myStream
                nextPutAll: myClass COMMENT;
                cr;
                cr.
            ].
    (myClass class methodDictionary select: [ :each | each selector = #NOTES ])
isEmpty
        ifFalse:
            [myStream
                nextPutAll: myClass NOTES;
                cr;
                cr.
            ].
    !


classMethodsOn: myStream
for: myClass
    "Private - Place class method documentation for myClass on myStream"

    | sourceStrings temp |
    myStream
        rtfBold;
        nextPutAll: 'Class Methods: ';
        rtfPlain;
        cr;
        cr.
```

Continued

```
        myClass class methodDictionary asSortedCollection
            do:
                [:each |
                sourceStrings := (each source asArrayOfSubstringsSeparatedBy: $").
                (sourceStrings at: 3 ifAbsent: [nil]) notNil
                    ifTrue:
                        [temp := (sourceStrings at: 2 ifAbsent: [nil]).
                        ]
                    ifFalse:
                        [ temp := nil. ].
                temp notNil
                    ifTrue:
                        [myStream
                            nextPutAll: ((sourceStrings at: 1) trimBlanks);
                            cr;
                            nextPutAll: '        ', temp;
                            cr;
                            cr]].
        myStream cr.
        !


classNameOn: myStream
for: myClass

    "Private - Place myClass name as a heading on myStream"
    myStream
        nextPutAllHeading1: myClass name;
        cr;
        cr.
    !


classPoolsOn: myStream
for: myClass

    "Private - Output class pools for myClass on myStream"
    myStream
        rtfBold;
        nextPutAll: 'Class Pools: ';
        rtfPlain;
        cr.
    myClass classPool
        keys do:
            [:each |
            myStream
                nextPutAll: '        ', each asString;
                tab].
    myStream cr.
!


classVariablesOn: myStream
for: myClass
    "Private - Output class variables for myClass on myStream"      *Continued*
```

```
        myStream
           rtfBold;
           nextPutAll: 'Class Variables: ';
           rtfPlain;
           cr.
        myClass classVarNames "allClassVarNamesGrouped"
           do:
              [:each |
              myStream
                 nextPutAll: '        ', each asString;
                 cr].
        myStream cr.
        !


instanceMethodsOn: myStream
for: myClass
   "Private - Output instance methods with comments for myClass on myStream"

   | temp |
   myStream
      rtfBold;
      nextPutAll: 'Instance Methods: ';
      rtfPlain;
      cr;
      cr.
   myClass methodDictionary asSortedCollection
      do:
         [:each |
         each source notNil ifTrue: [   temp := ((each source
asArrayOfSubstringsSeparatedBy: $") at: 2 ifAbsent: [nil])] ifFalse: [ temp :=
nil ].
         temp notNil
            ifTrue:
               [myStream
                  nextPutAll: ("each selector" ((each source
asArrayOfSubstringsSeparatedBy: $") at: 1 ifAbsent: [''])trimBlanks );
                  cr;
                  nextPutAll: '        ', temp;
                  cr;
                  cr]].
   "myStream cr."
   !


instanceVariablesOn: myStream
for: myClass
   "Private - Output instance variable names for myClass on myStream"

   myStream
      rtfBold;
      nextPutAll: 'Instance Variables: ';
      rtfPlain;
      cr.
```

Continued

```
myClass "allInstVarNamesGrouped" instVarNames
    do:
        [:each |
        myStream
            nextPutAll: '        ', each asString;
            cr].
    myStream cr.
    !

sharedPoolsOn: myStream
for: myClass
    "Private - Output listing of shared pools for myClass on myStream"

    myStream
        rtfBold;
        nextPutAll: 'Shared Pools: ';
        rtfPlain;
        cr.
    myClass sharedPools
        do:
            [:each |
            myStream
                nextPutAll: '        ', each asString;
                tab].
    myStream cr.
    !
subclassesOn: myStream
for: myClass
    "Private - Output list of subclasses for myClass on myStream"

    myStream
        rtfBold;
        nextPutAll: 'SubClasses: ';
        rtfPlain;
        cr.
    myClass subclasses
        do:
            [:each |
            myStream
                nextPutAll: '        ' , each name asString;
                tab].
    myStream cr.
    !

superclassesOn: myStream
for: myClass
    "Private - Output list of superclasses for myClass on myStream"

    myStream
        rtfBold;
        nextPutAll: 'SuperClasses: ';
```

Continued

```
            rtfPlain;
            cr.
        myClass allSuperclasses
            do:
                [:each |
                myStream
                    nextPutAll: '        ' , each name asString;
                    cr].
        myStream cr.
        ! !


!DocumentationGenerator methodsFor: 'public' !

documentationOn: myStream
for: myClass
    "Public - Answer contents for myClass using myStream"

    self
        classNameOn: myStream for: myClass;
        classDescriptionOn: myStream for: myClass;
        superclassesOn: myStream for: myClass;
        subclassesOn: myStream for: myClass;
        classVariablesOn: myStream for: myClass;
        instanceVariablesOn: myStream for: myClass;
        classPoolsOn: myStream for: myClass;
        sharedPoolsOn: myStream for: myClass;
        classMethodsOn: myStream for: myClass;
        instanceMethodsOn: myStream for: myClass.
    ^myStream "rtfPage;" truncate; contents!

documentationOn: myStream
forHandle: myClassHandle
    "Public - Answer contents for myClass using myStream"

    | myClass |
    myClass := myClassHandle value.
    self
        classNameOn: myStream for: myClass;
        classDescriptionOn: myStream for: myClass;
        classAnnotationsOn: myStream forHandle: myClassHandle;
        superclassesOn: myStream for: myClass;
        subclassesOn: myStream for: myClass;
        classVariablesOn: myStream for: myClass;
        instanceVariablesOn: myStream for: myClass;
        classPoolsOn: myStream for: myClass;
        sharedPoolsOn: myStream for: myClass;
        classMethodsOn: myStream for: myClass;
        instanceMethodsOn: myStream for: myClass.
    ^myStream "rtfPage;"
        truncate;
        contents! !
```

Continued

```
!DocumentationGenerator class methodsFor: 'Test' !

formattedTest
    | temp aStream |
    aStream := RTFStream on: (String new: 5000).
    temp := SortedCollection new.
    (TeamVInterface current cluster modules
        detect:
            [:each |
            each name = "'Application Development'" 'Test'])
        allDefinitionsDo:
            [:each |
            each isClass
                ifTrue: [temp add: each]].
    temp
        do:
            [:each |
            self newOn: aStream for: (each className) ].
    TextWindow
        new open;
        contents: (aStream contents).
    !


TEST
    | temp myStream myClassName myClass |
    myStream := (String new: 5000) asStream.
    myClassName := #DatabaseView.
    myClass := Smalltalk at: myClassName.
    self new documentationOn: myStream for: myClass.
    TextWindow
        new open;
        contents: (myStream contents).
    !


TEST2

    | temp aStream |
    aStream := (String new: 50000) asStream.
    temp := SortedCollection new.
    (TeamVInterface current cluster modules
        detect:
            [:each |
            each name = "'Application Development'" 'Test'])
        allDefinitionsDo:
            [:each |
            each isClass
                ifTrue: [temp add: each]].
    temp
        do:
            [:each |
            self newOn: aStream for: (each className).].
```

Continued

```
TextWindow
   new open;
   contents: (aStream contents).
  !  !


!DocumentationGenerator class methodsFor: 'Public' !

formattedDocs
   "Public - Generate Documentation for all classes in cluster 'Application
Development' and open in a text window"
   "DocumentationGenerator formattedDocs"

   | temp aStream |
   aStream := RTFStream on: (String new: 250000).
   temp := SortedCollection new.
   (TeamVInterface current cluster modules
      detect:
         [:each |
         each name = 'Application Development'])
      allDefinitionsDo:
         [:each |
         each isClass
            ifTrue: [temp add: each]].
   temp
      do:
         [:each |
         self newOn: aStream forClassDefinitionHandle: (each "className").
         aStream rtfPage].
   TextWindow
      new open;
      contents:
         (aStream
         rtfTail;
         truncate;
         contents).
   !

formattedDocsNoComment
   "Public - Generate Documentation for all classes in cluster 'Application
Development' and open in a text window"
   "DocumentationGenerator formattedDocsNoComment"

   | temp aStream |
   aStream := RTFStream on: (String new: 250000).
   temp := SortedCollection new.
   (TeamVInterface current cluster modules
      detect:
         [:each |
         each name = 'Application Development'])
      allDefinitionsDo:
         [:each |
         each isClass
            ifTrue: [temp add: each]].
```

Continued

```
        temp
            do:
                [:each |
                self newOn: aStream for: (each className).
                aStream rtfPage].
        TextWindow
            new open;
            contents:
                (aStream
                rtfTail;
                truncate;
                contents).
        !


generateDocumentationFor: aClass
    "Public - Generate documentation for aClass and display in a TextWindow. The
contents can then be saved to a filename.rtf, and imported into your favourite
word processor"

    | temp aStream |
    aStream := RTFStream on: (String new: 25000).
    temp := SortedCollection new.
    (Smalltalk at: aClass asSymbol ifAbsent: [nil]) notNil
        ifTrue:
            [temp add: (Smalltalk at: aClass asSymbol).
            temp
                do:
                    [:each |
                    self newOn: aStream for: (each)].
            TextWindow
                new open;
                contents:
                    (aStream
                    rtfTail;
                    contents).
            ]
        ifFalse:
            [MessageBox warn: 'No Class Found. Please check the number and dial
again.']!


generateDocumentationNoCommentFor: aClass
    "Public - Generate documentation for aClass and display in a TextWindow. The
contents can then be saved to a filename.rtf, and imported into your favourite
word processor"

    | temp aStream |
    aStream := RTFStream on: (String new: 25000).
    temp := SortedCollection new.
    (Smalltalk at: aClass asSymbol ifAbsent: [nil]) notNil
        ifTrue:
            [temp add: (Smalltalk at: aClass asSymbol).
```

Continued

```
    temp
        do:
            [:each |
            self newOn: aStream for: (each)].
        TextWindow
            new open;
            contents:
                (aStream
                rtfTail;
                contents).
        ]
    ifFalse:
        [MessageBox warn: 'No Class Found. Please check the number and dial
again.']!

newOn: myStream
for: myClassOrClassName
    "Public - Answer myStream's contents after generating a description for
myClassOrClassName"

    myClassOrClassName isClass
        ifFalse: [self new documentationOn: myStream for: (Smalltalk at:
myClassOrClassName ifAbsent: [^nil])]
        ifTrue: [self new documentationOn: myStream for: myClassOrClassName].
    ^myStream contents.!
newOn: myStream
for: myClassOrClassName
rtf: isRTF
    "Public - Answer myStream's contents after generating a description for
myClassOrClassName"

    myClassOrClassName isClass
        ifFalse: [self new documentationOn: myStream for: (Smalltalk at:
myClassOrClassName ifAbsent: [^nil]) rtf: isRTF]
        ifTrue: [self new documentationOn: myStream for: myClassOrClassName
rtf: isRTF].
    ^myStream contents. !


newOn: myStream
forClassDefinitionHandle: myClassDefinitionHandle
    "Public - Answer myStream's contents after generating a description for
myClassOrClassName"

    self new documentationOn: myStream forHandle: myClassDefinitionHandle.
    ^myStream contents.! !


!RTFStream methodsFor: 'appending' !

cr
        "Write the line terminating character (carriage-line-feed)
        to the receiver stream."
```

Continued

```
            self nextPutAll: '\par '.
        super cr.!

nextPutAll: aCollection
    "Public - Modified for RTF. Write each of the objects in aCollection to
the receiver stream. Answer aCollection."

    | result |

    result := aCollection
        inject: (String new: (aCollection size + 100)) asStream
        into:
            [:newStream :each |
            (each asciiValue = 13)
                ifTrue:
                    [newStream
                        nextPutAll: '\par';
                        cr]
                ifFalse:
                    [newStream nextPut: each].
                newStream.].
    super nextPutAll: result truncate contents.
    !

nextPutAllHeading1: aString
    "Public - Make aString have the format for the heading1 style"
    self rtfBold; rtfLarge; nextPutAll: aString; rtfNormal
    ! !

!RTFStream methodsFor: 'rtf fonts' !

rtfArial
    "Public - Place a marker to start the Arial font"

    self nextPutAll: '\f1 '!

rtfTimes
    "Public - Place a marker to start the Times font"

    self nextPutAll: '\f0 '! !

!RTFStream methodsFor: 'rtf font sizes' !

rtfLarge
    "Public - Place a marker to start the Large (18 Point) font size"

    self nextPutAll: '\fs36 '!

rt      fNormal
    "Public - Place a marker to start the Normal (12 point) font size"

    self nextPutAll: '\plain \fs24 '!
```

Continued

```
rtfSmall
    "Public - Place a marker to start the Small (9 point) font size"

    self nextPutAll: ' \fs19 '! !

!RTFStream methodsFor: 'rtf page formats' !

rtfHeader
    "Public - Appears at the top of an RTF file, should be called first"
    self nextPutAll:
'{\rtf1\ansi \deff0{\fonttbl{\f0\froman Times
New;}}{\colortbl\red0\green0\blue0;}{\stylesheet{\fs20 \snext0
Normal;}}\margl1440\margr1440\ftnbj\ftnrestart \sectd \sbknone\endnhere \pard
\s10 '!

rtfPage
    "Public - Place a marker to skip to the next page"
    self nextPutAll: '\page '
!

rtfTail
    "Public - Place the last information for the RTF file. Should be called last
    self nextPutAll: '}'
! !
!RTFStream methodsFor: 'rtf font styles' !

rtfBold
    "Public - Place a marker to start the Bold font style"

    self nextPutAll: '\b '!

rtfItalic
    "Public - Place a marker to start the Italic font style"

    self nextPutAll: '\i '!

rtfPlain
    "Public - Place a marker to reset the font styles and sizes to plain"

    self nextPutAll: ' \plain \fs24 '!

rtfUnderline
    "Public - Place a marker to start the Underline font style"

    self nextPutAll: '\ul '! !

!RTFStream class methodsFor: 'as yet unclassified' !

on: anIndexedCollection
        "Answer a new instance of the
        receiver on anIndexedCollection."
```

Continued

```
        ^(super on: anIndexedCollection) rtfHeader.
    ! !
DocumentationGenerator comment: '"Provides automatic document generation
based on the stored comments for each class.

To use:

""This line generates documentation for all classes in the cluster called
''Application Development'' ""
DocumentationGenerator formattedDocs

""This line generates documentation for a single class""
DocumentationGenerator generateDocumentationFor: #BusinessObject

-----------------------------------------------------------------
In order for the documentation to appear correctly, the code must be documented
consistently. Class comments can be stored in PVCS or class methods #COMMENT
#NOTES, both of which should return a string. Each method should have the
methodname, followed by a comment that will be used for documentation, stat-
ing Public or Private, and then the code.

This class uses RTFStream to create a Rich Text Format stream that can be
imported into your favourite word processor.
"'!
```

LISTING 2.13 An example documentation program.

This example program does not solve all of the documentation needs. It does not provide for any class purpose, examples, data item descriptions, or typesetting of the output. Reading the example, it is easy to see how it can be expanded to cover additional requirements, but the development effort required to create a complete documentation application is large, so it may be wise to consider a commercially available product like Class Publisher for VisualSmalltalk.

Class Publisher

Class Publisher, formerly called Synopsis, provides a complete documentation solution for the VisualSmalltalk programmer. It parses the Smalltalk source code, like the preceding example program, but provides a high-quality output in a formatted text version (RTF) or for on-line browsing within or outside of the Smalltalk environment.

The product centers around production of a class encyclopedia, and contains an interface to allow input and browsing of the documentation for classes within the Smalltalk environment while the programmer is coding. The format of the output is customizable so that the documentation may match any format needed. A sample of a Class Publisher page appears in Figure 2.4.

SynRTFTranslatorWithLimit

This object reads RTF and translates it via writing onto a SynWpStream. Given an input stream of RTF text and an output stream, it sends messages to the output stream to add the text and all formatting information represented by the RTF text.

Unlike its superclass, this class allows you to translate only a portion of some RTF text. You specify how much you want translated in terms of the number of paragraphs you want translated. Refer to method maxParagraphs: for details.

Superclasses:

SynRTFTranslator SynRTFReader SynObject Object

Instance Methods:

maxParagraphs

Answer the number of paragraphs that are to be translated when the read: message is sent to the receiver. A value of nil means that there is no limit, and all of the RTF text will be translated.

Instance Methods (private):

numbParagraphs numParagraphs:

Instance Variables:

maxParagraphs numParagraphs

Instance Variables (from superclasses):

directivesTable inputStream outputStream startOfDirective

FIGURE 2.4 Class Publisher, a commercial product, provides capabilities to enhance documentation of Smalltalk programs.

Summary

In this chapter, you have seen that there are some definite issues involved in style and programming quality. Smalltalk is quite good at helping the programmer to be most productive, but there are many ways to improve the process by which you create your Smalltalk code. You have seen several techniques to manage Smalltalk code and to document your Smalltalk programs. In the next chapter, you will further explore one of many interesting features of Smalltalk that can lead to better Smalltalk programs, the elusive dependency mechanism.

3

Dependencies

In this chapter you will explore the dependency mechanisms of Smalltalk. The dependency mechanism is one of the most powerful features of the Smalltalk environment, yet it is often not used or used poorly in Smalltalk programs. When applied properly, it can speed the development process and insulate classes from the changes that occur during an evolutionary development process. We will discuss:

- how the dependency mechanism works
- some real-world examples of the dependency mechanism
- the steps involved in using the dependency mechanism
- reasons to use the dependency mechanism
- common methods to call
- common methods to implement
- special methods available in some versions of Smalltalk
- some pitfalls to avoid in using the dependency mechanism
- how dependencies are used in the Model-View-Controller (MVC) paradigm present in the initial version of Smalltalk-80
- how dependencies are used in some of the alternatives to MVC

What Are Dependencies and What Is the Mechanism?

Dependencies are relationships between objects in Smalltalk. For example, for the following code:

```
add: first plus: second
"Public - Add first to second and return the result"
| result |
result := first + second.
^result
```

LISTING 3.1   A simple addition method.

The variable `result` is dependent on both `first` and `second`. For this example, the relationship is clear and explicit. If `first` changes and this code is executed, the `result` will change. If `second` changes and this code is executed, the `result` will also change. If both `first` and `second` change, then `result` will change, but based on this fragment, if `first` changes, `second` does not necessarily change and if `second` changes, then `first` does not necessarily change.

This example is simple and not one to which the dependency mechanism would apply, but it illustrates the concept of dependency and change. In the real Smalltalk world, the dependencies for which we would use the mechanism can be extremely complicated. The relationships may not all be explicitly known, having only been constructed piece by piece as the application evolved. We may have one dependency registered causing an update that, in turn, causes another dependency to be updated, and so on.

The real benefit of dependencies comes when growing or changing code. It is equally easy when writing code (and sometimes easier) to explicitly change a dependent object. But changing a dependent object creates a tight association between two types of objects and reduces the ability of an object to live alone in the object world. Dependencies improve encapsulation by removing the knowledge that one object has about another. Instead of coding an object to look inside something on which it is dependent, or to call a dependent's set of accessor functions (which must be consistent across the entire family of eligible objects), the dependency mechanism provides a well-formed and consistent way for two objects to communicate without deep knowledge of the other.

If a programmer were to write code that explicitly updated dependents, code would have to be written for each dependent to receive the types of changes expected. If the expected changes were altered, then both sides would have to be revised. If additional types of objects were added, or additional instances of objects, then the updates of these objects would also have to be coded into the application. Additional protocols might be required to send data to the dependent, and if the number or variety of arguments changed, both sides of the code would have to change. You can see the need for a mechanism that reduces the coupling of two or more different types of objects and, in addition, does not require the existence or knowledge of the dependents, but places the burden of requesting the information on the higher level of code.

How It Works

To illustrate the concept of dependencies in the Smalltalk environment, I have employed a stereotypical man and woman from the United States in the 1950s, a time of relative uniformity and predictability. I can use one class, Man, to abstractly represent all instances of men and one class, Woman, to abstractly represent all instances of women. If we have one primary instance of Man, named Chester, and one primary instance of Woman, named Linda, as in Figure 3.1, and a single instance of class IRS, called UncleSam, we can look at the dependencies between them. Linda and Chester are the typical Ozzie and Harriet couple.

UncleSam is a single global instance of IRS containing dependencies for all registered or reported instances of Man, Woman, and other significant objects in the system like Corporation, Foreign Corporation, and so on. UncleSam is analogous to the single class variable for Object that holds the dependencies. At this time, there is no entry in UncleSam for any object or

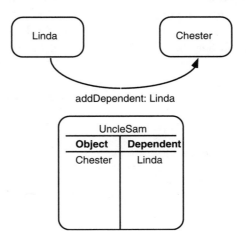

FIGURE 3.1 Basic dependencies, 1950's couple.

any dependents. Inspecting UncleSam reveals that it is an empty instance of IdentityDictionary.

Within UncleSam, there is currently no entry for Chester in the dependents area. If we execute the marry: method for Chester with Linda as the parameter, it will perform the following code:

```
marry: theRightWoman
"Private - can only be called by self or theRightWoman but only cooperatively
unless a shotgun is involved"
| |
self performMarriageCeremony.
self wife: theRightWoman.
self honeymoon.
self moveInTogether.
self addDependent: theRightWoman.
self changed: #marriage with: self.
```

LISTING 3.2 A marry: method for the Man class.

This method does some basic things for Chester, such as performing the marriage ceremony, going on a honeymoon, and moving in with the new bride. The method also serves to register Linda as a dependent of Chester, storing that association with UncleSam, who now maintains an entry associated with Chester. Inspecting UncleSam at this point would reveal that the instance of IdentityDictionary contains Chester as the key, with an instance of OrderedCollection containing Linda as the first and only entry. The changed:with: method will cause update:with: methods to execute within Chester's dependents (determined by looking inside UncleSam) which only includes Linda at this moment.

Linda's update:with: method, executed by the internal Smalltalk machinery because of Chester's changed:with: call, looks like the following:

```
update: aSymbol with: anObject
"Private - only called when notified by an object on which I'm dependent"
| |
(aSymbol = #marriage) ifTrue:
  [
  self husband: anObject.
  self husband isDeadBeat ifFalse:
    [
    self father removeDependent: self.
    ].
  ].
^self
```

LISTING 3.3 An update:with: method for the class Woman.

This method checks to see what message type is received (if many message types are received, the type can be converted into a message selector and executed against self—an efficient "case statement" of sorts from the C language). `Linda`'s husband is set to be `anObject` (which hopefully is the husband, `Chester`)! Before removing `Linda` from her father's list of dependents, we check to see if it is a wise decision by sending the selector `isDeadBeat` to `Chester` (which may not be the best place to find out the truth; `UncleSam` might be a better source of information). `Linda` is then removed from her father's list of dependents and becomes solely a dependent of `Chester`.

A few years down the road, `Chester` and `Linda` decide to have some children. Each time a child is born (after sending the `makeWhoopie` selector to the couple), the child must be added as a dependent of `Chester` (see Figure 3.2).

The instance method (in class `Woman`) looks something like the following:

```
giveBirth
"Private - can only be sent by self or instances of Stork"
| theBaby |
theBaby := Child new.
```
Continued

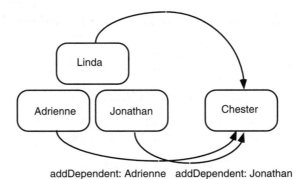

addDependent: Adrienne   addDependent: Jonathan

UncleSam	
Object	**Dependent**
Chester	#(Linda Adrienne Jonathan)

FIGURE 3.2 Extending dependencies, 1950's nuclear family.

```
theBaby name: (ChildrensNames randomPick).
self children add: theBaby.
self husband addDependent: theBaby.
```

LISTING 3.4 A `giveBirth` **method in the class** Woman.

After each execution of this method, UncleSam's entry in the IdentityDictionary for Chester contains an OrderedCollection of Linda first, followed by each child in the order that they were added.

With the dependencies now set up between Chester and Linda and the children, events that affect Chester are now automatically shared by Chester when the changed methods are sent to self by Chester. So if Chester loses his job, the method may look something like the following:

```
lostJob
"Private - try to keep this one very quiet"
| |
self salary: nil.
self changed: #noJob with: self.
```

LISTING 3.5 A `lostJob` **method in class** Man.

And once the changed: method is executed, Linda (and the children's) update: methods will be executed and may look like the following:

```
update: aSymbol with: anObject
"Private - only called when notified by an object on which I'm dependent"
| |
(aSymbol = #marriage) ifTrue:
   [
   self husband: anObject.
   self husband isDeadBeat ifFalse:
      [
      self father removeDependent: self.
      ].
   ].
(aSymbol = #noJob) ifTrue:
   [
   self husband encourageToWork.
   self mother callForSupport.
   ].
```

LISTING 3.6 The `update:with:` **method for the class** Woman.

The children's update: method will probably stay the same:

```
update: aSymbol with: anObject
"Private - Children do what Children do"
| |
self cry.
self sleep.
self eat.
self wet.
```

LISTING 3.7 The `update:with:` method for a child.

We could have simplified the `update:with:` method to simply `update:` and implemented it separately for `Linda`, but for purposes of showing one approach to extending the method, we did not. Sometimes in development, I choose to direct each of the `update:` type of methods to one final method. In that way, only one location exists for the true update functionality instead of spreading it among several. The best reason to keep them separate occurs when there is a clear division of functionality between the types of `update:` methods that will be called. For instance, you may wish to keep the messages for basic changes simple without the arguments. You may also wish to improve speed by reducing the additional number of calls that occur when redirecting routines to one single update method.

A Real-World Example

One of the projects on which I worked serves as an excellent example of how the dependency mechanism can work. The project used ObjectStudio under OS/2 to provide a prototype in both the user interface and the functionality of a customer service system. The project implemented a mission-critical client/server system providing workstation connections to a dozen different types of mainframe applications. The project could also have interfaced to a network-based SQL server based on the architecture (discussed in the SQL Database chapter), and may very well be doing so in the near future. The example presented here is similar in nature to the project's implementation.

The use of the dependency mechanism is rather interesting. Since the requirements stated that the user should be allowed to pursue any valid action at any time, even while data transaction responses were pending, an asynchronous notification mechanism was used. In addition, the data received by the application needed to be stored locally on the workstation. This meant that the dependency mechanism would be used to coordinate incoming messages from any of the mainframes while allowing other functions (including other outgoing and incoming transactions) to occur while a particular transaction was still pending.

Due to these requirements, the design embodied an intermediate layer that consisted of data (`Query` and `Update` class) objects. These data objects, when instantiated, had the GUI window instances set up as dependents of the data objects, using the `addDependent:` method. This method was called (message sent) immediately after the object was instantiated, as follows:

```
makeRequest
"Public - Make a sample request from the data layer"
| theRequest |
theRequest := Query new.
theRequest addDependent: self.
self requests add: theRequest.
"Simplification of request criteria usage"
theRequest query: { #'Account Name' }.
theRequest use: { #'Account Number' '123-456-789' }.
theRequest sendOnFailure: [:theRequestObject | self sendFailed:
theRequestObject ].
```

LISTING 3.8 The `makeRequest` method for a database query.

Since `theRequest` is a temporary variable scoped to the level of the method, after the method completes execution, the reference to the object is no longer needed, and `theRequest` may be garbage collected (except that `theRequest` is still referenced in the `Dependency` dictionary as a key). For this reason, and ease of manipulating `theRequest`, it is maintained in an instance variable (or even a class variable or pool since we use an accessor). When this instance receives an `update:` from `theRequest`, `theRequest` may be removed from the requests storage area. The request is simply filled with a desired data item from the application's data dictionary, with a search criterion and its key. The request is then sent (through another process, external to the system) with a failure-to-send routine installed through the one argument block supplied. If the request is successfully sent, the program can continue to respond to user requests and other database responses until the request is completed.

When the request returns to Smalltalk (through an external C callback that places a message to the data object, `theRequest`, at the end of the message queue) the data object will update itself with the returned data or error if data was not found. The data object can then use the `changed` method as follows:

```
externalResponse
"Private - received an external response from the mainframe/server. Check for
validity and notify dependents"
```

Continued

```
| |
self responseData isNil
ifTrue:
    [
    ^self changed: #errorNoData with: (self responseError).
    ].
self changed: #gotData with: self.
```

LISTING 3.9 The `externalResponse` method for an asynchronous data receiver.

The `update:with:` instance method in the requesting class is written to respond to the symbols `errorNoData` and `gotData` and to handle these conditions appropriately. In the case of `errorNoData`, the application would then branch to a routine that determines the action to take based on the reason for the error (that is, resend the transaction if a time-out occurred, notify user or other objects if the search key is inappropriate in format or not found). The `update:with:` instance method looks like the following:

```
update: aSymbol with: anObject
"Public - we will be notified if we are dependent on another object"
| |
(aSymbol = #errorNoData) ifTrue:
    [
    ^self doTheErrorThing
    ].
(aSymbol = #gotData) ifTrue:
    [
    self storeData: anObject.
    ^self doTheRightThing
    ].
^self doNothing
```

LISTING 3.10 The `update:with:` method for a data object.

How to Use Dependencies Step by Step

The first step in using the dependency mechanism is to analyze which dependencies should be placed under the control of this mechanism. Not all dependencies are appropriate for use; usually the best ones are those that have a cause-and-effect data change. GUI events that produce a data change are not typically placed under this mechanism. Rather, the GUI events are directly given to the dependent object (usually associated with a window or control). The events travel from the user, through the GUI, and into the instance of the window object. The window object may then manipulate and massage the data, causing other actions to occur and sending `self` `changed` messages (which causes an `update` message to be posted on the message queue). Control will then revert to the user event loop until either another user event occurs or an `update` event occurs.

The second step is to register the dependencies. This can be accomplished by using the `addDependent:` method. The action in this method depends on whether the class is a subclass of `Object` alone or a subclass of `Object` and `Model`.

If the class inherits the method from `Object`, the dependency is stored in a class variable for `Object`. The variable is most commonly called `Dependency`, but it is also known as `DependentsFields` in VisualWorks and `Dependents` in VisualAge. It consists of an instance of `Identity` `Dictionary` that will be initially empty. Since it is a class variable, it exists only once in the system, and stores all dependencies not specific to any `Model` (see upcoming). The entries in this `IdentityDictionary` consist of a `key`: the object that has dependents, and an `OrderedCollection` of the instances of other objects that depend on the key object. If there is only one dependent, it is still contained in an `OrderedCollection`. As the `addDependent:` method is called, dependents are added after the existing set of dependents. Since each entry in the dictionary is for an instance of an object, different instances of the same class can have dependents of different types, or different instances of the same class, and so on. This means that the dependency mechanism can register any object to be a dependent of another.

If a class inherits from `Model`, the dependencies are stored in an instance variable with the instance of the class. In this way, they are available for local manipulation if necessary, and get garbage collected at the end of the useful life of the `Model` subclass instance.

The third step is to write code to handle the `update:` messages in each of the dependents. This is generally the most time-consuming process because it involves deciphering the type of messages, the associated data items, and performing the action(s). The code may be simple or may be split into the various varieties of `update:` messages; the code may be a long set of `ifTrue:` statements, or the programmer may opt for a more dynamic approach, converting the first argument representing the type of change into a message send to `self` as follows:

```
update: aSymbol
"Private - receive messages from those that we care about deeply"
| |
"Check that we have a valid message before sending"
(self respondsTo: aSymbol) ifTrue:
```
Continued

```
    [
    self perform: aSymbol
    ].
```

LISTING 3.11 An `update:` method

The fourth step is to write code that causes dependency flags to be set. Whenever a variable or data item that a dependent may be interested in changes, a `self changed` message must be posted to the message queue. Additionally, an object may send messages explicitly to its dependents. Use of the `broadcast:` selectors will notify all dependents of the object of some change, and cause them to perform a message send contained in the symbol argument.

Why Use the Dependency Mechanism?

The primary reason to understand and make use of the mechanism is that it frees the programmer from having to worry about writing the code to update the dependent variables. It also frees the programmer from the task of ensuring that code to support each and every dependent is updated, especially when the program changes over time, which is typical of the Smalltalk programming approach of a rapidly evolving application.

Why Not Explicitly Update?

There are several arguments against explicitly updating dependents. The foremost is that explicitly updating violates the notion of encapsulation. Encapsulation provides the notion of insulating the internals of an object from the object world outside its bounds. It is only through a well-defined API that the object may be manipulated. This means that accessor methods (those methods that allow setting or getting the value of an instance variable directly) should not always be provided as a standard set of methods. They may be provided, but only for those properties that need to be externally manipulated to have a sensible functionality for the object.

Pitfalls

Generally, the dependency mechanism is safe, unlike the `become:` messages that can kill entire towns of objects with one single message send. There are two major problems to avoid: cyclical dependencies (the dog object chasing its tail), and overly persistent objects (living far beyond their useful lifetime).

Cyclical dependencies rarely occur when the programmer has a thorough understanding of the dependency mechanism. They can occur frequently when overdoing the dependencies. A simple example of this is as follows:

```
Object subclass: #MyObject
instanceVariableNames: ''
classVariableNames: ''
poolDictionaries: ''
class Methods

crashAndBurn
"Public - demonstrate the cyclical dependencies"
| me you them |
me := MyObject new.
you := MyObject new.
them := MyObject new.
me addDependent: you.
you addDependent: them.
them addDependent: me.
me changed.
```

LISTING 3.12   An example of cyclical dependencies.

If `MyObject` is defined such that the `update` messages that it receives cause other `changed` messages to be sent, the system will chase these dependencies in a circular fashion. The `update:` instance method looks like the following:

```
update: aSymbol
"Private - receive updates here"
| |
self changed.
```

LISTING 3.13   Another example of cyclical dependencies.

Executing the first set of code with `MyObject` defined with the preceding `update:` method causes the stack to overflow with changed and update messages in Digitalk Smalltalk. This is because first me sends the `changed` message. Then, in the `update:` method of you, the `changed` message is sent, which causes the `update:` method in them to execute, which causes again the `changed` method to be sent with an ensuing `update:` to me. Finally we're back where we started with a `changed` message being sent to me.

This is an obvious example; no real problems that exist in code will be this simple. They usually involve the GUI, with dependencies either set in both directions (GUI->window object *and* window object->GUI instead of just window object->GUI), or through improper use of the window objects.

The dependencies for the GUI should exist only in the direction from the objects to the GUI. The GUI code should directly send messages to the window. The reason for this one-sided dependency is to avoid the circular dependency problem that will cause the system to loop indefinitely.

The second pitfall of the dependency mechanism involves objects that never get garbage collected. They persist forever because the code that used `addDependent:` never used the `removeDependent:` message to clean up the dependency dictionary. Because the dependent is never removed from the dictionary, it is still referenced in the Smalltalk environment and may not be garbage collected. With the preceding example, after three runs of the `crashAndBurn` method, nine entries will exist in the dependents `IdentityDictionary`. For each of these entries, there is also an `Ordered Collection`, and a reference to the single dependent. It is easy to see from this example how memory will be quickly exhausted without the object cleanup.

To clean up the dependency dictionary, the programmer may manually remove items, access the dependents dictionary to manipulate it through code, or most important, write code that cleans up after itself! The preceding `crashAndBurn` method could be rewritten as follows to clean up after itself:

```
crashAndBurn
"Public - demonstrate the cyclical dependencies"
| me you them |
me := MyObject new.
you := MyObject new.
them := MyObject new.
me addDependent: you.
you addDependent: them.
them addDependent: me.
me changed. "<--- Here's the crash and burn!"
me removeDependent: you.
you removeDependent: them.
them removeDependent: me.
```

LISTING 3.14 Cyclical dependencies cause problems.

The program will now clean up after itself, only if execution passes the me changed statement (by commenting it out!).

Dependency Methods

Methods to Call

The following methods are those common to the various Smalltalk implementations. They are the minimum set necessary to program the dependency behavior. The methods in this section are those that are called by the program when creating or deleting dependencies and notifying dependents of changes. The next section contains those methods that must be implemented in the dependent object in order to receive dependency messages.

addDependent: anObject

Adds anObject *to the list of dependents for the receiver. This means that for a subclass of* Object *that is not also a subclass of* Model *or an equivalent, that* anObject *is stored in the* Object *class variable holding the dependencies. The argument* anObject *is stored in the array of objects associated with the key corresponding to the receiver. For subclasses of* Model *or equivalent, the argument* anObject *is sorted with other dependents in an instance variable.*

allDependents (Visual Smalltalk, ObjectStudio)

dependents (SmalltalkAgents, VisualWorks)

Answers the array of dependents associated with the receiver. Obtained from the class instance variable in Object *or from the* Model *instance variable if the receiver is a subclass of* Model *or an equivalent.*

broadcast: aSymbol
broadcast: aSymbol with: anObject

Causes the value of aSymbol *to be sent to each of the dependents as a selector. If* aSymbol *contains* hello, *then each of the dependents in the receiver's dependency list will be sent the message* hello. *If the receiver does not understand the message, the usual exceptions will occur, such as the debugger opening with a complaint about the dependent not understanding* hello. *The* with: anObject *extension will cause an argument (*anObject*) to be placed on the stack. In this case,* aSymbol *should contain something like* hello:, *and the dependent should have a method defined for* hello: anArgument *where* anArgument *is equal to* anObject.

```
changed
changed: aSymbol
changed: aSymbol with: anObject
```

```
changed: aSymbol with: anObject with: anotherObject (Visual
Smalltalk, ObjectStudio)
```

Usually sent to self, *causes the* update *message to be sent to each dependent.*

```
removeDependent: anObject
```

Removes anObject *from the dependency list for the receiver. This means that for a subclass of* Object *that is not also a subclass of* Model *or equivalent, that* anObject *is removed from the* Object *class variable holding the dependencies. The argument is removed from the value associated with the key corresponding to the receiver. For subclasses of* Model *or equivalent, the argument* anObject *is removed from the dependents stored in an instance variable. It is a good idea to use this method to dispose of the dependency stored in the* Object *class variable so that the object can be garbage collected. Failing to use this method means that the lifetime of the dependent will be indeterminate, and the dependent will not be marked for garbage collection, resulting in additional memory usage and overhead.*

Methods to Implement

```
update: aSymbol
update: aSymbol with: anObject
```

```
update: aSymbol with: anObject from: aSender (VisualWorks)
```

```
update: aSymbol with: anObject with: anotherObject (Visual Smalltalk,
ObjectStudio)
```

The implementation of this method is crucial to receive any notification of changes from any object on which the receiver depends. This method is called by the Smalltalk engine and is the mechanism through which dependents (in this case, self) are notified of a significant change. The implementation of one or many of these is necessary in order for the dependency mechanism to function. Typically, aSymbol is a criterion that indicates the type of change that occurred. The types of criteria that can be used in aSymbol are as varied as Smalltalk applications, so just about any criteria can be considered correct. Some examples are: the name of a variable (or data item) such as cost; the type of event that occurred such as mouseClick or communicationsResponse; a flag indicator such as linkDown or gameOver.

Special Methods

The following methods, grouped by product name, are also available in some implementations of Smalltalk. While many of them are useful extensions, none of them is required to make the dependency mechanism functional. They are mentioned here for reference for the reader; details of each method can be found in the appropriate vendor's on-line or paper documentation.

SmalltalkAgents

These methods primarily are provided to handle the semantic message sends supported in STA. Semantic messages check to see if the receiver understands the message before sending it, and, in the case of dependencies, they are stored with the other semantic messages.

```
allReferences
allReferencesDo:
broadcast:withParameters:
dependencySelector
dependentsDo:
on:evaluate:
on:send:
on:send:to:
on:send:to:with:
on:send:to:withParameters:
removeAllBehaviorsWithReceiver:
removeBehaviorsForSelector:
removeBehaviorsSatisfying:forSelector:
removeBehaviorsWithReceiver:forSelector:
smSelectorsUnderstood
```

 VisualWorks

These methods extend the basics of dependency and provide features geared toward the Model-View-Controller paradigm present only in ParcPlace Smalltalk. The myDependent *methods exist to be overridden in* Model *so that the dependencies are stored in the instance variable.*

```
expressInterestIn:anAspect for: anObject sendBack: aSelector
retractInterestIn: anAspectfor: anObject
performUpdate: aSymbol
performUpdate: aSymbol with: anObject
updateRequest
updateRequest:
changeRequest
changeRequest:
changeRequestFrom:
asDependentsAsCollection
asDependentsWith:
asDependentsWithout:
myDependents
myDependents: dependentsOrNil
```

Continued

```
breakDependents
setDependents
CLASS - initializeDependentsFields
```

 ## VisualSmalltalk Enterprise

One additional method to provide a complementary method for add
Dependent:
dependsOn:

 ## VisualAge

No additional methods of interest for dependencies were identified.

 ## Enfin

*These additional methods exist primarily for the Enfin concepts of linking the
database access with the dependents (note the use of the word field throughout).*

```
addDependent:field:
changed:type:
changedField:pos:type:
changedField:type:
changeReferencesTo:
dependencies
dependents
dependsOn:
getActualDependent
hasDependent
removeDependent:field:
removeSelfFromDependents
startAccessUpdateDependent:field:
swapReferencesTo:
update:with:with:with:
```

Separating the Model from the ViewController

The concept Model-View-Controller(MVC) has been around since the first
GUI (a Xerox Star running Smalltalk). Since that time, a somewhat differ-

ent model of GUI events and interaction has become the standard. For this and other historical reasons, the only commercially available Smalltalk that truly supports MVC is ParcPlace.

As far as dependencies are concerned, the approach to MVC is similar to that of a non-MVC approach: The Controller (the item that the user clicks, types, and so on from the keyboard/mouse) directly sends messages to the model. The Model (repository for data, main coordinator of all program functionality and computation) will send `changed` messages to itself after registering the view(s) as dependents using `addDependent:`. The View (the visual data, providing feedback for some controllers and just views of data for others, some with no controller) executes `update:` messages as a result of the model's `change` messages and manages to update the screen.

Non-MVC Dependency Models

I have seen little use of dependencies in non-MVC programs. This doesn't mean people are not using them, because they do exist. For instance, dependencies are maintained in Digitalk's ViewManager Class similar to the way they are in ParcPlace's model class, but each item on the screen is both the view and the controller combined, as we find most of the GUIs available these days. The use of dependencies is not widespread because they are not required for the GUI to work. It might make the work a little easier to maintain and change if used, but many may not encounter an approach to using it.

My approach to using dependencies in the non-MVC world is to use direct calls from the user to the program and the dependencies from the code to the user. In this way, the program can respond immediately to the user's actions and update the display when needed or required. Use of the dependency mechanism may also remove some of the need to enable and disable drawing to resolve incorrect and untimely updates of the screen, sometimes seen as flashing on the screen as the display refreshes repeatedly. This nonforce approach requires a different approach to these non-MVC GUI's, which are usually programmed by force in the non-Smalltalk world.

Summary

In this chapter you have seen examples of the dependency mechanism in use and learned some reasons to use it. You have also explored step by step how to implement the dependency mechanism in programs so that you have yet another tool in your arsenal of programming abilities. A reference was also provided to the commonly used methods in this area for each of the major Smalltalk versions. You will use the dependency mechanism further in this book where appropriate, as you explore some of the other magic behind Smalltalk.

4

Processes and Threads

The notion of running various tasks in parallel is appealing because it allows the division of labor to be organized into distinct units that can be run on multiple workstations. Currently, it is difficult to parallel process in mainstream versions of Smalltalk across workstations or processes, but the capability to run parallel processes within the same machine does exist. This chapter will cover:

* an overview of the concepts of processes and threads
* a definition of Smalltalk processes and threads
* how Smalltalk threads coordinate with each other
* examples of when and how to use threads in Smalltalk
* reference for classes and methods important to using threads in Smalltalk

Processes vs. Threads

In operating system terms, a process carries a lot more weight than a thread. The operating system, if multitasking, contains one or more processes. Each process contains its own memory space, stack, and program execution pointer. These processes can in turn contain one or more threads if the operating system is also multithreaded. All threads within a process share memory space and have separate program execution pointers. The process/thread concept is illustrated in Figure 4.1.

Since the Smalltalk environment runs within one operating system process, it is capable of containing one or more threads based on the capabilities of the operating system and the version of Smalltalk. ObjectStudio, for example, only runs one Smalltalk thread, although it runs in two operating system threads under OS/2. Since version 4.1 runs in a single thread and does not support multiple Smalltalk threads or Smalltalk processes, it will not be discussed in this chapter, although additional threads can be run in the process in C or another low-level language, just not Smalltalk, as shown in Figure 4.2.

Any of the Smalltalks can effectively create side threads in other low-level, non-Smalltalk languages, as shown in Figure 4.3. These are typically created from the low-level language, which is usually C, using operating system calls. These threads can do tasks like monitoring a communications input or managing an interprocess communications link. These threads are dependent on the capability of the workstation operating system.

Smalltalk threads are not dependent on the underlying workstation operating system. These threads are often called processes within the Smalltalk environment although they don't exactly fit the definition for a thread or process. Regardless of what they are called (thread will be used here), they give the programmer the capability to schedule and prioritize the seemingly parallel execution of various code modules. It is not truly parallel because the Smalltalk environment serializes the execution of each thread in order for the single CPU workstation to process the code.

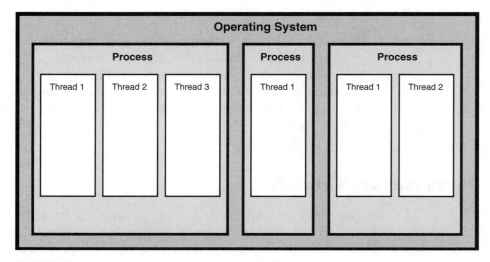

FIGURE 4.1   Operating system processes and threads.

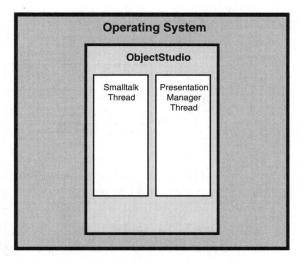

FIGURE 4.2 The ObjectStudio process with its threads and an auxiliary C thread.

Though the implementations vary in details from one Smalltalk to the next, the basic capabilities are quite similar, and the approach to using the threads is nearly the same. Figure 4.4 shows a set of Smalltalk threads at different priority levels within the system. The higher numbers represent a higher priority, and execution will occur at the higher priorities before the lower. The threads in Figure 4.4 will serve as an example of execution for comparison of nonpreemptive and preemptive multitasking within Smalltalk.

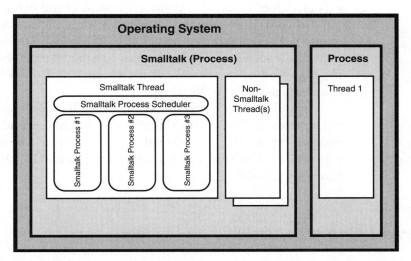

FIGURE 4.3 Non-Smalltalk threads running in parallel with Smalltalk threads and processes.

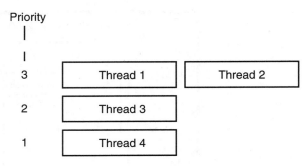

FIGURE 4.4   A set of threads at different priority levels within the Smalltalk operating system process.

In the case of VisualWorks and VisualSmalltalk Enterprise, the Smalltalk Processes are not time-slice preemptive. This means that two processes scheduled for execution at the same priority will not occur simultaneously by switching back and forth automatically. An example of how the threads are executed is shown in Figure 4.5.

The first thread scheduled at the level will execute first and run to completion or a `yield` statement. The second thread will then run at the priority, and then the third, and so on. Once the final thread has completed at this level, and the execution of all yielded processes has completed at this level, processes at lower levels will get executed. Note that execution of the highest-priority threads occurs before any execution of the lower-priority threads, so if priority level 4 threads are always executing, a level 3 thread will never get executed. Remember this point when writing and debugging programs.

In IBM Smalltalk and SmalltalkAgents, the thread model is fully preemptive. This means that processing time is given to each of the threads at the same level equally, or as close as possible to equal based on the scheduling algorithms. An example of the execution of threads within these environments is shown in Figure 4.6.

The first thread scheduled at a given level will be executed first, then the second, and so on. The difference is that the second thread will begin to execute before the first thread has completed. The exact nature of the scheduling algorithm can be understood better by observing behavior of threads in action.

Thread Coordination

So, now you've rewritten your programs to have dozens of threads executing. But since your algorithms are no longer executing serially in the same

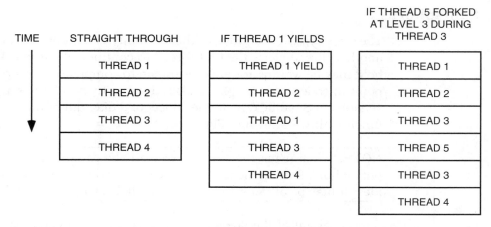

FIGURE 4.5 Execution order of nonpreemptive multitasking in Smalltalk.

fashion, problems are appearing and the results are less than perfect. You need the thread coordination mechanisms within Smalltalk to serialize some of the activities of these threads. Many times, one thread must complete or reach a certain point in code before execution of another thread can continue; or one thread needs to pass information to another. Mechanisms to coordinate the threads exist in Smalltalk and can solve problems that come from parallelization.

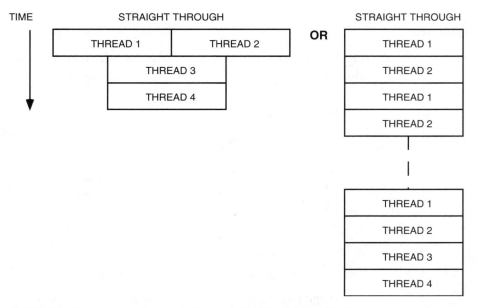

FIGURE 4.6 Execution of preemptive multitasking in Smalltalk.

Semaphores

The class Semaphore provides the capability to put one thread on hold until another thread alerts the first thread to continue execution. The thread on hold may be waiting for another thread to complete, or just reach a certain point in code. The Semaphore class does pretty much the same thing in all versions of Smalltalk. A simple conceptual diagram of the Semaphore class functionality is shown in Figure 4.7.

NOTE: When using the Semaphore class, be careful of which threads you put on hold. Putting the user interface thread on hold is probably not a good idea. It may be difficult to wake Smalltalk back up!

A variant of the Semaphore class is the Delay class that provides that capability to make a thread wait for a specified period of time and then begin execution. This is useful when a period of time needs to pass before execution. It can be used when interacting with the world outside Smalltalk where delays may be necessary to coordinate with outside events and their time lags.

Another interesting variant of the Semaphore class is the Promise class. The Promise class makes the process of evaluating such things as separate mathematical equations easier by using the concept that the second thread will finish calculating and fulfill the promise of calculating something. This class is available in VisualWorks.

Queues

The class Queue and the variants like SharedQueue allow the passing of data from one thread to another. To use Queue, both threads must have access to

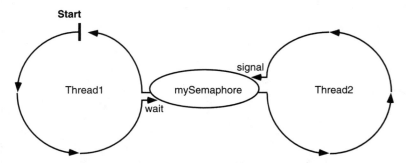

Note: Execution occurs through the Process Scheduler, not mySemaphore.

FIGURE 4.7 A conceptual diagram of how the Semaphore class operates in Smalltalk.

the same instance of Queue. This can be done by storing the instance of Queue in:

- ♦ a global:
  ```
  Smalltalk at: #MyQueue
  ```

- ♦ a pool:

  include the pool in the class definition or

  ```
  (Smalltalk at: #MyPool) at: #MyQueue
  ```

- ♦ a variable from the method that forks the processes:
  ```
  | myQueue |
  myQueue := Queue new.
  [ "Thread 1" ] fork.
  [ "Thread 2" ] fork.
  ```

- ♦ a method from another shared object:
  ```
  | anotherObject |
  anotherObject := MyAwesomeClass new.
  [ "Thread 1" ] fork.
  [ "Thread 2" ] fork.
  ```

SharedQueue (available in VisualWorks) combines the behavior of Queue with that of Semaphore. It allows a process to wait on a queue until an element appears in the queue. This is useful for coordinating algorithms that use input from other processes.

When and Why to Use Threads

Threads can be useful for performing processes at various levels of priority. For example, the user may be performing various input and manipulation activities, but when a communications response comes into the workstation, user activity may be interrupted to receive the information.

The Smalltalk environment uses various processing levels for its own activities. Incremental garbage collection takes place at a very low level, while the user is not interacting with the workstation. When memory runs low, the user activity will be suspended while a higher level thread takes over to garbage collect.

Other problems that can be solved with threads are background processing, like sorting or equation solving, while the user continues to work with the interface.

Examples

 VisualWorks

The VisualWorks thread model executes code in a serialized order and priority-based fashion. Threads are executed from highest to lowest priority, with the threads at each priority running in the order in which they were scheduled. Lower-priority threads do not get executed until higher-priority threads have been completed, including those that have yielded. The following code serves as an example of this:

```
[Transcript show: 'High'; cr. ] fork.
[Transcript show: 'Medium'; cr. ] fork.
Transcript show: 'Low'; cr.
```

produces:

```
Low[cr]
High[cr]
Medium[cr]
```

which shows the current thread completing first (low), followed by the first scheduled (high), and then the second scheduled (medium).

More examples:

```
[Transcript show: 'High'; cr. ] forkAt: 30.
[Transcript show: 'Medium'; cr. ] forkAt: 40.
Transcript show: 'Low'; cr.
```

produces:

```
Low[cr]
Medium[cr]
High[cr]
```

And:

```
| mySemaphore |
mySemaphore := Semaphore new.
[Transcript show: 'High'; cr. mySemaphore signal. ] forkAt: 30.
[mySemaphore wait. Transcript show: 'Medium'; cr. ] forkAt: 40.
Transcript show: 'Low'; cr.
```

produces:

```
Low[cr]
High[cr]
Medium[cr]
```

because the main thread keeps on going, followed by the `forkAt: 40` block, which suspends execution awaiting the semaphore `mySemaphore` to be signaled. The `forkAt: 30` process then executes, and after `mySemaphore signal` is evaluated, the `forkAt: 40` process continues.

 VisualSmalltalk Enterprise

An easy way to create a thread in VisualSmalltalk Enterprise is to send the `fork` message to an instance of `ZeroArgumentBlock`.

```
"This code sample will sound the bell"
[ UserLibrary messageBeep: -1 ] fork.
```

If several processes are forked at the same time, and the level of the processes is the same, they will be executed in the order of oldest (first created) to newest (most recently created). The pitches here will be: High, Medium, Low.

```
"This code sample will go down in pitch"
| mySpeaker |
mySpeaker := PARTSSpeakerDLL open.
"High Pitch"
[ mySpeaker beep: 5000 for: 500 ] fork. "Implied priority of 4"
"Medium Pitch"
[ mySpeaker beep: 2500 for: 750 ] fork. "Implied priority of 4"
"Low Pitch"
mySpeaker beep: 500 for: 1000. "Implied priority of 4"
"Close the DLL and invalidate mySpeaker"
mySpeaker close.
```

If several processes are forked at the same time and the level of the processes is different, the highest-priority processes will be executed first in the order in which they were created (oldest to newest). The priorities are then iterated over until the level of the original priority is reached, and execution will resume there. Once the original process has yielded or terminated, lower-level priorities will execute. The pitches here will be: Low, Medium, High.

```
"This code sample will go up in pitch"
| mySpeaker |
mySpeaker := PARTSSpeakerDLL open.
"High Pitch"
[ mySpeaker beep: 5000 for: 500 ] forkAt: 2.
"Medium Pitch"
[ mySpeaker beep: 2500 for: 750 ] forkAt: 3.
"Low Pitch"
mySpeaker beep: 500 for: 1000. "Implied priority of 4"
"Close the DLL and invalidate mySpeaker"
mySpeaker close.
```

If the execution of a routine is to wait for the completion of one or more threads, a semaphore may be used. The pitches here will be: Medium, Low, High.

```
"This code sample will go Medium, Low, High in pitch"
| mySpeaker mySemaphore |
mySpeaker := PARTSSpeakerDLL open.
mySemaphore := Semaphore new.
"High Pitch"
[ mySpeaker beep: 5000 for: 500. mySemaphore signal.] forkAt: 2.
"Medium Pitch"
[ mySpeaker beep: 2500 for: 750 ] forkAt: 3.
"Wait for mySemaphore signal to occur"
mySemaphore wait.
"Low Pitch"
mySpeaker beep: 500 for: 1000. "Implied priority of 4"
"Close the DLL and invalidate mySpeaker"
"Better put it in a background, lowest level process or it
may be gone before the above processes finish executing"
[ mySpeaker close. ] forkAt: 1.
```

If the process that sends the semaphore is level 3, the higher-priority code at level 4 will be executed before the level 2 code. The pitches here will be: Medium, High, Low.

```
"This code sample will go Medium, High, Low in pitch"
| mySpeaker mySemaphore |
mySpeaker := PARTSSpeakerDLL open.
mySemaphore := Semaphore new.
"High Pitch"
[ mySpeaker beep: 5000 for: 500. ] forkAt: 2.
"Medium Pitch"
[ mySpeaker beep: 2500 for: 750. mySemaphore signal.] forkAt: 3.
"Wait for mySemaphore signal to occur"
mySemaphore wait.
"Low Pitch"
mySpeaker beep: 500 for: 1000. "Implied priority of 4"
```

Continued

```
"Close the DLL and invalidate mySpeaker"
"Better put it in a background, lowest level process or it
may be gone before the above processes finish executing"
[ mySpeaker close. ] forkAt: 1.
```

 IBM Smalltalk/VisualAge

The IBM Smalltalk/VisualAge thread model executes code in a much more parallel fashion than VisualSmalltalk Enterprise. The completion of threads is not in a serial fashion; rather, the CPU time is divided among threads of the same priority. The following code serves as an example of this:

```
[Transcript show: 'High'; cr. ] fork.
[Transcript show: 'Medium'; cr. ] fork.
Transcript show: 'Low'; cr.
```

produces:

```
Low[cr]
HighMedium[cr]
[cr]
```

which is not as seen in VisualSmalltalk Enterprise. The more significant paralleling that goes on in IBM Smalltalk/VisualAge differentiates it from VisualSmalltalk Enterprise. The general approach and coding is similar.

More examples:

```
[Transcript show: 'High'; cr. ] forkAt: 2.
[Transcript show: 'Medium'; cr. ] forkAt: 3.
Transcript show: 'Low'; cr.
```

produces:

```
Low[cr]
Medium[cr]
High[cr]
```

And:

```
| mySemaphore |
mySemaphore := Semaphore new.
[Transcript show: 'High'; cr. mySemaphore signal. ] forkAt: 3.
[mySemaphore wait. Transcript show: 'Medium'; cr. ] forkAt: 4.
Transcript show: 'Low'; cr.
```

produces:

```
Low[cr]
High[cr]
Medium[cr]
```

because the main thread keeps on going, followed by the `forkAt: 4` block, which suspends execution awaiting the semaphore `mySemaphore` to be signaled. The `forkAt: 3` process then executes, and after `mySemaphore signal` is evaluated, the `forkAt: 4` process continues.

There is a danger in using semaphores. If the preceding code reads as follows:

```
| mySemaphore |
mySemaphore := Semaphore new.
[Transcript show: 'High'; cr. mySemaphore signal. ] forkAt: 3.
[Transcript show: 'Medium'; cr. ] forkAt: 4.
mySemaphore wait.
Transcript show: 'Low'; cr.
```

it will hang up the user interface thread, awaiting the semaphore. The semaphore signal is never sent, probably because all threads are dependent on the user interface thread remaining active. This is a scheduling issue in IBM Smalltalk/VisualAge that is an artifact of the way processes are scheduled more in parallel, and reflects a different underlying mechanism from the other Smalltalks.

SmalltalkAgents

Here's an example of running a thread to beep the speakers. The life of this thread entails beeping the speakers then dying.

```
Thread run: [Speakers beep.].
```

To create a thread without immediately executing the thread, first create the thread with the `Thread>>(class)new: aBlock` message, then initiate it by sending the thread the message `executionState:` with an argument of 1:

```
| theThreadInstance |
"Create the thread."
theThreadInstance := Thread new: [Speakers beep.].
```

Continued

```
"Start the thread running."
theThreadInstance executionState: 1.
```

In order to get efficient, extremely lightweight threads that take the least amount of CPU time, use the following approach: SmalltalkAgents threads all maintain an event queue, and they are automatically awakened whenever an event is posted into this queue. For the most complete "interrupt-driven" style of thread usage, this fact can be used as shown in the following code:

```
| myThread |

myThread :=
    Thread run: [
        [true] whileTrue: [

            | mask anEvent |

            [mask := thread disableSignals.
            (anEvent := thread nextEvent) notNil] whileTrue: [

                thread enableSignals: mask.
                anEvent send].
            thread enableSignals: mask; sleep.].
```

The disabling of signals in the preceding code ensures that other threads can run only while each event being processed is running. This minimizes the possibility of an event coming in just before going to sleep and getting caught in the queue.

Messages could be added to this thread's queue with code like the following:

```
myThread send: #beep to: Speakers
    "tell the thread to beep."
myThread send: #with: to: List with: 1
    "tell the thread to create a new <List>, {1.}."
```

To perform idle time actions such as blinking a selection, an object can be set up to receive idle notification through the scheduler, the sole instance of UIScheduler. The scheduler keeps a list of objects that are interested in receiving idle notification and sends these objects the message IdleTask (capital I) when it obtains idle time during its main event cycle. A minimum amount of time (currently, 12 ticks) must pass from the time when idle events are processed at one point to the time when they will next be processed. When they are processed, all objects are notified at one time, and their handler methods are synchronously executed. For this reason, processing done at idle time should be restricted to actions that are extremely simple and fast.

Objects register interest in receiving notification of idle events by sending the message `addIdleTask: anObjectInterestedInIdleTasks` to the `scheduler`.

Idle notification can also be handled by sending the same `addIdleTask:` message to a window. In this case, the object receives the message `idleTask` (small i) when idle tasks are being processed. In the window implementation of idle tasks, the window is the only object registered directly through the `scheduler`. Whenever it receives idle task notification, it in turn sends a notification to the list it keeps of objects interested in idle events. Thus the scheduler never knows about the existence of the objects registered with the window, and as soon as the window is removed from the `scheduler`'s task list, all objects registered through the window are also effectively removed.

Reference

 VisualWorks

BlockClosure

Instances of `BlockClosure` are created when a block is evaluated and is represented in source code by square brackets [].

fork	Create and schedule a process running the code in the receiver. Answer the new process.
forkAt: priority	Create and schedule a process running the code in the receiver. The priority of the process is the argument, priority. Answer the new process.
newProcess	Answer a new process running the code in the receiver. The process is not scheduled.
newProcessWith Arguments: anArray	Answer a new process running the code in the receiver. The receiver's block arguments are bound to the contents of the argument, `anArray`. The process is not scheduled.
promise	Answer a promise that represents the result of evaluating the receiver. See class `Promise` for more information.

promiseAt: aPriority	Answer a promise that represents the result of evaluating the receiver at the given priority. See class `Promise` for more information.

Process

Class process represents an independent path of control in the system. This path of control may be stopped (by sending the instance the message suspend) in such a way that it can later be restarted (by sending the instance the message resume). When any one of several paths of control can be advanced, the single instance of `ProcessorScheduler` named `Processor` determines which one will actually be advanced partly using the instance's priority.

interruptWith: aBlock	Force the receiver to interrupt whatever it is doing and to evaluate `aBlock`. The result of the evaluation is discarded. When the evaluation is completed, the receiver goes back to whatever it was doing before (including, if relevant, waiting on a semaphore). Only one interrupter allowed at a time.
resume	Allow the process that the receiver represents to continue. Put the receiver in line to become the `activeProcess`. Fail if the receiver is already waiting in a queue (in a `Semaphore` or `ProcessScheduler`).
suspend	Stop the process that the receiver represents in such a way that it can be restarted at a later time (by sending the receiver the message resume). If the receiver represents the `activeProcess`, suspend it. Otherwise, simply remove the receiver from the list of waiting processes, either in the scheduler or a semaphore.
suspendUnconditionally	Stqp the process that the receiver represents in such a way that it can be restarted at a later time (by sending the receiver the message resume). If the receiver represents the `activeProcess`, suspend it. Otherwise, simply remove the receiver from the list of waiting processes, either in the scheduler or a semaphore.

terminate	Terminate the receiver process, by sending the `Process terminateSignal`.
priority	Answer the priority of the receiver.
priority: anInteger	Set the receiver's priority to `anInteger`. Note that if the receiver is the currently active process, the new priority is lower, and there are higher-priority processes ready to run, the active process will be preempted.
uninterruptablyDo: aBlock	Execute the block, without interrupts (from `Process>>interruptWith:`) with respect to the receiver (process), which may or may not be the currently active process. Note that this does not prevent preemption by higher-priority processes. Use this facility *very* sparingly!!
(class) terminateSignal	Answer the `Signal` that is sent to terminate a process.

ProcessorScheduler

The single instance of class `ProcessorScheduler`, named `Processor` (`Smalltalk at: Processor`), coordinates the use of the physical processor by all instances of `Process` requiring service.

activeProcess	Answer the currently running `Process`.
highestPriority	Answer the number of priority levels currently available for use.
highestPriority: newHighestPriority	Change the number of priority levels currently available for use.
processesAt: priority	Answer the number of processes at priority-level priority.
remove: aProcess ifAbsent: aBlock	Remove `aProcess` from the list on which it is waiting for the processor. If it is not waiting, evaluate `aBlock`.
suspendFirstAt: aPriority	Suspend the first `Process` that is waiting to run with priority `aPriority`.
yield	Give other processes at the current priority a chance to run.
Process Priorities	These priorities are accessed as class methods. The highest priority is 100 and the lowest is 1. The processes normally run at 50 unless otherwise set.

```
systemRockBottomPriority   (1)
systemBackgroundPriority   (10)
userBackgroundPriority   (30)
userSchedulingPriority   (50)
userInterrupPriority   (70)
lowIOPriority   (90)
highIOPriority   (98)
timingPriority   (100)
```

Semaphore

Class `Semaphore` provides synchronized communication of a single bit of information (a "signal") between processes. A signal is sent by dispatching the instance the message `signal` and received by sending it the message `wait`. If no signal has been sent when a `wait` message is sent, the sending `Process` will be suspended until a signal is sent.

signal   Send a signal through the receiver. If one or more processes have been suspended trying to receive a signal, allow the first one to proceed. If no process is waiting, remember the excess signal.

wait   The active `Process` must receive a signal through the receiver before proceeding. If no signal has been sent, the active `Process` will be suspended until one is sent.

Promise

A `Promise` represents a value that is being computed by a concurrently executing process. An attempt to read the value of a `Promise` will wait until the process has finished computing it. If the process terminates with an exception, an attempt to read the value of the `Promise` will raise the same exception.

value   Answer the value computed by the child process. If the child terminated with an exception, raise that exception in the parent instead of answering a value.

(class)
example1

```
" This is an example of a successful Promise evaluation. "
| prom |
prom := [3 + 4] promise.
^prom value
```

SharedQueue

Class `SharedQueue` provides synchronized communication of arbitrary objects between processes. An object is sent by dispatching an instance the message `nextPut:` and received by sending it the message `next`. If no object has been sent when a `next` message is sent, the `Process` requesting the object will be suspended until one is sent.

next	Answer the object that was sent through the receiver first and has not yet been received by anyone. If no object has been sent, suspend the requesting process until one is.
nextPut: value	Send a value through the receiver. If a `Process` has been suspended waiting to receive a value through the receiver, allow it to proceed.
peek	Answer the object that was sent through the receiver first and has not yet been received by anyone, but do not remove it from the receiver. If no object has been sent, answer `nil`.
size	Answer the number of objects that have been sent through the receiver and not yet received by anyone.
isEmpty	Answer whether any objects have been sent through the receiver and not yet received by anyone.
(class) new	Answer a new instance of `SharedQueue` that has 10 elements.
(class) new: anInteger	Answer a new instance of `SharedQueue`, allocating space for the given number of elements.

Delay

Class `Delay` represents a real-time delay in the execution of a `Process`. An instance of `Delay` will respond to the message `wait` by suspending the active process for a certain amount of time. The time for resumption of the active process is specified when the `Delay` is created.

The resumption time can be specified relative to the current time with the messages `Delay forMilliseconds: anInteger` and `Delay forSeconds: anInteger`. `Delays` created in this way can be sent the message `wait` again after they have finished a previous delay.

The resumption time can also be specified at an absolute time with respect to the system's millisecond clock with the message `Delay untilMillisecond: anInteger`. Delays created in this way cannot be sent the message `wait` repeatedly.

delaySemaphore	Answer the semaphore that will be signaled when the delay expires.
resumptionTime	Answer the value of the system's milli-secondClock at which the receiver's suspended `Process` will resume.
disable	Remove the receiver from the queue of delayed processes to be serviced.
startup	Signal the delay's semaphore in the amount of time specified when the receiver was initialized.
wait	Suspend the active process for an amount of time specified when the receiver was initialized.
inProgress	Answer `true` if the delay is still pending.
(class) forMilliseconds: millisecondCount	Answer a new instance that will delay the active process for `millisecondCount` milliseconds when sent the message `wait`.
(class) forSeconds: secondCount	Answer a new instance that will delay the active process for `secondCount` seconds when sent the message `wait`.
(class) untilMilliseconds: millisecondCount	Answer a new instance that will delay the active process until the system's millisecond clock value is `millisecondCount` when sent the message `wait`.
(class) millisecond ClockValue	Answer the current value of the system's millisecond clock.

VisualSmalltalk Enterprise

Process

The current process is stored in the global `CurrentProcess` (`Smalltalk at: CurrentProcess`).

isUserIF	Answer `true` if receiver is a user interface process.

makeUserIF	Make the receiver be the user interface process.
name	Answer the process name.
name: aString	Set the process name to aString.
priority	Answer an integer representing the receiver process priority.
priority: aNumber	Change the priority of the receiver process to aNumber. aNumber is between 1 and 8.
resume	Resume the receiver process.
terminate	Terminate the receiver, causing all protection blocks to be executed.

ProcessScheduler

Process Priorities   These priorities are accessed as class methods. The highest priority is 7 and the lowest is 1. The processes normally run at 4 unless otherwise set.

```
idleTaskPriority    (1)
backgroundPriority  (2)
lowPriority  (2)
standardPriority  (4)
userPriority  (4)
highPriority  (6)
realTimePriority  (6)
topPriority  (7)
```

fork: forkBlock	Create a new process to execute the forkBlock and schedule it at the same priority as the active process.
fork: forkBlock at: priorityLevel	Create a new process to execute the forkBlock and schedule it at the given priorityLevel.
yield	Give other processes at the priority of the currently running process a chance to run.

Semaphore

signal	Increment the receiver's signal count. If there are processes waiting on the semaphore,

	resume the longest waiting. Upon exit, interrupts are always enabled.
wait	Force the current process to be suspended until the receiver semaphore is signaled. Upon exit, interrupts are always enabled.

ZeroArgumentBlock

fork	Create and schedule a new process for the expression in the receiver block, at the current priority. Answer the forked `Process`.
forkAt: aNumber	Create and schedule a new process for the expression in the receiver block, at priority `aNumber`. Answer the forked `Process`.

 IBM Smalltalk

PlatformFunction

This class allows the program to execute an external method (written in a low-level language like C or Assembly) to be executed in a separate operating system thread. This thread is a non-Smalltalk thread and does not execute Smalltalk code. It is useful for executing external functions asynchronously so that the Smalltalk environment doesn't get hung up waiting for the code to complete.

Block

fork	Create a new `Process` that is scheduled by the `ProcessScheduler`. The new process executes the receiver by sending it the message `value`. The new process is created with the same priority as the `activeProcess`. Answer the receiver.
forkAt: aPriority	Create a new `Process` that is scheduled by the `ProcessScheduler`. The new process executes the receiver by sending it the message `value`. The new process is created with priority `aPriority`. Answer the receiver.

newProcess	Create a new `Process` that is in suspended state by the `Process Scheduler`. The new process executes the receiver by sending it the message `value`. The new process is created with the same priority as the `activeProcess`. Answer the newly created process.
newProcessWith: arguments	Create a new `Process` that is in suspended state by the `Process Scheduler`. The new process executes the receiver by sending it the appropriate value message that matches the number of arguments. The new process is created with the same priority as the `activeProcess`. Answer the newly created process.

Process

priority	Answer the receiver's priority.
priority: anInteger	Set the receiver's priority to be `anInteger`. The change is not noticed by the process scheduler until the next process switch operation.
queueInterrupt: aBlock	Add `aBlock` to the queue of blocks that will be run the next time asynchronous messages are enabled for the receiver. If the receiver is the active process and asynchronous messages are enabled, `aBlock` will be evaluated immediately. `aBlock` will always be evaluated with asynchronous messages disabled.
resume	Tell the process scheduler to add the process to the ready-to-run queue.
suspend	Tell the process scheduler to suspend the process.
terminate	Tell the process scheduler to terminate the process.

ProcessorScheduler

Process Priorities	These priorities are accessed as class methods. The highest priority is 7 and the lowest is 1. The processes normally run at 3 unless otherwise set.

```
systemBackgroundPriority  (1)
userBackgroundPriority  (2)
userSchedulingPriority  (3)
userInterruptPriority  (4)
lowIOPriority  (5)
highIOPriority  (6)
timingPriority  (7)
```

activePriority	Answer the priority of the active process.
activeProcess	Answer the active running process. This primitive cannot fail.
signal: aSemaphore atTime: millisecondTime	Signal `aSemaphore` at the time specified by the `millisecondTime` value.

Semaphore

(class) forMutual Exclusion	Answer a `Semaphore` that has one signal operation on it. The first process to wait on this semaphore will not block.
(class) new	Answer a `semaphore`.
critical: aBlock	Evaluate `aBlock` under mutual exclusion of the receiver. Answer the result of evaluating `aBlock`.
signal	Signal the receiver. Resume in FIFO any process that has been waiting.
wait	Wait on the receiver. If the count is negative, suspend the waiting process.

 SmalltalkAgents

Thread Description

`Thread` is a concrete class that provides the structure and behavior for lightweight Virtual Machine (VM) thread objects (units of execution). The

Smalltalk compiler defines a pseudovariable, thread, that is always actively executing the Thread instance. By definition, there is always a thread, since, without it, no Smalltalk code would be executing.

Threads are preemptively time-sliced in SmalltalkAgents; the time-slice swapping is scheduled by the scheduler (UIScheduler instance) thread. The thread time-slice signals are generated by the VM, based on its current state configuration. The VM provides the ability to block thread slice signals and ensures that when a thread is swapped in or out it is always safe to issue any memory manager or other environment/host system service requests.

The Thread class is a subclass of LinkedListElement and therefore is capable of being queued into a preemptive/reentrant safe LinkedList instance. In general, the entire SmalltalkAgents environment has been designed for safe, preemptively threaded operations. Many of the classes have had critical code sections written to operate as atomic operations to ensure that they will be safe from not only preemptive threads, but also from any side effects of asynchronous signals (VM interrupts).

The Thread class defines a class pool variable, ThreadList, that contains all the environment's threads that can be scheduled for execution. When the scheduler is told to scheduleNextThread, it will either schedule itself or it will schedule the next appropriate thread from the ThreadList. The only threads that are not in the ThreadList are the scheduler and any "dead" or "debugged" threads. If a thread is not in the thread list, then it cannot be swapped in. If you attempt to force a thread that is not in the ThreadList—other than the scheduler—to be swapped in, you will crash the VM.

The environment fully supports Semaphore objects. However, it is strongly suggested that you design your code without them. In a multiplatform environment with distributed threads, a semaphore-based design will fail. The suggested design architecture is to use semantic event messages for communication between threads. Every thread has its own eventQueue and will be awakened and scheduled for work whenever events are posted on its queue. The thread can then process the events as part of a main event loop, or it can process them during its swappingIn method (to do so it must add an instance-specific method or install a swapHook handler object. See the swappingIn and swappingOut methods.)

Comments

The default scheduling implementation uses a straightforward round-robin scheme and ignores the thread's priority, starting time, and elapsed execution time. The scheduler thread always gives itself special priority to ensure that it can process user interface activity very quickly. If there is no user interface activity, the `scheduler` will sleep in between processing user interface idle-time (task) events.

Properties and Attributes

`activeSemaphores`	This is a reserved attribute.
`aehFrame`	This is the active exception handler frame. It is used by the VM and the thread when it is walking through the pending message send frames looking for dynamic exception handlers.
`breakpoints`	If not nil, this attribute contains a list of breakpoint descriptors that the VM will use to control break-pointing on the thread while it is actively executing. The VM supports per/thread breakpoints on any methods in the Environment. As a result, one can use a thread to debug system features without breaking the entire Environment.
`currentFrame`	This is a private attribute that belongs to the VM.
`debugger`	If not nil, then this is the object that controls the breakpoints and will receive any unhandled exceptions and any breakpoints that occur while the thread is executing.
`eventQueue`	This is a queue that holds any events that the thread has received. The events are kept in the order they are received. The thread will be notified when an event is added to its queue; it typically will request that it be scheduled for execution.
`exception`	This is a private attribute that belongs to the VM.
`exceptionHandler`	If not nil, this exception handler will get first crack at any (catchable) exceptions that occur while the thread is executing. See the Exception description for details on exceptions, and see the `catchException:` method for its actual usage.
`exceptionSubcode`	This is a private attribute that belongs to the VM.
`executionState`	This attribute contains a `SmallInteger` value that indicates what state the thread is in vis-à-vis execution. The VM and the thread itself may manipulate this value. The following is a chart of the values and their names.

Execution States

0	"new"	New Thread
1	"waiting"	Waiting (Ready To Run) Thread
2	"running"	Running (Current `thread`) Thread
3	"sleeping"	Sleeping (Not Ready To Run) Thread
4	"halted"	Halted (Not Executable—Exception) Thread
5	"zombie"	Finished (Execution Completed) Thread
6	"swappingIn"	Interval Where The Thread Is Being Activated
7	"swappingOut"	Interval Where The Thread Is Being Deactivated

`gcs`
This attribute holds the thread graphic context stack (its stack of graphic ports).

`groupID`
This is a public attribute that is used for group broadcasting and other related actions.

`id`
This is a public (read-only) attribute that is guaranteed to be unique for the thread. The VM provides this value when the thread is instantiated. Its value will always be 1 for the active `scheduler` thread.

`identifier`
This is a public attribute that holds an object for uniquely identifying a thread. This will usually hold a string descriptor that has the thread's name.

`interruptFrame`
This is a private attribute that belongs to the VM.

`maximumSize`
This attribute specifies the maximum size of the thread object. All objects in SmalltalkAgents are resizeable including threads. As a thread executes, it may execute recursive calls and deep message calls that require more (stack) space than it currently has. If that occurs, the VM will automatically grow the thread to accommodate. The VM will not grow the thread larger than the `maximumSize` attribute—it also won't grow the thread if there is insufficient memory.

`parentID`
This is the ID of the (parent) thread that was executing when the (child) thread was (spawned) instantiated. This is normally 1 because most threads are spawned by the `scheduler`.

`pendingSemaphores`
This is a reserved attribute.

`priority`
This is a public attribute that is intended to hold some form of thread ranking or priority scheduling value. The current `scheduler` method, `schedule`

	`NextThread`, that performs round-robin thread scheduling, does not use it.
processTime	This is the amount of time (in ticks) the thread has spent executing. The VM automatically maintains this value as part of its swapping activities.
reserve1	This is a private attribute that belongs to the VM.
reserve2	This is a private attribute that belongs to the VM.
resumable	This is a private attribute that belongs to the VM.
startTime	This is the time (in ticks) that the scheduler was first swapped in/spawned. This value is (should be) automatically set by the VM; it is currently set by the `beginExecution` method. It should also be corrected/updated when the environment is relaunched.
startupBlock	For non-scheduler threads, this is the object that will be evaluated when the thread begins execution. See the `beginExecution` method for its exact usage. It will usually be an instance of `BlockClosure`.
swapHook	If not nil, this object will be evaluated whenever the thread is swapped in or out. See the `swappingIn` and `swappingOut` methods for details.
swapTime	This is the time (in ticks) that the thread was last swapped (in or out). If this value is `nil`, the VM will perform time accounting for this thread.
executionState: n	Set the execution state of the thread. Values for n are: es_new =0, es_waiting =1, es_running =2, es_sleeping =3, es_halted =4, es_zombie =5, es_swappingIn =6, es_swappingOut =7
priority: n	Currently, we do not use priorities to schedule threads. Threads are scheduled by executing the first valid candidate in the `ThreadList` queue. When a thread is swapped out, it places itself at the end of the queue. If we use priorities, they will be used to affect the decision process of `scheduleNextThread` and the actions taken by `swappingOut`.
wakeup	Set our state to being awake so that we will not be scheduled to run until our state changes.
yield	Set our state to waiting and put ourselves last in the queue so another thread can run. Note: Yielding the

	scheduler has no effect since it is not in the process queue.
(class) new: aBlock	Create an instance of `Thread` that will run `aBlock`. Do not activate the thread. Send the instance the message `executionState: 1` to begin running.
(class) run: aBlock	Create an instance of `Thread` that will run `aBlock` and immediately begin running the thread.

UIScheduler Description

`UIScheduler` is a concrete class that provides the structure and behavior for VM scheduler thread objects. Instances of this class handle all the scheduling and processing of synchronous user interface events, thread scheduling, and VM (interrupt) signal handling.

Comments

The `UISchedule` has only one "real/active" instance at any given time, which the Smalltalk compiler defines through the pseudovariable `scheduler`. If the `scheduler` has a fatal exception the VM will create a new `scheduler` and will give it all the public attributes of the previous (halted) `scheduler`.

The `scheduler` has a wide range of responsibilities. It provides an asynchronous timer task queue, the cursor motion-task list, the user interface idle-task list, the methods for shutting down the VM, all the methods for handling the VM signals (see `signal:` and `raiseSignal:`).

The `scheduler` is also responsible for scheduling all the threads in the environment, including itself. It uses an unprioritized, round-robin scheme. It gives special preference to itself to ensure rapid user interface response time. See the `scheduleNextThread` method for the exact implementation.

Semaphore Description

Semaphore is a concrete class that provides the structure and behavior of semaphore objects (mutex controllers). A semaphore is usually implemented via an atomic access counting scheme that is based on two messages, `signal` and `wait`.

Comments

When a thread is executing code that needs access to a shared resource/service, it will typically request the resource's/service's semaphore to `wait`. If the resource/service is not in use by any other object, then the `wait` request will decrement the `signalLevel` and proceed with execution of the thread. If, on the other hand, the resource/service is in use by another object, then the `signalLevel` will be negative and the sending thread will be put to sleep until the service/resource (`signalLevel` ≥ 0) becomes available again. When the code that "locked-up" the semaphore via a `wait` message is through with its use of the resource/service, it will send a `signal` message to release the semaphore. If the semaphore had any other threads that were waiting for (sleeping on) the semaphore, the next one in line (FIFO) will be scheduled for execution (awakened).

Semaphores can be used to provide contention control to enable synchronized access to resources and services in a multithreaded environment. However, in multiprocess distributed environments, semaphores are not suitable, and therefore, event messaging between threads is the suggested method for synchronization of services and resources. Event messaging enables a (process) thread to sleep until any of a number of actions occur to which it can respond. Whereas a semaphore implies a strictly serial/Von Neumann architecture of one-action handling capability at a time because a semaphore takes control of the (process) thread, and semaphores only relate/implement contention control for a single entity/event.

It would be very useful if there were a test and set capability for semaphores that would enable a caller to ask for control of the semaphore, like `wait`. If, however, the semaphore were busy, it would simply return a flag indicating that the semaphore was busy (as opposed to putting the thread to sleep in a wait queue).

Implementation Notes

The `Semaphore` class stores queue (waiting) threads in its indexed variable slots in the order in which the `wait` requests are received. It dequeues (wakes up) threads in the reverse order, thus the oldest waiting thread will be the first thread awakened (in response to a `signal`).

Examples

Assuming that access to a resource/service is controlled by using a semaphore, `theSemaphore`, then any code that needs to have access to the resource/service would "bracket" its code as follows (the reader is also referred to the `Semaphore>>critical:` method):

```
theSemaphore wait  "Wait until we have exclusive access"
...Perform operations that require our
    exclusive use of the resource/service...
theSemaphore signal  "Indicate that we are now finished with our exclusive
usage"
```

Warnings

If there is only one thread (the scheduler) then it is not possible for it to really sleep. As a result the sole thread will sit in an idle-loop (see Thread>>sleep). If this occurs, it is very important that you, the designer, ensure that there is some valid mechanism for "raising" the signal on the semaphore that put the sole thread to sleep.

critical: block	Evaluate the block only if the semaphore signalLevel is positive. Otherwise, wait until the signal level becomes positive before executing the block.
signal	signalLevel < 0 If we have any suspended threads, then unqueue the thread and set it as ready to run. Otherwise, raise the signal level by 1 to a maximum of 0.
wait	signalLevel ≥ 0 atomically decrement the signalLevel < 0 sleep current thread or if not sleepable drop into a loop waiting for the signal level to get positive.

Summary

This chapter gave a brief overview of processes and threads, with emphasis on how they exist in Smalltalk. The concepts of the Smalltalk threads were presented, along with some ways to coordinate these threads. You saw sample code for the four versions of Smalltalk that have threads and processes, and a reference was provided for these versions.

Threads are used when you are presented with that annoying walkback window that you know and love, which appears at the worst possible moment when an error in code occurs. The next chapter, Exception Handling, talks about those annoying walkback windows, and provides you with the tools to prevent them from appearing!

5

Exceptions

Exception handling is the process of handling an exception. With that clear, perhaps you'd like to know what it really is all about. Exceptions are errors (or exceptional events like crashing hard disks). The exceptions can either crash the program, bring up a debugger, or do something a little less disastrous like correcting the problem. Exception handlers are usually blocks of code that are registered early in the program or right before executing another block. These exception handler blocks are executed whenever something goes wrong in a method.

In this chapter, you will discover exceptions, signals, and exception handlers. Topics include:

- ◆ comparative example of exception handling versus other approaches
- ◆ examples of common exceptions
- ◆ a detailed look at how each of the Smalltalks handles a divide-by-zero error
- ◆ some notes on how to do your own exception handling
- ◆ references to the classes and methods for exception handling in four commercial Smalltalks

Exception Handling by Example

Since exception handling can seem to be such a complicated set of processes, a simple example may make it more digestible. Consider a typical Save . . . dialog box that appears in so many applications these days, as shown in Figure 5.1, this one taken from VisualSmalltalk.

The program logic to support this dialog can vary depending on time available to build the application and expectations of possible errors. Many times shortcuts are taken because the program has to be done "yesterday," or there is little understanding and analysis of possible error conditions. Figure 5.2 shows a very general flowchart for a function utilizing the Save dialog. This flowchart does not include any mention of error or conditions that could cause any of the steps to fail. It rather naively assumes that everything will go well, and when it doesn't, will present the user with a nasty default error message and an uncertain course of action. Though execution may continue, the system will no longer be in a known state and side effects of the error may be seen.

In order to deal with some of the error conditions that can occur as the program executes, a rough flowchart for a more complete, error-handling

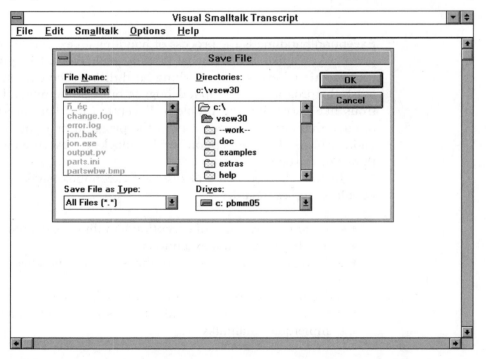

FIGURE 5.1 A typical Save dialog serves as a good example of possible error handling.

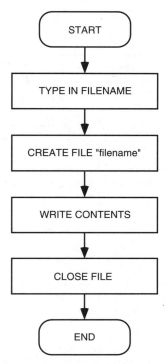

FIGURE 5.2 Program flow for a typical program performing Save functionality that crashes frequently.

program is shown in Figure 5.3. With the right amount of up-front analysis, this program will handle each error that occurs and is tested in a known, pre-determined fashion. It is possible that this approach to error handling will solve the need for error processing in the system. It does, however, require additional code to be inserted in every step that could possibly branch when an error occurs, and requires some top notch coding practices to handle problems like unraveling the layers of execution when an error is processed if execution is to reoccur from prior methods, as shown by the arrows on the right traveling back up to prior steps.

Using exception handling, as shown in Figure 5.4, the system can be organized differently for error handling. Whenever an error occurs in the processing of this section, an exception is created (differently in the various Smalltalks). This instance of exception then goes through the stack to find an appropriate exception handler, which is usually a one-argument block of code that takes the instance of exception as its argument. Based on the functionality of the exception handler, execution can then continue in a variety of ways.

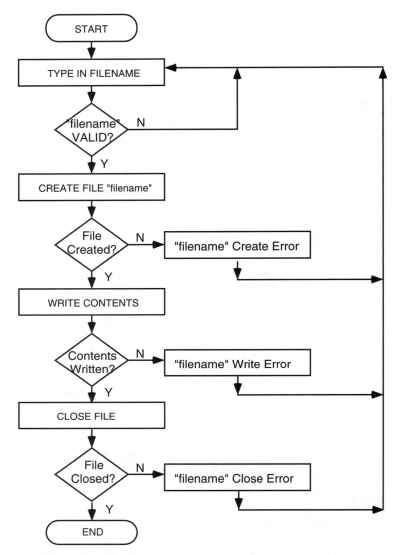

FIGURE 5.3 A better program flow with typical error-handling techniques that handle each and every error explicitly.

There are five distinctive types of responses that an exception handler can make. The responses are the last step in the exception handler and occur after other processing has completed. The five Rs of exception-handling responses are:

1. *Resume normal processing right after the code that raised the exception.* The type of exception determines whether the exception can

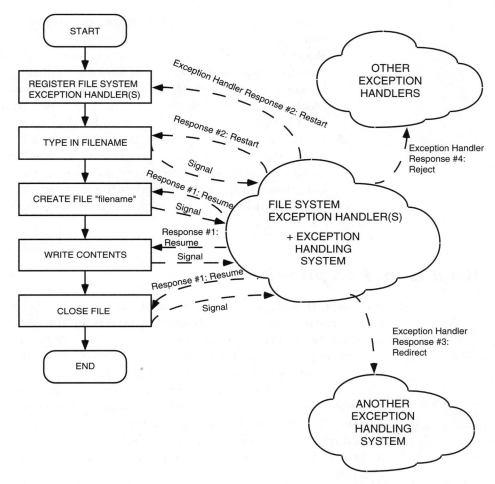

FIGURE 5.4 An even better program flow that uses exception-handling mechanisms to deal with errors.

be resumed. Usually, if it is to be resumed, a value will be returned to use in place of the exception argument; or processing will occur that will resolve the problem so that the calling code that raised the exception can continue.

2. *Restart normal processing from the point at which the exception handler was registered.* If the exception is to restart the processing, then all work accomplished in the routines lower on the stack will be thrown away in an attempt to recover. This is usually done after undoing some critical steps in the processing.

3. *Redirect the exception to another handler by changing the exception type.* Passing the buck is not usually done, but sometimes a raised

exception is a symptom of another problem, or to fix it requires creating another error. Use this sparingly.

4. *Reject the instance of exception so that the exception tries to find another exception handler.* This is done frequently when several handlers may be registered on the same exception and the same block of code. The exception will walk the stack trying to find the right handler, and does not get offended if rejected.

5. *Return or exit the code after the point at which the exception handler was registered.* Exiting the program is done when a fatal error occurs. This is not a preferred option because it gives the user low confidence in the system, trashes the user's work, and so on. You should try to handle the exception whenever possible.

What Is an Exception?

An exception is an exceptional circumstance in data or events that is known as an error to common folks. Some may take exception with this definition, but then they've probably got handlers to deal with the exception.

Perhaps the most important, unmentioned benefit of exception handling is encapsulation of error-handling code and reuse of error-handling code. These benefits are achieved through the organization and globally available use of error-handling code provided by the exception-handling system. Through the use of the exception handler, code that might have been duplicated throughout an application to handle common errors, such as input/output errors, can be consolidated into a central repository for exception-handling code.

There are two types of exception handling encountered in Smalltalk programming. The first type can be referred to as **local exception handling** in that it occurs on a case-by-case basis and is specific to a certain type of routine. The other type can be called **global exception handling,** and involves a comprehensive and global solution to the problem of dealing with exceptional events.

Most Smalltalk programmers are familiar with local exception handling through use of routines that accept a block to execute on failure. An example of this is the `remove:ifAbsent:` method present in most collection subclasses. This routine accepts the index or item to be removed and a block to execute when that item does not exist in the collection. The use of this method rather than the `remove:` method is usually the result of experience. Many times code is rewritten to use this type of method after the programmer has experienced failures at this point.

While local exception handling is adequate in many situations, for a complete solution to the problem of exceptional events or data, a global approach must be taken. This is where the consistent use of the exception-handling system comes into play. Global exception handling indicates that there is some integral exception-handling system in the environment.

The Exception-Handling System

Each implementation of an exception-handling system differs by Smalltalk version, though there are some common concepts that seem to exist in all the systems. A general description of the process of exception handling is presented here before the detailed discussion of a divide-by-zero exception later in this chapter.

An exception-handling system exists to deal with exceptions. Thus, in the system, some of the items that exist are exceptions and exception handlers. There are two views on how the exception-handling system works: the view from the point at which an error occurs, and the view of the program as a whole including setting up handlers for exceptions.

Execution from when an error is detected consists of "raising" an exception, identifying an exception handler to handle the exception, and passing the exception into the exception handler.

In the larger-scale view of program execution, the handlers are the first items encountered, as they are registered with the exception-handling system. Exception handlers can be created to handle any level of abstraction within an application, from application global to one line of code. They are registered in the beginning and remain dormant until code that detects an error sends a `raise` message to the exception-handling system. It is important to remember that exception handling does not begin with the error, but with the expectation of the error in the beginning of the program.

Default Exception Handling

Every Smalltalk version has a default exception handler that catches raised exceptions that are not handled by any other exception handler. You are probably familiar with these windows called Walkback windows, Exception windows, or various other terms. IBM Smalltalk is different in that it directly presents the debugger.

For simplicity, the first window that appears due to a default exception will be called the Walkback. This window is familiar because it appears each time an unhandled exception occurs, a breakpoint is hit in code, or a `self`

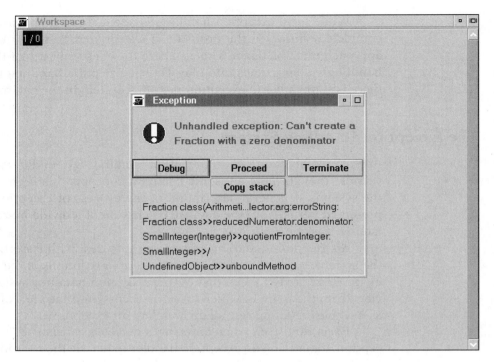

FIGURE 5.5 The VisualWorks default exception handler window.

`halt` is encountered. Typically, the window shows a few steps back on the Smalltalk stack, and provides the option to resume, restart, or abort the process. The windows for the default exception handlers, the Walkback windows, are presented for the Smalltalks in Figures 5.5, 5.6, 5.7, and 5.8. Additionally, the Debugger window for SmalltalkAgents is presented in Figure 5.9 because very little functionality and little information exists in the Walkback window, and it is useful to understand what the available options are for each default exception handler.

Examples of Exceptions

Some common examples of the types of errors commonly handled by built-in exception handlers are mentioned here. An exception handler could be called when you:

- ◆ read past the end of file
- ◆ create a file that already exists
- ◆ write to read-only or locked file

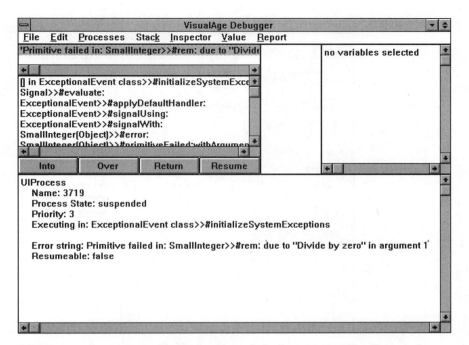

FIGURE 5.6 The IBM Smalltalk/VisualAge default exception handler window.

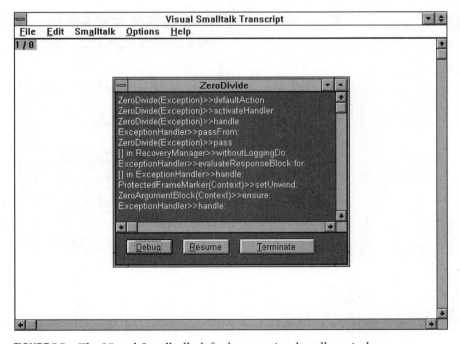

FIGURE 5.7 The Visual Smalltalk default exception handler window.

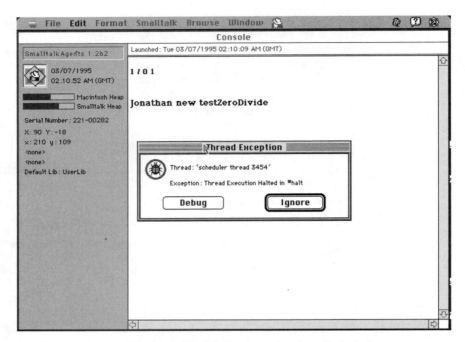

FIGURE 5.8 The SmalltalkAgents default exception handler window.

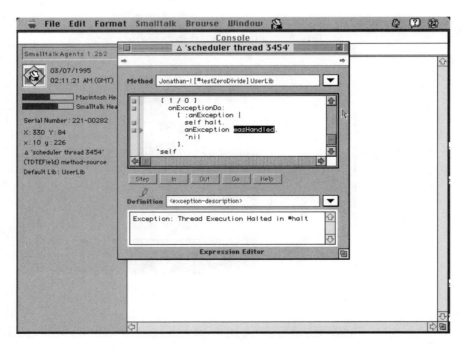

FIGURE 5.9 The SmalltalkAgents Thread Debugger window showing the thread with the exception.

- ♦ divide by zero
- ♦ reference an item out of the bounds of an `IndexedCollection`, `Array`, or `List`
- ♦ create a kill signal
- ♦ create an interrupt signal
- ♦ time-out waiting for something
- ♦ have a communications connection problem or status query

This is by no means an exhaustive list of exceptions, and not all environments have all these exceptions. But many do, and could have exception handlers to handle these exceptions explicitly for your application needs.

Detailed Examples: Discussion of Divide-by-Zero

In this section, a step-by-step account of the action for a divide-by-zero error is covered. Each of the Smalltalks that contains an exception-handling system is covered. Since each Smalltalk has a different implementation of the system, each is covered separately, but in the same manner. For each Smalltalk, the code 1 / 0 was evaluated in a Workspace. The default exception handler for a divide-by-zero error was executed by Smalltalk, and a Walkback window was presented, except for IBM Smalltalk, which directly presents the Debugger.

The execution stack is then shown, with the methods listed in order from the most recent (top of the stack) to the oldest (bottom of the stack). The entire contents of the stack is not listed. The listing extends to the division operation in each.

The methods that are invoked are then presented in reverse order from the stack frames. This means that the first method to be executed is presented first. The first method in each case is the division method /. A running commentary accompanies the method listings, and should help you to understand how each Smalltalk version processes exceptions internally.

 VisualWorks

The general concept of the VisualWorks exception-handling system is shown in Figure 5.10, and serves as a graphical overview of the processing that occurs during an exception. Refer to this figure while reading the details of the exception system to see how the significant steps are performed across several methods.

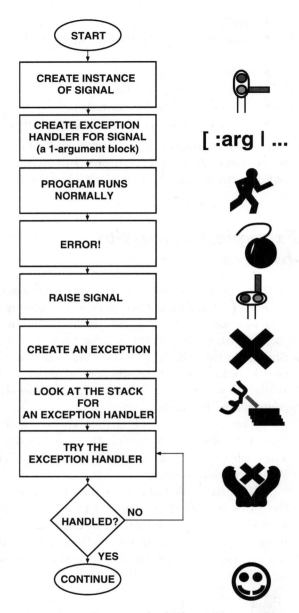

FIGURE 5.10 A graphical overview of the Visual-Works exception-handling system.

Stack

The stack for the divide-by-zero error in VisualWorks lists methods from the most recently executed to the initial divide method and looks like the following:

```
Fraction class (ArithmeticValue
    class)>>raise:receiver:selector:arg:errorString:
Fraction class>>reducedNumerator:denominator:
SmallInteger(Integer)>>quotientFromInteger:
SmallInteger>>/
```

SmallInteger>>/

This method appears in the `SmallInteger` class and contains functionality for division. The method is sent by the evaluation of the expression: `1 / 0`. An exception will occur if the primitive fails, `aNumber` is not an instance of `SmallInteger` or one of its subclasses, the result is not a whole integer (fractional amount), or the argument `aNumber` is zero. In the example, the argument `aNumber` is zero, therefore the primitive will fail and the `quotientFromInteger:` method will be called with `self` as the argument and `aNumber` as the receiver, thereby reversing `self` and `aNumber` in the next method.

```
/ aNumber
    "Answer the result of dividing the receiver by the argument aNumber. Fail
if the result is not a whole integer, or if the argument is 0 or is not a
SmallInteger."

    <primitive: 10>
    ^aNumber quotientFromInteger: self
```

SmallInteger(Integer)>>quotientFromInteger:

With this method call, the argument `aNumber` (`self` in the preceding) does not cleanly divide the receiver self (`aNumber` in the preceding) to give another instance of `SmallInteger`. The method calls the class method `reducedNumerator:denominator:` in the `Fraction` class.

```
quotientFromInteger: aNumber
    "Answer the result of dividing receiver by the argument,
    anInteger, if the division is exact."

    ^Fraction reducedNumerator: aNumber denominator: self
```

Fraction class>>reducedNumerator:denominator:

In this method, the denominator that is passed by the program flow is zero. The denominator is sent the method `isZero`, to which the answer is true, causing the `ifTrue:` block to be evaluated. The block uses the `Arithmetic-Value` class method `raise:receiver:selector:arg:errorString:` to pass in the values to create a `divisionByZeroSignal`.

```
reducedNumerator: numInteger denominator: denInteger
    "Answer a new Fraction numInteger/denInteger."

    | gcd denominator numerator |
    denominator := denInteger truncated abs.
    denominator isZero
        ifTrue: [^self raise: #divisionByZeroSignal
                receiver: numInteger
                selector: #/
                arg: denInteger
                errorString: 'Can't create a Fraction with a zero
denominator'].
    denInteger negative
        ifTrue: [numerator := numInteger truncated negated]
        ifFalse: [numerator := numInteger truncated].
    gcd := numerator gcd: denominator.
    denominator = gcd ifTrue: [^numerator // gcd].
    gcd = 1 ifTrue: [^self basicNew setNumerator: numerator denominator:
denominator].
    ^self basicNew setNumerator: numerator//gcd denominator:
denominator//gcd
```

Fraction class(ArithmeticValue class) >>raise:receiver:selector:arg:errorString:

This method takes the arguments sent by the block in the previous example and raises an error signal. The instance of `Signal` used is determined by the argument `signalName`, which is sent to `self` to retrieve the instance of `Signal`. The instance of `Signal` is then sent the `raiseRequestWith:errorString:` message with arguments consisting of an instance of `MessageSend` and `String`. The `MessageSend` instance contains the information necessary to populate the Walkback window or to write a log entry to disk. This method causes the Walkback window to appear with the stack listed in the preceding, since this is the default exception-handling behavior. The message to the instance of `Signal` creates an instance of `Exception` that walks through the stack looking for an exception handler; and finding none, it uses the default. The `raiseRequest` method does not appear in the Debugger window with the stack trace because the stack is stripped up to this point once the correct exception handler has been found.

```
raise: signalName receiver: anObject selector: aSymbol arg: anArg
errorString: aMessage

    ^(self perform: signalName) raiseRequestWith: (MessageSend receiver:
anObject selector: aSymbol argument: anArg) errorString: aMessage
```

Signal>>raiseRequestWith:errorString:

Here the instance of Exception is created and sent various messages to fill it with the appropriate data necessary to find the registered exception handler that is most appropriate. The raiseRequest message causes the action to occur after the instance of Exception has been fully populated.

```
raiseRequestWith: parameter errorString: aString
 "Raise the receiver, that is, create an exception on the receiver and have
it search the execution stack for a handler that accepts the receiver, then
evaluate the handler's exception block. The exception block may choose to pro-
ceed if this message is sent. The exception will answer the first argument
when asked for its parameter, and will use aString as its error string"

    ^self newException
      parameter: parameter;
      errorString: aString;
      originator: thisContext sender homeReceiver;
      raiseRequest
```

Exception>>raiseRequest

At this point, the context for the exception is set. The context is kept as one of the pieces in the stack and contains the parameters that distinguish one state from the next. The context set is of the sender's sender, and this is carried for comparison operations. Now the exception will propogateFrom: the initial context down the stack to find an exception handler appropriate to the Signal type for a divide-by-zero error.

```
raiseRequest
   "Actually raise this exception (proceedable)."

   initialContext isNil ifTrue:
     [ initialContext := thisContext sender sender ].
   signal mayProceed ifFalse:
     [^Signal wrongProceedabilitySignal newException
       parameter: signal;
```

Continued

```
                    searchFrom: initialContext;
                    raise].
            originatorSet ifFalse: [ originator := thisContext sender homeReceiver].
            self proceedBlock: [ :value | ^value ].
            ^self propogateFrom: initialContext
```

Exception>>propagateFrom:

The argument `startContext` supplied is used as the `initialContext` for the exception, and the `firstUnwindContext` is set to signify that this is the first attempt at finding an exception handler and that it has not been rejected by any handler yet. The private method `propagatePrivateFrom:` is called using the `startContext`.

```
propogateFrom: startContext
    "Search for, and run, an appropriate handler."

    initialContext := startContext.
    firstUnwindContext := nil.
    ^self propagatePrivateFrom: startContext
```

Exception>>propagatePrivateFrom:

At this point, the handler will be found using the `findHandlerFrom:` method. If the handler is found, the block is executed with the argument `self` (the exception). The block can then do corrective things and return `result`. The value of `result` is then passed into `noHandlerAction:` to determine the future action. At this point, for the divide-by-zero example, the exception Notifier window is created, and the stack unwound to the point of the `Fraction` class where the error condition occurred.

```
propagatePrivateFrom: startContext
    "Search for, and run, an appropriate handler.
    This is called both initially and after a reject.
    In the latter case, we don't reset firstUnwindContext."
    | handler ex2 result |
    handler := self findHandlerFrom: startContext.
    handler == nil ifTrue:
        [(Signal noHandlerSignal accepts: signal)
            ifTrue:
                ["If this was already an unhandled exception
                exception that was rejected, just start the
                emergency handler—parameter is the exception
                that couldn't be handled originally"
                ^EmergencyHandler value: parameter value: parameter
initialContext]
            ifFalse:
```

Continued

```
    ["No handler Convert this exception into
    an unhandled exception exception
    (no, you're not seeing double here.)"
    ex2 := self class new
        signal: Signal noHandlerSignal;
        parameter: self;
        proceedBlock: nil.
    handler := ex2 findHandlerFrom: initialContext.
    handler == nil ifTrue:
        ["No handler for this either Emergency!"
        ^EmergencyHandler value: self value: initialContext].
    result := handler value: ex2.
    "The handler returned without choosing an option."
    ^ex2 noHandlerAction: result]].
result := handler value: self.
"The handler returned without choosing an option."
^self noHandlerAction: result
```

 Visual Smalltalk

The general concept of the Visual Smalltalk exception-handling system is shown in Figure 5.11, and serves as a graphical overview of the processing that occurs during an exception. Refer to this figure while reading the details of the exception system to see how the significant steps are performed across several methods.

Stack

```
ZeroDivide(Exception)>>defaultAction
ZeroDivide(Exception)>>activateHandler:
ZeroDivide(Exception)>>handle
ExceptionHandler>>passFrom:
ZeroDivide(Exception)>>pass
[] in RecoveryManager>>withoutLoggingDo:
ExceptionHandler>>evaluateResponseBlock:for:
[] in ExceptionHandler>>handle:
ProtectedFrameMarker(Context)>>setUnwind:
ZeroArgumentBlock(Context)>>ensure:
ExceptionHandler>>handle:
ExceptionHandler>>findHandler:
ZeroDivide(Exception)>>activateHandler:
ZeroDivide(Exception)>>handle
ZeroDivide(Exception)>>signal
ZeroDivide class>>dividend:
Fraction(Number)>>zeroDivisor
Fraction>>numerator:denominator:
```

Continued

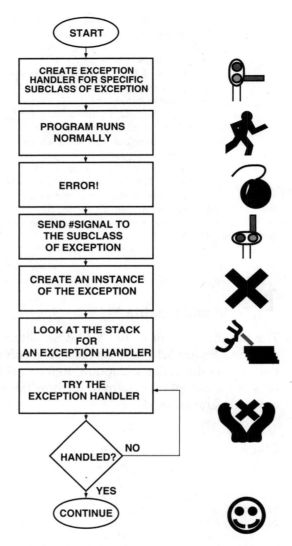

FIGURE 5.11 A graphical overview of the Visual Smalltalk exception-handling system.

```
Fraction class>>numerator:denominator:
SmallInteger(Integer)>>/
```

SmallInteger(Integer)>>/

This method appears in the SmallInteger class and contains functionality for division. The method is sent by the evaluation of the expression: 1 / 0.

The class method `numerator:denominator:` is called in class `Fraction` with `numerator` equal to 1 and `denominator` equal to 0.

```
/ aNumber
        "Answer the result of dividing
        the receiver by aNumber."
    | numerator denominator gcd |
    aNumber isInteger
        ifFalse: [^ ( aNumber reciprocal * self ) ].
    aNumber negative
        ifTrue: [
            denominator := aNumber negated.
            numerator := self negated ]
        ifFalse: [
            denominator := aNumber.
            numerator := self ].
    (gcd := numerator gcd: denominator) = denominator
        ifTrue: [^numerator // gcd]
        ifFalse: [
            ^Fraction
                numerator: numerator // gcd
                denominator: denominator // gcd]
```

Fraction class>>numerator:denominator:

An instance of `Fraction` is created, with `numerator` 1 and `denominator` 0.

```
numerator: n denominator: d
        "Answer an instance of class Fraction and
        initialize both numerator and denominatior
        instance variables to n and d respectively."
    ^self basicNew numerator: n denominator: d
```

Fraction>>numerator:denominator:

The new instance of `Fraction` has the `denominator` tested for 0. Since `denominator` is 0, the method `zeroDivisor` is called.

```
numerator: n
denominator: d
    "Private - Answer the receiver. The numerator
        and denominator of the receiver are set to the
        n and d arguments respectively."
    d = 0
        ifTrue: [^self zeroDivisor].
    d negative
        ifTrue:
            [numerator := n negated.
            denominator := d negated]
```

Continued

```
        ifFalse:
            [numerator := n.
             denominator := d]
```

Fraction(Number)>>zeroDivisor

Inherited by all subclasses of Number, the class ZeroDivide, a subclass of Exception, is sent the message dividend: with self as the argument.

```
zeroDivisor
        "An attempt was made to divide the receiver by zero."
    ^ZeroDivide dividend: self
```

ZeroDivide class>>dividend:

An instance of ZeroDivide is created, and aNumber is stored within the instance. The method signal is then called to signify that the exception has occurred.

```
dividend: aNumber
        "Signal that an attempt was made to divide the argument by
zero."
    | ex |
    ex := self new.
    ex dividend: aNumber.
    ^ex signal
```

ZeroDivide(Exception)>>signal

First the exception is checked for a circular case of exception raising, then the context for the currently executing exception is stored by sending exceptionEnvironment to the global CurrentProcess. An attempt to handle the exception is then attempted.

```
signal
        "Signal that this exception has occurred,
        find and execute the appropriate handler."
    self isActive ifTrue: [
        ^ControlError signal: 'Signaling an already signaled
exception'].
    self signalEnvironment: CurrentProcess exceptionEnvironment.
    ^self handle
```

ZeroDivide(Exception)>>handle

The exception handler for this exception is found here, with the result determining whether to resume the process by returning result, or redirect the exception as a different type by signaling the replacementException.

```
handle
        "Private - find the active handler for this exception and activate it."

    | result |
    result := self activateHandler: CurrentProcess exceptionEnvironment.
    result == self resignalContinuation
      ifFalse: [^result]
      ifTrue: [^self replacementException signal]
```

ZeroDivide(Exception)>>activateHandler:

If the environment in which to search for the exception, env, is nil, the
default action will occur. Otherwise, env is sent the findHandler: message
to locate an appropriate handler.

```
activateHandler: env
        "Private - Find and activate a handler"

    self resignalContinuation == nil ifTrue: [
        self resignalContinuation: [^self resignalContinuation]]. "the block
serves as its own flag value"
    ^env == nil
      ifTrue: [self defaultAction]
      ifFalse: [env findHandler: self].
```

ExceptionHandler>>findHandler:

A handler is sought for anException. If it is found, it is executed; otherwise
the default handler will be executed. The search starts with self, tests to
see if anException is of the type handled, and sends the message handle:
to the first handler found that handles anException.

```
findHandler: anException
        "If an active exception handler exists for the argument, activate it.
        Otherwise activate the default handler for the argument."

    | hndlr result oldH |
    hndlr := self.
    oldH := CurrentProcess exceptionEnvironment.
    " use default environment if an exception occurs while searching for
handler "
    CurrentProcess exceptionEnvironment: nil.
    [hndlr == nil] whileFalse:
        [(hndlr exception handles: anException)
            ifTrue: [
                CurrentProcess exceptionEnvironment: oldH.
                ^hndlr handle: anException].
          hndlr := hndlr previous].
```

Continued

```
CurrentProcess exceptionEnvironment: anException signalEnvironment.
 result := anException defaultAction.
CurrentProcess exceptionEnvironment: oldH.
^result
```

ExceptionHandler>>handle:

An instance of `ExceptionHandler` that handles the type of error in `anException`. An attempt is made to use `self` as the exception handler, with the use of `ensure:` to trap undesirable results of using the handler.

```
handle: anException
        "Private - the receiver is a handler for the argument exception.
Handle the exception."

    | result environment |
    environment := CurrentProcess exceptionEnvironment.
    [CurrentProcess exceptionEnvironment: self previous.
     anException activeHandler: self.
     result := self evaluateResponseBlock: self response for: anException
    ] ensure:
       [anException activeHandler: nil.
        CurrentProcess exceptionEnvironment: environment].
    anException isResumable ifTrue: [^result].
    self continuation value: result     "never returns"
```

ZeroArgumentBlock(Context)>>ensure:

The `ensure:` method is used to execute the code in the previous method, with `terminationBlock` to clean up any bad results. This is used to ensure that anything that gets botched up in unwinding the stack for exception execution can be fixed before trying the next handler.

```
ensure: terminationBlock
        "Return the result of evaluating the receiver. Before returning, but
after evaluating the receiver, evaluate the <terminationBlock>. The value of
the termination block is ignored. If a block attempts to return from a method
which (indirectly) invoked the receiver, either directly or indirectly,
evaluate the termination block before returning from the enclosing method.
        Implementation Comments: The receiver is evaluated by sending the
receiver the message #value."
    | result |
    result := self
        setUnwind:
            [:aContext :returnValue |
            terminationBlock value.
            aContext return: returnValue].
    terminationBlock value.
    ^result
```

ProtectedFrameMarker(Context)>>setUnwind:

This method evaluates the receiver (the instance of `ZeroArgumentBlock` in the preceding) with the caveat that if another exception occurs within this block, the `twoArgumentBlock` argument is evaluated.

```
setUnwind: twoArgumentBlock
        "Private - evaluate the receiver. If the system attempts to return
        from a method which (indirectly) invoked this one, evaluate the
        <twoArgumentBlock>. The first argument to the block is the context
        for the method being returned from, the second is the value being
        returned from that method. Implementation Comments: What will happen
        if the argument block is invoked and does not provide an explicit
        return is intentionally undefined."
    ^self valueMarked
```

[ ] in ExceptionHandler>>handle:

With the block ensured, the contents of the block are under execution. The parameters are set, and `result` is desired from the method `evaluateResponseBlock:for:`.

```
handle: anException
        "Private - the receiver is a handler for the argument exception.
Handle the exception."

        | result environment |
        environment := CurrentProcess exceptionEnvironment.
        [CurrentProcess exceptionEnvironment: self previous.
         anException activeHandler: self.
         result := self evaluateResponseBlock: self response for: anException
        ] ensure:
          [anException activeHandler: nil.
           CurrentProcess exceptionEnvironment: environment].
        anException isResumable ifTrue: [^result].
        self continuation value: result "never returns"
```

ExceptionHandler>>evaluateResponseBlock:for:

The `responseBlock` is evaluated with either no arguments or one argument, `anException`, as determined by querying `responseBlock`. The definition of `responseBlock` was made in the `RecoveryManager` `withoutLoggingDo:` method.

```
evaluateResponseBlock: responseBlock for: anException
        "Private - evaluate the first argument as the exception block but
first setup a continuation for result value."
```
Continued

```
responseBlock argumentCount = 0
   ifTrue: [result := responseBlock value]
   ifFalse: [
      self resultContinuation: [:result| ^result].
      result := responseBlock value: anException].
^result
```

[ ] in RecoveryManager>>withoutLoggingDo:

This method is executed by sending the message `value:` to the `responseBlock` in the previous method. It is the "doer" of the `responseBlock`. The block that is the exception handler takes one argument, `ex`, and sends the message `pass` to the exception.

```
withoutLoggingDo: aBlock
   "Don't log any expressions during the evaluation of <aBlock>
Answer the value of <aBlock>"

   | original terminated |
   original := self getShouldLog.
   original == nil
      ifFalse:
         [self cachedLog: original.
         self shouldLog: nil].
   [[^aBlock value]
         on: Error
         do:
            [:ex |
            terminated := true.
            self resetLogging: original.
            ex pass]]
      ensure:
         [terminated == nil
            ifTrue: [self resetLogging: original]]
```

ZeroDivide(Exception)>>pass

Since the exception handler decided to pass on handling the exception, an attempt will be made to find another handler. Had the previous handler done otherwise, execution could have resumed or the block been restarted.

```
pass
      "This handler does not want to handle the exception so activate any
      enclosing handlers."

   ^self exit: (self activeHandler passFrom: self)
```

ExceptionHandler>>passFrom:

Again, `theException` will try to be handled by obtaining the `result` from the method `handle`.

```
passFrom: theException
        "Activate any enclosing handlers for the argument exception."

    | result currentResultContinuation |
    currentResultContinuation := self resultContinuation.
    result := theException handle.
    theException activeHandler: self.
    self resultContinuation: currentResultContinuation.
    ^result
```

ZeroDivide(Exception)>>handle

The next handler on the list is located and sent the message `activateHandler:`.

```
handle
        "Private - find the active handler for this exception and
activate it."

    | result|
    result := self activateHandler: CurrentProcess exceptionEnvironment.
    result == self resignalContinuation
      ifFalse: [^result]
      ifTrue: [^self replacementException signal]
```

ZeroDivide(Exception)>>activateHandler:

At this point, there is no other handler available that deals with divide-by-zero errors. The argument `env` is nil, and the `defaultAction` method is sent.

```
activateHandler: env
        "Private - Find and activate a handler"

    self resignalContinuation == nil ifTrue: [
      self resignalContinuation: [^self resignalContinuation]]. "the block
serves as its own flag value"
    ^env == nil
      ifTrue: [self defaultAction]
      ifFalse: [env findHandler: self].
```

ZeroDivide(Exception)>>defaultAction

This is the end of the line for a divide-by-zero error. In the development environment, a Walkback window is presented with information about the runaway process. Note that the stack has not been cleaned up at all here and that the process is not resumable within the division method. In a delivered system, this would prompt a call from a user, and a need to find the bug or create additional functionality to remove possible sources of this exception.

```
defaultAction
        "This is the action that is performed if this exception is signaled
and there is no active handler for it."

    Process
        queueWalkback: self description
        makeUserIF: CurrentProcess isUserIF
        resumable: 1
```

VisualAge/IBM Smalltalk

The general concept of the IBM Smalltalk/VisualAge exception-handling system is shown in Figure 5.12, and serves as a graphical overview of the processing that occurs during an exception. Refer to this figure while reading the details of the exception system to see how the significant steps are performed across several methods.

Stack

The stack for the divide-by-zero error in VisualAge/IBM Smalltalk lists methods from the most recently executed to the initial divide method, and looks like the following:

```
[] in ExceptionalEvent class>>#initializeSystemExceptions
Signal>>#evaluate:
ExceptionalEvent>>#applyDefaultHandler:
ExceptionalEvent>>#signalUsing:
ExceptionalEvent>>#signalWith:
SmallInteger(Object)>>#error:
SmallInteger(Object)>>#primitiveFailed:withArgument:backUp:
SmallInteger(Object)>>#primitiveFailed
SmallInteger>>#rem:
SmallInteger(Integer)>>#'/'
```

SmallInteger(Integer)>>#'/'

This method appears in the Integer class and contains the functionality for division. It is sent by evaluating the expression: 1 / 0. An exception can occur if the argument aNumber is not an Integer or subclass of Integer, like SmallInteger, or if aNumber is zero. Since the argument aNumber is

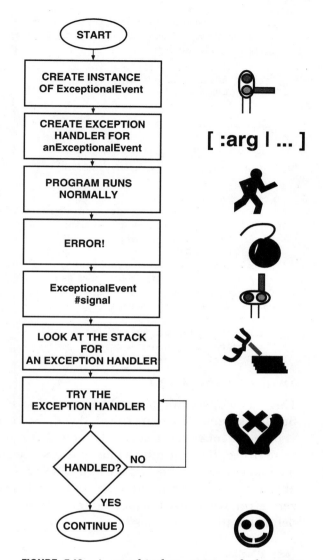

FIGURE 5.12 A graphical overview of the IBM Smalltalk/VisualAge exception-handling system.

zero, an exception will occur for this operation, but not within this method. The exception will occur below this level, in the `rem:` method.

```
/ aNumber

  "Answer a type of Number that is the result of
   dividing the receiver by the argument, aNumber.
   Note that since as much
```

Continued

precision as possible is retained, if the
division is not exact, the result will be an
instance of Fraction.

Fail if aNumber is not a type of Number.
Fail if aNumber is zero."

```
| numerator denominator gcd |

aNumber isInteger ifFalse: [
    ^self retry: #/ coercing: aNumber].

(self rem: aNumber) = 0
    ifTrue: ["Catches all cases of divide with
             no remainder where aNumber is an Integer."
             ^self quo: aNumber].
numerator := self * aNumber denominator.
(denominator := aNumber numerator) < 0 ifTrue: [
    denominator := denominator negated.
    numerator := numerator negated].
gcd := numerator gcd: denominator.
^Fraction newFraction
    numerator: (numerator quo: gcd)
    denominator: (denominator quo: gcd)
```

SmallInteger>>#rem:

This method, specific to SmallInteger makes use of a primitive (a non-Smalltalk function) to perform the division operation. If the primitive VMprSmallIntegerRem succeeds, a number representing the remainder will be returned. If the primitive fails, it is first checked to see whether the argument aNumber is an invalid type, in which case it will attempt to coerce the object into an appropriate type. Any other failure, including a divide-by-zero error, will cause the method to execute the primitiveFailed method defined in the Object class.

```
rem: aNumber

    "Answer a type of Number representing the remainder defined by dividing
    the receiver by aNumber with truncation toward zero.

    Fail if aNumber is not a type of Number. Fail if aNumber = 0."

    "Note that the Blue Book is unclear about what remainder returns for floats
    and fractions so this implementation returns the actual remainder whose
    class is the class of the receiver. For example, 4.5 rem: 2 = 0.5"

    <primitive: VMprSmallIntegerRem>
```

Continued

```
self primitiveErrorCode = PrimErrInvalidClass
   ifTrue: [^self retry: #rem: coercing: aNumber].
^self primitiveFailed
```

SmallInteger(Object)>>#primitiveFailed

This method obtains the primitive error code that tells the type of primitive error that occurred contained in the `primitiveErrorCode` and `primitiveBadArgumentNumber` methods. The argument supplied as the `backUp:` parameter tells where the primitive failed error stack frame is located.

```
primitiveFailed
   "Report to the user that a method that is implemented as a system primitive
   has failed."

   ^self  primitiveFailed:  self  primitiveErrorCode  withArgument:  self
primitiveBadArgumentNumber backUp: 1
```

SmallInteger(Object)>>#primitiveFailed:withArgument:backUp:

This method records the error information for the developer to browse. It also calls the `error` method that will cause a signal to be raised.

```
primitiveFailed: errorCode withArgument: argument backUp: backUp

   "Report to the user that a method that is implemented as a system
primitive as failed. Use errorCode and argument number report the problem"

   | errorString method |

   method := Processor activeProcess methodAtFrame: backUp + 1.
   errorString := 'Primitive failed in: ', method printString, ' due to
'.
   errorCode = PrimErrOSError
      ifTrue: [errorString := errorString , 'OS error ' , argument
printString]
      ifFalse: [
         errorString :=
            errorString , '"' , (
               PrimitiveErrorDescriptions
                  at: errorCode
                  ifAbsent: ['Unknown error (' , errorCode printString ,
')'])
               , '"'.
         argument ~= PrimArgNumNoArg ifTrue: [
            errorString :=
               errorString , ' in ' , (
                  argument = PrimArgNumSelf              Continued
```

```
                         ifTrue: ['receiver']
                         ifFalse: ['argument ' , argument printString])
            ]
        ].
    ^self error: errorString
```

SmallInteger(Object)>>#error:

This method uses the `ExError` instance of an `ExceptionalEvent` to raise a signal with the error message `aString`. To find out more about `ExError`, from a Workspace, evaluate the expression: `ExError inspect`. You will find among other things that `ExError` is nonresumable.

```
error: aString
     "Stop the currently executing process and display the error message
aString."


    ^ExError signalWith: aString
```

ExceptionalEvent>>#signalWith:

This method creates an instance of `Signal` to be used in handling the exception. The argument supplied, the error message, is bundled into an `Array` within signal, and the signal is passed into the `signalUsing:` method.

```
signalWith: arg1
   "Invoke the exception with a signal argument."

   | signal |
   (signal := Signal new)
      arguments: (Array with: arg1).
   ^self signalUsing: signal
```

ExceptionalEvent>>#signalUsing:

The signal created in the `signalWith:` method is supplied the instance of `ExceptionalEvent` (`self`) and a block, if the signal is resumable. A handler is then requested from the active process, and if it exists, it is called. Since a specific handler for this error has not been registered, the default handler is used.

```
signalUsing: aSignal
   "Invoke the exception using aSignal."
   | handler |
   aSignal
      exception: self;
      resumeBlock: [:value | ^value].
```
Continued

```
(handler := Processor activeProcess errorHandler) == nil
    ifTrue: [self applyDefaultHandler: aSignal]
    ifFalse: [handler value: aSignal].
self error: 'Execution should never reach this point'.
```

ExceptionalEvent>>#applyDefaultHandler:

The default exception handler for this error is identified for the instance of ExceptionalEvent. Each exception should have a default handler, and the inheritance tree for the ExceptionalEvent is searched for a defaultHandler. The default handler is then passed to the evaluate: method within the argument aSignal.

```
applyDefaultHandler: aSignal
    "Evaluate the defaultHandler for the receiver. If nil, the parent's
    defaultHandler is applied."

    | exception result |
    exception := self.
    [exception == nil] whileFalse: [
        exception defaultHandler == nil ifFalse: [
            aSignal evaluate: exception defaultHandler].
        exception := exception parent.
    ].
    self error: 'Unhandled exception: ', self description.

    "This code should never be executed but is the same code as the default han-
    dler for ExError, ExHalt and ExUserBreak (see the class method
    #initializeSystemExceptions). It is included here so ENVY/Packager will
    not find the methods sent by this expression as unused methods."
    ^Processor activeProcess
        reportError: (aSignal argument isString
            ifTrue: [aSignal argument] ifFalse: [aSignal description])
        resumable: aSignal resumable
```

Signal>>#evaluate:

The argument aBlock is the default block determined in the preceding. A block is set as the signal block for self (aSignal as in the preceding), which will be executed if self is signaled by the code contained in aBlock. Otherwise, the code is resumed once the block has evaluated. Since the default block is used, the behavior is to evaluate the default block defined in initializeSystemExceptions.

```
evaluate: aBlock
    "Evaluate aBlock. Return if the receiver is signaled. Resume the receiver
    if the execution of aBlock falls off the end."

    self signalBlock: [^self].
    self resumeWith: #resume with: (aBlock value: self).
```

[ ] in ExceptionalEvent class>>#initializeSystemExceptions

The default exception handler for the divide-by-zero error was registered in this method. The program trace lists this method because it is the source code location for the block. Be aware that this does not mean that this method is being executed in its entirety; only the appropriate block within this method is executed. The execution in this method occurs in the block defined in the `defaultHandler :=` assignment. The argument passed into the block is `signal` from the `evaluate` method. The block queries the `Processor` global for the `activeProcess` and sends the `reportError:resumable:` method to it. The contents of the error and the resumability of the process are determined from the argument `signal` and passed into the `reportError:resumable:` method. This method then causes the message box to display, from which the stack trace was obtained.

```
initializeSystemExceptions

    | defaultHandler |
    ExAll == nil ifTrue: [
       ExAll := ExceptionalEvent basicNew
          description: 'An exception has occurred.';
          resumable: false.
    ].


    defaultHandler := [:signal |
       Processor activeProcess
          reportError: (signal argument isString
             ifTrue: [signal argument] ifFalse: [signal description])
          resumable: signal resumable].

    ExError == nil ifTrue: [ExError := ExAll newChild].
    ExError
          description: 'An error has occurred.';
          defaultHandler: defaultHandler.


    ExHalt == nil ifTrue: [ExHalt := ExAll newChild].
    ExHalt
          description: 'A halt has occurred.';
          resumable: true;
          defaultHandler: defaultHandler.


    ExUserBreak == nil ifTrue: [ExUserBreak := ExAll newChild].
    ExUserBreak
          description: 'A break has occurred.';
          resumable: true;
          defaultHandler: defaultHandler.
```

SmalltalkAgents

The general concept of the SmalltalkAgents exception-handling system is shown in Figure 5.13, and serves as a graphical overview of the processing that occurs during an exception. Refer to this figure while reading the details

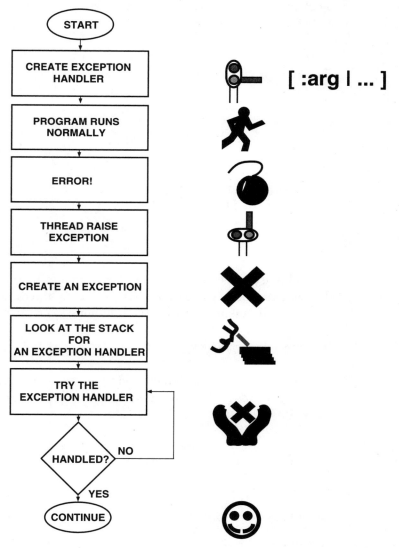

FIGURE 5.13 A graphical overview of the SmalltalkAgents exception-handling system.

of the exception system to see how the significant steps are performed across several methods.

Because SmalltalkAgents compiles the division directly into low-level code, the process of inspecting and observing an exception in progress is different from the other Smalltalks. For this illustration, a class was created in SmalltalkAgents, called `Jonathan`. One instance method was created in the class, `testZeroDivide`. The method sets an exception handler for the block of code that causes a Walkback window to appear. The method source code for class `Jonathan` is:

```
testZeroDivide

    | |

    § Directives Hidden §

    [ 1 / 0 ]
      onExceptionDo:
        [ :anException |
          self halt.
          anException wasHandled.
          ^nil
        ].
  ^self
```

This example uses the standard Smalltalk style exception handling, though exceptions can also be handled using the directives in a method. In the SmalltalkAgents Console, the following expression was evaluated:

```
Jonathan new testZeroDivide
```

The resulting Walkback window was instantiated by the block `onExceptionDo:`. Using the Debugger, the contents of the SmalltalkAgents stack are:

```
[#testZeroDivide-|-Jonathan]
[#onExceptionDo:-|-BlockClosure]
#catchException:-|-UIScheduler:Thread
#divideByZero-|-SmallInteger:Number
[#testZeroDivide-|-Jonathan]
#onExceptionDo:-|-BlockClosure
#testZeroDivide-|-Jonathan
#immediateEvaluation: ·Unbound·
```

which, when simplified to match the others, looks like:

```
Jonathan>>#testZeroDivide
BlockClosure>>#onExceptionDo:
UIScheduler(Thread)>>#catchException
SmallInteger(Number)>>#divideByZero
Jonathan>>#testZeroDivide
BlockClosure>>#onExceptionDo:
Jonathan>>#testZeroDivide
·Unbound·>>#immediateEvaluation:
```

As with the other examples, the stack will be discussed from the bottom (oldest) event of interest to the latest event that caused the Walkback window.

#immediateEvaluation:·Unbound·

This is the code that was executed in the console.

```
Jonathan new testZeroDivide
```

#testZeroDivide-|-Jonathan

This is the method that was written to test the divide-by-zero exception handler. Unfortunately, the default exception handler defined for the divide-by-zero evaluates to 1 in SmalltalkAgents 1.2 DR/2, so the default behavior does not allow inspection of the stack frames and the exception-handling mechanism. The block [1 / 0] is sent the onExceptionDo: message so that, if an exception occurs in the block, the block passed as an argument (the exception handler) will handle the error.

```
testZeroDivide

    | |

    § Directives Hidden §

    [ 1 / 0 ]
      onExceptionDo:
        [ :anException |
          self halt.
          anException wasHandled.
          ^nil
        ].
    ^self
```

#onExceptionDo:-|-BlockClosure

This is the source code that registers anExceptionHandlerBlock as the exception handler for self (an instance of BlockClosure created by compiling the block [1 / 0] in the preceding).

```
onExceptionDo: anExceptionHandlerBlock

    § Begin Directives §

        "Description: Evaluate the receiver block; if any exception
        occurs, the <anExceptionHandlerBlock> will be evaluated."

        Method Author:       'Andrew Demkin'.
        Method Created:      'Mon 08/15/1994 01:41:12 AM'.
        Method Protocol:     'exception-handling'.

        State Any.
        Access Public.

        Allow Undefined Identifiers: false.

        Routing Method.

        On Exception Do:
        [:exception |
            anExceptionHandlerBlock value: exception.
        ].

    § End Directives §

    ^self value
```

[#testZeroDivide-|-Jonathan]

Execution resumes in this method with the evaluation of the compiled block
[1 / 0] . Since this block is compiled into low-level machine code, the divide-
by-zero error occurs out of Smalltalk source code. The error method
divideByZero is called by the low-level routine for the receiver, in this case 1.

```
testZeroDivide

    | |

    § Directives Hidden §

    [ 1 / 0 ]
      onExceptionDo:
        [ :anException |
          self halt.
          anException wasHandled.
          ^nil
        ].
    ^self
```

#divideByZero-|-SmallInteger:Number

Inherited from `Number`, the `SmallInteger` 1 calls this method when an exception occurs. This method raises an exception called `'Numeric Exception'` that will in turn cause the `raiseException` method in `Object` to be executed. This method does not have source code visible, but causes the scheduler thread to execute the `catchException:` method.

```
divideByZero

    § Directives Hidden §

    ^0 raiseException: 'Numeric Exception'
```

#catchException:-|-UIScheduler:Thread

This method searches for the available exception handlers for the code generating `theException`. The code searches the frame stack for an exception handler, and tries to send `catchException:` to the handler. If the handler responds to the exception, then the handler has found a valid handler. If it does not respond, the next handler will be sought, until the default exception handler is used instead. For the divide-by-zero example, the exception handler is found.

```
catchException: theException

    | handler result |

    § Begin Directives §

        "Description: This method will intercept any exceptions and re-route
        them as required. It is a routing method so its actions will be trans-
        parent when doing sender and senderMethod operations. This message is
        sent directly from the VM when an exception occurs on the thread."

        Method Author:        'David Simmons'.
        Method Created:       'Wed 03/23/1994 01:31:00 PM (EST)'.
        Method Protocol:      'exception-handling'.

        State Any.
        Access Internal.

        Allow Undefined Identifiers: false.

        Routing Method.

    § End Directives §
```

Continued

```
"Look for the first special exception handler"
(handler := firstExceptionHandler) ifNotNil:
[
    "We uninstall the handler to prevent a double fault"
     firstExceptionHandler := nil.

    "Try to send it to the handler"
     (handler basicRespondsTo: #catchException:) ifTrue:
     [
        "If the handler executes a block far return then it
         is the handler's responsibility to re-set the thread's
         firstExceptionHandler attribute to itself"
         result := handler catchException: theException.
     ]

    "Re-install the handler"
     firstExceptionHandler := handler

    "See if the handler processed it"
     theException handled ifTrue: [^result].
].

"Look for an active exception handler in the frame stack"
[handler := self nextExceptionHandler] whileTrue:
[
    | aehFrameSave |

    "Restore the <aehFrame> parameter in case a far-return in the handler's
     #catchException: message cleared it."
     aehFrameSave := aehFrame.

    "Try to send it to the handler"
     (handler basicRespondsTo: #catchException:) ifTrue:
     [
         result := handler catchException: theException.
     ].

    "See if the handler processed it"
     theException handled ifTrue:
     [
         aehFrame := nil "Make sure we are nil as we return"
       ^result
     ].

    "Restore the <aehFrame> parameter in case a far-return in the han-
     dler's #catchException: message cleared it."
     aehFrame := aehFrameSave.
].

"Look for the last special exception handler"
(handler := lastExceptionHandler) ifNotNil:
 [
```

Continued

```
"We uninstall the handler to prevent a double fault"
lastExceptionHandler := nil.

"Try to send it to the handler"
(handler basicRespondsTo: #catchException:) ifTrue:
[
    "If the handler executes a block far return then it
    is the handler's responsibility to re-set the thread's
    firstExceptionHandler attribute to itself"
    result := handler catchException: theException.
]

"Re-install the handler"
lastExceptionHandler := handler

"See if the handler processed it"
theException handled ifTrue: [^result].
].

"theException asString vcpuDebug."

"If was not handled then punt it to the Debugger
By here, aehFrame is nil via #nextExceptionHandler"
^self raiseException: theException
```

[#onExceptionDo:-|-BlockClosure]

In SmalltalkAgents notation, the block around a frame stack item indicates that a block within the method is under execution, not the method from the normal entry point. In this case, the block anExceptionHandlerBlock is under execution. The reason that the block and code are not visible here is because SmalltalkAgents allows source code to be hidden, and the directives here are hiding the exception block functionality.

```
onExceptionDo: anExceptionHandlerBlock

    § Begin Directives §

        "Description: Evaluate the receiver block; if any exception occurs,
        the <anExceptionHandlerBlock> will be evaluated."

        Method Author:      'Andrew Demkin'.
        Method Created:     'Mon 08/15/1994 01:41:12 AM'.
        Method Protocol:    'exception-handling'.

        State Any.
        Access Public.
```
                                                                    Continued

```
        Allow Undefined Identifiers: false.

        Routing Method.

        On Exception Do:
        [:exception |
            anExceptionHandlerBlock value: exception.
        ].

    § End Directives §

  ^self value
```

[#testZeroDivide-|-Jonathan]

The execution is now in the exception handler that was registered at the beginning of the example. A `halt` message will be sent to `self`, and a Walkback window will be displayed.

```
testZeroDivide

    | |

    § Directives Hidden §

  [ 1 / 0 ]
    onExceptionDo:
      [ :anException |
        self halt.
        anException wasHandled.
        ^nil
      ].
  ^self
```

How to Do Your Own Exceptional Thing

The programmer of a robust application must expect the unexpected: the exceptional events or data. In addition, the programmer must be prepared to deal with these exceptions in a method appropriate for the project. In some cases, this means to crash and end the program (for hacks, prototypes, and products of unscrupulous vendors). For others, this means managing a budget of time used for additional functionality, something for which the customer can see the benefits, and time spent preparing for the worst, something the customer doesn't see until the project is completed! In my experience, often the customer must be reminded of these very essential tasks that have no immediate visual benefits. They can usually be won over by mentioning the problems with Microsoft Windows version 3.0, which was probably the most widely distributed buggy program.

Designing the exception handlers requires a different mind-set from that of programming the functionality of the system. It requires a data-oriented approach where each of the possible input parameters, be they from the user, a file, a network, or a product of another process, are analyzed for existence, proper type, range, and so on. It may seem like a lot of extra work for no apparent benefit, but for a higher-reliability application it is essential.

A simple example will illustrate the need and utility of using exception-handling code. For a simple application that uses a file system call in Digitalk's Directory class, the programmer has a choice in creating a new file: the programmer can use either `newFileNamed:` or `newFileNamed: ifExists:`. If the programmer uses the method supplying an `exception-Block` to execute when the file exists, the user will remain oblivious to the fact that an error has occurred, and the `exceptionBlock` can create a file with a slightly different name.

 VisualWorks

The following code fragments show simple examples of how to use the exception-handling system. They present only one approach to using the exception-handling system, as well as give available options.

Setup

Use an existing signal (see reference) or create a new signal.

```
aSignal := (Object errorSignal) newSignal.

aSignal := (Dictionary keyNotFoundSignal) newSignalMayProceed: false.
```

Use the signal to associate an exception handler with an error and watch a block of code.

```
aSignal
    handle:
      [ :anException |
      Transcript show: 'an exception has occurred'.
      anException proceed.
      ]
    do: [ self runTheSubSystem ].
```

Set a bunch of signals and handlers to watch the same execution block.

```
HandlerCollection new

    on: aSignal

        handle: [ :anException | self doException: anException ];

    on: anotherSignal

        handle: [ :anException | self doAnotherException: anException ];

    handleDo: [ self runTheSubSystem ].
```

When the Error Occurs

For a nonproceedable exception:

```
aSignal raise
```

For a proceedable exception:

```
aSignal raiseRequest
```

Exception Handler Block

The default action that will occur returns the value of the block.

```
[ :anException | ...... ].
```

The exception was not handled and another handler will be sought.

```
[ :anException | ...... anException reject ].
```

Exits the process from the point at which the exception handler was registered, using `nil` as the returned value.

```
[ :anException | ...... anException return ].
```

Exits the process from the point at which the exception handler was registered, using `aValue` as the returned value.

```
[ :anException | ...... anException returnWith: aValue ].
```

Continue execution from where `aSignal` was raised.

```
[ :anException | ...... anException proceed ].
```

Continue execution from where aSignal was raised, returning aValue.

```
[ :anException | ...... anException proceedWith: aValue ].
```

Redirect the exception to another exception type and handler.

```
[ :anException | ...... anException proceedDoing: [ anotherSignal raise ] ].
```

Try the top-level block at the point in the code at which the exception handler was registered, throwing everything since away.

```
[ :anException | ...... anException restart ].
```

Cleanup

Cleaning up after a nonproceedable exception can be necessary to close a file, terminate a transaction, and so on. These messages help to do this.

```
[] valueOnUnwindDo: [ ]
```

```
[] valueNowOrOnUnwindDo: [ ]
```

 VisualSmalltalk

```
Context>>on:exception do:handlerBlock
ExceptionHandler>>handle:exceptionClass(exception) with:handlerBlock during:
userBlock(self)
```

Setup

```
[ self runTheSubSystem ]

   on: ExceptionSubclass

   do: [ :anException |

     Transcript show: 'Boo Boo'.

     ].

[ self runTheSubSystem ]

   on: MyExcellentExceptionSubclass, YourCoolException

   do: [ :anException | ].
```

When the Error Occurs

```
ExceptionSubclass signal.

ExceptionSubclass signal: 'Boo Boo, ouch!'.
```

Exception Handler Block

```
[ ..... ].

[ :anException | ...... ].
```

Subclasses of Error are not resumable. Subclasses of Warning and Notification are resumable.

```
[ :anException | ...... anException exit: aValue ].

[ :anException | ...... anException resume: aValue ].

[ :anException | ...... anException return ].

[ :anException | ...... anException return: aValue ].

[ :anException | ...... anException retry ].

[ :anException | ...... anException retryUsing: [] ].

[ :anException | ...... anException resignalAs: ExceptionSubclass ].

[ :anException | ...... anException pass ].

[ :anException | ...... anException outer ].
```

Cleanup

If block1 completes successfully, block2 will be executed.

```
[block1] ensure: [block2]
```

If block1 fails to complete, block2 will be executed.

```
[block1] ifCurtailed: [block2]
```

VisualAge/IBM Smalltalk

Setup

```
myExceptionalEvent := ExAll newChild.

myExceptionalEvent description: 'sometext'.

myExceptionalEvent resumable: true.

myExceptionalEvent defaultHandler: [ :aSignal | ...... ].
```

When the Error Occurs

```
myExceptionalEvent signal

myExceptionalEvent signalWith:

myExceptionalEvent signalWith: with:

myExceptionalEvent signalWithArguments:
```

Exception Handler Block

```
[ :aSignal | ...... aSignal exitWith:aValue ].

[ :aSignal | ...... aSignal resumeWith:with:].

[ :aSignal | ...... aSignal retry ].
```

Cleanup

SmalltalkAgents

Setup

```
[] onExceptionDo: [ :anException | ....... ]
```

When the Error Occurs

```
0 raiseException: 'ExceptionType'.
```

Exception Handler Block

```
[ :anException | ....... anException wasHandled. ^nil ]
```

Cleanup

```
[] ensure: []
```

Classes Comprising the Exception-Handling System

 VisualWorks

```
Exception
HandlerCollection
Signal
SignalCollection
```

 VisualSmalltalk

Exceptions in VisualSmalltalk are defined as subclasses of Exception. The approach here is to override methods in the Exception class to define the different behavior for each of the exceptions being handled. The list of exceptions in VisualSmalltalk Enterprise is as follows:

```
Exception
 Error
  APICallError
   APICallEntryPointNotFound
   APICallInvalidArgument
   APICallUnknownPrimitiveFailure
  ArithmeticError
   ZeroDivide
  BindError
   BindDuplicate
   ClassShapeMismatch
   UnresolvedExternal
  ControlError
   MessageNotUnderstood
  FileError
   FileAlreadyExists
   FileErrorWriteProtected
   FileSharingViolation
   FileSystemAccessDenied
   TooManyOpenFiles
  UnknownImport
```

Continued

```
HostFileSystemError
Notification
 AboutToReplaceFile
 KeyboardInterrupt
 PessimisticRepositoryOnFirstEditRequest
  PessimisticRepositoryEditAnywayOnFirstEditRequest
  PessimisticRepositoryLockOnFirstEditRequest
 ProcessTermination
 RecompilationNotification
 RepositoryAmbiguousSpecNotification
 RepositoryConfirmation
 RepositoryInconsistencyNotification
  RepositoryDuplicateEntityInArchive
  RepositoryMissingArchiveNotification
  RepositoryMissingDataDirNotification
  RepositoryUnMappedArchiveNotification
  RepositoryUnMappedRevisionNotification
 RepositoryReconnectRequest
 TeamProgressMessageNotification
 TeamProgressPercentNotification
 VetoAction
 Warning
  LoggedWarning
PARTSGetExecutionContext
PVCSDLLError
RecoveryFailure
RepositoryError
 RepositoryClientError
  RepositoryNoLock
  RepositoryNoWrite
  RepositoryObjectAlreadyExists
   EntityRevisionAlreadyExists
   RepositoryDataAlreadyExists
   RepositoryEntityAlreadyExists
  RepositoryObjectDoesNotExist
   EntityRevisionDoesNotExist
   RepositoryDataDoesNotExistOnDisk
   RepositoryDoesNotExist
   RepositoryEntityDoesNotExist
  RepositorySystemPathCannotBeResolved
 RepositorySystemError
  RepositoryNoConnection
TeamVError
 SemanticError
  ClassDefinitionError
  ExistingHandleError
  ExistingReferencesError
  InvalidHandleError
  InvalidNameError
  MigrationConflictError
  UndefinedNameError
```

Other Classes:

```
ExceptionFilter
ExceptionHandler
ExceptionSet
```

 VisualAge/IBM Smalltalk

```
ExceptionalEvent
Signal
```

 SmalltalkAgents

```
BlockClosure
Thread
```

Summary

Hopefully, at this point you understand some of the mysteries of exception handling, and maybe even took a shot at trying exception handling in your own code. You saw an example of how error handling in general can benefit a program, learned some of the gory details of what exception handling is and how it works, looked at exception handling in action, got a few code snippets to try in your system, and have an idea of other items in the system to explore.

You probably can see that good error handling and good exception handling are part of a good overall design and understanding of the problems involved. The next chapter, on methodologies, should give you some ideas on how you can improve the process by which your programs materialize to improve the quality and cost of your software.

CHAPTER 6

Methodology and Project Management

One of the greatest problems facing the Smalltalk developer today is the lack of standard process. Many different approaches are taken to developing Smalltalk applications, some with great success, but most with moderate to disappointing results. Frederick P. Brooks, Jr., in his acclaimed book *The Mythical Man-Month, 20th Anniversary Edition*, points out that many failures in software development come from the process, not the technology. Smalltalk is mentioned as an exciting product (which we all know it is!) that has the necessary technology, but can fail just as miserably, or even more so, than the traditional programming languages like COBOL, Assembly, and FORTRAN. This chapter will shed some light on the necessary evils of Smalltalk project management, with a template for a project plan presented at the conclusion of the chapter.

In this chapter you will learn the following:

♦ phases of software development
♦ common methodologies for dealing with these phases
♦ the basics of a few object-oriented methodologies that deal with a limited subset of the problem, consisting of primarily analysis and design

139

- reasons why methodologies don't work
- ways to roll your own methodology
- a "cradle to grave" generic methodology for handling all phases of object-oriented development
- an example of development of an object-oriented system using this approach

Phases of Development

Developing software requires more than just hacking away at code. Phases of software development are presented in the order that they typically flow. These phases are: User Requirements, Analysis, Design, Prototype, Implementation, Testing, Delivery, and Maintenance.

User Requirements

The user requirements process determines, based on the business, what is required of the system to be built. This includes functional requirements (that is, the system must handle multiple accounts simultaneously), and performance requirements (the system must handle a maximum of four simultaneous queries against a single account, with an average of one query). The requirements from this phase should be thoroughly documented and very clearly stated to reduce misinterpretations in later phases of the project. The requirements must also be consistent to allow the later phases to handle the requirements in a structured manner. The requirements should also be quite stable, as changes here are magnified during later stages of some development processes.

Analysis

The analysis phase attempts to fit the user requirements together into a cohesive picture of the entire system. Though still in the "paper" phase, analysis takes into account both business needs and implementation-specific concerns such as target system, coordination of implementation groups, and so on.

Specification

Specification is the output product of the analysis step, enhanced to include all information necessary to describe the system. This phase typically takes place with analysis, and has quality assurances to reduce impacts of vague or incorrect requirements. This process may finish after analysis is complete, due to the time it takes to gather details and verify that the specification is complete and consistent. A complete specification will tell everything about a proposed system, and most specifications are not complete. Talking to the authors of the specification is often required to clarify details.

Design

The design comes out of analysis and allows system architects to design various ways for the system to work. The phase may result in several possible designs, and certain trade-off studies may occur in order to choose between the various designs to find the system that best solves the problem in the time frame and cost restrictions. Once the overall design has been decided, detailed designs for each significant module of the system can be done in parallel where possible. Many times the output of the design stage includes class diagrams representing inheritance, object diagrams representing the interaction of instances, and state diagrams, showing the changes in objects as time marches on. Often the work in this stage lacks consistency and detail since no standard has evolved that thoroughly describes the system.

Prototype

In some situations, a prototype may be necessary. Reasons for a prototype are as varied as projects, but may include the need for a vehicle to sell the project, education of the customer, experiments in new areas of technology, and so on. Prototyping is sometimes problematic because once some customers see a prototype, they may think that the final product will be completed in a matter of weeks, when in fact you've still got the database hookup, the reliability issues, the speed, and much of the underlying functional code to write.

Prototypes can also be extremely useful during the analysis, specification, and design phases. A prototype can be used during analysis to feed back interpretations of user requirements and ask "Is this what you meant?" It can be used as a specification by building a prototype and referencing "Use prototype X as specification for this requirement." Design phases can use a prototype of various internal architectures to evaluate speed and memory size constraints, and other possible components of the system, such as a communications scheme.

Implementation

The implementation can begin only after the problem is understood and a design has been produced. Starting with implementation can lead to such problems as software that doesn't meet the need, unsatisfied users, a system that will not grow into the future, and more. At this stage the development team may grow in size, during which "coders" are brought onboard. Most of the time in Smalltalk development, there is no ramp-up for implementation as the same team works through all phases of development.

Testing

The role of testing is often overlooked and underplanned. It is recommended that you plan twice to three times the amount of time you allot for testing as you have in the past if you plan to reuse the code and reduce the maintenance costs. There are three generic types of testing: module testing, integration testing, and system testing. Each of these should have a test plan prepared for every module that states how the testing will be performed and specific test cases that describe the inputs, functions, and outputs of each test.

Module testing provides for checking of code at the module level. In Smalltalk, the module may be a method, a class, a group of classes, or a source code repository entity. Not everything need be tested because the accessors are trusted to work correctly, the user interface is going to work— or not—regardless of your code, and constants are never constant. Each developer should be responsible for providing module testing for their code to prove that it works according to the specification. This assumes, of course, that the specification is correct!

Integration testing can be performed once several modules are interacting. For example, an object broker can be tested with a database connection service (two separate modules) to ensure that objects stored in the database appear as they were stored. This involves two modules that are probably integrated after being written separately, and this interaction must be tested.

System testing is the "end-to-end" testing of an entire software system and extends beyond the boundaries of the Smalltalk environment when external databases, communications, or users are involved. It is the last step before the users of the system will do their testing (the acceptance test) to determine whether the system is functioning as needed or requires more work.

When creating test plans and test cases, it is essential to get the most bang for the buck, and focus on the main areas of functionality. Often, the normal input data will be varied within range to provide coverage of the acceptable conditions, and inputs outside the acceptable range will also be tested to provide verification that errors occur when expected.

Delivery

Since you are all great developers and managers, the system has been documented thoroughly during development with plenty of time at the end to deal with final drafts of documentation, installation scripts, packaging, and distribution needs. Let's get real! No doubt, your project had such aggressive deadlines to begin with that you barely had time for lunch and worked through weekends and holidays to implement the greatest application since the knife was invented for slicing bread. There are, however, serious considerations to be given to delivery—above and beyond how much to tip the local pizza guy. These include documentation, installation scripts, packaging strategies, and distribution.

The minimum documentation required is an installation manual that tells the users how to install the software and configure it to perform properly. This document should include the required hardware and software, including RAM and hard disk storage and any special drivers or other products. It should also include a troubleshooting section to reduce the number of hours spent figuring out why it installs and runs on only half the user's machines.

An operating guide is also a recommended delivery option. It should detail the operation of the system and include a reference section and a "hands-on" tutorial. This is typically not written by the development organization, but rather by a training department.

Finally, all the documents that have been accumulated should be updated and coordinated to give the maintainers of the system a few hints on how to fix the big problems that could come five minutes or five years after delivery.

Installation scripts are usually required in order to insert the application into the user's computer. This should at a minimum prepare the machine, copy the software, and prompt the user as to how to proceed. In addition, a displayed release note and a test of the installed software are nice options.

Packaging and distribution may sound like something that occurs in the shipping room, but for Smalltalk, the packaging is an important part of how the application is delivered, and refers not to the box (if it will ship in a box) but to the types of "packages" that will be used for the run-time system. For example, in Visual Smalltalk Enterprise, the delivered code may be in the form of SLLs—Smalltalk Link Libraries—that may contain different pieces of functionality that can be swapped in and out of RAM as needed and updated independently by the maintainers. In SmalltalkAgents, the application can be added incrementally to an existing environment as the "engine" is only delivered once, and can run many applications simultaneously (preemptively, too!). Distribution may be in the form of a compressed archive, a set of diskettes, or an automated network download service. These issues should take into account the constant updates needed during maintenance, as well as the possibility of several versions deployed concurrently or on differing hardware platforms.

Maintenance

Now that the application is in the users' hands, the fun begins! Hopefully, they use the application that you've poured your lifeblood into, and it doesn't just sit there. If they do use it, they will probably need help (especially as they discover undocumented "features"), request enhancements and changes for their business, and ask you to update it to the latest operating system.

Your job is definitely made easier by the good quality of documentation maintained during development of the system, and by the fact that the people who wrote the application and its requirements really did a thorough job and captured the essence of the business. If not, then you are wading through the Debugger wondering what the programmer who wrote it was thinking. Figures as high as 90 percent have been touted to explain the time and expenses associated with maintenance, a misnomer for the continued evolution of the software product. Which is what Smalltalk does best!

Popular Methodologies

In this section, a brief overview of some of the very popular software development methodologies is presented. These methodologies range from the very structured (Waterfall) to the extremely unstructured (Build and Fix) and include some of the newer methodologies that pertain to Smalltalk. The hot methodologies for Smalltalk are Rapid Deployment, Evolutionary, and PARTS, but they are not the only approaches, and probably represent the minority of projects, especially in organizations with mandates to follow corporate procedures for all development. Each of the methodologies is described with a brief explanation, a functional flowchart, and a GANTT-type of activity versus time graph. The functional flowcharts may be familiar to many, while the GANTT-type charts are meant to assist project managers in the actual scheduling of projects, and are unique to this book.

Waterfall

Water splashes and is wasted in a waterfall.

The Waterfall model represents the classic approach to building a large system. It is used by large and small companies, government, and taught in our universities. It is the most popular approach because it allows different groups to have distinct and separate responsibilities, and for one group to drive another forward. It is used almost exclusively within the U.S. Federal Government and specified exactly in MIL STD 498, which details the documents generated in the various steps. The typical waterfall methodology steps are shown in Figure 6.1

The steps have an order, sometimes with one step feeding back to the previous step. The use of a prototype is not strict waterfall, but is common enough to fit this diagram. All methodologies visit these steps in this order, but none of the others "prohibits" the revisiting of the prior steps, and don't force the project to complete one step before moving into the next.

Figure 6.1 doesn't tell the whole story, though. It presents the steps in a logical, flowchart fashion, but does not give any indication as to how the steps would be scheduled in time. Figure 6.2 is a GANTT-type chart, where the activities are listed down the vertical axis, and the time span that these activities occupies is shown through the use of horizontal bars that represent the relative lengths of time, the component of the horizontal axis. This chart helps to illustrate how the steps are performed over time, and how they are performed for a subsequent version of the project.

Spiral

Spiral up or down? This methodology is heavily prescribed and represents a slightly different view of the Waterfall methodology. Each of the steps is performed in sequence, and the first step is revisited after the last step, as shown in Figure 6.3. In the first few runs around the spiral, the delivery and

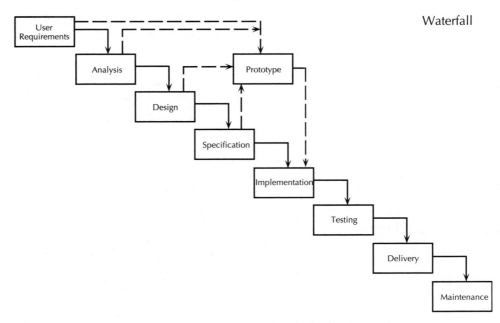

FIGURE 6.1 A functional flow diagram shows the steps involved in the various stages of the waterfall methodology.

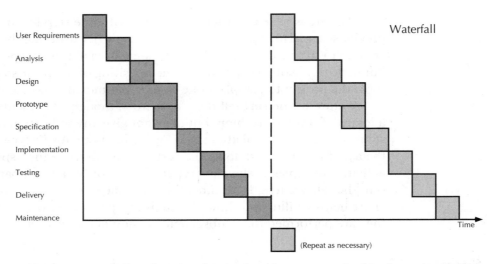

FIGURE 6.2 A time flow diagram shows when the steps involved in the various stages of the Waterfall methodology occur, and indicates the repeating steps.

maintenance steps may be skipped since no delivery is being made to external customers.

This methodology may be applied to an entire project, and scaled down to an individual piece of a project. For example, if you had three programmers working on a project, each of them may go once around the

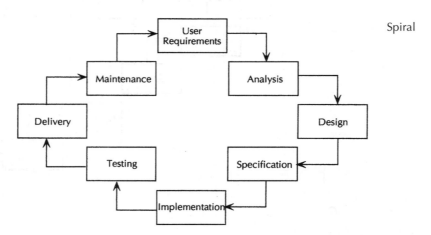

FIGURE 6.3 A functional flow diagram shows the steps involved in the various stages of the Spiral methodology.

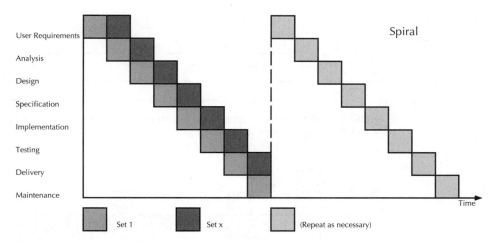

FIGURE 6.4 A time flow diagram shows when the steps involved in the various stages of the Waterfall methodology occur, and indicates the repeating steps.

spiral with the portion of the project for which each programmer is responsible. These three simultaneous spirals, when combined, would represent one project run around the spiral.

Figure 6.4 shows the steps that are performed in the Spiral method. Notice how they seem to be exactly the same as for the Waterfall. The difference is that each of the steps is performed in a much shorter time and that the normal repetition of steps can occur in days and weeks as opposed to years in the Waterfall. Also notice that two different tasks can occur simultaneously using Spiral, so that, for example, your analysts can tackle one piece, and then another, at the same time as the other teams (design, specification, implementation, and so on) perform their tasks.

Build and Fix

Sadly, **build and fix** is alive and well, as seen in Figure 6.5. This method for developing software must be the most widely used—and the least effective. It involves little attention to what to build until the construction begins. It can be likened to drawing the blueprints for a house as construction occurs, sometimes before the piece to be constructed, sometimes after. It results in many pieces of the system fitting together poorly, and much rework. One of the main reasons that this is still the most popular method is due to ignorance of process and its importance.

Figure 6.6 shows just how badly the methodology performs. The time spent fixing is incredibly long. The requirements, if visited, must be revisited,

Build and Fix

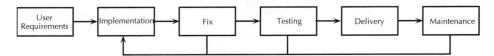

FIGURE 6.5   A functional flow diagram shows the steps involved in the various stages of the Build and Fix methodology.

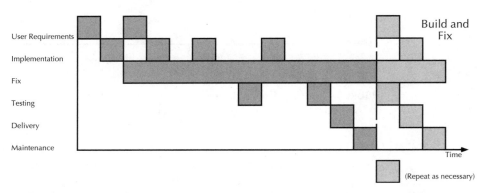

FIGURE 6.6   A time flow diagram shows when the steps involved in the various stages of the Build and Fix methodology occur, and indicates the repeating steps.

and the overall duration of the project is incredible when compared to other approaches. This is the result when the call to arms is "let's get coding!"

Rapid Deployment

Build and fix by another name? **Rapid deployment** is growing in popularity as development managers and customers demand a shorter development cycle. One major telecommunications company adopted this strategy as the only way to create a huge client/server system. This process, shown in Figure 6.7, is better than build and fix and compresses the time required by waterfall. However, it still ignores the problem of implementing the software before knowing exactly what the software is supposed to do.

The time required for each of the steps is shown in Figure 6.8. Notice that the user requirements stage is still going on during almost the entire implementation process. One problem not mentioned when discussing rapid deployment is the way people feel during this process. The implementors must rework and revise their work as the user requirements change. The prototype is nearly useless as it parallels real development and is subject to user requirements changes. People get weary of changing the same

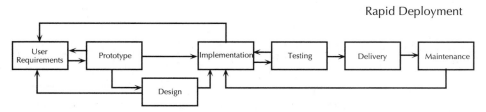

FIGURE 6.7   A functional flow diagram shows the steps involved in the various stages of the Rapid Deployment methodology.

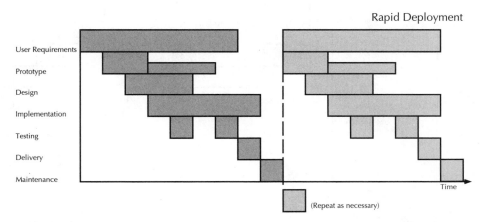

FIGURE 6.8   A time flow diagram shows when the steps involved in the various stages of the Rapid Deployment methodology occur, and indicates the repeating steps.

pieces of code or documentation, over and over, and the user requirements drive the other processes, so that changes to the requirements have major effects downstream.

Evolutionary

Son of build and fix? This process is similar to build and fix and rapid deployment. It is often spoken of as the way to "grow" software, and uses the same steps in the same sequence, with a shorter repetition period; it is shown in Figure 6.9. One process drives another, and feedback may occur between one step and the previous. The steps are all traversed quickly, with a growing subset of the problem, so that the end result is a larger and larger whole built on the same core. This results in incrementally more functional pieces of software, but assumes that the earlier steps in the process will be done correctly and with incredible foresight so that the original product meets the needs as the system grows. All Smalltalk development follows this

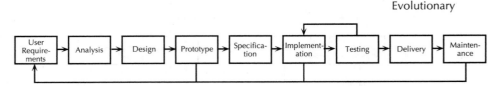

FIGURE 6.9   A functional flow diagram shows the steps involved in the various stages of the Evolutionary methodology.

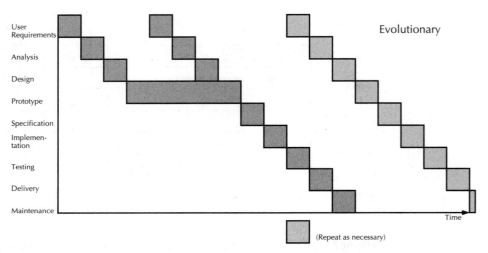

FIGURE 6.10   A time flow diagram shows when the steps involved in the various stages of the Evolutionary methodology occur, and indicates the repeating steps.

pattern to some degree, as the base image, the "already running application," is customized further and further.

The time necessary for these steps is shown in Figure 6.10. The repetition of these steps is rapid, with greater and greater functionality. The portions built in earlier stages can (hopefully) be reused without being rebuilt, and the system will evolve into better versions.

Component Software or PARTS

One of the latest ways to develop applications is with component-based software. Component-based software is a hot topic, and the Smalltalk version is known as PARTS, which stands for Parts Assembly and Reuse Tool Set. Both the VisualSmalltalk Enterprise and VisualAge products provide a PARTS approach.

This approach allows the team to divvy up the work between Smalltalk experts and problem domain experts. Some of the work must be done by hardcore Smalltalkers and the balance done by more business-oriented individuals, who can assemble the "parts" into a whole, in a process that is commonly referred to as "programming in the large" because it involves using large modules of software to create a final product, without worrying about many of the programming issues, instead focusing on the business and requirements (see Figure 6.11).

The time allotted for each of these steps is shown in Figure 6.12. The time cycle that is required for a final product is compressed, and since the component builders are separated from the application builders, the user requirements can change more freely without far-reaching impacts. The architecture of the system is known and the application assemblers tend to be less programmers and more users of the system being constructed.

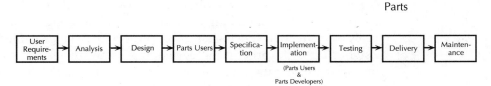

FIGURE 6.11 A functional flow diagram shows the steps involved in the various stages of the Component Software/PARTS methodology.

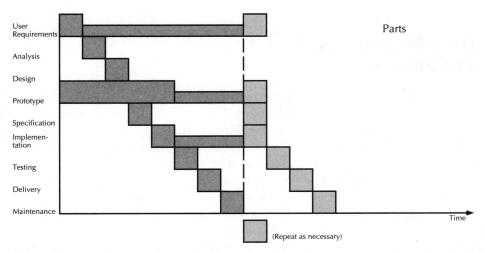

FIGURE 6.12 A time flow diagram shows when the steps involved in the various stages of the Component Software/PARTS methodology occur, and indicates the repeating steps.

As you can see, there are many different ways to build software, with two varieties particularly suited to Smalltalk development; evolutionary and components. These two approaches share both the rapid deployment required by managers and users, along with the flexibility to grow and change, which meets long-term strategic objectives of many organizations.

Why Choose a Methodology?

So, why choose a methodology? Many people do so because they want to follow a "cookbook" approach to development. While they may not know everything about the development process, they are assured that they will cover all the bases because the people who created these methodologies must surely know how to build software the right way.

There are other advantages to following a known path toward a goal. These include knowing the direction you will travel and the steps that will take you to your goal; being able to track the progress of the project more easily and effectively; using a base of project knowledge gained from others' insights into the process of developing software; easier communication among team members and external people like managers and customers; better preparations before steps are executed due to better planning. These advantages and others make it desirable to adopt a known methodology as opposed to making one up as you go along.

Hot Methodologies for Analysis and Design

You may have heard about many of the popular object methodologies of the day: Booch, Rumbaugh, Coad, Objectory, Responsibility-Driven Design (Digitalk), Object Behavior Analysis (ParcPlace), Class-Responsibility-Collaborator (CRC) Cards, and so on. Methodologies (not necessarily object-oriented) have been around for a long time. While these object-oriented methodologies are very useful, there are many steps in the software development process that these methodologies do not cover. They are primarily for the analysis and design stages of development and take you part of the way into specification and implementation.

As the authors of the methodologies join forces, these methodologies have merged. Two major forces now exist in the methodology war: IBM, with its Wisdom methodology, and Rational Inc., with the combined forces of Booch, Rumbaugh, Objectory (Jacobsen), and CRC Tools.

All of the methodologies capture most of the same information, but differ in name and symbol. This information includes classes, objects, relationships (including inheritance), attributes, methods, and state. The essential information can be captured in generic types of diagrams used in each methodology: class, object, and timing.

Booch

The Booch notation uses three types of views of the information, called **behavior, data,** and **architecture.** It uses three diagrams to represent the information, called **timing, object,** and **entity-relationship.** A tool, called Rational Rose, is available for Smalltalk that will provide diagramming, modeling, and Smalltalk code generation. In addition, it will perform reverse-engineering of existing Smalltalk code for documentation, understanding, and analysis.

Rumbaugh

The Rumbaugh notation uses three types of diagrams to represent the information, called **entity-relation, state,** and **data flow.** It has been combined with the Booch method, and is available as the Unified Booch-Rumbaugh method in tools from Rational Inc.

Coad

Coad is also a popular methodology, and can be used in software through the Playground program from Object International Inc. It is also known as Extended ERD, and comes from the Yourdon approach to software engineering, one of the most popular for structured analysis (the predecessor of object-oriented analysis).

Objectory

Objectory, the methodology of Ivar Jacobson, is probably the most complete methodology offered today, with its mature set of tools and the most thorough coverage of issues central to system engineering. Jacobsen recently joined Rational, combining forces with Booch and Rumbaugh. He was the primary force behind the Objectory methodology derived from his work in telecommunications. He makes extensive use of "use-cases" which are descriptions of how "actors" (people or other systems) interact with the system under design.

Responsibility-Driven Design (RDD)

This methodology uses CRC cards, and is the recommended methodology of Digitalk, and is taught in their classes. It makes use of the CRC cards for designing the system, and does not possess great amounts of notation, automated tools, or a large following outside of the Smalltalk marketplace.

Object Behavior Analysis

Originally a ParcPlace methodology emphasizing scenarios, this methodology is slated to be merged with RDD from Digitalk to create a new ParcPlace-Digitalk methodology.

Synchronicity

Synchronicity is the data modeling and object brokering set of tools from VMARK software for use with the ObjectStudio version of Smalltalk, and may become available for other versions of Smalltalk. It offers analysis and data modeling tools and a prebuilt architecture for accessing and manipulating data from relational databases through the included object broker.

Why Methodologies Don't Work

There are many reasons that a methodology does not work for a particular situation, customer, or project. The reasons vary as much as the problems that they are intended to solve. If a methodology does not work because of certain restrictions, it is not usually because the methodology is "wrong" or "bad," but rather that it is unsuited to solve the problem at hand.

Sometimes you may pick the right methodology (your own perhaps), but it does not work even though all indicators indicate that it will. This is often due to conditions beyond your control. Some of those conditions are correctable or avoidable, some are not. Some of these conditions are discussed next, with a few ideas on how to overcome the conditions.

♦ *No time:* Time will be saved by learning how to do "it" right the first time, and then doing so. More time will be wasted over the life of the project if no method is used, and it is much easier to track the progress.

- *Customer doesn't want it:* A sick child may not want medicine that tastes bad, but it may save the child. Does the customer really know better or know the consequences?
- *Hard to learn and use:* Smalltalk was hard to learn, too, but you can see its benefits. One way to ease the burden is to have someone who knows the method help you to use it the first time around. The second time, you can do it on your own.
- *Doesn't cover all phases of development:* This is the all-or-nothing argument. It is true that most of these methods don't cover all the phases of development, but they can be used for the portions they do cover, and a nonobject-oriented development methodology will provide most of what you need for the other phases.
- *Doesn't work with Smalltalk:* So pick one that does, or you'll have to do lots of extra work to make the method work with Smalltalk. There are many choices and tools available for Smalltalk to assist in your efforts.

Roll Your Own Methodology

Many people, after studying the methodologies, decide that they know better and will pick and choose pieces of the methodologies that work for them. That works great if you have budgeted the time to create a methodology for Smalltalk development, and have prior experience with Smalltalk. Otherwise, better to pick one and go with it.

A Generic Smalltalk Methodology

In addition to everything you've read about Smalltalk methodology here and elsewhere, there is one new idea to present in the context of a generic methodology for Smalltalk development: Make the Smalltalkers experts in the subject area.

They will end up being experts in the subject area at the end of the project, so why not speed up the learning process of the Smalltalker and reap the benefits of the knowledge early in the project? Smalltalk programming can take years to master, and every Smalltalk programmer has become a master in many subject areas as they developed systems and learned the full breadth of the class library, so they are in an excellent position to understand the business early and build it based on that understanding.

Figure 6.13 shows the project schedule for the generic Smalltalk methodology. Even if you decide not to make your Smalltalkers experts, you

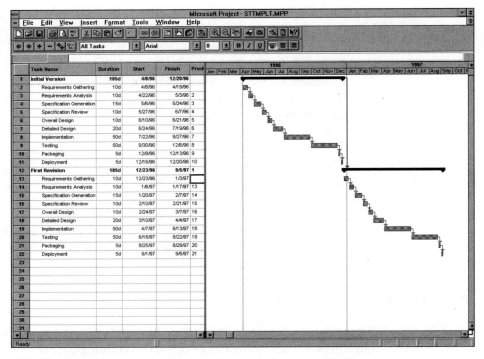

FIGURE 6.13   A Microsoft project template plan for a Smalltalk project.

can use this schedule, enclosed in soft copy on the disc, to prepare a project plan for your project.

Summary

You've read about the various steps in the software development process, seen various methodologies that address them, and learned a little about the object-oriented methodologies available. You have also noted that there are specific methodologies best suited for Smalltalk, including Component Software, Rational Rose Smalltalk, and Objectory. You saw a reusable generic Smalltalk methodology that can be customized to give you a project plan for Smalltalk development.

In the next chapter, you will see the generic Smalltalk methodology in action, with an example of a system built with it, a Personal Information Manager.

7

Methodology Applied:
A Personal Information
Manager (PIM)

An example of a full development example is presented here. The application is a personal information manager (PIM), and the material is offered as it might appear in project documentation.

Requirements

These requirements are similar to what you might be faced with when working with a potential user of the application. They don't come for free, and usually users will respond "Yeah" as you describe functionality that you think might be necessary to accomplish their task. The requirements may range from simple and ambiguous to complex and daunting, and they are gathered by the person who talks with the customer about his or her needs. The customer may be an internal manager, a client, or a group of individuals identified as the "target market" and interviewed by the marketing department.

This example starts with the simplest of requests: "I need to manage my contacts—you know, names and addresses." This may be all that is forthcoming from the customer, so it must be enhanced and embellished to cover all the things the user might have meant by the remark. Remember: Build what the customer really needs, not what the customer says he or she needs.

User requirements can typically be broken down into two types of requirements: functional and performance. The functional requirements are usually the most apparent, and are often the only ones mentioned by the customer. They refer to the "what" of the application.

Functional Requirements

The functional requirements for the personal information manager are:

1. Create, modify, delete records.
2. Manage people, companies, agencies, phone, fax, e-mail, and the relationships between them.

and so on. . . .

Performance Requirements

The performance requirements for the personal information manager include:

1. Enter a new contact in five seconds.
2. Return a search for a contact in less than 10 seconds.

and more. . . .

Analysis

Once the seed of the application has been sown, it is time to really determine what the application is supposed to do. This means studying the requirements, asking many questions, and understanding the answers. All work should be documented in writing, and ideally traced from the source of the work, whether that be a specific requirement, a conversation, a memorandum, a letter, or another product or prototype.

The key to this stage is understanding the need without beginning to dictate how the need will be met. By placing a division between understanding (analysis) and solving (design and implementation), work will not have to be revised or thrown away as the understanding of the problem increases.

Some design questions and answers to consider:

Q1: What details are necessary to know about a person in the system? (requirement 2)

A1: A person should include first name, last name, middle initial or middle name, birthday, address, office phone number, fax number, home phone, car phone, employer, organizational affiliations, spouse's name, children's names, and a few comments about golf handicap and personal interests.

Design

Once the understanding of the application is complete (which may never happen) and documented, it is time to begin to construct a design of the application. This can occur in many ways, and may use some of the off-the-shelf design methodologies.

Once you've completed a few applications, you may be able to "see the objects" in your mind without following a methodology. At this point, though, it is still good practice to use the available design tools to communicate ideas to others, so that a team may work on the application with complete understanding, or the application may be modified or maintained in the future.

In this example, the PIM may be designed in many ways. One design solution is shown in Figure 7.1. This diagram was generated from Rational Rose and includes the major classes and variables for the classes in the system. The methods are not shown in this example. The process that led to this design was lengthy and not well documented. It was created in 1991 for use with the SmalltalkAgents product, and has been redesigned and rebuilt many times on each of the versions of Smalltalk.

Of interest in the design is the abstraction of addresses, e-mail addresses, and phone numbers into a generic superclass, called a **locator.** Since each of these types serves as a way to locate a person, they are similar, and a person may have many. Also interesting is the abstraction of the person's employer, membership in user groups, associated companies, and so on, which are all types of **organization.**

Specification

Once the design has been completed, a specification (or "spec") can be generated that will be provided to "coders" who will create the system. If you are working solo, then this will serve as an exercise to determine exactly

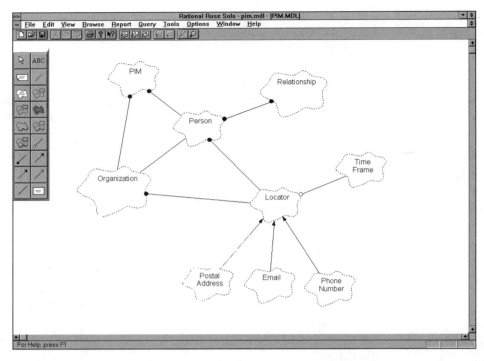

FIGURE 7.1 The design of the personal information manager (PIM) in Rational Rose.

what you will create, and what you *won't* create (which is much more important). This specification can be kept in the head, but if it is to stand the test of time, it should probably be written down and maintained. Since this example uses Rational Rose for design, the design diagram is probably sufficient for the specification purpose. After all, this is a solo mission; the result is presented next.

Implementation

It's finally time to code. If you were drawn to computer programming because you like to write programs (like me) then you probably skipped the preceding steps and started here. Skipping the previous steps may make the application impossible to complete, however, so a little time should be spent on them, even if it's only scratching a few notes down about the application before coding.

The code is presented in Listing 7.1 for an implementation of a personal information manager. This is the generic model for a PIM that is very portable between different versions of Smalltalk. Since the graphical user interface is not portable, a separate user interface, along with a customized version of this code, is required for each of the major versions of Smalltalk. This is left to the reader.

```
Object
    subclass: #PIMModel
    instanceVariableNames: 'comments'
    classVariableNames: ' '
    poolDictionaries: ' ' !

PIMModel
    subclass: #PIMInterval
    instanceVariableNames: 'start end increment units'
    classVariableNames: ''
    poolDictionaries: ''!

PIMModel
    subclass: #PIMLocators
    instanceVariableNames: ''
    classVariableNames: ''
    poolDictionaries: ''!

PIMLocators
    subclass: #PIMElectronicAddress
    instanceVariableNames: ''
    classVariableNames: ''
    poolDictionaries: ''!

PIMElectronicAddress
    subclass: #PIMEmail
    instanceVariableNames: 'username host'
    classVariableNames: ''
    poolDictionaries: ''!

PIMModel
    subclass: #PIMOrganization
    instanceVariableNames: 'locators name'
    classVariableNames: ''
    poolDictionaries: ''!

PIMModel
    subclass: #PIMPerson
    instanceVariableNames: 'firstName middleName lastName birthDate
organizations relationships locators'
    classVariableNames: ''
    poolDictionaries: ''!

PIMModel
    subclass: #PIMPIM
    instanceVariableNames: 'people organizations'
```

Continued

```
        classVariableNames: 'CurrentPIM'
        poolDictionaries: ''!


PIMLocators
        subclass: #PIMPostalAddress
        instanceVariableNames: 'street suite city stateProvince country
postalCode'
        classVariableNames: ''
        poolDictionaries: ''!


PIMModel
        subclass: #PIMRelationship
        instanceVariableNames: 'name from to'
        classVariableNames: ''
        poolDictionaries: ''!


PIMElectronicAddress
        subclass: #PIMTelephone
        instanceVariableNames: 'countryCode areaCode number'
        classVariableNames: ''
        poolDictionaries: ''!


PIMModel
        subclass: #PIMTimeFrame
        instanceVariableNames: 'intervals beginning ending'
        classVariableNames: ''
        poolDictionaries: ''!


!PIMEmail methods!

host
        "Generated accessor. Return the value of the variable <host>."

        ^host!


host: anObject
        "Generated accessor. Set the value of the variable <host>."

        host := anObject!


initialize
        host := String new.
        username := String new.!


printOn: aStream

        aStream
            nextPutAll: username;                           Continued
```

```
            nextPut: $@;
            nextPutAll: host!

username
      "Generated accessor. Return the value of the variable <username>."

      ^username!

username: anObject
      "Generated accessor. Set the value of the variable <username>."

      username := anObject! !

!PIMInterval methods!

end
      "Generated accessor. Return the value of the variable <end>."
      ^end!

end: anObject
      "Generated accessor. Set the value of the variable <end>."

      end := anObject!

increment
      "Generated accessor. Return the value of the variable <increment>."

      ^increment!

increment: anObject
      "Generated accessor. Set the value of the variable <increment>."

      increment := anObject!

initialize
      end := Date new.
      start := Date new.
      units := 'Days'.
      increment := 1.!

printOn: aStream

      aStream
          nextPutAll: start;
          nextPutAll: ' to ';
          nextPutAll: end;
          nextPutAll: ' by ';
```

Continued

```
            nextPutAll: increment;
            space;
            nextPutAll: units!

start
        "Generated accessor. Return the value of the variable <start>."

        ^start!

start: anObject
        "Generated accessor. Set the value of the variable <start>."

        start := anObject!

units
        "Generated accessor. Return the value of the variable <units>."

        ^units!

units: anObject
        "Generated accessor. Set the value of the variable <units>."

        units := anObject! !

!PIMModel methods!

comments
        "Generated accessor. Return the value of the variable <comments>."

        ^comments!

comments: anObject
        "Generated accessor. Set the value of the variable <comments>."

        comments := anObject!

initialize
        ! !

!PIMModel class methods!

new
        "Public - Force initialization of instances on creation"

^super new initialize! !

!PIMOrganization methods!
```

Continued

```
initialize
     locators := Set new.
     name := String new.!

locators
     "Generated accessor. Return the value of the variable <locators>."

     ^locators!

locators: anObject
     "Generated accessor. Set the value of the variable <locators>."

     locators := anObject!

name
     "Generated accessor. Return the value of the variable <name>."

     ^name!

name: anObject
     "Generated accessor. Set the value of the variable <name>."

     name := anObject!

printOn: aStream

     aStream nextPutAll: name! !

!PIMPerson methods!

addRelationshipNamed: aName to: anotherPerson

     relationships add: (PIMRelationship new from: self; to:
anotherPerson; name: aName).!

birthDate
     "Generated accessor. Return the value of the variable <birthDate>."

     ^birthDate!

birthDate: anObject
     "Generated accessor. Set the value of the variable <birthDate>."

     birthDate := anObject!

firstName
     "Generated accessor. Return the value of the variable <firstName>."
```

Continued

```
        ^firstName!

firstName: anObject
        "Generated accessor. Set the value of the variable <firstName>."

        firstName := anObject!

initialize
        organizations := Set new.
        relationships := Set new.
        locators := Set new.
        firstName := String new.
        lastName := String new.
        birthDate := Date new.
        middleName := String new.
        !

lastName
        "Generated accessor. Return the value of the variable <lastName>."

        ^lastName!

lastName: anObject
        "Generated accessor. Set the value of the variable <lastName>."

        lastName := anObject!

locators
        "Generated accessor. Return the value of the variable <locators>."

        ^locators!

locators: anObject
        "Generated accessor. Set the value of the variable <locators>."

        locators := anObject!

middleName
        "Generated accessor. Return the value of the variable <middleName>."

        ^middleName!

middleName: anObject
        "Generated accessor. Set the value of the variable <middleName>."

        middleName := anObject!
```

Continued

```
organizations
     "Generated accessor. Return the value of the variable
<organizations>."

     ^organizations!

organizations: anObject
     "Generated accessor. Set the value of the variable <organizations>."

     organizations := anObject!

printOn: aStream

     aStream nextPutAll: firstName;
     space;
     nextPutAll: middleName;
     space;
     nextPutAll: lastName!

relationships
     "Generated accessor. Return the value of the variable
<relationships>."

     ^relationships!

relationships: anObject
     "Generated accessor. Set the value of the variable <relationships>."

     relationships := anObject! !

!PIMPIM methods!

initialize
     people := Set new.
     organizations := Set new.!

newOrganization

     self organizations add: (self class organizationClass new).!

newPerson

     self people add: (self class personClass new).!

organizations
     "Generated accessor. Return the value of the variable
<organizations>."
```

Continued

```
        ^organizations!

organizations: anObject
        "Generated accessor. Set the value of the variable <organizations>."

        organizations := anObject!

people
        "Generated accessor. Return the value of the variable <people>."

        ^people!

people: anObject
        "Generated accessor. Set the value of the variable <people>."

        people := anObject!

printOn: aStream

        aStream
            nextPutAll: 'People';
            cr.
        self people
            do:
                [:each |
                each printOn: aStream.
                aStream cr.
                ].
        aStream
            nextPutAll: 'Organizations';
            cr.
        self organizations
            do:
                [:each |
                each printOn: aStream.
                aStream cr.
                ].
        !

show
        self class viewClass new openOn: self.! !

!PIMPIM class methods!

current
        CurrentPIM isNil ifTrue: [ CurrentPIM := PIMPIM new ].
        ^CurrentPIM!

organizationClass
        ^PIMOrganization!
```

Continued

```
personClass
    ^PIMPerson!

viewClass
    ^PIMView! !

!PIMPostalAddress methods!

city
    "Generated accessor. Return the value of the variable <city>."

    ^city!

city: anObject
    "Generated accessor. Set the value of the variable <city>."

    city := anObject!

country
    "Generated accessor. Return the value of the variable <country>."

    ^country!

country: anObject
    "Generated accessor. Set the value of the variable <country>."

    country := anObject!

initialize
    city := String new.
    country := String new.
    postalCode := String new.
    stateProvince := String new.
    street := String new.
    suite := String new.!

postalCode
    "Generated accessor. Return the value of the variable <postalCode>."
    ^postalCode!

postalCode: anObject
    "Generated accessor. Set the value of the variable <postalCode>."

    postalCode := anObject!

printOn: aStream

    aStream
        nextPutAll: street;
```

Continued

```
                    space;
                    nextPutAll: suite;
                    cr;
                    nextPutAll: city;
                    comma;
                    space;
                    nextPutAll: stateProvince;
                    space;
                    nextPutAll: postalCode!

stateProvince
        "Generated accessor. Return the value of the variable <stateProvince>."


        ^stateProvince!

stateProvince: anObject
        "Generated accessor. Set the value of the variable <stateProvince>."


        stateProvince := anObject!

street
        "Generated accessor. Return the value of the variable <street>."


        ^street!

street: anObject
        "Generated accessor. Set the value of the variable <street>."


        street := anObject!

suite
        "Generated accessor. Return the value of the variable <suite>."


        ^suite!

suite: anObject
        "Generated accessor. Set the value of the variable <suite>."


        suite := anObject! !

!PIMRelationship methods!

from
        "Generated accessor. Return the value of the variable <from>."


        ^from!

from: anObject
        "Generated accessor. Set the value of the variable <from>."
```

Continued

```
        from := anObject!

initialize
        from := String new.
        to := String new.
        name := String new.!

name
        "Generated accessor. Return the value of the variable <name>."

        ^name!

name: anObject
        "Generated accessor. Set the value of the variable <name>."

        name := anObject!

printOn: aStream

        aStream
            nextPutAll: from;
            space;
            nextPutAll: name;
            space;
            nextPutAll: to!

to
        "Generated accessor. Return the value of the variable <to>."

        ^to!

to: anObject
        "Generated accessor. Set the value of the variable <to>."

        to := anObject! !

!PIMTelephone methods!

areaCode
        "Generated accessor. Return the value of the variable <areaCode>."

        ^areaCode!

areaCode: anObject

        "Generated accessor. Set the value of the variable <areaCode>."

        areaCode := anObject!
```

Continued

```
countryCode
    "Generated accessor. Return the value of the variable <countryCode>."

    ^countryCode!

countryCode: anObject
    "Generated accessor. Set the value of the variable <countryCode>."

    countryCode := anObject!

initialize
    areaCode := 101.
    countryCode := 011.
    number := 5551212.
    !

number
    "Generated accessor. Return the value of the variable <number>."

    ^number!

number: anObject
    "Generated accessor. Set the value of the variable <number>."

    number := anObject!

printOn: aStream

    aStream
        nextPut: countryCode;
        nextPut: $-;
        nextPutAll: areaCode;
        nextPut: $-;
        nextPutAll: number! !

!PIMTimeFrame methods!

beginning
    "Generated accessor. Return the value of the variable <beginning>."

    ^beginning!

beginning: anObject
    "Generated accessor. Set the value of the variable <beginning>."

    beginning := anObject!
```

Continued

```
ending
    "Generated accessor. Return the value of the variable <ending>."

    ^ending!

ending: anObject
    "Generated accessor. Set the value of the variable <ending>."

    ending := anObject!

initialize
    beginning := Date new.
    ending := Date new.
    intervals := Set new.!

intervals
    "Generated accessor. Return the value of the variable <intervals>."

    ^intervals!

intervals: anObject
    "Generated accessor. Set the value of the variable <intervals>."

    intervals := anObject!

printOn: aStream

    aStream
        nextPutAll: beginning;
        space;
        nextPutAll: ending;
        space;
        nextPutAll: intervals! !
```

LISTING 7.1 A simple personal information manager model.

Testing

After the code has been written, and many of the bugs fixed, it is time to test it. You probably tested various pieces of the code as you went, or things wouldn't run at all. Additionally, you can test whole sets of the code, or let real users of the application get their hands on it and really put it to work! One caution about releasing the software "before it's time" is that user perception of software is crucial to success. An early release of the software that is prone to failure or hard to use will doom future releases. Better to get the software tested by some typical users, and listen to what they have to say about how the software works for them.

Delivery

Now that your application is perfect, it's time to send it out to the users. You may want to create a huge image, or split it into Parcels, PIPO's, DLLs, or SLLs, all packaging elements of the various Smalltalks. It's also time to wonder about how it will get installed on the users' machine, and how it will be updated. How much RAM do they have? What video card are they running? Do they have VGA, SVGA, or XGA? Is the software built to run on their machine? These questions need to be anticipated, and early delivery to a few "beta testers" should point out weaknesses.

Maintenance

Once the users have the software, it changes the way that they work. And so the system must again change to accommodate their needs. Is the appropriate feedback loop set up so that developers can receive their comments graciously? Are changes and fixes batched so as to minimize impact to both development and users? Since this example involves the ultimate, complete, do-everything personal information manager ever conceived, it will need no maintenance or enhancement. Or will it?

Summary

This has been a fast, quick overview of end-to-end Smalltalk development of a personal information manager. Most projects take months if not years to pass through all these stages, and a chapter in a book cannot replace the experience of being on a project. Perhaps you'd like to design and code your own personal information manager and use it to manage your contacts. It will certainly give you a better feel for how your customers will use your applications.

8

Frameworks

Just what is a framework? And how is it useful? These questions are asked often, and the answers are literally right under your nose. In your Smalltalk image. Several frameworks live in there, and additional frameworks can be purchased, borrowed, or created to enhance your development experience.

Definition

An object-oriented framework provides a subsystem of functionality. It is more rigorously defined than a class library, and is used to accomplish a programming goal. A framework is different from a class library in that it shows relationships of the pieces in terms of how they interact at runtime. A class library merely provides classes that are related by inheritance, but not functional relationships. A framework goes one step further by defining the relationships between instances of the classes, and describes how those instances should interact at runtime. Figure 8.1 shows a framework of a building. This rough sketch is familiar to most people, in that they can see the same elements used repeatedly throughout the building.

Figure 8.2 is a more specific view of one side of the building. It contains more detail and is an example of the use of a framework. While patterns may

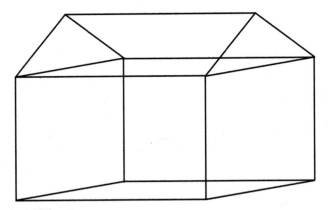

FIGURE 8.1   Picture of house framing—a framework.

exist in this example, discussion of these is deferred to the next chapter on patterns. This example deals with concrete instances of items, pieces of wood: 2″ × 4″ × 10′ lumber, 4″ × 8″ × 10′ lumber, and sheets of 4′ × 8′ × ½″ plywood. It is also understood that nails and screws are used to hold this framework together. This diagram not only itemizes the items to be used, but also points out the relationships between them; for example, the corner framing piece is connected at each end to the header and the footer, and so on.

A class library is similar to Figure 8.3 in that it is a collection of classes of objects, but the exact relationships to accomplish a goal are not defined. This is like a lumberyard, where all the classes are available and plenty of instances of those classes are available. The process of using a framework achieves a

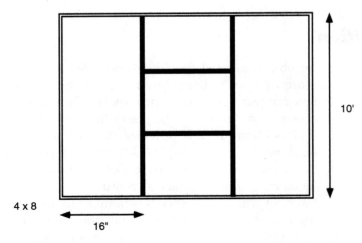

FIGURE 8.2   Picture of one side of the house—an example of the framework in action.

Class Library

FIGURE 8.3   Picture of construction parts—a class library.

goal. A class library does not direct the user to accomplish a specific goal, but merely provides the components necessary for any desired functionality.

A framework provides an implementation of a solution to a particular problem. It is customizable to meet the specific needs of a programmer, and provides that solution in a particular area. It implements inheritance to reuse a common protocol within specialized instances of classes; and callback methods that are uniformly defined to allow customization to occur at runtime, providing a dynamic system.

Examples

Smalltalk

The Smalltalk development environment is itself a general application framework. It provides that ability to inherit and customize classes, and solves the problem of providing a generic GUI application. In essence, the programmer is always customizing the Smalltalk application framework to derive a unique solution application that suits the requirements.

GUI

Graphical user interfaces (GUIs) are very popular places in which to incorporate an object-oriented framework. There are many frameworks for GUIs that vary by operating system platform and development language. They are also different for each version of Smalltalk, which is one of the main reasons that the user interface portion of any Smalltalk application is not portable from one version to another. The classes, use of classes, and mechanisms by which they are used vary greatly from one version to the next. The ANSI standard for Smalltalk will not solve this problem either, as it steers clear of this very sticky area. Smalltalk is not alone in facing this issue. User interfaces developed in C++ using the Microsoft Foundation Classes do not work if a different user interface framework is used, say the Common User Interface library from IBM.

MVC

The original GUI framework in Smalltalk survives under the covers of many Smalltalk applications today. In fact, the framework was in use in the VisualWorks Smalltalk development tools. The major problem with this framework is the difficulty people had in comprehending it. This is a common problem that may be repeated in many frameworks to come; specifically, there is no accepted or complete way to document a framework at present.

VisualWorks

This GUI framework evolved from the MVC framework and exists in the ParcPlace version of Smalltalk. The MVC framework coexists with this framework for compatibility, but is superseded by the enhanced functionality of this new GUI framework.

ViewManager, WindowBuilder, ApplicationCoordinator, and PARTS

The Visual Smalltalk product (formerly Smalltalk/V) has at least four GUI frameworks available at present. The original GUI framework, ViewManager, was elaborated and served as the basis for the WindowBuilder framework from ObjectShare systems. The ApplicationCoordinator framework came from the Macintosh version of Smalltalk/V and has found its way into the OS/2 and Windows versions. The PARTS framework is totally different from the others in that it provides an instance-based user interface (as opposed to creating a new class for each user interface) and provides visual programming capabilities. The PARTS framework is disliked by many who are familiar with the older way of building windows in classes, and is not nearly as rich as the IBM VisualAge version of PARTS.

The Visual Smalltalk GUI framework shakedown will probably leave two frameworks intact: the WindowBuilder framework for its comprehensive GUI solution, and the PARTS framework, for those who need the visual programming capability.

IBM Smalltalk, VisualAge, and WindowBuilder Pro

IBM Smalltalk contains a GUI framework that provides platform-independent graphical user interfaces. It is loosely based on the X Windows model, which is itself a platform-independent, nonobject GUI framework. This means that having knowledge of the X-Window system makes it easier to understand the IBM GUI framework.

In addition to the basic GUI framework, a visual programming framework is available that provides all the capability of the PARTS Digitalk framework, with many enhancements. This framework is an excellent choice for integrating components developed by different people at various levels of expertise. If the visual programming framework is not needed, then the WindowBuilder Pro framework can be used within IBM Smalltalk (or VisualAge). This framework is similar to the WindowBuilder framework in Visual Smalltalk; in fact, a translating tool exists to help developers move their GUI applications from Visual Smalltalk to IBM Smalltalk, if they use the WindowBuilder framework. This is the first example of vendor translation of the GUI framework, and is a positive step toward freeing the developer from committing to a particular Smalltalk for all applications.

Generic GUI Framework

Listing 8.1 provides a simple, portable GUI framework that can serve as the beginning for a cross-Smalltalk portable GUI. Though not complete, the framework serves to generalize the visual components into groups, and then allows various flavors within the group to be created. Look for further updates on this framework on the author's Web site.

```
Object
    subclass: #GUIModel
    instanceVariableNames: ''
    classVariableNames: ''
    poolDictionaries: ''
    category: 'PortableGUIFramework'!

GUIModel
    subclass: #GUIComplex
    instanceVariableNames: ''
    classVariableNames: ''
    poolDictionaries: ''
    category: 'PortableGUIFramework'!

GUIModel
    subclass: #GUIMeasure
    instanceVariableNames: ''
```

Continued

```
    classVariableNames: ''
    poolDictionaries: ''
    category: 'PortableGUIFramework'!


GUIModel
    subclass: #GUIOrganizer
    instanceVariableNames: ''
    classVariableNames: ''
    poolDictionaries: ''
    category: 'PortableGUIFramework'!


Object
    subclass: #GUISmalltalkBrand
    instanceVariableNames: ''
    classVariableNames: ''
    poolDictionaries: ''
    category: 'PortableGUIFramework'!


GUISmalltalkBrand
    subclass: #GUIENF
    instanceVariableNames: ''
    classVariableNames: ''
    poolDictionaries: ''
    category: 'PortableGUIFramework'!


GUISmalltalkBrand
    subclass: #GUISTA
    instanceVariableNames: ''
    classVariableNames: ''
    poolDictionaries: ''
    category: 'PortableGUIFramework'!


GUISmalltalkBrand
    subclass: #GUIVA
    instanceVariableNames: ''
    classVariableNames: ''
    poolDictionaries: ''
    category: 'PortableGUIFramework'!


GUISmalltalkBrand
    subclass: #GUIVSE
    instanceVariableNames: ''
    classVariableNames: ''
    poolDictionaries: ''
    category: 'PortableGUIFramework'!


GUISmalltalkBrand
    subclass: #GUIVW
    instanceVariableNames: ''
    classVariableNames: ''
```

```
        poolDictionaries: ''
        category: 'PortableGUIFramework'!

GUIOrganizer
    subclass: #GUIWidget
    instanceVariableNames: ''
    classVariableNames: ''
    poolDictionaries: ''
    category: 'PortableGUIFramework'!

GUIWidget
    subclass: #GUIClicker
    instanceVariableNames: ''
    classVariableNames: ''
    poolDictionaries: ''
    category: 'PortableGUIFramework'!

GUIWidget
    subclass: #GUIDecorator
    instanceVariableNames: ''
    classVariableNames: ''
    poolDictionaries: ''
    category: 'PortableGUIFramework'!

GUIWidget
    subclass: #GUIPicker
    instanceVariableNames: ''
    classVariableNames: ''
    poolDictionaries: ''
    category: 'PortableGUIFramework'!

GUIWidget
    subclass: #GUITyper
    instanceVariableNames: ''
    classVariableNames: ''
    poolDictionaries: ''
    category: 'PortableGUIFramework'!

PARTSNonvisualPart
    subclass: #MyPart
    instanceVariableNames: 'object'
    classVariableNames: ''
    poolDictionaries: ''
    category: 'PortableGUIFramework'!

!GUIModel class methodsFor: 'as yet unclassified'!

map
    "Public - Answer the map for the appropriate brand of Smalltalk"

    ^(self smalltalkBrand) map!
```

Continued

```
smalltalkBrand
    "Public - Answer the current brand of Smalltalk"
! !

!GUISmalltalkBrand class methodsFor: 'as yet unclassified' !

Clickers!

Complexes!

Decorators!

Measures!

Organizers!

Pickers!

Typers! !

!GUISTA class methodsFor: 'as yet unclassified' !

Clickers!

Complexes!

Decorators!

Measures!

Organizers!

Pickers!

Typers! !

!GUIVA class methodsFor: 'as yet unclassified' !

Clickers!

Complexes!

Decorators!

Measures!

Organizers!
```

```
Pickers!

Typers! !

!GUIVSE class methodsFor: 'as yet unclassified' !

Clickers
    #(Button Checkbox RadioButton)!

Complexes!

Decorators
    # (StaticText GroupBox)!

Measures!

Organizers!

Pickers
    #(ListBox DropDownList ComboBox ExtendedListBox MultipleSelectListBox)!

Typers
    # (EntryField TextPane)! !

!GUIVW class methodsFor: 'as yet unclassified' !

Clickers!

Complexes!

Decorators!

Measures!

Organizers!

Pickers!

Typers! !

!MyPart methodsFor: 'as yet unclassified' !

doesNotUnderstand: aMessage
    ^self object perform: aMessage selector withArguments: aMessage arguments!

object
    ^object
!
```

Continued

```
object: anObject
    object := anObject
!


partEvents


    ^PARTSInterfaceList new items: (self object class instanceClass method-
Dictionary keys asSortedCollection) defaultItem: nil!


partMessages


    ^PARTSInterfaceList new items: (self object class instanceClass
methodDictionary keys asSortedCollection) defaultItem: nil.! !
GUIModel comment: '"Graphical User Interface (GUI) portable components "'!
GUIOrganizer comment: '"Organizes GUI widgets "'!
GUITyper comment: '"User types "'!
GUIPicker comment: '"User picks from a set "'!
GUIClicker comment: '"Elements in the system that are clicked by the user "'!
GUIMeasure comment: '"A portable measure for GUI placement "'!
GUIDecorator comment: '"A Decoration that does not have behavior. "'!
GUIComplex comment: '"A complex of GUI widgets "'!
```

LISTING 8.1 The beginnings of a cross-Smalltalk GUI framework.

Other

Although GUIs are very popular places in which to create a framework for Smalltalk development, it is not the only place that frameworks show up in Smalltalk. A framework exists for handling errors, storing objects to relational or object databases, and in many business domains, including accounting, banking, and science.

Exception Handling

The exception handling portion of the Smalltalk development environment is really a framework, as well as a portion of the class library. In order to use it effectively, you subclass existing types of signal classes or create instances of new signals. Then you use these new classes to handle errors encountered as the application is run. The exception-handling systems in the different Smalltalks are not directly compatible, although the ANSI standard does bring them closer. The exception handling system is a class library, because it contains many related classes. It is a framework because it accomplishes a specific goal, provides the capability to subclass and specialize, and defines the operational relationships between instances of the classes.

Persistent Object Frameworks

Persistent object frameworks provide the capability to store objects to disk, a relational database, or an object database. The simplest way to do this is to save the image, but when certain objects, as subclasses of defined objects, are written to disk or a database independently as demanded by the program, those objects make use of a persistency framework that allows them to be saved and retrieved.

Domain Frameworks

Frameworks do not have to address a generic programming need, but can consist of classes that provide functionality for a particular program area. The personal information manager presented in the previous chapter is an example of a domain framework. The domain is personal information, and the goal is to manage that information. Used as-is, without modification, the framework is an application; but when the classes are in turn subclassed to provide more specific details and behavior, the set of classes can be interpreted as a domain framework.

Sources

Now that you've got an idea of what a framework is, you are probably hungering to find more frameworks and more information about frameworks. The number of frameworks available is growing, but discerning between them is a difficult task. Since the framework concept is similar to component software, there is more available to help in this area. Topics like SOM and DSOM, OLE, and OpenDoc all address some portion of development needs that are also dealt with by frameworks. These advances provide a way for frameworks to be developed that are platform- and language- (not to mention Smalltalk vendor) independent.

Internet

Here are a few sites on the Internet to discover more about Frameworks.

Taligent

Taligent offers somewhere on the order of 100 different frameworks. Check it out (and the neat People, Places, and Things UI) at:

```
http://www.taligent.com
```

Frameworks Homepage

An Internet effort at organizing information on frameworks can be found at:

```
http://www.pt.hk-r.se:80/~michaelm/frameworks.html
```

Framework List (FWList) archive

An archive of a new defunct list server can be found at:

```
ftp://st.cs.uiuc.edu/pub/fwlist
http://www.eden.com/%7Emsm/fwlist/
```

Frameworks Frequently Asked Questions (FAQ)

A FAQ (Frequently Asked Questions) for frameworks can be found at:

```
http://www.pt.hk-r.se:80/~michaelm/fwfaqs.html
```

Frameworks Bibliography

A bibliography of published works on frameworks is at:

```
http://www.pt.hk-r.se:80/~michaelm/fwbibl.html
```

Products

Following are two of the commercially available products in which object-oriented Frameworks can be found.

TopLink

TopLink is an object persistence framework that allows the Smalltalk developer to make Smalltalk objects persistent in relational databases, and preserves relationships and identity of objects. It is available for VisualSmalltalk, VisualWorks, and IBM Smalltalk/VisualAge, and runs with most relational databases. An excellent example of an extremely useful framework. Find it at:

```
http://www.objectpeople.com
```

WindowBuilder

WindowBuilder and WindowBuilder Pro, from ObjectShare, are GUI frameworks for VisualSmalltalk and IBM Smalltalk/VisualAge. They provide more sophisticated graphical user interface capabilities, and make the task of creating custom UI components easy with the framework. ObjectShare also offers additional UI components for their framework and for the PARTS and VisualAge frameworks.

9

Patterns

Patterns have become hot in object-oriented programming. They can be useful when communicating ideas about how to solve problems, and even when determining whether the problems are in design, coding, or testing. An introduction to patterns is presented here, with a common pattern that you may see in your code. In addition, a new pattern makes its debut here, and serves as an example of how to create your own patterns. Applications of patterns are given, followed by resources available to pattern seekers.

Definition

Patterns are abstract solutions to software development problems. They do not specify exact classes, specific ways to implement, or code to do so. Rather, they suggest implementation, and provide a generic way to accomplish a development task. They are "discovered" or "found" rather than created. When a particular task is seen several times during a person's development career, this repetition can be considered a pattern, and then documented as such.

Patterns provide a way to think about systems in a more abstract way. This means that the analysis can occur at a higher level, by combining patterns as solutions to the individual problems encountered. Patterns, and

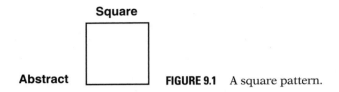

Square

Abstract

FIGURE 9.1   A square pattern.

more specifically, pattern languages for design, were first identified by an architect named Christopher Alexander in the 1970s as a way to provide architectural design for the masses. Almost immediately after publication of his text on the subject (Alexander et al., A Pattern Language, Oxford University Press, 1977), programmers recognized the applicability of patterns to the programming and software construction industry. Subsequently, the activity of understanding software through patterns began.

As research in the concept of patterns has proceeded, patterns for design, coding, and testing have been discovered. These patterns cover many areas of software development and can be used to document frameworks and other aspects of software design and implementation. Patterns exist in many places on the World Wide Web. These patterns can be navigated, and new patterns can be created in one of the existing sites or on your own Web site, using an HTML format for patterns. To better understand patterns, contrast Figure 9.1 with the figures in Chapter 8 on frameworks.

The square pattern provides a name for the pattern—square—a picture of the pattern, the problem solved by the pattern, and a detailed description of the pattern and how it is applied. In this case, the square pattern does not supply an exact specification (no representation of size or component choice) and only gives general guidelines on how to create the pattern. A framework would specify the exact dimensions and material to be used (for instance, metal versus pine, and 12 inches versus 12 feet for the square).

Examples

In order to better understand patterns, one simple pattern is presented to help make the connection between what patterns are and the purpose they serve. The pattern is called **singleton.** The name of a pattern is significant because a common name should exist for a particular pattern so that everyone is speaking the same language when using patterns during design exercises.

Singleton

Problem: What do you need to do to provide storage of a single, unique value that should not exist elsewhere? How about a global? But globals are bad. So what is the solution? A singleton.

Explanation: The singleton addresses these problems: a value must exist, but only in one place, and it must be unique and maintain that uniqueness. This is a simple pattern, and one that you may recognize. The first solution that comes to mind is to use a global. But that presents problems, in that it is accessible and changeable by any object in the system.

Solution: Better to use a singleton in the form of a class variable that has a public getter method, but no public setter method. That way the concern of having the value modified by any other object in the system is resolved, and the single value can be initialized to a valid value when it is requested the first time.

You can see that a pattern can be somewhat free-form and that it has some general properties. It has a title, a statement of the problem, a discussion of the issues related to the problem, and a recommended solution that indicates an implementation.

How to Write a Pattern

Following the example just given, and examples that you will find on the Web, you can begin to create your own patterns. These patterns need not be general, nor should they solve global problems. They can be specific to your company, project, or personal taste. Everyone has something to contribute, and patterns are an effective way to communicate these chunks of information.

An analogy that may help you to understand the role of patterns in programming is to compare them with the roles of various components in music. Musical notes are similar to program statements; musical phrases are similar to methods; symphonies are similar to complete programs; and leit-motifs are recurring themes that persist during the piece, similar to patterns. The patterns may be repeated, although they may not have the same structure in either methods or statements, variables, or class, but solve the same general problem.

The following is a pattern that I've identified in my work. I call it **RobustValue** because it contains a value and some additional state information related to that value, but not necessarily held within the value's instance variables.

RobustValue

Problem: Storing values directly in instance variables means that only the instance can have dependents, because each time the instance variable is changed, it holds a different object and a different object pointer. This means that all dependencies and change notifications must be handled through the class, which requires writing code for each class to handle the translation between the instance variable changes and the notifications to the dependents.

Explanation: This problem is encountered very frequently when creating a user interface for an application. It is solved to some degree in the VisualWorks product with the `ValueHolder` class, but does not go far enough and is not available directly in other classes. Instead of writing a fair amount of code to coordinate changes to instance variables and external notifications, the use of a third party to hold the value (a RobustValue) allows dependencies and notifications to be done at the instance variable level, providing greater granularity to the programmer and reducing the number of lines of code. Additional information about the validity of the value and the necessity for validation, as well as requirements for the database (such as whether the value can be a NULL—a nil in Smalltalk), cannot be coded into every object in the system without affecting all classes and greatly increasing the size of the image. By using a third party (a RobustValue) and setting the dependencies on that third party, changes can be made to the value in the RobustValue, and the results of changes can be broadcast via dependency or event mechanisms to appropriate user interface instances, validation, and data storage classes.

Solution: Use an additional entity in the system (a RobustValue) to maintain the identity for the value, by referencing only the RobustValue; to provide dependent notification and changed events; to provide additional state property information including the necessity, error state, and nill-able aspects of any value in the system. An example implementation of a pattern always helps, so refer to the CD for a version of RobustValue.

How to Apply Patterns

In order to apply patterns, they must first be studied, restudied, and discussed. Once each pattern has been assimilated into each of the development team member's vocabulary, the patterns can then be used.

Pattern Languages

Assuming that each of the patterns is understood by the team members, the patterns can be used in communication of design, implementation, and testing. The combination of the patterns into sentences (sequences of patterns) can be very powerful by covering a lot of functional ground without getting mired in technical details of how a particular class operates in one vendor's Smalltalk (or C++). We could say, for instance, that our application manager for the banking system is a singleton and that each instance of a domain class uses RobustValues to communicate with the object broker and the GUI. See? Patterns are very compatible with other terms like object broker (which really is a pattern because we are speaking of it in the abstract) and GUI (another pattern), and make for a good description of the system.

Finding Patterns

Patterns are pretty neat. They give lots of descriptive power to the developer to communicate complex ideas. They provide the encapsulation of much detail that can get in the way of the system to be developed. But where do patterns come from? Here are some places to find them:

The World Wide Web

Patterns Homepage at the University of Illinois:

`http://st-www.cs.uiuc.edu/users/patterns/patterns.html`

Portland Pattern Repository:

`http://c2.com/ppr/index.html`

Patterns Discussion Frequently Asked Questions:

`http://g.oswego.edu/dl/pd-FAQ/pd-FAQ.html`

Some examples of patterns:

`http://st-www.cs.uiuc.edu/users/patterns/EgPatterns.html`

List Servers

A list of lists:

http://st-www.cs.uiuc.edu/users/patterns/Lists.html

Subscribe and unsubscribe to the lists:

http://st-www.cs.uiuc.edu/users/brant/subscribe.html

An archive of Design Patterns mailing lists:

http://iamwww.unibe.ch/~fcglib/WWW/OnlineDoku/archive/DesignPatterns/

Conferences

Pattern Languages of Programming (PLoP)

See the Web page below for a list of conferences and archived information about them:

http://st-www.cs.uiuc.edu/users/patterns/Conferences.html

10

Smalltalk Bugs

The bugs in this chapter are identified along with their typical symptoms, an explanation of why they are bugs, and recommended solutions.

Incorrect Return Value

Symptom: Debugger with `"SomeClass doesn't understand: someMessage"`

Explanation: The class `SomeClass` does not have a method corresponding to `someMessage`. Either `SomeClass` needs to have the appropriate method created, or `SomeClass` is not the expected receiver. If `SomeClass` is not the intended receiver, it is likely that the value returned by a prior method is not consistent with the expected return value.

Solution: Either implement the message, if appropriate, in `SomeClass`, or look through prior messages that determine the receiver of the message, and check that code to ensure that the correct object or type of object is being returned. It is also sometimes helpful to inspect the instance of `SomeClass` to identify which method returned it.

Changing a Collection During Iteration

Symptom: A do:, collect:, reject:, select:, detect:, or inject:into: method doesn't answer the expected Collection, or fails during the loop.

Explanation: Changing a Collection while it is being iterated causes problems. The iteration assumes that the Collection will remain constant during the iteration, so items should not change, and the length of the Collection should not grow or shrink.

Solution: Use a temporary variable to house a new collection that will contain the modified values. This requires restructuring the affected code, and may require a new algorithm to accomplish your goal.

Subclasses of Collection Don't Copy Properly

Symptom: My own special subclass of Collection (or one of its children) has nil in its new instance variable after a copy.

Explanation: The information in the copy is not correct because the method used to copy the Collection subclass, copyEmpty: has not been overridden.

Solution: Create a method copyEmpty: in your subclass, and ensure that the new instance variables receive proper treatment. Refer to other subclasses of Collection for examples.

Add: Returns Its Argument

Symptom: For some strange reason, the Collection you returned from your method isn't a Collection, but the last value added to the Collection. Something must be wrong with the Collection class.

Explanation: The return value from add: and other methods in the system are not what you might expect. It actually returns the value added, and not the whole collection.

Solution: Append the message yourself to the cascade of add: in your method; for example: ^OrderedCollection new add: 'Jon'; add: 'Joe'; yourself

Changing a Copy of a Collection, Not the Original

Symptom: You added those items to the Collection, but they're gone! How can that be?

Explanation: Sometimes, when you are manipulating instances of Collection, it is hard to know which methods give you the same Collection and which give you a copy. If you modify a copy, the original will not contain the right information! A `Collection` returned from other classes can sometimes be a copy and sometimes the original.

Solution: If the `Collection` is inside another class, use or create accessors to modify the `Collection`. If it is inside the current class, modify the original `Collection`, not the processed, sorted, inverted, turbocharged copy.

Missing a ^

Symptom: Instead of the (insert any object here) I expected, I got an instance of the class (insert class name).

Explanation: A method answers (returns) the instance if nothing different is specified.

Solution: Place a ^ in the correct place.

Class Instance Creation Methods

Symptom: My class methods don't return the instances as I expect them.

Explanation: It is hard to know which methods are being sent to the class, which to the new instance, and which to super. A method `new` reading `^self new initialize` will cause a swift and fatal error to your program.

Solution: Code your class instance creation methods slowly and carefully. Use temporaries for clarity, creating the instance in one line, and performing the operations on other lines as necessary.

Assigning to Classes or Other Globals

Symptom: I try to send a message to create a new instance of (insert class name here) and get a debugger with `messageNotUnderstood`, but I know that this class has that message. I can't get it to come up in the code browser either.

Explanation: Uh-oh, somehow the class has been replaced with some other value and is now a global. If your image hasn't crashed by now, you might be wise to export your changes since the last save to see if the problem is recent. It may have been an assignment operation to the class instead of a message send.

Solution: Export your source code and reload into a fresh image. Identify the code that harmed the class by searching for references to that class.

Become:

Symptom: Crazy things are happening since I did `(anyItem) become: nil`.

Explanation: You were attempting to clean up unused, but still referenced objects. The become: operation can be very dangerous. A much better way to do away with unused objects is to start with a clean image.

Solution: Export all your source code and start with a fresh image.

Obsolete References to Classes and Globals

Symptom: A debugger comes up saying "Undefined Object does not understand: aMessage" in what looks like valid code.

Explanation: You used to reference a class called MyClass and compiled references into the method, but the class is missing and the code hasn't been recompiled, so Smalltalk hasn't warned you about the problems.

Solution: Export all your source code and reload into a clean image. Errors that you encounter when reloading the source show weak points and bugs within the code.

Scope in Methods and Blocks

Symptom: The variable X that I use in the block does not contain the proper value in the subsequent lines.

Explanation: Even if you use a variable in the scope of a method in a block, make sure that you don't use the same names in the block and in the method, and are a person in good standing, the value will not be modified in the block unless the block executes in the method, and is simply not passed to another method.

Solution: Send the message value to the block so that it executes before expecting a value in your method variable.

Cached Information

Symptom: I made a change to my GUI code, menu code, or database code, but the change doesn't seem to have taken effect.

Explanation: Sometimes information is cached in memory, usually when Smalltalk must deal with the world outside the image and faces limitations in how it works with the outside world.

Solution: The portion of the system, or the entire image, must be restarted and reinitialized. You may even need to reboot the machine, depending on the various "features" found in many operating systems.

Symbols vs. Strings

Symptom: I'm using a lot of `symbols` in my application and it seems to be getting geometrically slower.

Explanation: There is a single global pool of `symbols` in the system. Each `symbol` is guaranteed to be unique, but it must be looked up, and as the `symbol` table gets larger, this takes longer.

Solution: Use `strings` instead of `symbols` where possible. `Strings`, never guaranteed to be anything but a `String`, can be used in many places where you might use `symbols`.

asSet Is Slow

Symptom: I'm making sure that all my data sets are unique, but it sure is taking a long time with my 1.2 billion items.

Explanation: The `asSet` method creates a new collection and checks each item against the collection as it is added.

Solution: If at all possible, check the item before it is added to the collection on creation, or create an algorithm to deal with your large sets of data. Why aren't you using a `Set` in the first place?

collect: on a SortedCollection Gives a New Sort Order

Symptom: When I use `collect:` on a `SortedCollection`, the resulting collection is in a different order.

Explanation: You don't even get back an instance of `SortedCollection` when you use the `collect:` method; you get an `OrderedCollection`.

Solution: You may want to create a new method called `collectSorted:`, or send `asSortedCollection sortBlock: (OriginalCollection sortBlock)` to the result.

GUI is Frozen

Symptom: The GUI is frozen and I can't access anything.

Explanation: You've got a Smalltalk `Process` that is at a higher priority than the user interface, and since your version of Smalltalk is non-preemptive, the user interface will not get any processing time unless your `Process` yields or finishes. Either that or there was a power surge.

Solution: Try not to write `Processes` that might block user interface access. Get an uninterruptable power supply for your computer.

GUI Flashes and Image Crashes

Symptom: The GUI is flashing steadily during this piece of code that I'm running for a particular operation, and then Smalltalk crashes.

Explanation: There may be a stack overflow error that is in the user interface code, or some other block that causes the code to be executed over and over until it either works or dies.

Solution: Step through the code until the loop is found, or use the keyboard to interrupt the processing as soon as the flashing starts.

Stack Overflow

Symptom: A debugger appears with the message "stack overflow."

Explanation: A circular reference exists that is causing message send after message send to accumulate on the stack. You will probably see a repetition of a group of methods. It is in this group somewhere.

Solution: Identify the circular reference and sever it.

Summary

No one I know would ever write code that has any of these bugs in it. Well not more than once a day. Once an hour. Okay, so these bugs can get anyone, anywhere, even if you know about them. But recognizing that your problem is one of the aforementioned bugs and having the insight to resolve the problem will save hours of frustration and tears as you debug your code.

11

Development Tricks

People always seem to find out better ways to enhance the development experience by modifying the development process. Unfortunately, many of these tips and tricks are not documented, but are passed from one developer to another. In an attempt to document some of these shortcuts and enhancements, a `Development` class has been constructed to house development "tricks" that can enhance your Smalltalk development experience.

Development Techniques

A Development Utility Class

In order to keep all of your development tools separate and portable, it is a good idea to organize them into a single class. For example, the class might be called `Development`, and methods will exist primarily on the class side. No instances of the class will be created, but instead the class will act as a global repository of the development tool functionality.

In order for the `Development` class to be unobtrusive during runtime and testing, the code `Development beRunTime` can be evaluated to cause the development messages to become inert. To switch back to development mode with all utilities available, the code `Development beDevelopment` should be evaluated.

For runtime distribution of the program, it is best to replace the development class with a stubbed-out version that causes the messages to return `self`. If all the source code is then filed into a clean image, all messages sent to the `Development` class will be optimized out. The second best solution is to find all senders of the code and then remove them. This prevents the development and the delivery code from being the same if you wish to preserve the various bookmarks, breakpoints, and so on. At minimum, you should evaluate the code `Development beRunTime` to ensure that the `Development` utilities do not interfere with your delivered product.

Finding Code Examples

By executing the code `Development examplesFor: aSymbol` you can view examples of use of the method defined by `aSymbol`. The typical behavior of the `examplesFor:` method is to execute `Smalltalk sendersOf: aSymbol` to find all the places in the system that call the method `aSymbol` and provide an example of the code. Additionally, this method might be defined to answer certain methods on the class side that provide examples of use of the class.

Setting Conditional Breakpoints

On those occasions when you want to break the program execution in order to debug or inspect the results to that point, typically you send the message `halt` to any object and are presented with a debugger; and program execution always stops when it encounters that `halt`. If, however, you want to `halt` only sometimes during development, and never in the delivered product, you may wish to use a method in the `Development` class to conditionally halt, and do nothing in runtime.

Sending the message `Development break` causes execution to stop if the condition inside the `break` method is met. For example, the method can check to determine whether the Shift key is pressed, and only `halt` when it is pressed. You can define several types of breakpoints so that different keys can cause the various breaks to occur, without editing the source code of your program. You might, for example, have a `shiftControlBreak` method that will break only when both keys are being held down.

Another convenient feature of the conditional breakpoint is that all breakpoints of a certain type can be found, or all breakpoints can be found by executing the code `Development breakPoints`. A fancier version of the program might include a graphical user interface that is launched by the code `Development browseBreakPoints`.

Creating Logfiles (Logging to Transcript or File)

Printing information to the transcript can slow down a program significantly, but often may be the only way to identify certain problems or functional deficiencies. If you use the standard Stream protocols, then the Transcript can be swapped easily with a logfile, but code must be edited to switch from the global transcript to some other global.

An easier way to accomplish this is to use the `Development` utility class to log the information. You can use either a string, with the code `Development log: aString`, or the Stream protocol, such as `Development nextPutAll: aString; cr; anotherString; tab; yetAnotherString;cr`. Output of the `Development` class can be directed to the Transcript when desired by `Development logToTranscript` or to a file by `Development logToFileNamed: aFileNameString`.

The logging mechanism can also be made conditional, like the breakpoints just discussed, so that logging can be enabled for only certain types of information. One way to do this is to use a keypress as in the preceding, and another way is to use a slightly different protocol for each level of logging information. The message `Development log: aString` can be specialized into a suite of messages that identify the level of information. These messages are `Development logSevere: aString`, `Development logModerate: aString`, `Development logInformation: aString`. Yet another way to do this is through messages sent to the `Development` class along with its Stream protocol. These messages include: `Development severe; nextPutAll: aString; cr`, `Development moderate; nextPutAll: aString; tab; aString; cr`, `Development informational; nextPutAll: aString; cr`.

Bookmarks

Bookmarks are very useful for marking methods of interest for future retrieval. It is also a way to mark methods that fall into categories, as ObjectShare does with a `OSIGenerated` symbol in each method in their line of user interface products. The number and variety of bookmarks should be kept to a sensible minimum, but the mechanism should be flexible enough to allow on-the-fly bookmark creation. It would impede the thinking and exploring process too much to have to retrieve the `Development` class in order to add a new bookmark type.

In order to mark a method with a bookmark, the code `Development setBookMarkName` should be typed into the desired method, where the word "Name" is replaced with the desired bookmark type. If you use a new name, then make a note to add it to the `Development` class later on, or the `doesNotUnderstand:` method will pick it up and attempt to resume execution, after notifying you that the bookmark doesn't exist.

Setting a bookmark is no good unless there is a way to retrieve the bookmark and return to the marked method. The methods `Development browseBookMarks`, and `Development bookmarks` both answer the bookmarks that exist in the system. In addition, you may want to view only a subset of the bookmarks, so you would pick one first and then view it by evaluating `Development browseBookMarksFor: (Development browseBookMarkTypes)`. This can be shortened into `Development browseBookMarksByType` by hiding the previous code sample in that method. The bookmarks are retrieved in a browser by finding all the senders of the bookmark method.

pause

Sometimes it is important to pause execution of a program or process within the program. Evaluating `Development pauseForReturn` would wait for the Return key to be pressed before continuing and will always pause in that location. To pause only intermittently, then evaluating `Development pauseWhenShift` may be preferable in your method.

In order to track down the places that contain pauses, the evaluating `Development pauses` returns all the methods that create a pause. Listing 11.1 shows the source code for the `Development` class.

```
Object
    subclass: #Development
    instanceVariableNames: ''
    classVariableNames: ''
    poolDictionaries: ''
    category: 'DevelopmentTools'!

!Development class methodsFor: 'development tricks' !

bookMark
    "Public - Do nothing. Simply find senders of this to see code that is inter-
esting"!

checkLater
    "Public - Simply find senders of this to see code that must be checked
later"
    !

halt
    "Public - Halt processing only if the [Shift] key is currently down"
```

Continued

```
      Notifier isShiftKeyDown
          ifTrue: [super halt]!


  show: aString
      "Public - Show aString on the Transcript but only if the [Alt] key is down"


      Notifier isAltKeyDown
          ifTrue: [Transcript show: aString]! !


!Object methodsFor: 'development tricks' !


checkLater
    "Public - Do nothing. Simply find senders of this to see code that must be
checked later"! !


!Object methodsFor: 'development tricks' !


shiftHalt
    "Public - Halt processing only if the [Shift] key is currently down"


      Notifier isShiftKeyDown
          ifTrue: [self halt]! !


!Object methodsFor: 'development tricks' !


altShow: aString
    "Public - Show aString on the Transcript but only if the [Alt] key is down"


      Notifier isAltKeyDown
          ifTrue: [Transcript show: aString]! !


!Object methodsFor: 'development tricks' !


bookMark
    "Public - Do nothing. Simply find senders of this to see code that is inter-
esting"! !


!Object class methodsFor: 'development tricks' !


checkLater
    "Public - Simply find senders of this to see code that must be checked
later"! !
```

LISTING 11.1 Development class source code.

Using ValueHolders, and SharedValues to Maintain Identity and Dependencies

In Smalltalk, you can always directly identify an object, but not the objects that it contains if they are transient. That gives each object a unique identity, but does not provide a comparable identity for attributes within a class. For example suppose you have an instance of `Person` and an instance of `Address` in the instance variables of your class `PersonalInformationManager`. If you set `Address` as a dependent of `Person`, but then change the `Address` instance, the old `Address` will be a dependent of `Person`, not the new one. You have to write code that specifically removes the `oldAddress` as a dependent and adds the new address as a dependent. This is a simple example, but the complexity increases as does the number of instance variables and through the use of other classes that share the values of the instance variables.

A more complex example involves a screen for editing instances of `Person`. If the `Person` contains attributes `FirstName`, `LastName`, and `Weight`, then you cannot simply set the entry fields on the screen associated with `FirstName`, `LastName`, and `Weight` as dependents to ensure automatic updating between the screen and the object. The screen can be set as a dependent of the `Person` and the `Person` set as a dependent of the screen, but no action will take place unless code is written that specifically moves data between the instance variables of `Person` and the entry fields on the screen. This may seem like a little nuisance, but once you've written the code that maps instance variables to screens a few hundred times, it gets tedious and begs to be simplified.

There is a solution to this problem and others where two or more objects share a value, like an object broker that manages your object to relational database interface. It is through the use of a `SharedValue` or `ValueHolder`, both terms being similar and providing the same functionality. To implement this functionality in all versions of `Smalltalk`, we create a class called `IdentifiedValue` because the most important feature being added to `Smalltalk` is the concept of identity for attributes.

The operation of the `IdentifiedValue` class is simple, and it contains several enhancements that provide more than a `SharedValue` or a `ValueHolder`. `IdentifiedValue` contains an instance variable called `value`. This is where the data will be stored. The instance of `IdentifiedValue` can be used to add dependents to an instance variable, so that any user interface control or object brokering mechanism can receive update messages due to the changes. The source code for `IdentifiedValue` appears in Listing 11.2, along with test code for `IdentifiedValue` that provides examples of how the class works.

```
Object
    subclass: #IdentifiedValue
    instanceVariableNames: 'editable required error canBeNil value'
    classVariableNames: ''
    poolDictionaries: ''
    category: 'IdentifiedValue'!

TestCase
    subclass: #IdentifiedValueTestCase
    instanceVariableNames: 'anIDV'
    classVariableNames: ''
    poolDictionaries: ''
    category: 'IdentifiedValue'!

!IdentifiedValue methodsFor: 'as yet unclassified' !

canBeNil
    ^canBeNil!

canBeNil: aBoolean
    canBeNil := aBoolean!

editable
    ^editable !

editable: aBoolean
    editable := aBoolean!

error
    ^error !

error: aStringOrNil
    error := aStringOrNil!

inError
    "Answer false if error is nil or error is false. Answer true if error is a
string"

    ^error isString or: [ error isBoolean ifTrue: [ error ] ifFalse: [ false ] ]
!

initialize
    "Private - Init the extended attributes to defaults"

    editable := true.
    required := false.
    error := nil.
    canBeNil := true.
    value := nil.!
```

Continued

```
isEditable
    ^editable !

isEmpty
    ^value isNil!

isNil
    ^self evaluate isNil!

isRequired
    ^required notNil ifTrue: [ required ] ifFalse: [ false ]
!

notNil
    ^self evaluate notNil!

printOn: aStream
    "Append the print representation of the receiver to <aStream>."

    super printOn: aStream.
    aStream nextPutAll: ' on: '.
    self value printOn: aStream!

required
    ^required !

required: aBoolean
    required := aBoolean!

setCanBeNil: aBoolean
    canBeNil := aBoolean.
    self triggerEvent: #changed: with: self.
!

setEditable: aBoolean

    editable := aBoolean.
    self triggerEvent: #changed: with: self.
!

setError: aStringOrNil

    error := aStringOrNil.
    self triggerEvent: #changed: with: self.

!

setRequired: aBoolean
```

Continued

```
        required := aBoolean.
        self triggerEvent: #changed: with: self.
!

setValue: anObject
    "Set the value to <anObject> then generate a changed: event."

    value := anObject.
    self triggerEvent: #changed: with: self.!

update: aValue

    self value: aValue.!

update: anAspect with: aValue

    self perform: anAspect with: aValue.!

value
    "Answer the value."

    ^value!

value: anObject
    "Set the value to <anObject>."

    value := anObject!

valueInto: aPane

    aPane value: (self value).
    aPane setRequired: (self isRequired).
    aPane setError: (self inError).
    aPane setEditable: (self isEditable).! !

!IdentifiedValue class methodsFor: 'as yet unclassified' !

constructEventsTriggered
        "Private - Construct the set of events triggered by instances
        of the receiver."
    ^super constructEventsTriggered
        add: #requiredState: ;
        add: #errorState: ;
        add: #editState: ;
        yourself!

newOrderedCollection
    "Create a new instance whose value is a new OrderedCollection."
```

Continued

```smalltalk
    ^self new initialize; value: OrderedCollection new!

newString
    "Create a new instance whose value is a new String."

    ^self new initialize; value: String new!

on: anObject
    "Create a new instance whose value is <anObject>."

    ^self new initialize; value: anObject!

testSuite
    "Public - Answer the testSuite for this class"

    | test |
    test := TestSuite named: self name.
    test addTestCases: (Smalltalk at: ((self name , 'TestCase') asSymbol))
testCases.
    ^test! !

!IdentifiedValueTestCase methodsFor: 'as yet unclassified' !

setUp
    "Public - Setup this testCase to hold a new instance of IDV"

    anIDV := IdentifiedValue new!

tearDown
    "Release whatever resources you used for the test."

    anIDV := nil!

testAccessors
    "Public - Test the non-event raising accessors"

    anIDV initialize.
    anIDV
        value: 1;
        error: 'No Error';
        editable: false;
        required: true;
        canBeNil: false.
    self
        should: [anIDV error = 'No Error'];
        shouldnt: [anIDV editable];
        should: [anIDV required];
        should: [anIDV value = 1].
    self
```

Continued

```
        shouldnt: [anIDV isEmpty];
        shouldnt: [anIDV canBeNil];
        should: [anIDV inError];
        shouldnt: [anIDV isEditable];
        should: [anIDV isRequired].
!

testAsSharedValue
    "Public - Test the #asSharedValue method in Object to see if other classes
can be wrapped into an IDV"

    anIDV value: 1.
    self should: [(1 asSharedValue) = anIDV]!

testChangingAccessors
    "Public - Test the accessors that raise a #changed event"

    | theDependentPart |
    theDependentPart := IdentifiedValue on: 2.
    anIDV initialize.
    anIDV addDependent: theDependentPart.
    anIDV
        setValue: 1;
        setError: 'No Error';
        setEditable: false;
        setRequired: true;
        setCanBeNil: false.
    self
        should: [theDependentPart error];
        shouldnt: [theDependentPart editable];
        should: [theDependentPart required];
        should: [theDependentPart value = 1].
    !

testFail
    "Public - This method creates a failed test case. Use to see an example of
failure"

    anIDV value: 1.
    self should: [((IdentifiedValue on: 1) = anIDV) not]!

testInitialize
    "Public - Test the initialization of the IDV to verify that it does
not change from what is currently expected"

    anIDV initialize.
    self
        should: [anIDV isEmpty];
        should: [anIDV canBeNil];
        shouldnt: [anIDV inError];
```

Continued

```
                    should: [anIDV isEditable];
                    shouldnt: [anIDV isRequired].
            !


        testObjectAccessors
            "Public - Test the accessors that exist in Object"

                | anObject |
                anObject := Object new.
                anObject
                    setError: 'No Error';
                    setEditable: false;
                    setRequired: true.
                anObject valueInto: anIDV.
                self
                    should: [anObject inError];
                    shouldnt: [anObject isEditable];
                    should: [anObject isRequired];
                    shouldnt: [anObject isSharedValue];
                    shouldnt: [anIDV value = 1].!


        testOn
            "Public - Test the on: class method that creates a new instance populated
        with the argument"

                anIDV value: 1.
                self should: [(IdentifiedValue on: 1) = anIDV]!


        testValueInto
            "Public - Test the valueInto: method that places the value and it's prop-
        erties into the argument which is typically a subPane"

                | theDependentPart |
                theDependentPart := IdentifiedValue on: 2.
                anIDV initialize.
                anIDV
                    setValue: 1;
                    setError: 'No Error';
                    setEditable: false;
                    setRequired: true;
                    setCanBeNil: false.
                anIDV valueInto: theDependentPart.
                self
                    should: [theDependentPart error];
                    shouldnt: [theDependentPart editable];
                    should: [theDependentPart required];
                    should: [theDependentPart value = 1].
            ! !


    !IdentifiedValueTestCase class methodsFor: 'as yet unclassified' !
```

Continued

```
testCases
    "Public - Answer all the Test Cases to be performed for the target object
using this subclass of TestCase"

    ^#(testOn testAsSharedValue testInitialize testAccessors
testChangingAccessors testValueInto testObjectAccessors testFail) "Add
testFail to the list to cause a failure"
        inject: OrderedCollection new
        into:
            [:result :each |
            result
            add: (self selector: each);
            yourself].! !


!SubPane methodsFor: 'as yet unclassified' !

setRequired: aBool

    self propertyAt: #required put: aBool.
    (self propertyAt: #error) notNil
        ifTrue:
            [(self propertyAt: #error)
                ifFalse:
                    [self isHandleOk
                        ifFalse: [^self whenValid: #setRequired: with:
aBool].
                    aBool
                        ifTrue:
                            [ "Required Field"
                            self backColor: (self class requiredColor)]
                        ifFalse:
                            [ "Optional Field"
                            self backColor: (self defaultBackColor)].
                ]]! !


!Object methodsFor: 'as yet unclassified' !

inError
    "Answer false if error is nil or error is false. Answer true if
error is a string"
    | error |
    error := self propertyAt: #error.

    ^error isString or: [ error isBoolean ifTrue: [ error ] ifFalse: [ false
] ]
! !


!Object class methodsFor: 'as yet unclassified' !

asSharedValue
    ^IdentifiedValue on: self! !
```

Continued

```
!Object methodsFor: 'as yet unclassified' !

isEditable
    | answer |

    answer := self propertyAt: #editable .
    answer isNil ifTrue: [ answer := true ].
    ^answer! !

!Object methodsFor: 'as yet unclassified' !

required: aBool
    self propertyAt: #required put: aBool ! !

!Object methodsFor: 'as yet unclassified' !

isSharedValue
    ^false! !

!SubPane methodsFor: 'as yet unclassified' !

setEditable: aBool
"Public - Set the current GUI Widget to reflect aBool. Don't trigger #changed
because this is an #update method"

    self propertyAt: #editable put: aBool.
    aBool
        ifTrue:
            [ "Editable Field"
            self enable]
        ifFalse:
            [ "Read-Only Field"
            self disable]! !

!SubPane methodsFor: 'as yet unclassified' !

setError: aBool

    self propertyAt: #error put: aBool.
    aBool
        ifTrue:
            [ "Error Stricken Field"
            self backColor: (self class errorColor)]
        ifFalse:
            [ "No Error in Field"
            (self propertyAt: #required) notNil
                ifTrue:
                    [(self propertyAt: #required)
                        ifTrue: [self setRequired: true]
                        ifFalse: [self backColor: (self defaultBackColor)]]]! !
```

Continued

```
!Object methodsFor: 'as yet unclassified' !

valueInto: aSomething
    aSomething value: (self evaluate).! !

!Object methodsFor: 'as yet unclassified' !

asSharedValue
    ^IdentifiedValue on: self! !

!Object methodsFor: 'as yet unclassified' !

isRequired
    | answer |
    answer := self propertyAt: #required.
    answer isNil ifTrue: [ answer := false ].
    ^answer! !

!Object methodsFor: 'as yet unclassified' !

setEditable: aBool

    self propertyAt: #editable put: aBool.
! !

!Object methodsFor: 'as yet unclassified' !

setError: aBool

    self propertyAt: #error put: aBool.! !

!Object methodsFor: 'as yet unclassified' !

setRequired: aBool

    self propertyAt: #required put: aBool.! !

!Object class methodsFor: 'as yet unclassified' !

newIDV
    "Public - Answer an IdentifiedValue on a new instance of self.
    Make the IdentifiedValue dependent on the instance"

    | value result |
    value := self new.
    result := IdentifiedValue on: value.
    value addDependent: result.
    ^result! !
```

LISTING 11.2 IdentifiedValue class source code.

The IdentifiedValue contains additional information about the instance variable besides its value. It also contains Boolean state information that indicates that the value is inError, is required, or canBeNil. This information can be used to enhance the capabilities of the system by increasing information transmitted with any changes to the information, and encapsulates all the information associated with that instance variable within the IdentifiedValue. An example of this is to use the IdentifiedValue with a screen that turns the associated field red when it is in error, yellow when it is required, and red when it is required and in error.

Additionally, the IdentifiedValue can be used to validate the type of information passed to the object broker, so that a relational database does not give errors when NULL information (converted from nil) shows up in the records. An IdentifiedValue that answers false to canBeNil would have to have an instance inside it in order to be accepted by the object broker.

Exploring Variables

There are many global variables, stored within the topmost global variable in Smalltalk, called Smalltalk (or System). Inspecting this shows all visible class names, and many other global variables. By iterating over all the items in Smalltalk, you can identify the globals and pool dictionaries worth studying. The code in Listing 11.3 enables you to inspect only those items in the SystemDictionary instance called Smalltalk.

```
(Smalltalk reject:
    [ :each | (each isClass) or: [each isMetaClass] ]) inspect
```

LISTING 11.3 A way to inspect the globals that aren't classes.

Riding Along with the Debugger

Another technique necessary to mention here briefly is use of the Debugger. Unlike many other development environments, you can use the Debugger in Smalltalk to edit and play with your program. Placing halt statements will bring up the Debugger, and then you can hop, skip, and jump along with it. You can also edit and modify the source code, inspect variables, and send messages to these variables in the inspectors. Spending time understanding the Debugger and riding along with it can help to reveal much of the mystery behind some of the functionality.

Summary

You have seen two classes in this chapter that help you to do a better job, the first being the `Development` class, the second the `IdentifiedValue` class. In addition, a few other hints were sneaked in along the way to share a few of the secrets of Smalltalk.

12

Message Frequency

The power of Smalltalk makes it possible to easily write programs that analyze the code in the entire image or a part of it. One of the most useful statistics to know about a programming language with so much source code in the environment is how many times other programmers have written a certain method send in their code. This assists the Smalltalk developer to know about some of the most important methods to call in the system, and which methods others are using in their code. The most frequently written messages and the code that revealed these statistics is presented in this chapter.

The statistics for the most frequently written messages in each Smalltalk version have been calculated and appear in the following table. Then the source code used to calculate these statistics is presented. The execution time for these statistics varied between versions of Smalltalk and ranged between 2 and 12 hours. The order of speed for these calculations is rough and tests only a portion of the system, so it is not a fair comparison of the virtues of the vendors' Smalltalk products.

You can attempt additional calculations by varying this code to identify the most frequently implemented messages. Just change the `sendersOf:` to `implementorsOf:`.

VisualSmalltalk Enterprise

Messages

Times Sent	Message
2950	new
2234	isNil
1472	size
1422	at:
1319	notNil
1247	,
1181	value
1130	@
1121	class
1070	do:
1006	at:put:
860	value:
772	yourself
688	add:
686	y
660	x
643	new:
597	with:
577	contents
549	name
536	not
506	at:ifAbsent:
483	handle
468	current
449	invalidArgument
435	asString
405	includes:
404	nextPutAll:
390	close
373	printString
372	contents:
369	height
368	asParameter
359	isEmpty
346	font
325	initialize
312	first
290	propertyAt:put:
282	width
279	on:
271	error:

Continued

263	isHandleOk
252	max:
252	propertyAt:
250	extent
249	copyFrom:to:
247	leftTop
243	asSymbol
231	pen
224	font:
218	reference
218	setValue:
216	cr
215	partsIfOS2Do:partsIfWindowsDo:
213	key
212	asInteger
211	min:
210	collect:
203	label:
203	with:with:
202	isString
201	open
199	copy
197	on:do:
197	owner:
193	asArray
193	changed:
191	extent:
189	partNamed:
189	triggerEvent:with:
187	execute
185	left
179	framingBlock:
179	when:send:to:
176	top
173	addSubpane:
173	dbms
170	triggerEvent:
169	down:
165	foreColor:
164	indexOf:
161	part
160	selection
157	selector
155	implementedBySubclass
154	superWindow
153	paneAt:
151	extentFromLeftTop:
150	openOn:
147	event:

Continued

146	setFocus
145	right:
144	items:separators:defaultItem:
143	changeFor:
143	select:
141	rectangle
138	detect:ifNone:
137	right
136	nextPut:
136	receiver:selector:arguments:
135	addAll:
135	partEditor
133	disable
131	rightAndDown:
131	trimBlanks
130	bottom
128	backColor:
128	partWrapper
126	mainView
124	asSortedCollection
120	associationsDo:
119	clicked
119	enable
118	backColor
113	last
109	label
109	origin
108	selectedItem
106	constructEventsTriggered
106	fromBytes:
106	obsoleteMethod
106	selection:
103	boundingBox
103	doGraphics:
103	isInteger
101	position

Code to Gather Statistics

```
"Statistics Gathering"

massiveDictionary := Dictionary new.
(CompiledMethod allInstances collect: [ :each | each selector ])
    asSet asOrderedCollection
    do: [:each |
        massiveDictionary at: each put:
        ((ToolInterface current sendersOf: each in: (TeamVInterface
current))
        definitions size)].
```

Continued

```
massiveDictionary inspect.

| theFile |
theFile := (File newFile: 'D:\dictnry2.st').
self storeOn: theFile.
theFile close

self values asSortedCollection

self keyAtValue: 2950 new
self keyAtValue: 2234 isNil
self keyAtValue: 1472 size
self keyAtValue: 1422 at:

smallDictionary := (massive Dictionary asSortedCollection
descendingOrder select: [ :each | each > 100 ])
                            inject: Dictionary new into: [ :result
:each | result at: each put: (massiveDictionary keyAtValue: each);
yourself ].
smallDictionary inspect

smallDict2 := Dictionary new.
massiveDictionary keysAndValuesDo: [ :key :value | value > 100 ifTrue:
[ smallDict2 at: key put: value ] ].
smallDict2 keysAndValuesDo: [ :key :value | Transcript nextPutAll:
value printString; tab; nextPutAll: key printString; cr ]

myStream := Transcript.

myStream := (File newFile: 'D:\output2.txt').
myStream nextPutAll: 'Number of Times a message is sent in all methods';cr;
    nextPutAll: 'Times'; tab; nextPutAll: 'Message';cr;
    nextPutAll: '-----'; tab; nextPutAll: '-------';cr.
(smallDictionary keys collect: [ :each | each asInteger ])
asSortedCollection descendingOrder
    do: [ :key | myStream nextPutAll: key asString; tab; nextPutAll:
(smallDictionary at: key) asString; cr ] .
myStream close.
```

 VisualWorks

Messages

Times Sent	Message	
2714	==	
1906	new	
1838	+	*Continued*

1363	=
1192	at:
1166	size
1113	–
1048	value:
1007	@
871	class
844	value
828	<=
811	notNil
757	at:put:
756	do:
747	isNil
716	>
610	new:
508	on:
503	bounds
484	add:
468	,
455	nextPutAll:
436	<
411	name
392	not
370	copy
361	nextPut:
334	isEmpty
328	subclassResponsibility
323	max:
321	model:
313	at:ifAbsent:
304	first
298	with:
296	initialize
286	error:
285	extent
281	label:
275	y
272	min:
266	x
264	window
249	cr
245	contents
236	isKindOf:
230	>=
225	component:
222	layout:
220	bounds:
217	includes:
214	sensor

Continued

207	height
205	default
198	asSymbol
196	width
193	with:with:
189	controller
188	asString
187	paint:
186	/
179	printString
178	name:
173	extent:
172	~=
169	left
168	primitiveFailed
163	preferredBounds
162	space
160	bitShift:
157	top
156	collection:
152	collect:
148	last
147	basicAt:
144	close
143	asValue
140	extent:depth:bitsPerPixel:palette:usingBits:
139	invalidate
138	monoMaskPalette
132	view
131	writeStream
130	perform:
128	next
127	changed:
125	origin
123	right
122	printOn:
119	~ ~
116	rounded
115	model
107	removeDependent:
103	white
102	errorSignal
101	displayOn:at:

Code to Gather Statistics

```
'From VisualWorks(R) Release 2.0 of 4 August 1994 on 27 November 1995
at 3:31:55 am'!
```
Continued

```
Object subclass: #StatisticsTests
   instanceVariableNames: ''
   classVariableNames: 'massiveDictionary myStream smallDictionary '
   poolDictionaries: ''
   category: 'AAAJonathan'!


"-- -- -- -- -- -- -- -- -- -- -- -- -- -- -- -- -- -- "!


StatisticsTests class
   instanceVariableNames: ''!


!StatisticsTests class methodsFor: 'test'!


buildDictionary
   " StatisticsTests buildDictionary "
   massiveDictionary := Dictionary new.
   (CompiledMethod allInstances collect: [ :each | each who notNil
ifTrue: [ each who at: 2] ifFalse: [nil] ])
   asSet asOrderedCollection
   do: [ :each |
   massiveDictionary at: each put: ((Browser allCallsOn: each) size)
].!


buildSmallDictionary
   "StatisticsTests buildSmallDictionary"


   smallDictionary := (massiveDictionary asSortedCollection reverse
select: [:each | each > 100])
          inject: Dictionary new into: [:result :each | result at:
each put: (massiveDictionary keyAtValue: each); yourself]!


writeResultsToFile
   "StatisticsTests writeResultsToFile"


   myStream := (Filename named: 'D:\vwout.txt') writeStream.
   myStream nextPutAll: 'Number of times a message is written in all
methods'; cr; nextPutAll: 'Times'; tab; nextPutAll: 'Message'; cr;
nextPutAll: '-----'; tab; nextPutAll: '-------'; cr.
   (smallDictionary keys collect: [:each | each asInteger])
asSortedCollection reverse do: [:key | myStream nextPutAll: key
printString; tab; nextPutAll: (smallDictionary at: key) printString; cr].
   myStream close! !
```

VisualAge

Messages

Times Sent	Message
4175	new
2982	=
2610	+
2541	size
2013	at:
1975	do:
1886	class
1881	−
1344	new:
1331	add:
1209	value
1147	>
1139	at:put:
1126	<
890	name
824	signalEvent:with:
821	,
713	value:
701	with:
700	*
686	isEmpty
647	includes:
637	nextPutAll:
634	x
623	@
623	primaryWidget
604	uint32At:
595	y
584	uint32At:put:
547	subpartNamed:
537	height
516	printString
510	widget
507	at:ifAbsent:
500	//
486	width
437	bindWith:
431	default
420	first
420	key
409	execShortOperation:

Continued

385	featureNamed:put:
371	error:
367	indexedMsg:
366	==
363	with:with:
350	<=
347	>=
347	bitAnd:
347	cr
346	max:
345	newPart
342	symbol
338	current
333	finalInitialize
332	subpartNamed:put:
327	offset:
309	packagedImage
308	on:
307	initializeAttributeConnections
305	addAll:
301	~=
298	object:
296	collect:
294	not
292	updateOperation
291	nextPut:
289	abtSeparatedConstants
289	leftEdge:
288	topEdge:
286	uint16At:
285	initialize
281	primitiveFailed
276	uint16At:put:
275	attachment:
275	rightEdge:
272	framingSpec:
265	asString
264	min:
259	associationsDo:
257	callWith:with:
252	bottomEdge:
246	copyFrom:to:
240	items:
239	contents
235	notEmpty
231	addCallback:receiver:selector:clientData:
231	visualPart
218	\\
215	selectedApplication

Continued

215	selector
215	signature
209	object
206	bitOr:
204	abtAttachPart
204	partBuilder
202	int32At:
201	deferUpdate:
201	getMRIString:group:
200	asArray
200	isDestroyed
197	int32At:put:
197	valueOfAttributeNamed:put:
196	message:
195	bindWith:with:
194	top
191	primaryPart:
189	attachedTargetView:
189	partClass
188	copy
188	winSendMsg:mp1:mp2:
187	immediate:
185	items
185	parent
185	title:
183	attributeConnections
183	subclassResponsibility
182	uint8At:
181	bitShift:
181	callWith:
181	select:
181	x:
179	indexOf:
179	signalEvent:
177	window
175	asSymbol
175	connectSource:featureName:feature:
175	manageChild
175	replaceFrom:to:with:startingAt:
175	selector:
175	y:
174	target
173	between:and:
172	int16At:
171	asPSZ
167	int16At:put:
166	shell
165	extent:
165	timeStamp

Continued

163	replace:
162	residentMsg:
161	isString
161	last
160	primaryPart
160	uint8At:put:
157	address:
157	left
156	remove:ifAbsent:
155	callWith:with:with:
153	display
153	printOn:
152	receiver:
147	close
146	converterManager
146	gc
146	receiver:selector:
145	extent
145	handle
144	controller
144	preferredStringClass
144	width:
142	/
140	clicked
140	components
140	showBusyCursorWhile:
138	abtWhen:perform:
136	origin
135	marginWidth:
135	valueOfAttributeNamed:
130	application
130	height:
130	structAt:put:
129	managerInterface
129	textFontName:
128	buttonFontName:
128	detect:ifNone:
128	fontName:
128	labelFontName:
128	|
127	hash
127	methodClass
127	position
127	position:
127	setFocus
126	species
125	with:with:with:
124	includesKey:
123	library

Continued

122	getMRI:group:
122	target:
121	newMenu
120	asOrderedCollection
120	isAbtError
120	open
120	selectedItem
119	fullName
118	actionProvider:featureName:feature:
117	asSortedCollection:
117	signalWith:
116	isRealized
115	reason:
115	structAt:type:
114	asSortedCollection
114	converter:
114	execute
114	marginHeight:
113	IS_updateOperation
113	id:
113	keys
113	selectedApplications
112	callWith:with:with:with:
112	for:
111	IS_object
111	selectedClass
111	sortBlock
110	asSet
110	perform:
110	removeKey:ifAbsent:
109	bottom
109	classUpdate
109	superclass
107	attributeSettingNamed:put:
107	connectSource:variableFeatureName:featureSelector:toTarget:feature
107	selection
106	errorReporter
106	isKindOf:
106	label
104	columns
104	parentingWidget
103	add:label:enable:
101	freeFormEditPart
101	moduleName:

Code to Gather Statistics

```
Object subclass: #StatisticsTests
    instanceVariableNames: ''
```

Continued

```
        classVariableNames: 'ClassHierarchyRoots MassiveDictionary MyStream
SmallDictionary '
        poolDictionaries: ''!

!StatisticsTests class publicMethods !

allMethodsSending: selector
    "Open a browser on the methods sending the selector."

    | methods |

        methods := OrderedCollection new.
        self classHierarchyRoots do: [:cl |
            methods addAll: (cl allMethodsSending: selector)].
        ^methods
!


classHierarchyRoots

        "Answer a collection containing all of the classes which make up the
    roots of the class hierarchy. (ie. Their superclass is nil.)"

^ClassHierarchyRoots notNil ifTrue: [ ClassHierarchyRoots ]
    ifFalse: [
    ClassHierarchyRoots := OrderedCollection new.
    Class subclasses do: [:cl |
    cl isMetaclass ifTrue: [ClassHierarchyRoots add: cl
primaryInstance]].
    ClassHierarchyRoots ]!


createMassiveDictionary

    MassiveDictionary := Dictionary new.
    (CompiledMethod allInstances collect: [ :each | each selector ])
    asSet asOrderedCollection
    do: [:each |
    MassiveDictionary at: each put: ((self allMethodsSending: each)
size) ].!


createSmallDictionary

SmallDictionary := Dictionary new.
MassiveDictionary keysAndValuesDo: [ :key :value | value > 100 ifTrue:
[ SmallDictionary at: key put: value ] ].
SmallDictionary inspect.
"
(MassiveDictionary
asSortedCollection reverse
select: [ :each | each > 100 ])
```

Continued

```
inject: Dictionary new into:
[ :result :each | result at: each put: (MassiveDictionary keyAtValue:
each); yourself ].
"!

prepareReport

MyStream := (EtWorkspace
        new open).
MyStream nextPutAll: 'Number of Times a message is sent in all
methods';cr;
    nextPutAll: 'Times'; tab; nextPutAll: 'Message';cr;
    nextPutAll: '-----'; tab; nextPutAll: '-------';cr.
"(SmallDictionary keys collect: [:each | each asInteger ])
asSortedCollection reverse
do: [ :key | MyStream nextPutAll: key printString; tab; nextPutAll:
(SmallDictionary at: key) printString; cr ]."
SmallDictionary keysAndValuesDo:
    [ :key :value |
    MyStream
        nextPutAll: value printString; tab;
        nextPutAll: key printString; cr.]
"MyStream close."! !

StatisticsTests initializeAfterLoad!
```

 SmalltalkAgents

Messages

Times Sent	Message
1241	#==
1137	#+
1087	#notNil
956	#=
869	#–
847	#@
846	#new
819	#isNil
652	#isKindOf:
588	#&
570	#,
496	#size
478	#asString
400	#copy
395	#do:
383	#class
366	#at:

Continued

345	#basicNew
344	#*
337	#add:
323	#value
308	#<
298	#basicAt:
296	#value:
292	#bounds
267	#>
263	#|
249	#asBoolean
248	#top
242	#left
242	#popCanvas
242	#pushCanvas:
242	#to:do:
241	#//
241	#popPen
239	#windowPort
238	#basicSize
234	#enableSignals:
232	#extent:
232	#longAt:
229	#≠≠
221	#at:put:
221	#¬
219	#y
209	#shortAt:
207	#x
205	#disableSignals
194	#≠
189	#width
185	#name
179	#insetBy:
175	#right
173	#contentBounds
172	#shortAt:put:
170	#origin
167	#bottom
167	#height
167	#new:
166	#setDefault
164	#nextPutAll:
162	#≥
157	#at:ifAbsent:
154	#open
152	#setForeground
148	#≤
146	#erase

Continued

142	#position
141	#unsignedLongAt:
140	#basicNewStorage:
140	#basicRespondsTo:
140	#pointerAt:put:
139	#error:
137	#basicShallowCopy
136	#longAt:put:
132	#busy
129	#label:
129	#pushPen
127	#message:
125	#bounds:
124	#storageSize
121	#extent
120	#asRegion
120	#white
119	#draw
117	#pushPen:
112	#label
110	#asInteger
108	#raiseException:
107	#frame
107	#position:
103	#copyFrom:to:
101	#addComponent:
101	#clearObjectProperty:
101	#selector
101	#textFont:

Code to Gather Statistics

```
(Environment@#CompiledMethod) metaclass compileMethodSource: (
(Text from: 'instancesWhichReferenceSymbol: aSymbol

    | list |

   § Begin Directives §

      "Description: Return a list of all methods that are responders
      to a selector"

      Method Author:      ''David Simmons''.
      Method Created:     ''Thu 06/02/1994 08:55:57 PM (EST)''.
      Method Protocol:    ''calculation''.

Allow Undefined Identifiers: no.

      § End Directives §
```

Continued

```
        list := {}.

        self instancesDo:
        [:instance |
            (instance referencesSelector: aSymbol)
                ifTrue:
            [
                list add: instance
            ].
        ].

        ^list' styleRuns: ((ScrapStyle basicNewStorage: 400)
            storageFromHexString:
#'001500000000000B00090004010000090000000000000000001D000B0009000400000
0090000000000000000000002D000B0009000400000009666633330000000000033000B0009
00040000000900000000000000000003A000C000A00030000000900008000011B0000000 4
F000B0009000400000009000000000000000000058000C000A0003050000090000000000
0000000063000C000A000300000009000000000000000000095000B00090004000000090
00000000000000009E000C000A0003000000090000000000000000000AB000B0009000 4
00000009000000000000000000000B5000B00090004000000096666333300000000000C3000
B000900040000000900000000000000000000E2000B000900040000000966663333000000
0000F1000B0009000400000009000000000000000000122000B000900040000000966663
3330000000000132000B00090004000000090000000000000000014E000B000900040000
00096666333300000000016A000B000900040000000900000000000000000175000C000
A0003000000090000800011B000000187000B000900040000000900000000000';
            UnarchiveNotification: nil
        )
    ))!


Test reset
Gestalt gcMemory


MassiveDictionary FirstCollection

Q :=
    (CompiledMethod allInstances collect: [:each | each selector ])
    asSet asOrderedCollection.

Q4 := 0.
Q3 := Dictionary new.
Q
    do: [:each |
        "Transcript show: Q4.
        Q4 := Q4 + 1."
        Q2 := (CompiledMethod instancesWhichReferenceSymbol: each) size.
        Q2 > 100 ifTrue: [ Q3 at: each put: Q2 ].
        ].
Q3 inspect.

Q4 := Q3 inject: Dictionary new into: [ :result :each | result at: each
```

Continued

```
put: (Q3 keyAtValue: each); yourself ].
Q4 inspect.

Transcript nextPutAll: 'Number of Times a message is sent in all
methods'; cr;
nextPutAll: 'Times'; tab; nextPutAll: 'Message'; cr;
nextPutAll: '-----'; tab; nextPutAll: '-------'; cr.
((Q3 values collect: [ :each | each asInteger ]) asSortedList
sortBlock: [:a :b | a > b]) do: [ :key | Transcript nextPutAll: key
printString; tab nextPutAll: (Q3 keyAtValue: key) printString; cr ].

UserLib
                 name: #Test
           superclass: Environment@#Object
           properties: 0x0
                 tags: #('Kernel-Object')
   classVariableNames: #(massiveDictionary smallDictionary myStream)
instanceVariableNames: #()
  sharedVariableNames: #()
           namespaces: #(ToolPool)
    structureTemplates: #()
    defaultStorageSize: 0
!
(UserLib@#Test) metaclass compileMethodSource: (
(Text from: 'createMassiveDictionary
    massiveDictionary := Dictionary new.
    (CompiledMethod allInstances collect: [:each | each selector ])
    asSet asOrderedCollection
    do: [:each |
        massiveDictionary at: each put:
            ((CompiledMethod instancesWhichReference: each) size)].
            ' styleRuns: ((ScrapStyle basicNew)
        storageFromHexString:
#'000100000000000B00090004010000090000000000000';
        UnarchiveNotification: nil
    )
))!

(UserLib@#Test) metaclass compileMethodSource: (
(Text from: 'massiveDictionary
    ^massiveDictionary
    ' styleRuns: ((ScrapStyle basicNew)
        storageFromHexString:
#'000100000000000B00090004010000090000000000000';
        UnarchiveNotification: nil
    )
))!

(UserLib@#Test) metaclass compileMethodSource: (
(Text from: 'reset
    massiveDictionary := nil.
    smallDictionary := nil.
```

Continued

```
    myStream := nil.' styleRuns: ((ScrapStyle basicNew)
        storageFromHexString:
#'000100000000000B0009000401000009000000000000';
        UnarchiveNotification: nil
    )
))!
```

 ObjectStudio

Messages

Times Sent	Message
2085	new
1265	do:
1008	getValue
1000	name
966	add:
899	size
762	isNil
673	'++'
654	notNil
563	asString
531	isKindOf:
522	close
516	put:
480	class
422	hasElement:
409	asSymbol
391	copy
377	isEmpty
356	mainForm
353	collect:
319	to:do:
302	asArray
300	indexOf:
299	onError:
287	open
262	remove:
252	new:
248	setSelectionTo:
247	with:
244	getList
242	named:
221	y
219	object
215	formItem
214	changedField:pos:type:

Continued

213	sort
208	not
208	select:
208	x
205	nextPutString:
204	removeAt:
199	first
198	notEmpty
197	addAll:
187	name:
184	getSelection
177	associationsDo:
175	value:
173	controller
173	isMessage
172	store
171	includes:
169	triggerEvent:with:
161	model
160	detect:
156	error:
150	setFocus
147	value
143	initialize
142	isOpen
142	varAt:put:
140	'//'
138	put:select:
137	classMap
136	title:text:icon:buttons:action:controller:
133	concat:
132	keysAsArray
129	add:class:rect:options:form:
129	sendTo:args:
124	display:
124	respondsTo:
121	newEntries:
120	add:class:rect:options:form:text:
120	yourself
119	form
116	putLabels:
116	setInitialValueTo:
111	initializeInstanceVariables
108	remove
107	asMessage
105	setTitleTo:
104	disable
104	errorBoxMessage:
101	setMainFormTo:

Code to Gather Statistics

```
| theFile |

"
MetaClass allInstances
    inject: 0
    into: [ :result :each |
        result +
            (each selectors size) +
            (each instanceClass notNil ifTrue: [ each instanceClass
selectors size] ifFalse: [ 0 ]) ]
"
"17786"
"9566"
System at: AAAAJON put: (((
MetaClass allInstances
    inject: Set new
    into: [ :result :each |
        result
            addAll: (each selectors).
        each instanceClass notNil ifTrue: [ result addAll: (each
instanceClass selectors) ].
        result ]
) asOrderedCollection) inject: Dictionary new into:
    [ :result :each | result at: each put: ((Object sendersOf: each)
size) ]).

theFile := (FileStream createFile: 'D:\ENFSTATS.TXT').
(System at: AAAAJON) storeOn: theFile.
theFile close.

theFile := (FileStream createFile: 'D:\ENFPRN.TXT').
AAAAJON associationsDo: [ :key :value |
    value > 100 ifTrue: [
        theFile nextPutString: (value printString,' ', key
printString)
    ].
    ].
theFile close.
```

Summary

This information can be extremely useful as you advance your knowledge of Smalltalk. The code used to gather the statistics implements some of the internal code management facilities of the Smalltalk environment to identify and process statistics based on that information. Understanding the most frequently written messages and how the statistics were gathered can help to unlock more of the power inside Smalltalk.

13

The Most Useful Methods

This chapter provides a reference for the most commonly used methods in Smalltalk. It has been compiled based on the familiarity with the various versions of Smalltalk and the number of times each method is used or encountered. This list may appear obvious and uninteresting to a seasoned Smalltalker who should know each of these methods inside and out, but the novice through intermediate level programmer can use this list to study and become familiar with some of the typical methods used.

Each of these methods is presented in the following format:

```
methodName
description
example(s)
```

The `methodName` is shown as it is displayed in the Smalltalk image. The description discusses the value of the method, and at least one example follows each method to supply a context for how the method would appear in typical code.

A couple of tips on reading the definitions:

- The receiver is the object (instance of a class, instance method) in which the method is executing.
- The argument refers to the object passed to the method (follows the :).

General Methods

Most of these methods can be found in the class `Object`, and many of them can be found in subclasses of `Object`, as the default behavior of `Object` is overridden. One way to find these places is to use the code: `Smalltalk implementorsOf: #methodName`. (For `ObjectStudio`, use: `System implementorsOf:#methodName`).

♦ `printOn: aStream`

This method is implemented in `Object` and is meant to be implemented in each of your classes. It provides a textual description of the object and places it on `aStream`. The senders of this method can be any method that requires a textual description, or the `printString` method.

```
printOn: aStream
"Public - Place a description of myself on aStream"
aStream nextPutAll: (self class name asString); cr
```

♦ `asString`

Provides for conversion of the receiver object into the desired format and creation of a new instance in that format, leaving the receiver object in its original state.

```
1 asString
#Symbol asString
```

♦ `printString`

Slightly different from `asString`, this method provides for the appropriate delimiters around an object. If the object is not an instance of `String`, it provides an instance of `String` and places single quotes around the object. Calls the `printOn:` method.

```
#symbol printString
aStream nextPutAll: myObject printString
```

♦ `= anObject`

Equality: Answers `true` if `receiver` and `anObject` are equal as defined by each class. Default behavior in `Object` is to see if the objects are the same. Any implementation of this must also include an implementation of the `hash` method.

```
(myObject = yourObject) ifTrue: [ self equalButMayNotBeTheSame ]
```

♦ `== anObject`

Identity: Answers `true` if `receiver` and `anObject` are the same object.

```
(myObject == anotherObject) ifTrue: [ self sameObject ]
```

◆ `halt`

Used extensively when debugging software, this message can be sent to any object in the system. It causes an exception (where exception handling exists) and presents a debug window. An implementation for a derivative, `ShiftHalt`, is presented in the Development Tricks chapter.

```
self halt
aCollection collect: [:each | each halt firstName ]
```

◆ `inspect`

This message can be sent to any object to cause an `Inspector` to be opened. Any object in the system will respond by opening the appropriate type of inspector for itself. Most objects will have a standard inspector, `Collections` will have a collection inspector, and some versions of Smalltalk will open a class browser when the `inspect` message is sent to a class.

```
self inspect
anArray inspect
self class inspect
```

◆ `addDependent: anObject`

Places `anObject` into the list of dependents. `anObject` will be sent the `update` suite of messages when the receiver sends `changed` to itself. See the Dependencies chapter for further explanation.

```
myFather addDependent: me
myWindow addDependent: theModel
```

◆ `isNil`
◆ `notNil`
◆ `is__`

Answers `true` or `false` depending on whether the object is or is not a certain type. Is much more efficient than sending `Class` or `Class` name to identify types. Implemented in `Object` and in the identified class. `isNil` answers `true` in class `UndefinedObject` and `false` in class `Object` (and its subclasses). `notNil` answers `false` in class `UndefinedObject` and `true` in class `Object` (and its subclasses).

```
"If myObject already has a value, send it the #hasValue message, if it
doesn't have a value (isNil) then give it a value"
```

```
myObject isNil
    ifTrue: [ myObject hasValue]
    ifFalse: [ myObject := MyObject new ]

"Always answer a collection. If myObject is a Collection, then answer
it, otherwise answer a new collection with myObject as the only member"
^myObject isCollection
    ifTrue: [ myObject ]
    ifFalse: [ OrderedCollection new with: myObject ]
```

♦ perform: aMessage

Similar to sending aMessage directly to an object, but can calculate the message dynamically. The argument aMessage can be a symbol that is valid in the receiver that will be executed by the receiver, and the return value of performing the message will be answered.

```
"Same as anObject myMessage"
anObject perform: #myMessage

"Message varies. Two possible messages can be sent to anObject."
"They can be anObject cleanupOnFriday
or anObject cleanupOnNormal"
anObject perform: ( 'cleanupOn', (self isFriday ifTrue: [ 'Friday' ]
ifFalse: [ 'Normal' ] ) asSymbol
```

♦ removeDependent: anObject

Removes anObject from the dependent list so that it will no longer receive update messages when the changed message is sent to the receiver.

```
myFather removeDependent: me
```

♦ respondsTo: aMessage

Answers true if the receiver has a method defined for aMessage in itself or its superclass(es). Answers false if the receiver cannot process aMessage and sending of the message would cause an exception. This is a fairly expensive (slow) method, so use of the is_ type of message or of a method in the class that determines correct behavior is preferable.

```
myObject respondsTo: #close
    ifTrue: [ myObject close ]
    ifFalse: [ myObject manager close ]
```

♦ sender

Answers the sender of the message for the current Context (stack frame). Usually used as "self sender" to determine the object sending into the method, it can also be used to block private messages from being executed outside self. "This example sees if the sender of the message (the previous method) was inside self. If so, then the private action is performed; otherwise an error is raised."

```
(self sender = self)
   ifTrue: [ "Private Action" ]
   ifFalse: [ "Raise Error" ]
```

◆ copy

Performs a shallowCopy as shown next.

◆ deepCopy

Answers a new instance of the receiver, with a shallowCopy of each of the instance variables.

```
| myArray myCopy|
myArray := Array with: 'Item1' with: 'Item2' with: 'Item3'.
myArray == myArray deepCopy
      ifTrue: [ Transcript show: 'You should never end up here' ]
      ifFalse: [ Transcript show: 'You should always end up here because
the Object Oriented Pointer is different for a deepCopy' ]
myCopy := myArray deepCopy.
(1 to: myArray size) do: [ :each
 ((myArray at: each) == (myCopy at: each))
      ifTrue: [ Transcript show: 'You should never end up here' ]
      ifFalse: [ Transcript show: 'You should always end up here because
the Object Oriented Pointer is different for a deepCopy' ]
```

◆ shallowCopy

Answers a new instance of the receiver, with the instance variables pointing to the objects contained in existing instance variables.

```
| myArray myCopy |
myArray := Array with: 'Item1' with: 'Item2' with: 'Item3'.
myArray == myArray deepCopy
      ifTrue: [ Transcript show: 'You should never end up here' ]
      ifFalse: [ Transcript show: 'You should always end up here because
the Object Oriented Pointer is different for a shallowCopy' ]
myCopy := myArray deepCopy.
(1 to: myArray size) do: [ :each
 ((myArray at: each) == (myCopy at: each))
      ifTrue: [ Transcript show: 'You should always end up here because
the items in the array have the same Object Oriented Pointer (OOP) for
a shallowCopy' ]
   ifFalse: [ Transcript show: 'You should never end up here' ]
```

◆ yourself

Answers the receiver self. This simple behavior of answering self is useful when cascading several messages together when the messages don't answer self.

```
"Without the yourself message, this myCollection will
contain the string 'Third' because the add: message answers
the argument, not the collection."

| myCollection |
myCollection := OrderedCollection new
   add: 'First';
   add: 'Second';
   add: 'Third';
   yourself
```

♦ update: anAspect
♦ update: anAspect with: aValue

Implemented by each of your classes, these methods are called every time an object on which the receiver is dependent executes its changed method.

```
anAspect = 'halt' ifTrue: [self halt]
```

♦ when: anEvent do: aBlock

A newer mechanism that is becoming quite popular, this extends the changed and update methods to have anEvent trigger aBlock.

```
self when: #changed do:[ self dependents do:[ :each | each update: self ]]
```

Collection Methods

♦ do: aOneArgumentBlock

Takes each item in the receiver and sends aOneArgumentBlock the value: message with an argument of the item.

```
#( 'first' 'second' 'third' ) do: [ :each | Transcript nextPutAll: each;
cr ]
```

♦ collect: aOneArgumentBlock

Answers a collection of the same size as the receiver. The items in the collection are the result of each send of the message value: to aOneArgumentBlock with each element of the receiver as an argument.

```
#( $1 $2 $3 ) collect: [ :each | each asciiValue ]
```

♦ `reject: aOneArgumentBlock`

Answers a new collection of equal or lesser size than the receiver. The items in the collection are rejected based on the response of `aOneArgumentBlock` to the message `value:` with each element in the receiver passed as an argument. When the block evaluates to `true`, the element is rejected; when the block evaluates to `false`, the item is included in the answered collection.

```
#( 1 2 3 4 ) reject: [ :each | each > 2 ]
```

♦ `select: aOneArgumentBlock`

Answers a new collection of equal or lesser size than the receiver. The items in the collection are selected based on the response of `aOneArgumentBlock` to the message `value:` with each element in the receiver passed as an argument. When the block evaluates to `false`, the element is rejected; when the block evaluates to `true`, the item is included in the answered collection.

```
#( 1 2 3 4 ) select: [ :each | each > 2 ]
```

♦ `detect: aOneArgumentBlock`
♦ `detect: aOneArgumentBlock ifNone: aZeroArgumentBlock`

Answers the first item in the receiver that causes `aOneArgumentBlock` to evaluate to `true`. If no items are detected, an error will be raised, or `aZeroArgumentBlock` will be evaluated and the value will be answered.

```
#(1 2 3 4 ) detect: [ :each | each / 2 * 2 = each ]
#(1 2 3 4 ) detect: [ :each | each = 5 ]
#(1 2 3 4 ) detect: [ :each | each = 5 ] ifNone: [ 5 ]
```

♦ `inject: aValue into: aTwoArgumentBlock`

Answers a value that is the result of the final evaluation of `aTwoArgumentBlock`. Each item in the receiver is passed into `aTwoArgumentBlock` with the result of the previous evaluation. The first time through the result is `aValue` that serves to replace the need for a temporary variable.

```
#( 1 2 3 4 ) inject: 0 into: [ :result :each | each + result ]
#( 1 2 3 4 ) inject: Dictionary new into:
    [ :result :each | result at: each put: (each printString); yourself
]
```

♦ `at: anIndex`

Answers the item at `anIndex` in the receiver. Can also be used to access the storage area of some versions of Smalltalk.

```
#(1 2 3 4) at: 2
```

♦ `at: anIndex put: aValue`

Places `aValue` at `anIndex` in the receiver. Some Collections are fixed size and will cause an error if `anIndex` is outside of the current size.

```
#(1 2 3 4) at: 2 put: 4
Dictionary new at: 'One' put: 1
```

♦ `asSortedCollection`

Answers a copy of the receiver in the form of a `SortedCollection` with the default sorting in ascending order. The `printString` method is used to compare string representations of objects that do not have any specific comparison methods.

```
#( 1 4 3 2 ) asSortedCollection
```

♦ `sortBlock: aTwoArgumentBlock`

Changes the sorting of a `SortedCollection` to be more complex than the default of `[ :a :b | a > b ]`.

```
mySortedCollection sortBlock: [ :a :b | a lastName > b lastName ]
mySortedCollection sortBlock: [ :a :b | (a lastName > b lastName)
    and: [ a firstName > b firstName ] ]
```

♦ `remove: anObject`
♦ `remove: anObject ifAbsent: aZeroArgumentBlock`

Removes `anObject` from the receiver. If the receiver does not contain the object, raises an error or executes `aZeroArgumentBlock`. Answers `anObject`.

```
#(1 2 3 4) asOrderedCollection remove: 4
#(1 2 3 4) asOrderedCollection remove: 5
#(1 2 3 4) asOrderedCollection remove: 5 ifAbsent: [ nil ]
```

♦ `addAll: aCollection`

Appends `aCollection` to the receiver. The receiver is then a concatenation of the two collections.

```
'Hello ' addAll: 'there'
#( 1 2 3 4 ) asOrderedCollection addAll: #( 5 6 7 8)
```

◆ size

Answers the size of the receiver, usually the number of elements.

```
#(1 2 3 4) size
'Monday' size
```

◆ asSet

Answers a copy of the receiver as an instance of Set, removing all duplicated elements.

```
#(1 2 2 3 3 4) asSet
```

◆ asOrderedCollection

Answers a copy of the receiver as an instance of OrderedCollection. Many methods assume an OrderedCollection.

```
#(1 2 3 4) asOrderedCollection
'Hello' asOrderedCollection
```

Stream Methods

◆ on: aCollection

Uses aCollection for storage of data. aCollection can be a Collection in memory or an external storage mechanism like a file.

```
ReadWriteStream new on: (String new: 1000).
```

◆ atEnd

Checks the receiver to determine whether the position is currently at the end.

```
myStream atEnd whileFalse: [ self process: myStream nextLine].
myStream close
```

◆ contents

Answers the Collection that is accessed through the receiver.

```
(ReadWriteStream new) on: 'Hello'; contents
```

◆ next

Answers the next byte/character in the receiver.

```
myStream next = $! ifTrue: [ Transcript show: 'Bang!' ]
```

♦ nextLine

Answers the next line up to the current end-of-line character.

```
myStream nextLine includes: 'password' ifTrue: [ Transcript show:
nextLine]
```

♦ nextPut: anObject

Places anObject into the next position in the receiver's collection and increments the position counter. If the Collection under the Stream is resizeable and the limits are reached, grows the collection; otherwise, raises an exception.

```
myStream nextPut: $!
```

♦ nextPutAll: aCollection

Places aCollection in the next aCollection size places in the receiver's Collection and increments the position counter by aCollection size. If the Collection under the Stream is resizeable and the limits are reached, grows the collection; otherwise, raises an exception.

```
myCollection nextPutAll: 'Hello Hello!'
```

♦ truncate

Causes the size of the receiver to be adjusted to the current position.

```
(ReadWriteStream new) on: (String new: 1000); nextPutAll: 'Hello';
truncate
```

♦ cr

Places a carriage return in the current position and increments the position by one.

```
myStream nextPutAll: 'Hello'; cr; 'Goodbye'; cr
```

♦ space

Places a single space in the current position and increments the position by one.

```
myStream nextPutAll: 'Hello'; space; ' Goodbye'; cr
```

♦ flush

Causes the contents of the receiver, if an external stream, to be written to the medium.

```
myFileStream flush
```

◆ `upTo: anIndex`

Answers the contents of the receiver up to `anIndex`.

```
(ReadStream new) on: 'HelloGoodbye' upTo: 5
```

◆ `close`

Closes the receiver, causing the receiver to flush the contents.

```
myFileStream close.
```

◆ `asStream`

Answers the appropriate type of stream for a collection or other object.

```
'Hello' asStream
String new: 10000 asStream
```

◆ `position`
◆ `position: anInteger`

Sets or gets the current position in the receiver.

```
myStream position: (myStream position + 2)
```

◆ `skip: anInteger`

Advances the current position in the receiver by `anInteger`.

```
myStream skip: 2
```

Nonmethods: Keywords

◆ `super aMessage`

Like `self`, uses the current object for data, but finds `aMessage` in the superclass of the receiver.

```
^super new initialize
super initialize.
myVariable := Collection new.
```

◆ `self aMessage`

Refers to the current object in which the method resides.

```
self halt.
Transcript show: self
```

Summary

You can use this list to reference essential methods in Smalltalk or as a teaching tool when working with new Smalltalkers.

14

Team Work

In this chapter you will learn the ways that programmers can work together when developing Smalltalk programs. Topics include:

- ♦ qualities of a successful team
- ♦ the concepts behind the change log
- ♦ uses for the change log
- ♦ structuring the change process for various teams
- ♦ manual change control without change tools
- ♦ traditional C-style change controls
- ♦ Smalltalk-specific change control including VisualWorks change tools, Team/V, and ENVY

A Successful Team

The keys to working successfully on a programming project team are organization, communication, and respect.

SUCCESS = ORGANIZATION * COMMUNICATION * RESPECT

Organization involves creating a reasonable design based on documented requirements, partitioning of the work, and using good API definitions for each class and method. The design requires a good understanding of the requirements for the project. When the requirements are poorly understood, the design of the program will probably also be poor; and when the requirements are understood later, the design may not meet the need. Thus, the requirements should be known and agreed upon *before* the design is undertaken, with all questions answered. True, it is a significant investment to use a full methodology to develop the program with a modeling technique, but the payoff can be enormous if done properly.

The partitioning of work should be undertaken with the talents and desires of each programmer in mind. A successful team can be built from various levels of programmers, and it should be balanced with many backgrounds and skill levels. A team that is top-heavy (too many "hotshots") can cause much grief as each "hotshot" attempts to drive the project in a different direction. Further, when partitioning the work, the API should be defined for all classes. This can be accomplished through modeling or simple design techniques. The importance of this step cannot be stressed enough as it frees programmers from writing code with problems like poor encapsulation, unregulated use of methods, and so on. The APIs should be defined before any coding begins, and can be extended once the work is in progress.

Communication means maintaining a list of changed methods, the needs of other work domains, state of development of pieces, and a good understanding of the initial design with all the modifications that become necessary as coding takes place. The list of changed methods and classes can be maintained on a notepad placed beside each programmer's computer and then entered by a support person. The list can consist of a shared file or an electronic repository containing the list and the changes. The needs of another's work domain can include a defined class with public methods but no code, a fully finished class, or an entire subsystem of code. The state of development of each of the pieces (definition, API methods, private methods, external code calls) must be communicated to all team members so that code can be evaluated and tested against available functionality. Finally, every team member must be educated on "the big picture"—how all the pieces will fit together in the final product, what the individual's responsibilities to the group are, and updates regarding changes to the design and code as problems and details are uncovered. The larger the team, the more communication is required, and the greater the respect must be for individuals and the team structure and rules.

The respect factor of the success formula refers to meeting commitments, giving others confidence and information to enable them to meet theirs, and not working outside the boundaries of your responsibility. Programmers must meet the deadlines for individual pieces of code on the critical path. (Code not on critical path must also have deadlines, but critical code must be completed first.) The importance of these dates must be stressed so that the programmers maintain an awareness of how much the others on the team are depending on delivery. Therefore, code must be entrusted to individuals capable of producing the code. If problems arise, you should encourage the programmer in question to come forward with the problem, and work with the programmer to resolve the problem yourself or through another resource. Programmers must also be aware of their "turf", and be careful not to violate another's. This means that a renegade programmer who rewrites another's methods be prohibited from releasing that code. The code should, however, be supplied to the rightful author as a resource to draw on, and may be passed through a repository or through a file-in.

If these requirements can be met, then the chance of success for the project is greatly increased. Some factors, such as budget cuts, constantly changing specifications, unreasonable deadlines, and personality conflicts can cause project failure even if everything else on the project is perfect. Obviously, there is no guarantee for success, but factoring in the aforementioned elements will improve your chances.

The Change Log

There are several common issues to working with Smalltalk and with other Smalltalk programmers. The foremost issue centers on tracking changes to the base system. The Smalltalk environment ships to the customer in what is called the **base image.** This includes classes for use at runtime and all development classes. When it ships, the Smalltalk environment is a fully functional application. It contains features that allow the programmer to further customize the Smalltalk environment to be delivered as a different application. It is essential, however, that the changes programmer(s) make to the base image be managed properly.

There are various mechanisms within Smalltalk that enable you to manage these changes. These all revolve around logging changes to external or internal destinations. The primary mechanism for this is the change log. The change log automatically writes all changes made to a single workstation image to a text file so that the changes can be recovered in case of a catastrophic workstation failure or for other management purposes. The list of changes can also be compressed to retain only the most recent changes, and serves as a source to track changes made to existing classes in the system, known as system classes.

Automatic Logging of Changes

In nearly all of the Smalltalk environments, changes to the classes and methods are logged to an external Change Log file. This file contains, in addition to changes to the classes and methods, evaluations, do-its, image save date and time, and other operations particular to the version. The purpose for logging the changes is to document the history of how the application has evolved, to be referenced in case the development environment or the operating system crashes, or the developer just forgets to save the image. Clearly, this Change Log file can prove very useful and is worth understanding.

The Change Log file that ships with Smalltalk contains only one entry, the date and time that the base image was saved before being shipped to the customer. As changes are made within the Smalltalk environment, entries will appear following that line. The rule is that the most recent changes appear at the end of the file.

Each time a method is saved in the Smalltalk environment, via a browser or other tool, an entry is made in the Change Log. This entry consists of the name of the class, the name of the method, and the entire contents of the method. Every time the method is modified and saved, it is again written to the Change Log.

Additional entries in the Change Log include changes in a class definition (such as more variables, change in parenting), definition of a new class, image save time stamps, and evaluated expressions. Evaluated expressions include all those for which you either **do it, show it,** or **inspect it.** These are valuable in tracking steps of a particular programming construct, as each refinement is saved along the way.

Viewing Changes

VisualWorks provides a nice capability through which to view changes recorded in the Change Log or in another file, perhaps one that you may wish to File In to the image. This is the only version of Smalltalk that includes this specific capability.

From the VisualWorks Main window, you can access the Changes menu that contains the relevant tools, as shown in Figure 14.1. The options in the Changes menu include **Open Change List,** which will open a browser on the Change List that allows various types of viewing; **File Out Changes . . . ,** which lets you place all changes into a separate source file; **Changed Methods,** which shows how methods have been changed; and **Inspect ChangeSet,** which allows you to view changes in terms of a ChangeSet. These will be discussed further in this chapter under the VisualWorks Tools section.

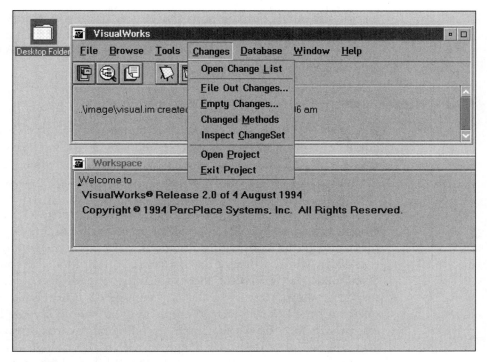

FIGURE 14.1 VisualWorks Main window showing the Changes menu.

Changes to System Classes

System classes can be thought of as the Smalltalk classes that ship with the Smalltalk environment in a clean image before any changes have been made and do not include development environment classes or extensions. The merits of changes to the system classes have been discussed in the chapter on style. The biggest problem with system classes is keeping track of what changes have been made, and where those changes occur. This is important to know when, for example, a new release of Smalltalk comes in the mail, you want to share changes with a friend, you are working in a team, or someone else gives you changes.

Probably the easiest way to track these types of changes is through the Change Log mechanism. Since all changes made to all classes are recorded in the Change Log, entries that correspond to a system class can be found either by searching through all entries for all system class names (not very effective), or by removing new classes from a copy of the Change Log to reveal any changes that exist for the system classes. Probably the most effective way to identify these changes, however, is through use of Smalltalk tools made for this purpose. VisualWorks contains these tools and some tools exist in the public domain or as shareware. Writing tools like these does not require great feats of strength and agility, but rather the patience to poke around in the Change Log mechanism to identify existing code to reuse for your own purposes.

Failure Recovery

One of the beneficial features of the Change Log capability is its capacity to enable the programmer to restore changes made to the system before a crash. As we all know, crashes do occur, and usually when we haven't saved the image in a while! Using the Change Log, you can recapture the changes that were made after the last image save.

To identify the changes made after the last image save and before the crash, look at the Change Log file for your version of Smalltalk. You should probably do this from within Smalltalk by opening the Change Log file in a text editor window or in a disk inspector. (Both tools are common to most Smalltalks. The text editor allows editing of one file at a time, while the disk inspector allows viewing of all files in a directory, displaying the contents of one at a time.) Scrolling to the bottom, you should see the last statement executed before the system crash. Scrolling backwards through the log file, you will be able to see all changes made in chronological order, with the most recent changes at the end of the file. While looking at the contents, you will find at some point a message stating that the image was saved, the date, time, and maybe even the image filename. All text below this point refers to the changes made to the image after the save, but before the crash.

You can highlight changes in the window and proceed to file them into the image (file-in). Do *not* highlight the message indicating the image save because it may not be valid Smalltalk syntax! Further, do not file-in the last statement that was executed, as it may cause the same problem to occur that caused the crash.

NOTE: Depending on the version of Smalltalk you are using, the actions and the image saves may only be seen as comments to the Smalltalk compiler. This means that, in some cases, highlighting the text for file-in causes no problems. But beware of a transcript that does not enclose image saves and evaluated expressions in comment quotes. These will cause many exciting and interesting effects, possibly including the crash from which you are trying to recover. Do not compress changes on the log file until you have brought the image up to date with the log file, and saved the image. Changes made after the image save will be removed from the Change Log file and lost forever!

Manually Condensing Changes

As stated, changes in the Smalltalk environment are recorded in a Change Log file, but this excludes ObjectStudio and SmalltalkAgents. This file records all changes from oldest to newest and serves as a record of changes to the system. Condensing changes means throwing away all changes except for those that are considered significant. The judgment for significance includes changes that are current in the system and different from the original classes. All other items can be discarded when the programmer compresses the Change Log. The procedure for this operation is as follows.

VisualSmalltalk

Evaluate the following expression:

```
Smalltalk compressChanges
```

VisualWorks

Evaluate the following expression:

```
SourceFileManager default condenseChanges
```

IBM Smalltalk/VisualAge

Use the **Smalltalk Tools** menu to pick the **System** submenu and then the **Compress Changes** item.

Development Team Structures

There are many ways that programmers work together. The effective size of a Smalltalk development team may well be smaller than that of a C programming team because of the productivity difference. Other, more significant reasons than size, however, mean that Smalltalk teamwork requires some different rules and processes.

One Person

The Smalltalk programming environment was designed for one programmer; there is no capacity for two or more developers to concurrently share an evolving image. Features that are missing include multiple version management and code module management.

Multiple Versions

When programming, it is necessary to maintain multiple versions of a code set. This need is not met directly in the Smalltalk environment by the base tools, and the only way to get to a previous method is through either the Change Log or by keeping a copy of the older method around. A simple trick for the latter option is to append a numeric character to the last character of a method name. In this way, you can keep as many versions as you like of the same method around. You should, however, be sure to make the numeric copy of the method first so that you don't have to save the new one under another name until the backup is created. The following example illustrates the concept:

```
takeOutTheGarbage
"Initial version of the method"
self collectGarbage.
self disposeOfGarbage.
^self
```

As changes are made, `takeOutTheGarbage` alters, so, in order to keep the original version around, you would have already had to save it as `takeOutTheGarbage1`; or save the new version as `takeOutTheGarbageTemp`, click on `takeOutTheGarbage`, rename it to `takeOutTheGarbage1`, and then click back on `takeOutTheGarbageTemp`, and rename it to `takeOutTheGarbage`, save and then delete `takeOutTheGarbageTemp`. The net result of this is the following:

```
takeOutTheGarbage1
"Initial version of the method"
self collectGarbage.
self disposeOfGarbage.
^self
takeOutTheGarbage
"Second version of the method"
self collectGarbage.
self disposeofGarbageByCurb.
^self
```

There are other ways to deal with many versions of the same method. Version management tools have been written for a couple of the Smalltalks and can be found in the Smalltalk Archive on the CD-ROM. The simplest approach to managing versions is to create an ordered collection of method sources for the methods, and allow the programmer to view methods in the order in which they were created. To create the code to do this, the tool must intercept the "save" method for the class browser, place the previous source for the method in the version collection, and then implement the default save behavior for the method. For instance, in the Visual Smalltalk environment, the behavior for the Class Hierarchy Browser's "save" method is located in the `accept:` method. In order to create a version-saving mechanism, an additional method call must be made to save the old version of the method before the new one is compiled.

It is possible to use the preceding approach for a small number of items, but then the image will start to grow in size. Therefore, changes should probably be written to an external file. An additional source file can be created to hold all versions of the method, but this requires managing yet another file. An alternative approach is to monitor changes going to the Change Log file. While this resolves the problem of dealing with an external file, it does not provide for versions since the last compression of the Change Log; it also does not provide for maintenance of the original version of the code.

Creating tools to manage versions of methods and classes is worthwhile, but can become a huge task in itself. Several commercial versions of teamware address these problems and are discussed toward the end of this chapter. Many examples of different approaches to solving versioning problems can be found in the Smalltalk Archive, and you should review them for additional ideas before launching into your own version management software.

Code Module Management

At some point in the development process, the application will start to get very large. Navigating the class hierarchy, with the various base classes interspersed with application code can become a problem. In addition, archiving the code to separate source files can become a daunting task as changes are made to existing classes. This can result in a transition to a new version of the Smalltalk environment that requires days or weeks of work.

There are some tools to help manage code modules, among them are VisualWorks Project tools, discussed later. Ideally, the single user working in a stand-alone environment should have all the tools that an entire team would have, including either Team/V or ENVY. Without one of these tools, though, you must maintain, either manually or on the computer, a list of all classes and methods that have been changed. The Change Log works well for this purpose, but all changes are listed in it serially without the benefit of any type of browser to inspect the changes, with the exception of VisualWorks. It is possible to work individually using the Change Log as the means of recording all changes, but when the team grows beyond one person, the rules change and a different approach must be taken.

Two People

As just discussed, the tools for a single user can be enhanced significantly to provide some of the functionality required for a serious application development environment. These niceties become more important as the number of members on a programming team increase. Let's look at how two Smalltalk programmers work together *without* sophisticated team tools to better understand the benefits of having the tools, as well as cover an approach for those who are developing on a tight budget.

File In, File Out

The primary method for working together without team tools is the file-in and file-out capabilities of Smalltalk. This allows developers to trade Smalltalk source code for the same Smalltalk environment. Currently, unfortunately, there is no standard for the Smalltalk chunk format, so developers are somewhat restricted in sharing code between various manufacturers (not to mention the differences in class hierarchies and methods).

The file-out is simply a text file that contains the source code for a class, method, or group of classes or methods. It is written in the "chunk" format specific to the Smalltalk version. The file can contain source code for a single method, a class, or a collection of methods and classes. Usually, the collections of methods and classes are created by concatenating the files.

File-in is the process of using the file-out text file (or concatenation of several) as source code for the Smalltalk environment. This means that as the source code is read from the file-in, it is compiled and retained in the image. The file-in will disappear if the image is not saved, but will persist if the image is saved. An example of extensive use of file-ins is Object Studio's LoadableApplication. Since all source files exist separately, the concept of LoadableApplication revolves around the use of a text file listing file-ins to dynamically load an application. ObjectStudio will read through the LoadableApplication text file and file-in each of the listed Smalltalk files one by one.

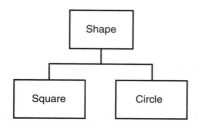

FIGURE 14.2 A class hierarchy diagram shows the relationship between Shape and its subclasses.

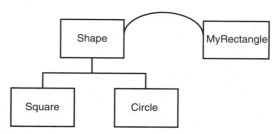

FIGURE 14.3 A class hierarchy diagram with a uses relationship for the MyRectangle class.

File-ins must be ordered because they may have dependents. If you have three Smalltalk classes Shape, Square, and Circle, and Square and Circle are subclasses of Shape, Shape must be filed-in first or errors will be encountered. A hierarchy diagram for these classes is shown in Figure 14.2.

In addition to inheritance, code that reference others for instance creation or class methods may not compile properly if the other class has not been filed-in. For example, the Shape class just described may use a class called MyRectangle. Without a definition for MyRectangle, the compile of methods that reference MyRectangle may fail. You must either file-in MyRectangle completely or just file-in or define the basic definition for MyRectangle (that it is a class and a subclass of another class). A hierarchy diagram showing a uses relationship is shown in Figure 14.3.

Coordinating all the filed-out pieces of a growing Smalltalk application and the order in which file-in occurs can become a major task. If the job of sharing code is not tracked closely, changes will be lost, corrections will not be shared, and when it comes time to deliver the application, pieces may be left out. There are ways to bring the list of source code file-outs under control, typically by using a version control system.

Small Team

When a team numbers three people, you really begin to need a formal and controlled change management system. You can continue to work manually, but there are a number of solutions available, and you'll find that with the ever-decreasing cost of these solutions, coupled with the increasing costs of developing quality software in a timely manner that can be easily maintained, the solutions will quickly pay for themselves. The main choices available to Smalltalk developers range from the traditional versions control system to a dynamic object-oriented system. These are discussed in the following section under change tools and include no tools, traditional change control, Team/V, and ENVY.

Large Team

For a large team, the issues arise from the size of the team, which often causes communication and coordination problems between developers. The members of the team will spend more time communicating and coordinating tasks than programming, and progress will slow. Implementing the best tools in this situation is recommended because the cost of the tools is minimal compared with the price of lost productivity generated as team members spend more time in meetings instead of producing programs. Encourage management to purchase the best tools available for a large team (more people than you can count on one hand) or they will face a larger development cost, longer development time, lower quality, and higher maintenance costs.

No Change Management Tools

As noted, you can work in Smalltalk without change management tools; many people do. Nevertheless, there are some steps you can take to improve the way that the programmers work to increase productivity, improve quality, and keep fistfights to a minimum. Some concepts for these topics are presented in this section, along with the manner of working with the different processes necessary to Smalltalk team development. These concepts include API definition, filing-out code, filing-in code, and management of versions.

Defining an API: Public vs. Private

One major issue that arises when working with teams of other programmers is agreeing on how the various programmers' code will work together. Much time can be devoted to this area during the design process, and each object can have a set of public methods defined. Since Smalltalk does not have any explicit mechanisms for public methods versus private methods, the first entry in the method's comment can declare the level of publicity. Further discussion of public, private, and the concept of "friends" can be found in the chapter entitled Style.

If a clear set of methods available to other programmers is defined for a particular object (and its class), then the process of creating the classes that make up the application can be divided among team members. If there are enough classes to go around, each developer can have a single class to work with, and each programmer must maintain the public application programming interface (API) for his or her assigned class. The programmer can then develop the rest of the code in the class in near isolation from the others in the system, enhancing and extending the code while maintaining the agreed-upon API.

Creating File-Outs

A file-out, created by the process of "filing-out" some portion of the Smalltalk environment, consists of text source code for Smalltalk. It is stored in a different file format for each Smalltalk version, and is mostly human-readable. A file-out can include source code for an entire application, a set of classes, a single class, a group of methods, a method, or any combination of these. It can also include code that, when evaluated, may create items in the system dictionary (global data) or other areas of the Smalltalk environment.

The process of creating a file-out is simple. The hard part is deciding what to file-out and how to consistently file-out the same code, identify new code to file-out, and manage the source code once it has been filed-out.

Filing-out code is accomplished by selecting **File-out** from the Class Browser or Class Hierarchy Browser on most systems. Options exist as to which code will be filed-out. You may file-out an entire class, an entire hierarchy of classes, or specific methods. In Visual Smalltalk, this is accomplished from the Class Hierarchy Browser by using either the Class menu or the Method menu. To file-out a class, you select the desired class, select **File Out** from the Class menu, and enter the filename for the file-out in the file dialog box that appears. To file-out an entire hierarchy, select the superclass that you desire to file-out with subclasses, select **File Out All** from the Class menu, and enter the filename for the file-out in the file dialog box that appears. To file-out a method, select the class, the method, and then **File Out** from the Method menu.

Each time that you file-out code, you need to file-out the same set of code with any additions or deletions of the set noted. The record keeping for this can be done on-line in a word processor, within a Smalltalk text editor, or on a sheet of paper. It is necessary to keep track of the pieces of the system in order to be able to share the pieces between developers. Since the programmer cannot forcibly be prevented from modifying code, the file-outs from two developers of the same project must be compared, even though there may be agreements not to modify certain portions of code. The reasons for this are numerous, and include quick fixes, hacks, mistakes in recording changes, and the need to have functionality when the other programmer(s) are not around.

One way to achieve a more consistent file-out is to write a small program that uses a list of classes or methods and file them out. In Visual Smalltalk, the file-out method for a class, called `fileOut`, is located in the `ClassReader` class and can be used to file-out classes over a list.

Once the pieces have been filed-out, the process of working together is not over. New files must be noted by all developers, and each common file must be evaluated for differences. One way to track differences is through the Change Log, but if the system crashes (which can happen due to many reasons outside of the Smalltalk environment) the Change Log may be less effective as a source of changes.

Another way to track changes is through a difference program that will show the exact differences between files. A typical difference program is diff, which exists in Unix, Macintosh, DOS/Windows, and OS/2. Available in many different versions, most of which are public domain, this program will read through two files and compare them line by line and report the lines that differ between the two files. The **diff** program can show what has been changed between two programmers' file-outs; it can also be used to find differences between a programmer's file-outs and the prior version's file-outs in order to track changes in the system as a whole.

Once differences have been determined, they can be evaluated and a release version of the code can be decided on. This can occur in a meeting where two conflicting changes to the same file are resolved. Much of this work is automated by versioning tools, but it is workable manually if the group is small and in close communication. You can create some simple tools to help automate this by using already written methods in the system, like the `ClassReader fileOut` method in VisualSmalltalk, which writes a class to a text file.

After all conflicts have been resolved, a set of files can be prepared for testing before a new release is made. The code is ready to be filed into the Smalltalk environment.

Filing-In Code

When filing-in code, it is best to start from a known state, which usually means that a known version of the image file is used each time the file-ins take place, and is used by all developers. The image may be the one that shipped with the system, or one that has additional code that has been determined to be stable and not subject to major changes. It is also beneficial when the image is pure enough that large amounts of possibly questionable code have not been executed; that is, the code has been loaded from the virgin image.

Before filing code into the Smalltalk environment, you need to determine whether there are any order-dependent pieces. Since the interdependencies can become quite complex as the application grows, this simple trick will reduce the amount of order dependencies in the system: create a file that contains the class definition for all classes to be filed-in. This file, call it `defines.st`, contains simply the definition of the class without any class method or instance method code, and looks like a file-out of a new class without any methods. Make sure that variables defined in the full class file-in are defined the same way as in `defines.st` to avoid a recompile of dependent code when the variables are added later.

To create `defines.st`, copy the definitions of all classes in every file-out and paste them into `defines.st`. (Note, however, that this approach will not work for Smalltalks that require a single class in a single file; in which case, separate definition files may be created and loaded first in any order, so that the other files may be loaded in any order.) To file-in the code, use the File-in menu choice from the File menu or equivalent. You can then pick the files to file-in, one after another. You can also create a Smalltalk code segment that uses the file-in mechanism directly. In Visual Smalltalk and others, the `FileStream` class contains behavior to load files and bring them into the Smalltalk environment. One approach to automating the procedure is to create a method that uses the `FileStream` class and the `fileIn` method to file-in each of the files in the order necessary.

Unfortunately, once the file-in process has begun, problems can occur. These can be due to conflicting definitions from different programmers, wrong order of dependent pieces, or missing modules of code. Once these problems have been ironed out, the process can complete and the application execute. Next, the source files need to be maintained for future reference.

Managing Versions

There are many techniques to managing versions. The simplest for the programmer is to use a version control system. Another is to use a different directory for each set of files associated with a release, naming the first directory `version1`, the second `version2`, and so on. In this way, the file-in code needs to reference the directory, but the filenames remain the same. Another approach is to name each of the files with a version such as `mycls1.st`, `mycls2.st`, and so on. The file-in code must then append the version number separately to each filename to file in the correct version. If this seems like a lot of extra work, too mundane to bother with, it is. Traditional change control tools solve this problem well.

Traditional Change Control

Many of the current version control systems have a file granularity and were designed for a file-by-file compilation system like C or FORTRAN. It is worth considering the use of these tools if they exist, but you must understand their limitations and the way these tools will work for you. ObjectStudio and Visual Smalltalk Enterprise (which includes Team/V) both work with the PVCS change control system. Other Smalltalks may not work as well with this type of system because the steps of the file-out and file-in process can be lengthy and must be followed the same as when no change management tools are used. To understand traditional change control tools, the concepts of file locking, building, testing, and branching must be defined.

File Locking

Traditional change control systems lock files for a single developer to modify. These products, like PVCS, SCCS, or RCS, are targeted to a programming environment that works on a file-by-file basis. Programming languages like C and C++ are commonly placed on this type of system, in which a single file is editable by one developer at a time. There may be many functions within the file, so at different times, different developers may be making changes to the file. Sometimes, however, there will be a need for more than one version of a file to exist. When a new release of Smalltalk becomes available, and bug fixes need to be made, changes to the file must be made for the new version. This leads to the concept of **branching,** where there may be two paths of change in the file's lifetime; the change to the earlier version of the file is referred to as a **minor branch.** In this model, fixes that have been made to the earlier version will probably need to be made to the main development branch.

File locking does not lend itself well to Smalltalk development because Smalltalk works on an image-wide state and does not break easily into separate files (with the exception of ObjectStudio where a class is likely to have its own file, or several files when a class is large). You could place the sources file under change control, but since there is only one of these files, it would not help much.

Another file locking approach to change management for Smalltalk is to use the file-in/file-out capabilities within Smalltalk to create separate files for each class, a set of classes, or a set of methods within a single class. This would certainly create smaller, more manageable chunks of program that would fit into the scheme of file-by-file management, but the process of consistently creating the right set of files for file-out, and knowing which files to input for file-in can become a major effort in itself.

This method does work well for ObjectStudio because of its granularity and mapping of one class to one or more files, but for other Smalltalks, a different mechanism is needed. Other factors to consider in using a traditional change management tool include the building of an application, coordination of versions for the build, testing of the application, and branching within the version tree.

Building the Application

When using a traditional change management tool, you must have not only a comprehensive list of files needed for each release of the application, but also a version ID for each file. When this list is assembled, the versions can be pulled from the archive and you can attempt to load all the pieces. It is important to coordinate the versions together for a release of the application, and maintain records of each version as the application is tested and corrected.

Coordinating Versions

In order to successfully build an application from a set of files, you must identify a version of the file to be used as the build version. In PVCS, revisions are marked with a number such as 1.20, and versions can be marked with any textual label such as `buildme`. Each version is coordinated to a revision number, so that the version `buildme` represents the 1.20 revision. Multiple versions can exist for a specific file, so every time a build is made, the revision used can be labeled for that release so that the 1.20 revision can be labeled as `buildme` and `release 4.0`. This labeling tracks each file's revision for the release. The `buildme` label identifies the version available for the next release, and may be moved by the manager of the file.

The process of building the application begins by moving the `buildme` label to the desired buildable version. The files are then retrieved from the archive and placed into the source directory. An attempt is then made to file-in or load all files. If this is not successful, the load order may be changed, class definitions may be created, or missing classes may be added to the archive. Once the load is successful, the build must be tested and corrected if problems occur.

Testing

Testing of the Smalltalk application can be accomplished by executing test code created specifically for the purpose of ensuring proper expected behavior of each component, or at least the major ones, in the system. This is probably the best way to test each piece before assembling the application, and it becomes more important as the size of the application increases.

Sometimes, testing consists of simply running the application and testing it from the user point of view. This may not help to identify the subsystems in question, but it can be performed by individuals who are not familiar with the Smalltalk language and environment or the structure of the application. If the application passes the tests, it can be delivered to the user, but this rarely happens. Usually, some type of correction must be made.

As faults are identified, the necessary corrections must be made to the files in the archive. If the file that has been used is not the tip version (the latest version in the archive), the tip version must be modified in addition to the version used for the build of the application. This means that the change has to be made twice (at least) in order to keep the same problem from appearing again. Once all changes have been made, and the version label for the release has been updated, then the application can be considered complete for the release and shipped to the users.

Group Programming Tools for Smalltalk

Group programming tools have been created for Smalltalk and vary in the way they work, the organizational model that they follow, and the platforms that they run on:

- ◆ For VisualWorks, the product ships with some elementary tools, and the ENVY product is available.
- ◆ For VisualSmalltalk, Team/V (included in Visual Smalltalk Enterprise) and ENVY are available.
- ◆ For VisualAge/IBM Smalltalk, ENVY is a standard component of the team version.
- ◆ For ObjectStudio, an interface to a standard file locking system is available.
- ◆ For SmalltalkAgents, currently no special tools are available.

 ### VisualWorks Tools

Shipping with the standard VisualWorks package is a set of tools to help one or more programmers work on a project. While these tools do not provide the versioning, instant network access, and other wonderful features of a full-blown team programming package, they do provide enough for an individual or a close group of disciplined programmers to build Smalltalk projects. The tools consist of three pieces: the project, the change list, and a change set.

The project shown in Figure 14.4 is a subspace within the Smalltalk environment. It contains a set of viewers and browsers that are in view only when the project is active, additional subprojects, and a separate record of changes made to the system while the project is active. This allows the work in the system to be segmented so that the project may contain only changes that are relevant to a certain subsystem; they may be filed-out together using the project's change set.

The ChangeSet shown in Figure 14.5 contains a list of the latest changes to the Smalltalk environment from within a project. Items in the ChangeSet include classes, methods, reorganization of categories, and changes to globals using the `evaluateAndRemember:` method. The contents of a ChangeSet may be filed-out to be shared with others and represent a subset of the change list.

The change list shown in Figure 14.6 contains a history of all changes made to the environment either since the last image save, for a project's change set, or for the entire Change Log. To view changes since the last

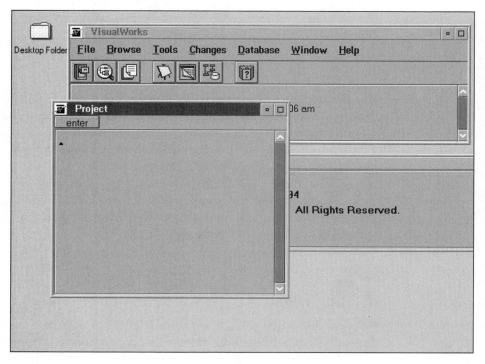

FIGURE 14.4   The VisualWorks project browser.

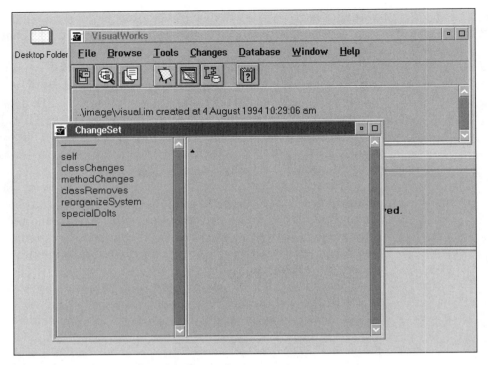

FIGURE 14.5 The VisualWorks ChangeSet.

image save, select **Recover Last Changes** from the Operate menu. To view changes for a project's change set, select **Display System Changes** from the Operate menu. To view changes for the entire Change Log file, select **Read File** from the Operate menu, and select the Change Log file, a `.changes` or `.cha` file type.

While these tools help in working together, they do not provide an exact mechanism or methodology for sharing code. Team/V and ENVY provide this capability, along with an archiving mechanism for versions, to some Smalltalk environments.

 Team/V

This product runs exclusively with Digitalk products, as it is produced by Digitalk. It has been merged into the corporate development kit available from Digitalk, and may not be available separately in the future. The infor-

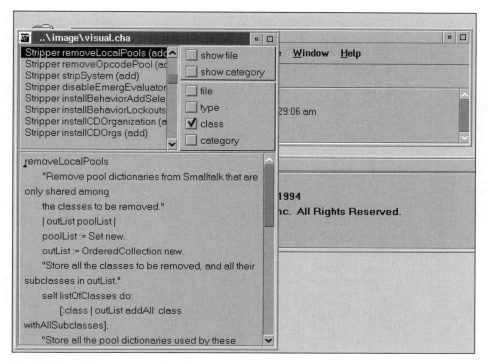

FIGURE 14.6 The VisualWorks change list.

mation presented here is from the Visual Smalltalk Enterprise version of Team/V.

In Team/V, all Smalltalk code, including classes, methods, variables, pools, globals, and initialization code is called a **definition.** Team/V organizes definitions into **packages.** Packages can have various revisions, similar to a file in traditional version control systems. Team/V can then organize packages of Smalltalk code into **clusters.** Clusters contain one or more packages that are associated in some way.

Team/V can store the various revisions of packages in normal file system files or by using PVCS. The interface to PVCS is hidden from the user, and other than response times, the interface to file-based and PVCS archive storage is the same.

Since the two versions of Visual Smalltalk are becoming more similar, porting code between the two versions is becoming easier, though Visual Smalltalk for Windows seems to still lead the OS/2 version. For portable code, the system should work for both versions; for nonportable code, different code must exist for the two operating systems. This may mean creating separate, operating system-dependent packages and writing code to initialize the packages and clusters into the system, based on platform. Since the user interface and operating systems are different, external code and custom GUI widgets may need to be separate.

Team/V is a solution that works for anyone using Visual Smalltalk, and may be the de facto choice for buyers of Visual Smalltalk Enterprise since it is included in the box. For those of you who may need to work between Visual Smalltalk Enterprise, VisualWorks, and IBM Smalltalk/VisualAge, ENVY provides a repository that will share code among these three platforms.

Listing 14.1 provides a few simple methods that are extremely useful when attempting to get a Team/V repository under control. These methods add functionality to Team/V to show the latest revision of loaded entities, unloaded entities, and locked entities.

```
!TeamVInterface class methodsFor: 'as yet unclassified' !
pvcsRevisionCheck
    "Public - Populates a window with a list of currently loaded PVCS
entities that are not at the latest revision"
    "
    TeamVInterface pvcsRevisionCheck
    "

    | temp temp2 answerStream |
    temp := OrderedCollection new.
    answerStream := (String new: 1000) asStream.
    answerStream
        nextPutAll: 'Entity, Current Version, Latest Version';
        cr.
    TeamVInterface current cluster
        allModulesDo:
            [:each |

            each repositoryEntity notNil ifTrue: [
            temp2 := (each repositoryEntitySpec
existing RepositoryEntityMatchIn: ((RepositorySystemPath repositoryName:
"'YourRepository'" (each repositoryEntity repository name)) resolve
)).].
            temp2 notNil
                ifTrue: [temp add: (Array with: each with: temp2) ].
            ].
    temp2 := (temp
        reject:
            [:each |
            ((each at: 2) revisionNumberList last asString) = ((each at:
1) revisionNumber asString)]).
        temp2
```

Continued

```
        do:
            [:each |
            answerStream
                nextPutAll: ((each at: 2) specification type);
                nextPutAll: ': ';
                nextPutAll: ((each at: 2) specification name);
                comma;
                tab;
                nextPutAll: ((each at: 1) revisionNumber asString);
                comma;
                tab;
                nextPutAll: ((each at: 2) revisionNumberList last
asString);
                cr].
    TextWindow
        new open;
        contents: (answerStream contents printString)! !


!TeamVInterface class methodsFor: 'as yet unclassified' !


pvcsLockCheck
    "Public - Populates a window with a list of currently loaded and
locked PVCS entities"
    "
    TeamVInterface pvcsLockCheck
    "


    | temp temp2 temp3 answerStream |
    temp := OrderedCollection new.
    temp3 := OrderedCollection new.
    answerStream := (String new: 1000) asStream.
    answerStream
        nextPutAll: 'Entity, Locked By';
        cr.
    TeamVInterface current cluster
        allModulesDo:
            [:each |
            temp2 := (each repositoryEntitySpec
existingRepositoryEntityMatchIn: ((RepositorySystemPath repositoryName:
'YourRepository') resolve)).
            temp2 notNil
                ifTrue: [temp add: temp2].
            ].
    temp2 := (temp
        reject:
            [:each |
(temp3 add: ((each revisionNumberList) detect: [ :each2 | (each
lockerOf: each2) notNil ] ifNone: [ nil ]) isNil)

            "((each lockerOf: (each revisionNumberList last)) isNil)" ]).
```

Continued

```
        temp2
           do:
               [:each |
               answerStream
                   nextPutAll: (each specification type);
                   nextPutAll: ': ';
                   nextPutAll: (each specification name);
                   comma;
                   tab;
                   nextPutAll: ((each lockerOf: (each revisionNumberList
last)) asString);
                   comma;
                   cr].
      TextWindow
         new open;
         contents: (answerStream contents printString)! !


!TeamVInterface class methodsFor: 'as yet unclassified' !


pvcsAllLockCheck
   "Public - Populates a window with a list of currently loaded and
locked PVCS entities"

   | temp temp2 answerStream |
   temp := OrderedCollection new.
   answerStream := (String new: 1000) asStream.
   answerStream
      nextPutAll: 'Entity, Locked By';
      cr.
   ((RepositorySystemPath repositoryName: 'YourRepository') resolve)
      componentsDo:
         [:each |
         temp add: each].
   (temp
      reject:
         [:each |
         (each revisionNumberList) isEmpty
            ifTrue: [false]
            ifFalse: [( "(each lockerOf: (each revisionNumberList
last))"((each revisionNumberList) detect: [ :each2 | (each lockerOf:
each2) notNil ] ifNone: [ nil ]) isNil)]])

         do:
            [:each |
            each revisionNumberList isEmpty
               ifTrue:
                  [temp2 := 'No Revisions'.
                  ]
               ifFalse:
                  [temp2 := "((each lockerOf: (each revisionNumberList
last))"
```

Continued

```
(each lockerOf: ((each revisionNumberList) detect: [ :each2 | (each
lockerOf: each2) notNil ])) asString].
        answerStream
            nextPutAll: (each specification type);
            nextPutAll: ': ';
            nextPutAll: (each specification name);
            comma;
            tab;
            nextPutAll: temp2;
            comma;
            cr].
    TextWindow
      new open;
        contents: (answerStream contents printString)! !


!TeamVInterface class methodsFor: 'as yet unclassified' !


pvcsAllUnloadedCheck
    "Public - Populates a window with a list of PVCS entities that are cur-
rently not loaded"


    | temp temp2 answerStream loadedModules |
    temp := OrderedCollection new.
    answerStream := (String new: 1000) asStream.
    answerStream
      nextPutAll: 'Repository: Entity, Latest revision';
      cr.
loadedModules := OrderedCollection new.
    TeamVInterface current cluster
        allModulesDo:
            [:each |
            loadedModules add: each repositoryEntity ].
RepositoryServices current repositories do: [ :eachRepository |
    eachRepository
    "((RepositorySystemPath repositoryName: 'YourRepository') resolve)"
        componentsDo:
            [:each |
            (loadedModules includes: each) ifFalse: [
            temp add: each]]].

    temp
        do:
            [:each |
            each revisionNumberList isEmpty
                ifTrue:
                    [temp2 := 'No Revisions'.
                    ]
                ifFalse:
                    [temp2 := (each revisionNumberList last) asString]. *Continued*
```

```
        answerStream
          nextPutAll: (each repository name);
          nextPutAll: ': ';
          nextPutAll: (each specification type);
          nextPutAll: ': ';
          nextPutAll: (each specification name);
          comma;
          tab;
          nextPutAll: temp2;
          comma;
          cr].
    TextWindow
      new open;
      contents: (answerStream contents printString)! !
```

LISTING 14.1   Team/V methods for repository management.

ENVY

Definitely the best (and one of the most expensive!) product for Smalltalk development, ENVY extends the Smalltalk environment to provide features for change management for one or more developers. The expense of the system can be recaptured quickly in programmer productivity. It provides capabilities that go far beyond the traditional check-in/check-out model for file change management. ENVY is available for VisualAge, Visual Smalltalk (older version), and IBM Smalltalk/VisualAge.

In the ENVY model of object storage, the classes are grouped into applications, each of which can contain as many classes as desired. They can be dependent on other applications, and can contain other applications (subapplications). The object repository is located on a shared network server that allows programmers to load and unload code from their local environments.

The approach for keeping changes to files is different from most change control systems. Programmers are allowed to change code as needed and to update the code to the server, but only one person, the manager of the portion of code, can ever make the next release. A release of code, known as a version, is created by the manager of the portion of the application, and may come from the work of one or more programmers who have contributed code in the form of editions. This differs from many systems in that most allow only one person to change code at a time, whereas ENVY allows all programmers that option—but, again, only one person can create the release. A configuration of specific releases of applications and subapplications is stored in a config map, to assist in the loading and unloading of releases.

Another major feature of the ENVY system is its capability to store common Smalltalk code for a variety of platforms. The platforms can be for the same Smalltalk on different machines (say, Windows versus OS/2) or for two or more different versions of Smalltalk (code for both VisualWorks and Visual Smalltalk). This allows for more reusable code and truly independent Smalltalk code.

Summary

You have seen many ways to work with teams in Smalltalk. There are many options, and no one way will work for everyone. It is important to set up a process that works for the team as well as the client or corporation, thus drawing from these diverse approaches to custom-craft the one suited to the way you do business. Once the team has finished the application, it must be prepared for delivery. But before it is delivered, it must be tuned for performance. The next chapter discusses the ways that Smalltalk code can be profiled and then tuned to yield optimal performance.

15

Profiling/Tuning

Often, when programs are written, factors such as lack of definition, limited time, or technological restrictions produce code that runs slowly and eats a great deal of memory. In this chapter you will learn:

- how to monitor the time and memory use of your programs
- how to interpret the gathered information
- how to improve the speed of your programs
- how to reduce the memory requirements of your programs

With these concepts in hand, your programs can run faster and smaller, but be aware that the techniques presented here do not exhaust all possible ways of improving program speed and memory size. Items such as virtual machine tuning, reanalysis of algorithms, and differing implementations are too detailed or specific to the various Smalltalk versions. Further information can be found in the Smalltalk documentation and technical notes for each platform.

Steps for Optimizing Programs

In order to properly optimize your Smalltalk code, do the following three steps. They are the essential and obvious steps, but they may be forgotten when working deeply on a programming problem.

Step 1: Write Code

The first thing to do before profiling your code is to write it! The program or routine should be fairly well written and debugged before you begin profiling. This does not mean that as you complete pieces of code you cannot profile them. But due to the typical pressures to complete the code, profiling and tuning may—and often should—be saved until last in order to get the code working and out there.

You should also be aware of the various techniques available to write faster code in the first place. Optimizing code should be done at the end, too, because you will not know which routines are being called the most and taking the longest to execute. Once the code is written, then you can evaluate which portions are taking the longest to execute, and optimize those portions. If you begin optimizing code before the application is complete, you may spend a great deal of time optimizing a routine that may be called only occasionally, that never makes it into production, or isn't a big performance hog.

Step 2: Profile Code

Once you have assembled your application and it is up and running, you can begin to think about the performance bottlenecks, and plan to optimize portions of your application. Profiling tools exist for all the Smalltalk versions and provide the same general types of information. Each of these tools has its strengths and its weaknesses, so it may be wise to experiment with them before committing to using them for production work.

Many people prefer third-party profiling tools because some of the vendor tools do not provide much guidance in terms of identifying where the problems are. One very popular choice for VisualSmalltalk is the Profiler/V product, from First Class software. It provides better statistics about the code, so that you can more easily identify methods for optimization.

The profiling available in Smalltalk occurs during the program run. No commercial tools exist at this time that provide static analysis of source code to identify potential bottlenecks, but they are sure to become available soon with the identification of good and poor Smalltalk patterns and the market demand for better tools.

There are three types of statistics gathered by the profiling tools during a program run: the number of times a method is called, the accumulated duration of a calls to a method, and the number of objects created and garbage collected during execution. The first two types of information can be combined to determine the average execution duration of the methods, so you can isolate those that, on average, are slow.

Number of Calls

The first statistic to look at is the number of calls made to each method. (Another way of stating this is the number of times a method is executed.) Look at the methods that have the highest incidence of calls. These may be ripe for optimization, but if they are primitives or system methods, they probably are already optimized. A better statistic to use to determine the methods to optimize is the duration of call statistic.

Duration of Call

This statistic is not generated by all profiling mechanisms, but it can be extremely useful alone or in combination with the number of calls to a method. Look for the methods that take the longest to execute. If these methods are long and do many tasks, consider refactoring the code into separate, smaller methods that accomplish one task. Then rerun the profiling and you'll be able to identify any extremely slow section in any of those methods.

Once you identify methods that are taking a very long time to execute, you can take these methods and find the number of times that they are called, multiply the number, and find the total cumulative time for the method. Some profilers provide the total time taken by all calls to a method, which is the same number.

If your tool has the capability, or you use a spreadsheet, you may want to sort your number of calls statistic and your duration of call statistic by method name, and then multiply the two to find the biggest processing hogs.

Object Creation

Creating objects requires memory and speed, and cleaning up after them—using the built-in garbage collection—can be extremely costly in terms of performance, especially if there are large numbers of objects, even if small.

Since profilers, for the most part, don't provide special features to track object creation and dereferencing, it is up to you to find all the places that you create objects, and then try to reduce the number of objects generated to improve the speed of the program. Since the garbage collection goes on in the background, the reduction in object disposal should improve overall performance of the system, during and after the method that is creating or disposing of the objects.

Interpreting the Profile

Understanding the resulting statistics from the profile run can be tedious and difficult if you don't have a good tool to manipulate the information. A spreadsheet is an excellent way to provide very flexible analysis of the pro-filing results. Depending on the tool that you use to profile, you may need to prepare the raw profile output by parsing the fields and inserting commas or tabs to separate the fields.

Using a spreadsheet to assist in the analysis of the profiling informa-tion can provide quick sorting capabilities, the ability to combine several fields to get customized results, and good printing capability so that you can quit the spreadsheet application to free up that needed RAM for Smalltalk!

Step 3: Tune Code

After you have identified the methods that will deliver the best gain when optimized, you must identify how you intend to improve the code. There are many goals to consider when analyzing a method for optimization. These drivers include the need to reduce the execution time of the method, the number of objects created in a method, the number of objects dereferenced (and then garbage collected) in a method, the type of storage in a method, and the number of messages sent to accomplish a task.

Performance techniques to assist in meeting these performance tuning goals are itemized in the next section. Another big performance gain for Smalltalk is to tune the garbage collection mechanism. Specific details about this can be obtained from each of the Smalltalk vendors, as this mechanism is specific to the version and platform you are using.

Performance Techniques

Reuse Objects

Every time a new object is created and then released, the memory allocation and garbage collection mechanisms go into action. These two mechanisms can slow application execution to a crawl. By reusing objects, you can avoid many of the slowdowns when generating and discarding hundreds or thou-sands of objects.

Of course, if possible, you should reduce the number of objects created in the first place. Sometimes, in an enumeration loop, you create hundreds of objects to avoid the use of a temporary variable. The same holds true for a method when the thought is to avoid using a temporary or instance vari-able in favor of creating an object each time it is needed. Listing 15.1 shows a reuse objects technique.

```
myWastefulMethod
   "Public - Use temporary variables and don't reuse objects"
   | theString theStream |
   theString := String new: 1000.
   theStream := Stream on: theString.
   self doSomethingWithStream: theStream.
   ^(theStream truncate) contents


myBetterMethod
   "Public - Use an instance variable to hold onto the string"
   theString isNil ifTrue: [ theString := String new: 1000 ].
   theStream isNil ifTrue: [ theStream := Stream on: theString ].
   theStream reset.
   self doSomethingWithStream: theStream.
   ^(theStream truncate) contents
```

LISTING 15.1   Before and after reuse objects technique.

Reduce Conversion between Types

Another way to reduce the number of objects is to watch for the "asSomething" methods. If you have an OrderedCollection and send it the message asSet followed by asSortedCollection, you will be creating two new copies of the original OrderedCollection and disposing of one entire copy of the OrderedCollection. Since you rarely see the impact of garbage collection directly, but only in terms of slower performance, or processing "hiccups," it is easy to overlook the mass creation and destruction that occurs during conversions.

Precompute Certain Items

A long time ago, in a laboratory far, far, away, I remember the tremendous difference in performance on my Z-80 CP/M machine between calculating the sine of a degree value and referring to a lookup table of the sine, rounded to the nearest whole degree. I can't remember exactly the performance increase, but it must have been somewhere between 10 and 100 because my programs really took off after I made the change. This important lesson can be referenced today in Smalltalk development, by precomputing certain items as constants.

The technique is to create tables of values either during program startup (slow) or before the product is delivered, and store them in the image. Then, instead of calculating them with great precision, you use the closest value to get a reasonably accurate result, as shown in Listing 15.2.

```
initializeComputation
    resultTable := IdentityDictionary new.
    (1 to: 360) do: [ :each |
        resultTable at: each put: (each sine) ].


sineOf: aNumber
    ^resultTable at: (aNumber truncate).
```

LISTING 15.2 Precompute technique.

"Hide" Delays

On occasion, a certain delay in code will be less noticeable if placed in a different location. For instance, if you have a complex method that needs to execute, and it goes as fast as it can, you can execute that method at some point when the user is busy. A good time to do this is during the GUI displaying period, as it places the blame for slowness on the operating system. The absolute best time is right after a user closes a window, since the user will take a second or two to respond to the window closing. Take a look at Listing 15.3 for an example of this technique.

```
commitObject
    "Public - Store to database"
    self commitToDatabase.
    self closeWindow.


commitObject
    "Public - Store to database"
    [ self commitToDatabase ] fork.
    self closeWindow.
```

LISTING 15.3 Before and after hide delays technique.

Streams

One of the biggest improvements can be realized by using Streams properly to manipulate collections. Every time a comma is used to concatenate two Collections or Strings, a new object is created that houses the two old strings, and it is likely that the old ones will be thrown away, causing large amounts of garbage. It is estimated that combining two collections with a comma breaks even with using a Stream only when there is one comma! Two or more, and the performance is enhanced by using a Stream. Listing 15.4 shows this technique in action.

```
asCompleteAddress
    "Public - Answer the complete address as a String"
    ^self street asString, '
```

Continued

```
', self apartment asString, '
', self city asString, '
', self state asString, '
', self zipcode asString, '
', self country asString

asCompleteAddress
   "Public - Answer the complete address as a String"
   | myStream |
   myStream := (ReadWriteStream on: (String new: 256)).
   self street printOn: myStream.
   myStream cr.
   self apartment printOn: myStream.
   myStream cr.
   self city printOn: myStream.
   myStream cr.
   self state printOn: myStream.
   myStream cr.
   self zipcode printOn: myStream.
   myStream cr.
   self country printOn: myStream.
   ^myStream truncate contents
OR


asCompleteAddress
   "Public - Answer the complete address as a String"
   | myStream |
   myStream := (ReadWriteStream on: (String new: 256)).
   myStream
      nextPutAll: self street printString;
      cr;
      nextPutAll: self apartment printString;
      cr;
      nextPutAll: self city printString;
      cr;
      nextPutAll: self state printString;
      cr;
      nextPutAll: self zipcode printString;
      cr;
      nextPutAll: self country printString.
   ^myStream truncate contents
```

LISTING 15.4   Before and after streams technique.

Overallocating

When creating new objects, you may be very cautious about allocating too much memory, or you may not specify the amount of memory to allocate at all. The problem is that if your allocation falls short, even by one byte, the object will be grown to meet the needs of the operation. The problem with growing objects is that the new object is allocated slightly larger than the old object, and `become:` is used to make the new object replace the old one. The more times this happens, the slower the operation, due to the growing and the garbage collecting of the old object.

The way to get around this grow slowdown is to overallocate. This means that when you create a new variable-sized object like a `Collection` or a `String`, you specify a length for the object and ensure that the length is liberally larger than what you expect to need. See Listing 15.5.

```
asString
   | result |
   result := String new.
   result
      addAll: firstName; "re-allocates result"
      add: $ ; "re-allocates result again"
      addAll: lastName. "re-allocates result again!"
   ^result

asString
   | result |
   result := String new: 100. "Only allocates once"
   result
      addAll: firstName;
      add: $ ;
      addAll: lastName.
   ^result
```

LISTING 15.5   Before and after overallocating technique.

Symbols vs. Strings

`Symbols` are extremely useful because they are guaranteed to be unique and can be any set of characters permitted. Ironically, this is also the downfall of `Symbols`. Because they are guaranteed to be unique, all instances of `Symbol` are stored in a table deep inside Smalltalk. They take up space, even when they are no longer being referenced, and are much slower to reference than an instance of another object.

Using instances of `String` is preferred to `Symbol` because the `String` does not use any global lookup to ensure uniqueness. This saves a lot of time, and eventually memory as the `Symbols` never die without your executing code to remove them. See Listing 15.6.

```
(guiWidgetCollection at: #OKButton) enable
(guiWidgetCollection at: #'OKButton') enable
```

LISTING 15.6   Before and after strings technique.

Message Ordering

The order in which methods are executed can have a significant impact on performance. Knowing which methods cause lengthy operations to occur can help you to identify the appropriate order for sending messages. An example of this involves the sorting of a collection. If you have any type of collection, and determine that it must be converted into a sorted collection, an approximate factor of two performance gain can be realized by using the second version of the sample code, as illustrated in Listing 15.7.

```
myCollection
    asSortedCollection
    sortBlock: [ :a :b | a value > b value ]


SortedCollection
    sortBlock: [ :a :b | a value > b value ]
    on: myCollection
```

LISTING 15.7 Before and after order of messages technique.

In the first version of code, a copy of `myCollection` is created as an instance of `SortedCollection`. The values are sorted using the default `sortblock`. Then the values are sorted again when the message `sortBlock:` is sent to the `SortedCollection`.

In the second version of code, a new, empty `SortedCollection` is supplied with a new sort block with the message `sortBlock:`. Since there are no items in the collection, no sorting occurs with the default sort block or the new sort block until items are added. Essentially, the first version sorts the list twice, while the second version sorts the list only once, a performance gain of approximately two.

Cache Items

When an item requires a lengthy operation to create its value, and then is answered in a method, the next time the method is called the operation must be repeated. Instead of doing this each time, the use of a variable to cache the information can give significant performance gains. See Listing 15.8.

```
allTables
    ^myDatabase executeSQL: 'select * from SYSIBM.SYSTABLES'


allTables
    "Now we have an instance variable called tables"
    tables isNil ifTrue:
```

Continued

```
[ tables := myDatabase
              executeSQL: 'select * from SYSIBM.SYSTABLES' ].


^tables
```

LISTING 15.8 Before and after cache items technique.

Defer Execution

Often, a lengthy operation can be deferred until it is really needed. This can be done by creating a block that contains the operation, and then sending the message `value` when the value is finally needed. Another approach is to use the class `Promise` that provides the value when referenced, executing the supplied block automatically.

Background Threads

When a continuous or lengthy process must occur, it is possible to do that operation in the background, at a lower priority than normal execution. The operation will take longer to complete, but has the advantage that the user can continue to use the application as more results are obtained. This is particularly useful when working with collections or lists that require each item to be manipulated.

```
list := self retrieveListFromDatabase.
self changed: #list with: list.
"Execution waits for preceeding to complete"

[ list := self retrieveListFromDatabase.
  self changed: #list with: list ] forkAt: 3.
"Execution continues while preceeding is processing"
```

LISTING 15.9 Before and after background threads technique.

Summary

In this chapter, some ideas common to all methods of profiling and improving the memory footprint and execution speed of your Smalltalk programs have been presented. Hopefully, all your Smalltalk programs will run faster and smaller in the future. It is important to remember to save profiling and tuning for the final stages of a project, just before the application is prepared for delivery, as you will see in the next chapter on Application Delivery.

16

Application Delivery

The process of delivering a "double-clickable" application in Smalltalk can be very difficult to understand because it does not mirror the way applications built in other languages like C, C++, or BASIC are delivered. The approach is simple, as you will see in this chapter. You will learn:

- ♦ the general concepts in creating a runnable Smalltalk application
- ♦ how to create a Digitalk stand-alone application
- ♦ how to create a ParcPlace stand-alone application
- ♦ how to create a VisualAge/IBM Smalltalk stand-alone application
- ♦ how to create a SmalltalkAgents stand-alone application
- ♦ how to create an ObjectStudio stand-alone application

Application Delivery Process

In preparing to deliver a Smalltalk application, you must first realize there is there is no big procedure to follow. Unlike C/C++, the application that you develop with the Smalltalk environment is part of the application being delivered. The simplest way to think of this is that Smalltalk is already a running application that you are customizing. Thus, instead of having to build an application, you simply remove the development tools from the application, and then you have the application.

In all the Smalltalk versions, the process of building an application is similar, but there is a great difference in the steps required to accomplish application delivery. In each case, a deliverable image must be created, auxiliary files like DLLs must be included, the virtual machine (executable) must be included, and code must be written to handle application startup and shutdown. This process is illustrated for each of the Smalltalk vendors in the following sections.

 VisualSmalltalk (Digitalk)

The VisualSmalltalk approach to creating an application is simple, but it is not totally automated. The image is saved from the transcript File menu, and then the appropriate files are copied. A Startup Method gets the application going.

From the VisualSmalltalk Transcript window shown in Figure 16.1, select the **File** menu and the item **Save Image As.** You will then see the Save

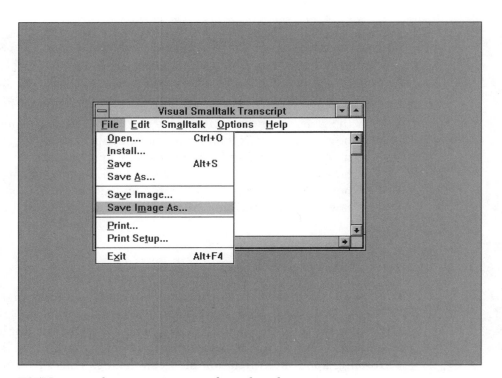

FIGURE 16.1   Select **Save Image As** from the File menu.

Image As window, pictured in Figure 16.2. This is where you will name your application, provide an icon associated with the application, and enter code for the `startUpApplication` method.

The filename of the application that you specify will be the name of the executable that will contain the basic executable and the image for the application. The filename can be any valid operating system filename, and should not overwrite any of the existing VisualSmalltalk files (choose something other than `v.exe` or `vdevw.exe`.

The Default Icon is shown below the filename entry field, and can be changed by clicking on the **Set Icon** button at the bottom of the Save Image As window. Clicking on this button lets you select any icon from the system through a standard file dialog. If you change the icon for the application, the changed icon will appear as the Default Icon.

The Startup Method can contain any code that you want the application to execute on startup. The method name in the Startup Method editor pane is `startUpApplication` and is contained in the `NotificationManager` class. Another example of the `startUpApplication` use can be found in the `startUpSampleApplication` method also found in `NotificationManager`.

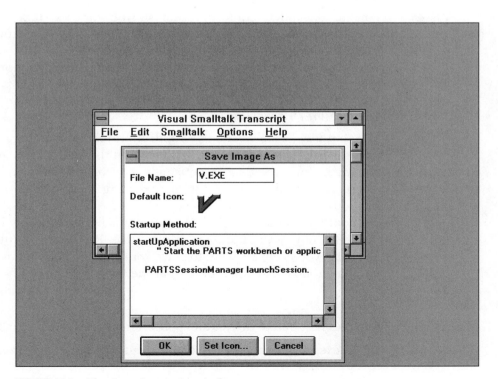

FIGURE 16.2 The Save Image As window.

Note the use of the `Smalltalk isRunTime` message to determine behavior of the program after delivery as opposed to during development.

Once the parameters have been verified, press the **OK** button. The VisualSmalltalk Transcript window title will change to VisualSmalltalk Transcript: MYAPP.EXE (where MYAPP is the name of your application). After it has completed, you may exit VisualSmalltalk and attempt to run your application.

With VisualSmalltalk, you will not be able to remove any methods that you do not need, unless you do it by hand, very carefully. This marks a departure from the other Smalltalk versions, in which tools exist to help strip the image. However, the need to strip the image in VisualSmalltalk is less prevalent than the others, due to image size, separation of the executable into many DLLs, and the small size and number of tools included.

Problems that occur after the runtime image has been created, can usually be found in the file `error.log` which contains a listing of all messages displayed to the user depending on the type of error, either Smalltalk debugger information or a machine register dump.

Startup Processing

For more explicit control of the startup process, take a look at the `startupSession` method in the `SessionModel` class. This method exposes many of the lower-level system details and should not be modified by a novice programmer because it can greatly affect the functionality (or lack thereof) of VisualSmalltalk.

Shutdown Processing

The shutdown code can do any application-related cleanup, including stopping the user from exiting the application if the attempt is made at an inappropriate time (there is an outstanding server transaction). One place to insert shutdown code is the `SystemDictionary` class `exit` instance method, which calls the `Session Model` class `exitSession` instance method. The `exitSession` method contains more of the low-level code that can get a novice programmer into trouble. Remember, with any of these methods, you probably want to place your code in front of any existing code in the methods; and don't forget that the code is there!

Files

The files required to deliver an application created with VisualSmalltalk are:

> v.exe (or yourapp.exe)—main executable and image, minimum size of 1.3MB

> dll subdirectory—DLL and SLL files, depending on features selected

VisualWorks (ParcPlace)

VisualWorks has the simplest of application delivery procedures. You can simply save your image, and then deliver it with the executable to run on any platform that VisualWorks supports. Additional steps can be performed to reduce the size of the image file by removing unneeded classes. The process of removing these classes and preparing the image for delivery is known as "stripping the image."

The stripping tool can be found in the VisualWorks directory, in the `utils` subdirectory. The stripper is not installed into the image file, and must be filed-in in order to make use of it. Use the Tools menu item File Editor to select the file `stripper.st` from the `utils` subdirectory, as shown in Figure 16.3.

Select **file in** from the popup menu in the second pane with the file list. Then evaluate `Stripper open` from the transcript. You will see a screen like that in Figure 16.4. You have two options on this screen. The first option instructs VisualWorks to remove the compiler classes that will render your

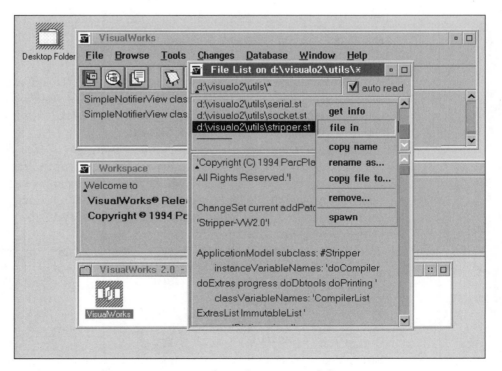

FIGURE 16.3 Select `stripper.st` from the `utils` subdirectory.

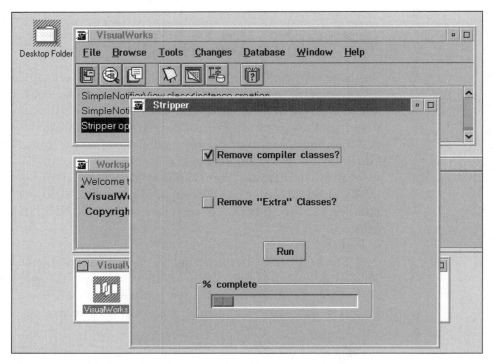

FIGURE 16.4 The VisualWorks Stripper tool.

image incapable of compiling and changing code. This is a good option to prevent users and other programmers from altering your product. The second option instructs VisualWorks to remove all "Extra" classes, as defined in the Stripper class method named `InitExtras`.

Certain basic operations are done regardless of the option chosen. Pressing the **Run** button will remove all development tools from the image, both in binary and class form; all variables associated with development will be removed. Additionally, the error notifier, which during development provides detailed debugging information, is removed from the system and replaced by a simple error notifier.

Other stripping operations can be performed by redefining the `preStrip` and `postStrip` methods. Detailed analysis of your needs should be performed when doing so, and you should take a closer look at the Stripper's built-in functionality.

Startup Processing

Since VisualWorks starts up in the state at which it was left upon saving the image, little needs to be done to cause the application to start in the beginning. All that is needed is to have an open application window visible when the image save occurs. There are other ways to cause actions to happen on startup, but these are not necessary, unlike other Smalltalk environments.

Files

The files required to deliver an application created with VisualWorks are:

> OE20.EXE or ST80.EXE—executable. 685KB
>
> visual.im—image file. 4.2MB

VisualAge/IBM Smalltalk (IBM)

VisualAge and IBM Smalltalk have a slightly different way of delivering applications. The VisualAge product has an additional capability that automatically puts together an application, whereas the IBM Smalltalk product has a few more steps that can be used to provide a more customized solution to the application delivery process. The IBM Smalltalk process is presented because it allows more and involves Smalltalk programming.

The steps required to create a stand-alone runnable program built using IBM Smalltalk include using the Application Packager browser to create .APP files, creation of a .CNF file to specify files to be loaded at runtime, and merging the .APP, .CNF and other files into the finished product. These files should all be collocated in a single directory for the application where they will be merged into the final application.

Creating an .APP file requires you to evaluate Smalltalk code that will unload the application and subapplications to .APP files. Some of the common applications in IBM Smalltalk are included in the basic runtime image file, ABTRTI20 for VisualAge and IBMRTI20 for IBM Smalltalk. These are:

- ◆ CommonFileSystem
- ◆ CommonGraphics
- ◆ CommonWidgets
- ◆ Kernel
- ◆ PlatformEvents
- ◆ PlatformFramework
- ◆ PlatformInterface
- ◆ PlatformWidgets

In order to create your own .APP files, you must evaluate the following code (assuming the application is named MyApp and it will be stored in MyApp.APP).

```
ApplicationDumper new
       unlinkInstancesOfClasses: (Array with: EmLibraryPointer);
       dumpApplications: MyApp withAllSubApplications
       dumpIntoFileNamed: '.\MyApp.APP'.
```

This code needs to be executed for each application to be included in the runtime distribution. Fortunately, VisualAge automates this task for VisualAge users. IBM Smalltalk users need to do this repeatedly.

The next step before merging the files into the final application is to copy the .APP files into an empty directory, followed by either runtime image (ABTRI20 or IBMRTI20), the executable file (ABT.EXE or IBMST.EXE), ESVM13.DLL, CURSORS.OBJ, and RGB.TXT. The runtime image file needs to be renamed to IMAGE.

You must now use a text editor to create a .CNF file that lists each of the .APP files on a separate line. The order of the .APP files is significant in that dependents must be loaded after the classes on which they are dependent. The process will fail and the .CNF file will need to be reorganized if the dependents do not follow. The .CNF file should be named ABTAPP.CNF for VisualAge users or IBMSTAPP.CNF for IBM Smalltalk users.

The packaging can begin by running ABT.EXE for VisualAge or IBMST.EXE for IBM Smalltalk. The results of the packaging will be detailed in either ABTAPP.LOG or IBMSTAPP.LOG depending on what you are using. If there is a failure, look at the .LOG file for hints on how to resolve the problem. During the process, a window named **MyApp/App Startup Status** will be displayed.

Once the process has completed successfully, rename the .CNF file to .CNX and retain it for future revisions. Run ABT.EXE or IBMST.EXE again, and since there is no .CNF file present, it will run the image and the application should start.

Startup Processing

Startup processing occurs in the method called runtimeStartUp, which exists as a class method in the class of the same name as your application. This means that if your application is called MyApp, then in the class MyApp, the runtimeStartUp method would be defined to execute startup processing code, typically to open a window. An example of what this method looks like is:

```
runtimeStartUp
"Public - Initialize and run MyApp in a delivered application"
MyAppTopWindow new open.
^self
```

Files

The files required to deliver an application created with VisualAge are:

cursors.obj—5KB

esvm13.dll—287KB

rgb.txt—17KB

abtrti20 or ibmrti20—renamed to `image`

additional DLL and APP files, depending on features

 SmalltalkAgents (QKS)

The SmalltalkAgents environment contains a product called Application Delivery Toolkit (ADT). The ADT consists of two pieces, the ADT Environment, a specialized version of the SmalltalkAgents Environment (read Image) and the Stand-alone Shell, a customized version of the SmalltalkAgents virtual machine.

To begin the process of creating a stand-alone application, you should first create platform-independent portable object (PIPO) files containing your entire application. This can be one file or a set of files. To create a PIPO file from within SmalltalkAgents, your code must be organized into a **project.** By default, all code written in SmalltalkAgents is saved into the project called User Scratch Library, so it is available for export via PIPO. Select the **Smalltalk** menu and the **Open Project Browser** item from the menu. You will then be presented with a screen like that in Figure 16.5.

From within this project browser, you may select the desired project library for export to PIPO format. The final step to create the PIPO file is to select the **Export Project** item from the Project, as shown (in tear-off form) in Figure 16.6. You will then be presented with a standard save file dialog in which you can name the PIPO file. At this point, you have saved the application to be bundled into the runtime portion of SmalltalkAgents.

After exiting SmalltalkAgents, open the **Application Delivery Toolkit** folder on the desktop within the SmalltalkAgents folder. Double-click on the ADT 1.2b2 icon, as shown in Figure 16.7. This will start the Application Delivery Toolkit. The first screen presented in the ADT is shown in Figure 16.8. It states that you should use the standard load file dialog on the following screen to select the desired PIPO file.

For example, you can select the **QuickStartTutorial-1.2.pipo** file from the QuickStartTutorial folder, as shown in Figure 16.9. Pressing the **Open** button will confirm the choice of PIPO file and go to the next screen. The

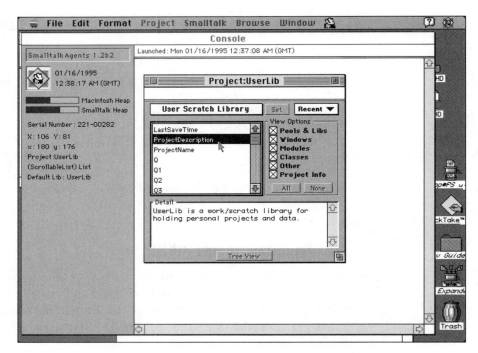

FIGURE 16.5 The Project Browser window.

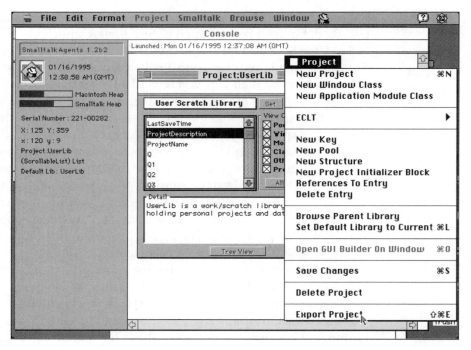

FIGURE 16.6 The Export Project menu item.

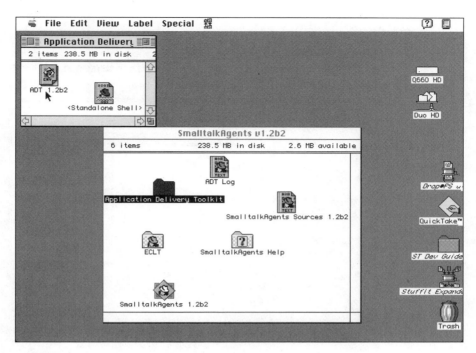

FIGURE 16.7   The Application Delivery Tool (ADT) icon.

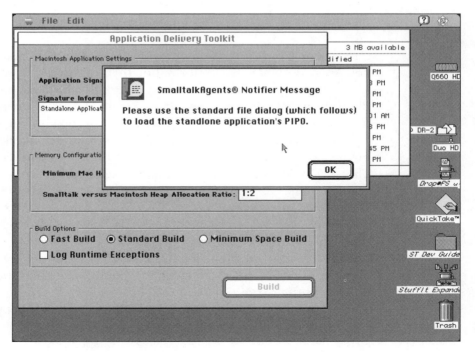

FIGURE 16.8   The first screen in ADT.

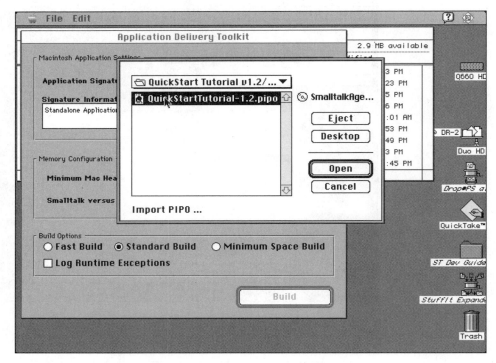

FIGURE 16.9 Select a PIPO file from the File dialog.

screen shown in Figure 16.10 contains the message: Unarchive Request: Do You Approve? which is a confirmation that this is the correct PIPO file. The second line in this dialog contains a description of the content of the PIPO file from its creation as a project in SmalltalkAgents. Pressing **OK** at this point will take you to the Application Delivery Toolkit main screen.

The main screen of the Application Delivery Toolkit is shown in Figure 16.11. There are three main groupings of controls on the screen. The first is Macintosh Application Settings, which contains information specific to the creation of the application in the Macintosh File System and the primary module, typically a GUI window module. The second grouping of controls, called Memory Configuration, includes absolute memory specifiers and a ratio for the two types of memory: Smalltalk and Macintosh. The third set of controls called Build Options contains choices for the level of stripping to occur and a switch to control the handling of exceptions during runtime. The final control on the screen starts the Build process, which can take anywhere from a few minutes to a half-hour depending on the desired final image size, complexity of application, and processor speed.

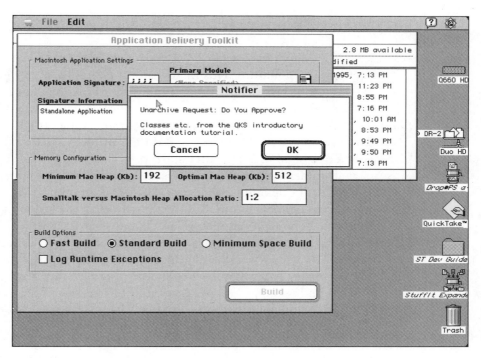

FIGURE 16.10 The PIPO archive file description.

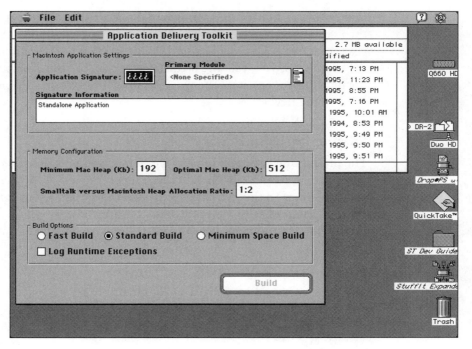

FIGURE 16.11 The main screen of the Application Delivery Toolkit.

The Macintosh Application Settings allow you to specify a Macintosh Application Signature. This field is a four-character identifier that can contain any four characters, though many combinations have been registered with Apple for specific Macintosh application programs. The default of ???? is standard for a nonregistered program and is an acceptable entry. The Primary Module should contain the primary GUI module that will be sent a new open message after startup.

The Memory Configuration settings allow you to set a Minimum Mac Heap size, the default of which is 192KB. This amount of RAM is adequate for most types of applications, but the size can be increased for applications that require it. The Optimal Mac Heap default is at 512KB, which again is adequate for most configurations. The parameter that may require tuning is the Smalltalk versus Macintosh Heap Allocation Ratio. The default value is 1:2, but a smaller ratio may be better for an application that generates fewer objects, and a value of 1:3 or higher may be necessary for an object instantiation-intensive application. The trade-off here is between required RAM and the frequency and duration of garbage collection.

The Build Options settings control how many passes the ADT will make through the image to dispose of unnecessary classes, methods, and libraries. The Fast Build setting causes two passes to be made, the Standard Build causes eight passes to be made (stopping after five if no gains were made on the fifth), and Minimum Space Build will keep making passes through the image until no further gains can be made. The Log Runtime Exceptions checkbox will cause the application to create a log file each time the program is run, placing error messages in the file. This is useful for diagnosing failures in the system by reading the file or shipping the contents back to the developer.

Startup and Shutdown Processing

The processing required for startup of the system is the standard that occurs when a new window is open. The callback sequence for the main GUI window specified in the Primary Module is the same as that for any other window, so code should be placed in the appropriate places. The shutdown processing should occur in the main GUI window close routines.

Files

The files required to deliver an application created with SmalltalkAgents are:

    ADT—Application Delivery Toolkit. 2.4MB
    <Standalone Shell>—244KB

ObjectStudio (VMARK)

Under VMARK's ObjectStudio product, the creation of a stand-alone run-time is done through the Program Generator. Since VMARK does not recommend saving the ObjectStudio image regularly, unlike the other Smalltalk environments, there are options and processes to organize the ObjectStudio application components into loadable applications. It is useful to organize the ObjectStudio classes into applications prior to using the Program Generator, preferably early in the development process.

Loadable Application Support

It is convenient to package your application ahead of time for easy and convenient loading into the ObjectStudio environment. To do this, simply create an ASCII text file that lists each of the classes (by filename and directory) to be loaded into the ObjectStudio environment. The order in which the class files are specified is very important because dependent classes must be loaded after the class on which they are dependent. Typically, a subclass must be loaded after its superclass, and classes that reference another class must be loaded after that class. Once the list of class filenames has been created in the text file, it can be loaded with either an **-l** option on startup, or by inserting a line of code into the `lappiniw.cls` file contained in the `cls` subdirectory of the top-level ObjectStudio directory. The following is an example of how to create a loadable application.

For purposes of this example, we will create a file called `myapp.txt` as a loadable application. Open a text editor on this file, and enter the following lines:

```
myparent.cls
child1.cls
child2.cls
child3.cls
orphan.cls
```

Save this file to disk in the ObjectStudio top-level directory. Other examples of loadable application text files can be found in the `lappiniw.cls` file. The contents of the `lappiniw.cls` are as follows:

```
IdentityDictionary subclass: #LoadableApplicationDictionary
instanceVariableNames: ''
classVariableNames: ''
poolDictionaries: '' !

! LoadableApplicationDictionary class methods !
```

Continued

```
initialize
   | dict |
   dict := LoadableApplicationDictionary new.
   dict at: #'EDA/SQL' put: 'eda.txt'.
   dict at: #'EHLLAPI Generic' put: 'gehllapi.txt'.
   dict at: #'EHLLAPI Rumba' put: 'rehllapi.txt'.
   dict at: #'Extended Services Database' put: 'extdb.txt'.
   dict at: #'Profiler' put: 'profiler.txt'.
   dict at: #'APPC DCA' put: 'appc.txt'.
   dict at: #'Oracle Ver6 Database' put: 'oracle.txt'.
   dict at: #'Oracle Ver7 Database' put: 'oracle7.txt'.
   dict at: #'SQLBase Database Ver5' put: 'sqlbase.txt'.
   dict at: #'DBase Database' put: 'ebase.txt'.
   dict at: #'RDB Database' put: 'rdb.txt'.
   dict at: #'SQLServer Database' put: 'sqlserv.txt'.
   dict at: #'ODBC' put: 'odbc.txt'.
   dict at: #'TCPIP' put: 'tcpip.txt'.
   dict at: #'Workplace Demo' put: 'wpdemo.txt'.
   dict at: #'Load Tutorial Data' put: 'demoload.txt'.
   dict at: #'Load DBaseTutorial Data' put: 'dbDemo.txt'.
   dict at: #'DLL Generator' put: 'dllgen.txt'.
   dict at: #'OLE' put: 'ole.txt'.
   dict at: #'CommBuilder' put: 'commbldr.txt'.
   LoadableApplications := dict.
   LoadedApplications := IdentityDictionary new.
   LoadedApplicationOrder := Array new.
   LoadAppInitSource := (self class sourceDict) at: #initialize.
!"end initialize"


!"End of LoadableApplicationDictionary class methods block"
```

Next we must edit the `lappiniw.cls` file. Open a text editor on the file, and you will see the display of Figure 16.12. Edit the text in the display to include the `lappinit.cls` file to look like Figure 16.13. Save this file and close the text editor. Now you can use the ObjectStudio Loadable Application Browser to load the file.

To load the application, use the right mouse button in the ObjectStudio main window (known as the Workplace Shell) and pick the item labeled **Load Application.** The menu is shown in Figure 16.14. The Loadable Application Browser should now appear as shown in Figure 16.15. Don't be surprised when the application that you have just defined does not show up in the list. Press the **Refresh** button and the list will be reloaded from the `lappinit.cls` file. You will need to use the Refresh button each time you restart ObjectStudio unless you save the image. Make sure that if you do save the image that you haven't actually loaded your application—unless that is your intention! Simply hit Refresh and then close the Loadable Application Browser.

```
┌──────────────────────────────────────────────────────────────────────────┐
│ ─                       Notepad - LAPPINIW.CLS                       ▼ ▲  │
├──────────────────────────────────────────────────────────────────────────┤
│ File   Edit   Search   Help                                               │
├──────────────────────────────────────────────────────────────────────────┤
│ IdentityDictionary subclass: #LoadableApplicationDictionary           ▲   │
│ instanceVariableNames: ''                                                 │
│ classVariableNames: ''                                                    │
│ poolDictionaries: '' !                                                    │
│                                                                           │
│                                                                           │
│ ! LoadableApplicationDictionary class methods !                           │
│                                                                           │
│                                                                           │
│ initialize                                                                │
│         | dict |                                                          │
│         dict := LoadableApplicationDictionary new.                        │
│         dict at: #'EDA/SQL' put: 'eda.txt'.                               │
│         dict at: #'EHLLAPI Generic' put: 'gehllapi.txt'.                  │
│         dict at: #'EHLLAPI Rumba' put: 'rehllapi.txt'.                    │
│         dict at: #'Extended Services Database' put: 'extdb.txt'.          │
│         dict at: #'Profiler' put: 'profiler.txt'.                         │
│         dict at: #'APPC DCA' put: 'appc.txt'.                             │
│         dict at: #'Oracle Ver6 Database' put: 'oracle.txt'.              │
│         dict at: #'Oracle Ver7 Database' put: 'oracle7.txt'.             │
│         dict at: #'SQLBase Database Ver5' put: 'sqlbase.txt'.            │
│         dict at: #'DBase Database' put: 'ebase.txt'.                      │
│         dict at: #'RDB Database' put: 'rdb.txt'.                          │
│         dict at: #'SQLServer Database' put: 'sqlserv.txt'.               │
│         dict at: #'ODBC' put: 'odbc.txt'.                                 │
│         dict at: #'TCPIP' put: 'tcpip.txt'.                               │
│         dict at: #'Workplace Demo' put: 'wpdemo.txt'.                     │
│         dict at: #'Load Tutorial Data' put: 'demoload.txt'.          ▼   │
├──────────────────────────────────────────────────────────────────────────┤
│ ◄                                                                    ►   │
└──────────────────────────────────────────────────────────────────────────┘
```

FIGURE 16.12   Edit the `lappiniw.cls` file.

```
┌──────────────────────────────────────────────────────────────────────────┐
│ ─                       Notepad - LAPPINIW.CLS                       ▼ ▲  │
├──────────────────────────────────────────────────────────────────────────┤
│ File   Edit   Search   Help                                               │
├──────────────────────────────────────────────────────────────────────────┤
│ IdentityDictionary subclass: #LoadableApplicationDictionary           ▲   │
│ instanceVariableNames: ''                                                 │
│ classVariableNames: ''                                                    │
│ poolDictionaries: '' !                                                    │
│                                                                           │
│                                                                           │
│ ! LoadableApplicationDictionary class methods !                           │
│                                                                           │
│                                                                           │
│ initialize                                                                │
│         | dict |                                                          │
│         dict := LoadableApplicationDictionary new.                        │
│         dict at: #'1. MyApp' put: 'myapp.txt'.                            │
│         dict at: #'EDA/SQL' put: 'eda.txt'.                               │
│         dict at: #'EHLLAPI Generic' put: 'gehllapi.txt'.                  │
│         dict at: #'EHLLAPI Rumba' put: 'rehllapi.txt'.                    │
│         dict at: #'Extended Services Database' put: 'extdb.txt'.          │
│         dict at: #'Profiler' put: 'profiler.txt'.                         │
│         dict at: #'APPC DCA' put: 'appc.txt'.                             │
│         dict at: #'Oracle Ver6 Database' put: 'oracle.txt'.              │
│         dict at: #'Oracle Ver7 Database' put: 'oracle7.txt'.             │
│         dict at: #'SQLBase Database Ver5' put: 'sqlbase.txt'.            │
│         dict at: #'DBase Database' put: 'ebase.txt'.                      │
│         dict at: #'RDB Database' put: 'rdb.txt'.                          │
│         dict at: #'SQLServer Database' put: 'sqlserv.txt'.               │
│         dict at: #'ODBC' put: 'odbc.txt'.                                 │
│         dict at: #'TCPIP' put: 'tcpip.txt'.                               │
│         dict at: #'Workplace Demo' put: 'wpdemo.txt'.                ▼   │
├──────────────────────────────────────────────────────────────────────────┤
│ ◄                                                                    ►   │
└──────────────────────────────────────────────────────────────────────────┘
```

FIGURE 16.13   The `lappiniw.cls` file after changes.

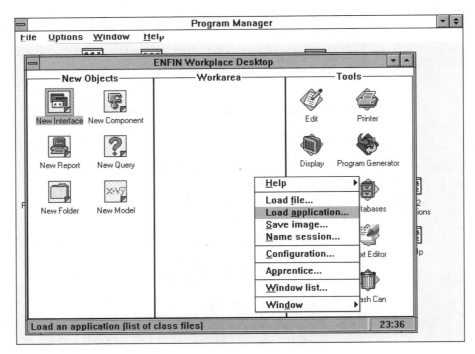

FIGURE 16.14   The Load Application menu item.

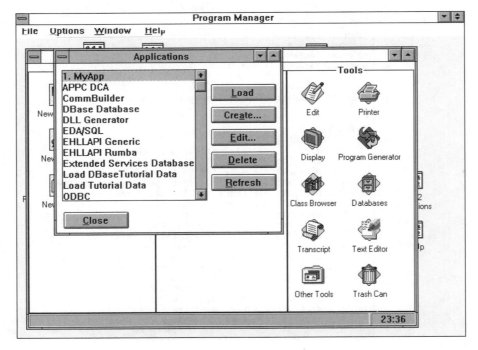

FIGURE 16.15   The Loadable Application Browser.

Program Generator

The Program Generator can be accessed through the main desktop of the ObjectStudio product as one of the development icons on the right. Either double-click on the Program Generator icon, or drag a controller icon onto the icon. An example of the drag-and-drop functionality is shown in Figure 16.16.

The Program Generator in ObjectStudio is the first step in preparing to package and deliver an application. You must identify a controller (an ObjectStudio top-level GUI class) that will serve as the initial screen for the application. In many cases, this will be your program's main window or program desktop, depending on the GUI metaphor that you are following.

When you are ready to use the Program Generator, quit then restart ObjectStudio. After loading the ObjectStudio application into memory, do not run the application before using the Program Generator. This ensures that the image size created by the Program Generator contains the minimum number of objects required to run that application, and that the ObjectStudio environment is at a known state that can be repeated for subsequent releases. Globals and class variables have been known to cause

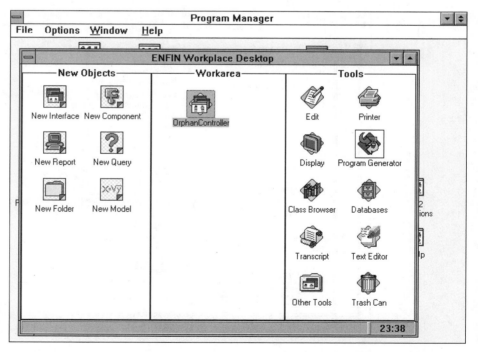

FIGURE 16.16 ObjectStudio Desktop showing drag-and-drop onto Program Generator.

problems when code does not explicitly initialize them on startup. Be on the safe side and generate the program before running your application.

To begin the example of Program Generator use, load the Loadable Application example from the preceding by using the Loadable Application Browser. Once the application has been loaded, press the **Close** button in the browser to return to the ObjectStudio desktop. Use the left mouse button to drag the OrphanController icon, and drop the icon on the Program Generator icon. The Program Generator should then appear as in Figure 16.17.

Various options in the Program Generator can now be set. These items include the program's main controller (Application name), the image file-name, a splash-screen logo to be shown when the program is run, a list of classes to be removed from the image, options for deleting method source and unused classes, and a list of controllers to be removed.

The first item, the main controller, has already been filled in because you used the drag-and-drop interface to the Program Generator. Had you simply double-clicked on the Program Generator icon, you would need to fill this item by selecting an application controller for the application from the list in the upper right corner of the window. It is important to note that you

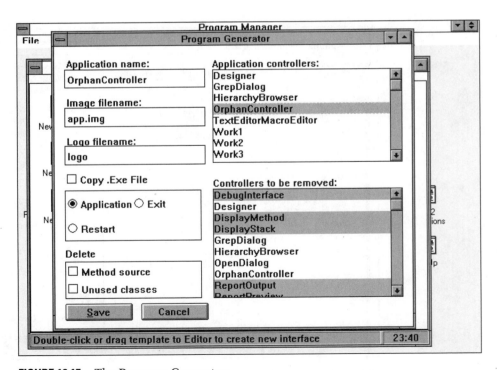

FIGURE 16.17 The Program Generator.

can have only one main application controller in the application, and that this window is opened as the final step of the application startup process.

The second item is the Image filename. It is only important to remember the name of the image when delivering the files. Reasons to change it could be for different versions of the application, or different applications altogether.

The third item is the Logo filename. It should be left blank if no startup splash-screen is desired. The default entry for this field is the VMARK ObjectStudio logo, so you may wish to clear this field, unless you want the end users to see the logo. The Logo filename should be the first eight characters of a DLL file, with the extension of .dll. To create a DLL file with Logo, you should use the included example file to generate the DLL, replacing the ObjectStudio logo with one of your choice. This step requires use of a C compiler on each delivery platform.

A few miscellaneous items follow, the first being a checkbox labelled `Copy .Exe File`, which simply copies the file `enfin.exe` into the same name as the image with an .exe suffix (`myapp.exe`). This step is not necessary for the program to run, and could be accomplished simply by copying the exe file. The next group of radio buttons determines the state of ObjectStudio after the application has been generated. You have the option of running the application, exiting from ObjectStudio, or restarting ObjectStudio as though you had exited and started from the program icon.

The second to last item is a grouping of checkboxes that govern the deletion of Smalltalk source. The first checkbox removes the method source if selected. This makes the application delivery without any source code, which assists in protecting the confidentiality of source code. The second checkbox removes unused classes through an internal ObjectStudio algorithm.

The last item in the Program Generator window is the Controllers to be removed listbox, containing all the GUI windows (subclasses of Controller) that will be removed from the system. This is the place to manually specify controllers unneccesary to the runtime application. This is a multiselect listbox and contains the ObjectStudio development system controllers as the default set of selections.

Startup Processing

The startup processing for ObjectStudio can take place completely within the main Application controller for your application. Since the main Application controller is the first window to be opened on startup, you can place code into the `openIntialization` or the `postOpenInitialization` methods for that class to perform the various startup actions that you require. Make sure that code that depends on the window being visible occurs in postOpenInitialization!

Shutdown Processing

The shutdown processing for the application can occur in the close method for the main Application controller. It is most likely, based on the way ObjectStudio works, that the main Application controller will exist the entire time the application is running. If it does not, then you will need to insert code in as many main windows that exist. The other alternative is to hide the main Application controller, but to still use it as the highest-level window in your windowing hierarchy, thereby reducing the amount of code to be written in each close method.

Files

The files required to deliver an application created with ObjectStudio are:

enfin.exe—693KB
app.img—(image file) 2.7MB
E41?????.DLL—Required/Optional DLLs.

Summary

You have now seen how to transform your Smalltalk program from development to delivery. The steps for doing so have been illustrated for each of the Smalltalks. You can now prepare your own applications for delivery. But before you ship your diskettes, test, test, and retest your application. And, remember, the user would probably appreciate some documentation on how to install and use the application. Then you can compress the files onto floppy disks, a CD-ROM, or a network delivery directory, and invite the users to begin using your wonderful Smalltalk application.

17

Primitives and External Code

It has become increasingly important to reuse code that exists outside of the Smalltalk world. The investment an organization has made in legacy systems cannot be overlooked by Smalltalkers as this represents one additional way to justify the use of Smalltalk. In this chapter, you will learn:

♦ ways to call code external to the Smalltalk environment
♦ how to use the Generic External Library interface to call external code
♦ how to write Smalltalk primitives

Note that it is not currently common practice to use Smalltalk to write the non-GUI portion of a system or to build libraries that are called from other programming environments. Some successful projects have been written in Smalltalk with no GUI present, but the interfacing of Smalltalk to another GUI is rare. The difficulty lies in placing the Smalltalk engine in a secondary position, where operations such as garbage collection can be subordinate to the functioning of the GUI portion of the application. Successful use of Smalltalk for non-GUI can be accomplished by using interprocess communication mechanisms on a multitasking platform, which removes

Microsoft Windows and MacOS from possible platforms, as neither possesses true preemptive multitasking.

Primitives vs. Generic External Library

There are many reasons to interface to code outside of the Smalltalk environment. These reasons range from the need to interface with existing libraries outside the environment, like operating system and existing code, to the need for speed, such as external sort and retrieval engines. Almost everything in Smalltalk that deals with the platform operating system, communication packages, or databases must use external code.

There are two approaches to interfacing to the world outside Smalltalk. Although these may be named differently by the Smalltalk vendors, they form two distinct types of interfaces: **primitives** and **Generic External Library.** The primitive is the original approach, and allows external code to be called as if it is a Smalltalk method. The Generic External Library interface is a more recent innovation, and provides an easier way to access the external code. Both methods accomplish the same general task: interfacing to external code.

What Are Primitives?

The primitive approach creates methods in a class that directly call external code instead of Smalltalk code. These are known as primitives and are the smallest building blocks of the Smalltalk environment. In the original Smalltalk design, there were a finite number of primitives defined within the virtual machine. Today, much code is written in the form of primitives to interface to the world outside the Smalltalk environment. The primitive varies greatly between Smalltalk vendors and between the platforms on which the Smalltalk engine runs. A primitive is generally regarded as more complex to write, as will be demonstrated later. They are, however, generally more convenient once written because they can be called in the same general manner as any method.

Primitives can appear in any class; they do not have to have a separate area. In some cases, they can even appear in-line, although this is not recommended because it does not provide good encapsulation of the external interface. Primitives act just like methods. They can accept arguments passed in, they can call other methods in Smalltalk, and answer a Smalltalk object as their result. Primitives truly are primitive Smalltalk methods that are written in code other than Smalltalk, which tends to be C code.

The Primitive type of external call has its drawbacks, too. You must worry when creating the external code about the impact of the garbage collection mechanism on the arguments passed in on the stack, the validity of other objects created in the method that could be garbage collected, the difference between the Smalltalk memory space and the external operating system memory space and in Windows versions, the 16- and 32-bit versions of code, and the various mechanisms to manage the different types of resources.

What Is the Generic External Library Interface?

The second flavor of interface is the Generic External Library. Typically, it is referred to as a Generic C interface because many people are interfacing to an external C API. This approach can be simpler to create because it requires fewer C worries, but it has the drawback of requiring additional Smalltalk code.

Your instance of the Generic External Library is a separate class, usually a subclass of DLL or some External Library class. The new class contains a method for each of the calls into the external library, defined in a way that maps the Smalltalk arguments into external representations of the data. The class also contains a reference to the external library for binding and identification.

With the Generic External Library interface it is very important that the External Library class you create have another class that provides encapsulation of the needed data, when arguments and return values must be cached; an error-trapping interface; and higher-level functionality. This also serves to isolate the calling methods from the details of the external library, so one can be replaced with another without modifying the Smalltalk Public API.

Generic External Calling

The Generic External Code interface in the various versions of Smalltalk provides a safe, quick, and easy way to interface to external code. It provides an easier way for mere mortals (anyone less than a Smalltalk guru) to write effective production code without worrying about many of the issues inherent to writing user primitives.

The drawbacks to using the Generic External Code interface are elegance of the solution, limits in data transfer, no access to Smalltalk variables, and reduced encapsulation.

Generic Code Example DLL: TESTDLL.DLL

For the Generic External Code interface examples, I have created a sample DLL: TESTDLL.DLL. This library provides simple functionality that can be used in all the generic DLL examples. It was written in C, so some familiarity with the C language helps in understanding the code. The C source code file for the DLL appears in Listings 17.1 to 17.3. These files contain three simple functions with varying arguments.

```c
/*
 * TestDLL.C - Source code to the TestDLL.
 * Example of a Generic External DLL
 */


long MyFunction( int theInteger, char* theStringPointer);
int MyFunction1( int theInteger);
float MyFunction2( float theFloat, float theOtherFloat);


/*
 * MyFunction - takes theInteger and the first character
 * of theStringPointer minus the value of '0' and multiplies them
 * returning the result. Example: input: 2, "2345" = 4.
 */
long MyFunction( int theInteger, char* theStringPointer)
{
return ((theStringPointer[0] - '0') * theInteger);
}


/*
 * MyFunction1 - takes theInteger and returns it.
 * Pretty boring.
 */
int MyFunction1( int theInteger)
{
return theInteger;
}


/*
 * MyFunction2 - takes theFloat and theOtherFloat,
 * multiplies them, and returns the result as another
 * float.
 */
float MyFunction2( float theFloat, float theOtherFloat )
{
float theReturnFloat;

theReturnFloat = theFloat * theOtherFloat;
```

Continued

```
return theReturnFloat;


}
```

LISTING 17.1 File: TESTDLL.C. The C source code for the TESTDLL.DLL used in the Generic DLL examples.

```
LIBRARY     TESTDLL
EXETYPE     WINDOWS
CODE        PRELOAD MOVEABLE DISCARDABLE
DATA        PRELOAD MOVEABLE SINGLE
HEAPSIZE    1024
EXPORTS
            _MyFunction
            _MyFunction1
            _MyFunction2
```

LISTING 17.2 File: TESTDLL.DEF. The Definitions file needed to build TEST-DLL.DLL.

```
# Microsoft Visual C++ generated build script - Do not modify

PROJ = TESTDLL
DEBUG = 1
PROGTYPE = 1
CALLER =
ARGS =
DLLS =
D_RCDEFINES = /d_DEBUG
R_RCDEFINES = /dNDEBUG
ORIGIN = MSVC
ORIGIN_VER = 1.00
PROJPATH = D:\ENFINWIN\JON\
USEMFC = 0
CC = cl
CPP = cl
CXX = cl
CCREATEPCHFLAG =
CPPCREATEPCHFLAG =
CUSEPCHFLAG =
CPPUSEPCHFLAG =
FIRSTC = TESTDLL.C
FIRSTCPP =
RC = rc
CFLAGS_D_WDLL = /nologo /G2 /Za /Gy /W3 /Zi /ALw/Od /D "_DEBUG" /FR /GD
/GEe /Fd"TESTDLL.PDB"
CFLAGS_R_WDLL = /nologo /W3 /ALw /O1 /D "NDEBUG" /FR /GD
```
Continued

```
LFLAGS_D_WDLL = /NOLOGO /NOE /PACKC:61440 /ALIGN:16 /ONERROR:NOEXE /CO/MAP:FULL
LFLAGS_R_WDLL = /NOLOGO /NOD /NOE /PACKC:61440 /ALIGN:16 /ONERROR:NOEXE
/MAP:FULL
LIBS_D_WDLL = libw ldllcew
LIBS_R_WDLL = oldnames libw ldllcew commdlg.lib olecli.lib olesvr.lib
shell.lib
RCFLAGS = /nologo
RESFLAGS = /nologo
RUNFLAGS =
DEFFILE = TESTDLL.DEF
OBJS_EXT =
LIBS_EXT =
!if "$(DEBUG)" == "1"
CFLAGS = $(CFLAGS_D_WDLL)
LFLAGS = $(LFLAGS_D_WDLL)
LIBS = $(LIBS_D_WDLL)
MAPFILE = nul
RCDEFINES = $(D_RCDEFINES)
!else
CFLAGS = $(CFLAGS_R_WDLL)
LFLAGS = $(LFLAGS_R_WDLL)
LIBS = $(LIBS_R_WDLL)
MAPFILE = nul
RCDEFINES = $(R_RCDEFINES)
!endif
!if [if exist MSVC.BND del MSVC.BND]
!endif
SBRS = TESTDLL.SBR


TESTDLL_DEP =

all: $(PROJ) .DLL $(PROJ) .BSC


TESTDLL.OBJ: TESTDLL.C $(TESTDLL_DEP)
        $(CC) $(CFLAGS) $(CCREATEPCHFLAG) /c TESTDLL.C


$(PROJ) .DLL:: TESTDLL.OBJ $(OBJS_EXT) $(DEFFILE)
        echo >NUL @<<$(PROJ) .CRF
TESTDLL.OBJ +
$(OBJS_EXT)
$(PROJ) .DLL
$(MAPFILE)
d:\msvc\lib\+
d:\msvc\mfc\lib\+
$(LIBS)
$(DEFFILE) ;
<<
    link $(LFLAGS) @$(PROJ) .CRF
    $(RC) $(RESFLAGS) $@
    implib /nowep $(PROJ) .LIB $(PROJ) .DLL
run: $(PROJ) .DLL
```

Continued

```
    $(PROJ) $(RUNFLAGS)

$(PROJ) .BSC: $(SBRS)
    bscmake @<<
/o$@ $(SBRS)
<<
```

LISTING 17.3 File: TESTDLL.MAK. The make file to build the test DLL in Visual C++ under MS-Windows 32-bit.

 ObjectStudio

The key to using Dynamic Link Libraries (DLLs) in ObjectStudio is the class `Module`. It provides all the functionality necessary to call an external routine in a DLL, such as the function name, the arguments and types, the type of function, and the return value.

The function can be written in any language that supports the DLL convention. This means that you can call DLLs created from C, Pascal, Assembly Language, and so on. You need not even have the source code, but simply the DLL! In some cases, you may be provided with a DLL and a specification on which functions are available. This is enough to interface to the DLL, by following the next example, and enhancing and customizing the code to suit your needs.

To define an external function through the Generic DLL interface, two instance methods are available in the ObjectStudio `Module` class:

```
defineExternalProc: theProc
 paramTypes: theTypes
 returnType: theReturnType
 callingConvention: theCallingConvention
 defineExternalProc: theProc
 paramTypes: theTypes
 returnType: theReturnType
 callingConvention: theCallingConvention
 ordinalNumber: theOrdinalNumber
```

In these two instance methods, the argument `theProc` is an instance of `Symbol` corresponding to the function name in the DLL; for example: `MyFunction` or `MYFUNCTION`.

The argument `theTypes` is an instance of `Array` containing any symbols related to the types of parameters available. This includes `#byte`, `#word`, `#dword`, `#float`, `#double`, `#string`, `#structure`, and `#pointer`; for example: `#( #word #string )` or `Array with: #word with: #string`. Optionally, each element in the array can be a two-item array itself. The first argument would be as in the preceding, with the second argument either #value or #reference. This symbol flags the Module class to either pass the value along so that it cannot be modified (make a copy and send that along) or send it so it can be modified (send a pointer to the real thing). For example: #(#(#word #value) #(#string #reference).

NOTE: To verify your available data types, execute the code: Module dataTypes out, and read the System Transcript.

The argument theReturnType is an instance of Symbol corresponding to the type of the returned argument. It can be any of the values just listed for theTypes which are: #byte, #word, #dword, #float, #double, #string, #structure, and #pointer; for example: #dword.

The argument theCallingConvention is the type of DLL calling convention used. It refers to how the linking was performed during compile and can be: #C or #Pascal. The convention varies depending on which tool created the DLL and when it was created. For your own DLLs, you may want to use #System, and explicitly set it for your compiler; for example: #System.

NOTE: To verify your available calling conventions, execute the code: Module callingConventions out, and read the System Transcript.

An alternative way to identify the DLL function is to use theOrdinalNumber. It is an instance of SmallInteger, and can be used instead of the theProc argument in accessing DLLs. Note that not all DLLs will be accessed this way, and some do not give function names, but simply ordinals; for example: 1 or 100.

The upcoming simple example of how to use these methods is based on calling an external function written in C that looks like the following:

```
LONG MyFunction( INT theInteger, CHAR* theStringPointer) ;
```

Using the first ObjectStudio method looks like the following:

```
| myModule |

myModule :=
    Module
        name: 'THEDLL' "From the file 'THEDLL.DLL'"
        onError: [ "Tell the user an error occurred" ].

myModule
```

Continued

```
    defineExternalProc: #MyFunction
    paramTypes: ( #word #string )
    returnType: #dword
    callingConvention: #System
```

or

```
| myModule |

myModule := Module name: 'THEDLL'. "From the file 'THEDLL.DLL' "

myModule
    defineExternalProc: #MYFUNCTION
    paramTypes: #( #word #string )
    returnType: #dword
    callingConvention: #System
```

If case-sensitivity is turned off for the DLL, all names appear in uppercase. The default setting in the ObjectStudio DLLs is case-sensitivity off, so check your setting if you have any problems, and try uppercase function names if you have problems.

Once you have installed the external functions for the DLL, you may call them from Smalltalk. In order to do so, you must send a message to the instance of Module that was created in the previous example.

```
| myModule returnValue |

myModule := Module name: 'THEDLL'. "From the file 'THEDLL.DLL' "

myModule
    defineExternalProc: #MYFUNCTION
    paramTypes: #( #word #string )
    returnType: #dword
    callingConvention: #System.

returnValue := myModule callExternalProc: #MYFUNCTION with: #( 123 'abc').
```

You can expect that returnValue in this program will be what the external function returns, converted into a Smalltalk object.

Conversions that occur between ObjectStudio Smalltalk and the outside world (C, Pascal, Assembly) allow you to pass an object in Smalltalk to the outside function with automatic conversion to that format. Of course, not all objects are converted into each external type. Valid classes of Smalltalk objects for conversion and their possible types are shown in Table 17.1. Returned values go through a reverse conversion, with a default type as the return. The only types that can be returned are simple, such as byte, word, and dword.

TABLE 17.1 ObjectStudio Classes and the Converted External Data Types

Class Name	External Types
Character	byte, word, dword
SmallInteger	word, dword
LongInteger	word, dword
PMHandle	word, dword
Float	float, double
String	string

Strings and structures cannot be returned. The pointers to these items exist outside the Smalltalk memory space, and cannot be referenced in Smalltalk. In order to pass more complex data back from the DLL, including strings and structures, you must employ the structure mechanism. The class `Structure` provides the functionality necessary to create C style structures in Smalltalk.

An instance of `Structure` can hold many types of data. Table 17.2 provides a list of the types of data fields held in the structure and the appropriate lengths of the fields.

The following Smalltalk program for ObjectStudio Smalltalk interfaces to the test DLL.

```
| myModule returnValue |

myModule := Module name: 'TESTDLL'.

"Module callingConventions inspect."

returnValue := myModule
    defineExternalProc: #_MyFunction
    paramTypes: #{ #word #{ #string #reference} }
```

TABLE 17.2 Data Types Available in ObjectStudio Structures

Element	Size
#byte	1
#double	8
#dword	4
#float	4
#reference	4
#string	0
#structure	0
#word	2

```
      returnType: #dword
      callingConvention: #C.


returnValue := myModule
   defineExternalProc: #_MyFunction1
   paramTypes: #{ #word }
   returnType: #word
   callingConvention: #C.


returnValue := myModule
   defineExternalProc: #_MyFunction2
   paramTypes: #{ #{#float #reference} #{#float #reference} }
   returnType: #float
   callingConvention: #C.


returnValue := myModule
             callExternalProc: #_MyFunction
             params: #{ 2 '10' }.


('MyFunction = ', returnValue) out.


returnValue := myModule
             callExternalProc: #_MyFunction1
             params: #{ 5 }.


('MyFunction1 = ', returnValue) out.


returnValue := myModule
             callExternalProc: #_MyFunction2
             params: #{ 1.22 2.44 } .


('MyFunction2 = ', returnValue) out.


returnValue inspect.


myModule freeModule.


"To determine valid options for dataTypes and callingConventions,
   execute the following code in quotes:"
"
Module dataTypes out.
Module callingConventions out.
"
```

LISTING 17.4 File: TESTDLL.ST. The ObjectStudio Generic DLL code to interface to TESTDLL.DLL

SmalltalkAgents

The External Code Linking Tool (ECLT) is the heart and soul of the SmalltalkAgents external code interface. Since the DLL is still a new invention on the Macintosh, object code must be linked into the environment statically using the ECLT. The primary class of interest in Smalltalk agents for external code is the class `ExternalMethod`. And in particular you should study the methods `selectorType` and NOTES as they have the latest details of the interface.

When creating the external methods, attempting to find an existing method, or learning which methods are already written, you can find all external code modules in a pool called `ExternalCodeModules`. A tool for browsing pool modules allows easy access to `ExternalCodeModules`.

The steps to create an external method in SmalltalkAgents are:

1. Create External Library Spec.
2. Create external code from ECLT menu of Proj.Browser.
3. Create external library glue code.
4. Compile the glue code with the external code as a resource of type ECLT.
5. Install the ECLT resource in the SmalltalkAgents project.

An example of this interface can be seen in the external Musical Instrument Digital Interface (MIDI) class, supplied with the SmalltalkAgents product.

 VisualSmalltalk

To create a VisualSmalltalk External Interface, follow these steps:

1. Create a subclass of `DynamicLinkLibrary`.
2. Create instance methods for each of the external methods to be called.
3. Map external variable types between Smalltalk and C.
4. Create an encapsulation class for your functional piece (typically a subclass of `Object`). This will serve to encapsulate the external functions (hiding the external functions and possible changes to it from the other classes).
5. Write Smalltalk code in the encapsulation class to access and manage external functions. Public methods should be created that do not presume knowledge of the external data types. Private

methods should be created that convert and coerce the data into the correct types and manage the external interface.

6. Test and retest the interface.

Example:

```
DynamicLinkLibrary variableByteSubclass: #TestDLL
classVariableNames: ''
poolDictionaries: ''

myFunction: theInteger string: theString
<api: '_MyFunction' long struct long >
^self invalidArgument

myFunction1: theInteger
<api: '_MyFunction1' long long >
^self invalidArgument

myFunction2: theFloat anotherFloat: theOtherFloat
<api: '_MyFunction2' float float float>
^self invalidArgument

myFunction3: theStruct string: theString stringLength: theStringLength
<api: '_MyFunction3' struct struct long long>
^self invalidArgument
```

Once you've created your interface, it is likely that you will have some problems. In order to determine these problems with the interface, you will need to check the types of arguments sent into the DLL call, whether you are getting return values, and whether changes to the interface or the code affect the parameter. Table 17.3 shows the argument types in Smalltalk, the classes associated with the types, and the associated C language types with their lengths in bytes.

TABLE 17.3 Passed Argument Types in VisualSmalltalk

Argument Type	Object Class	C Type	Length
boolean	Boolean	BOOL	4
double	Float	DOUBLE	8
handle	ExternalHandle	HANDLE	4
long	Integer	LONG	4
self	Object	OOP	4
short	SmallInteger	SHORT	2(4)
struct	ExternalBuffer	PSZ	4
ulong	Integer (positive)	ULONG	4
ushort	SmallInteger (positive)	USHORT	2(4)

Table 17.4 shows the types of information that can be returned from a DLL call. The return type is specified in the definition of the external call; the object class type tells you which class the answered instance will be; and the C type and length show the mapping of returned C argument types that correspond to the Smalltalk types.

VisualAge/IBM Smalltalk

VisualAge contains an entire kit specifically designed to provide a quick and easy interface to external code in both C and COBOL. The external code interface is well documented, and even provides the capability to determine whether the external call is accomplished synchronously (while Smalltalk waits) or asynchronously (while Smalltalk continues processing).

Primitives

The easiest way to create Smalltalk primitives for C code is to use the External Code Library Tool (ECLT) for SmalltalkAgents from QKS. With the tool, you simply select the file to be converted in a dialog box, and you are then presented with a full description of the API. The tool even takes care of linking the code into the system if you are using SmalltalkAgents on Macintosh, PowerMac, or Windows. There are, however, some limitations on what it can do: it won't write any additional code for you to do useful things like placing values into instance or class variables or calling other Smalltalk methods from C.

The second easiest way to create Smalltalk primitives for C code is to use the C Programmer's Object Kit from ParcPlace systems. It will automat-

TABLE 17.4 Returned Argument Types in VisualSmalltalk

Return Type	Object Class	C Type	Length
boolean	Boolean	BOOL	4
double	Float	DOUBLE	8
handle, ulong	String	HANDLE	4
long	Integer	LONG	4
none	UndefinedObject (nil)	VOID	0
short	SmallInteger	SHORT	2
struct	ExternalBuffer	PSZ	4
ulong	Integer (positive)	ULONG	4
ushort	SmallInteger (positive)	USHORT	2

ically create a Smalltalk class and its associated methods by parsing a C header file. Of course, you can do this only if you are using ParcPlace Smalltalk and you are interfacing to C. If you're using ParcPlace and your legacy code isn't in C, it is probably simpler to create a C interface to your code, and then use CPOK.

Issues

The drawback to primitives is not in how they are accessed in Smalltalk, but in the actual writing of the primitive. You cannot simply insert existing C code into a primitive template and go. There are some things that must be planned for when writing the primitive code.

The first dilemma, and the most difficult to get right, is how to deal with the garbage collector. The garbage collector is always running, and can throw away items that may be on the stack if you pop them off the stack before your primitive has finished executing. And because the garbage collector disposes of any unreferenced objects, temporary items that appear on the stack as arguments to your primitive may be garbage collected as they are popped off the stack. A better way to write the primitive is to use the items from the stack by referencing them on the stack, without popping them off the top until the primitive is about to return.

Second, you can call methods written in Smalltalk from the primitive. It is more work than calling them from Smalltalk, but a C interface does exist. It is tricky business, though, because you must create Smalltalk objects, put them on the stack in the right order, construct the message, and evaluate it. You must also keep track of how many items are on the stack, and make use of the returned item from the message send. The better way to do this is to call Smalltalk code from Smalltalk, and only return an appropriate value from the primitive.

The third problem you may encounter has to do with object pointers. In C programming, the programmer ideally is in control of the memory allocation and freeing in the program. The programmer may get a pointer to a data area and save that pointer for use in a later function. The problem occurs when the C programmer saves a pointer to a Smalltalk object. Since Smalltalk is constantly garbage collecting and managing memory, the pointer may not be valid when it is time to use it again. Therefore, the C program cannot store a Smalltalk pointer and assume that it will be valid in the future. Instead, the code must be written to point to an object when it is time to manipulate it.

The final problem is a real hair-puller. It has to do with the flags that are set on the C compiler. In one instance, a week was spent while the "bug" was tracked down. Unlike Smalltalk, C and other languages have options on the compilers that change the way code is compiled and linked. One common error in writing primitives is to have the wrong type of linkage in the generated C code. For example, the IBM C/C++ compiler for OS/2 by default uses an optimized linking algorithm called Optlink. Unfortunately, Smalltalk cannot understand this format, so the proper flag to set the linking to System must be set when compiling the C code.

ObjectStudio

Template—Listing 17.5 is a template for use with ObjectStudio.

```
/********************
 *
 * ObjectStudio primitive template
 *
 ********************/

/* For debugging purposes */
/* Comment this line out when not debugging */
#define DEBUG 1

/* Include the standard enfin library of c type primitive actions */
/* This file contains a wealth of information */
#include "../../enfinlib/enfinlib.h"

/* Primitives are of the following format */
VOID EXPENTRY PrimitiveTemplate (VOID);

/***********************************
 * Function: PrimitiveTemplate
 * Description: Primitive does ....
 * Input(s): Non explicit (uses Smalltalk stack)
 * Output(s): Non explicit (uses Smalltalk stack)
 ***********************************/
VOID EXPENTRY PrimitiveTemplate()
{
/*
 * Expected Stack on Entry: (Top to bottom)
 * argument(s) - optional arguments depending on number expected
 * self - the receiver
 *
 * The assumption is that the arguments have been pre-checked for validity
 * in the Smalltalk environment by a public method before calling the private
 * primitive method.
 */
```

Continued

```
/* Pointers to Smalltalk Objects */
OPTR oArg1, oArg2, oSelf;

#ifdef DEBUG
/* Print to transcript */
Out ("Entering PrimitiveTemplate");
#endif

/* Get the pointer to the form from the top of the stack, but leave the
object on the stack so that it doesn't get garbage collected. */

/* This is for two arguments. Should always start at top and work down. */
oArg2 = PTOS();
oArg1 = PTOS1();
oSelf = PTOS2();
/* If one argument:
   oArg1 = PTOS();
   oSelf = PTOS1();
   If no arguments:
   oSelf = PTOS();
*/

/*
 *
 * Insert your code here....
 *
 */

/* pop argument2 off the stack */
PPop(); //oArg2
/* Stack:
 *    argument1
 *    self
 */

/* pop argument1 off the stack */
PPop(); //oArg1
/* Stack:
 *    self
 */
/* pop self off the stack - only if you're returning something! */
PPop(); //self
/* Stack:
 */

/* push self onto stack - not returning anything else - need default of self
*/
PPush(oSelf);
/* Stack:
 * self
 */
```

Continued

```
#ifdef DEBUG
/* Print to transcript */
Out("Primitive: PrimitiveTemplate Completed!");
#endif


/* self is on the stack, so it will be that argument returned */
/* Very important not to leave more than one item on the stack, and not */
/* to remove too many! */
```

LISTING 17.5   An ObjectStudio primitive template.

Sample Primitive

To demonstrate writing a primitive for ObjectStudio, a sample primitive is presented in Listing 17.6. The function of the primitive is to obtain the pixel rectangle for a GUI object, an instance of a subclass of FormItem, passed in as an argument. This primitive is written in C, like so many for Smalltalk, and was written to query OS/2 for the pixel coordinates. To convert the code to work with Windows, simply replace the pixel querying routines with those for Windows.

```
/********************
 * Sample Primitive for ObjectStudio 4.1
 * This code, along with the sample class file
 * enhances FormItem and its subclasses to return the pixel boundaries
 * of any FormItem widget
 *
 * Written in C for OS/2 2.1
 ********************/

/* Include window defines */
#define INCL_WIN

/* For debugging purposes */
/* Comment this line out when not debugging */
#define DEBUG 1

/* Include the standard enfin library of c type primitive actions */
/* This file contains a wealth of information */
#include "../../enfinlib/enfinlib.h"

/* Define the third indexed variable slot of a formItem as the operating
system handle to the widget */
#define fHWND 3

/* Primitives are of the following format */
VOID EXPENTRY PrimitiveGetPixelRect(VOID);
```

Continued

```
/************************************
 * Function: PrimitiveGetPixelRect
 * Description: Primitive gets the pixels from aFormItem passed as argument
 * Input(s): Non explicit (uses Smalltalk stack)
 * Output(s): Non explicit (uses Smalltalk stack)
 **********************************/
VOID EXPENTRY PrimitiveGetPixelRect()
{
/*
 * Expected Stack on Entry: (Top to bottom)
 * aFormItem - an instance of FormItem (the one we want the pixels from)
 * self - the receiver
 *
 * The assumption is that the arguments have been pre-checked for validity
 * in the Smalltalk environment by a public method before calling the
 * private primitive method.
 */

/* Pointers to Smalltalk Objects */
OPTR oHwnd, oForm, oRect;

/* Operating System Handle to Window */
HWND hwnd;
SWP theSWP;
PSWP pSWP=&theSWP;
POINTL aptlPoint;

#ifdef DEBUG
/* Print to transcript */
Out("Entering PrimitiveGetPixelRect");
#endif

/* Get the pointer to the form from the top of the stack, but leave the object
on the stack so that it doesn't get garbage collected. *

oForm = PTOS();

/* Look inside the indexed storage for aFormItem for the host window handle

oHwnd = ObjVar (oForm, fHWND);

/* Convert the handle to the host native type */
hwnd = (HWND) ObjHandle (oHwnd);

/* Find the class PMRectangle in the global space, "System" */
oRect = GlobalLookup(SymbolHash("PMRectangle"));

/* Put it on the stack */
PPush(oRect);
```

Continued

```
/* Stack:
 * PMRectangle - class (an instance of MetaClass of course)
 * aFormItem
 * self
 */

/* Send Smalltalk message "new" to PMRectangle (already on stack)

*/
PSend(0,SymbolHash("new"));

oRect = PTOS();

/* Stack:
 * aPMRectangle - instance of PMRectangle returned from "new" message
 * aFormItem
 * self
 */

#ifdef DEBUG
/* Print to transcript */
Out("Successfully created a PMRectangle");
#endif

/* Get the window rectangle in pixels */
WinQueryWindowPos (hwnd, pSWP);
/* A good C program should check for an error return here */

#ifdef DEBUG
/* Output to transcript */
Out("TheRect: Left:%d, Bottom:%d, Right:%d, Top:%d /n",
     pSWP->x, pSWP->y, pSWP->cx, pSWP->cy);
#endif DEBUG

/* create a Long as an argument from the integer aptlPoint.x */
PPush(LongAllocate(apt1Point.x));
/* Stack:
 * aXLong - instance of Long for aptlPoint.x
 * aPMRectangle
 * aFormItem
 * self
 */

/* send the message "left" with the above argument to aPMRectangle */
PSend(1,SymbolHash("left:"));
/* Stack:
 * aPMRectangle - instance of PMRectangle returned from left: (^self)
 * aFormItem
 * self
 */
```

Continued

```
/* create a Long as an argument from the integer aptlPoint.y */
PPush(LongAllocate(aptlPoint.y));
/* Stack:
 * aYLong - instance of Long for aptlPoint.y
 * aPMRectangle
 * aFormItem
 * self
 */


/* Send the message #bottom: to aPMRectangle with aLong as the argument */
PSend(1,SymbolHash("bottom:"));
/* Stack:
 * aPMRectangle - instance of PMRectangle returned from bottom: (^self)
 * aFormItem
 * self
 */


/* create a Long as an argument from the integer aptlPoint.cx */
PPush(LongAllocate(aptlPoint.cx));
/* Stack:
 * aCxLong - instance of Long for aptlPoint.cx
 * aPMRectangle
 * aFormItem
 * self
 */


/* Send the message #width: to aPMRectangle with aLong as the argument
PSend(1,SymbolHash("width:"));
/* Stack:
 * aPMRectangle - instance of PMRectangle returned from width: (^self)
 * aFormItem
 * self
 */


/* create a Long as an argument from the integer aptlPoint.cy */
PPush(LongAllocate(aptlPoint.cy));
/* Stack:
 * aCyLong - instance of Long for aptlPoint.cy
 * aPMRectangle
 * aFormItem
 *     self
 */


PSend(1,SymbolHash("height:"));
/* Stack:
 *   aPMRectangle - instance of PMRectangle returned from height: (^self)
 *   aFormItem
 *   self
 */
```

Continued

```
/*
 * We've still got the Rect on the stack, so return.
 * Pop aPMRectangle off the stack, but make no other calls to Smalltalk
 * so that it doesn't get garbage collected!
 */
oRect = PPop();
/* Stack:
 * aFormItem
 * self
 */

/* pop aFormItem off the stack */
PPop(); //oForm
/* Stack:
 * self
 */

/* pop self off the stack */
PPop(); //self
/* Stack:
 */

/* push aPMRectangle back onto the stack */
PPush(oRect);
/* Stack:
 * aPMRectangle
 */

#ifdef DEBUG
/* Print to transcript */
Out("Primitive: PrimitiveGetPixelRect Completed!");
#endif

/* aPMRectangle is on the stack, so it will be that argument returned */
/* Very important not to leave more than one item on the stack, and not */
/* to remove too many! */
```

LISTING 17.6 An ObjectStudio sample primitive.

 VisualSmalltalk

Template and Sample Primitive

A template for creating a primitive for VisualSmalltalk can be found on the CD-ROM. This template can be filled in with the appropriate C code and then compiled and called from the Smalltalk environment. A sample primitive for VisualSmalltalk is also included. This primitive makes use of the primitive template and shows a typical example of the calling mechanism. Smalltalk code is provided to call the primitive.

 VisualWorks

VisualWorks DLL and C Connect is a product available for the VisualWorks Smalltalk version that allows you to access user-written primitives. This toolkit is not required to create primitives, but I don't know how to do it without this kit.

Summary

You have learned in this chapter that the Generic External Interface is limited in the types of return arguments unless you use a structure, that it requires extensive setup code in Smalltalk, and that you should use an additional layer to encapsulate objects and hide external functions. The Generic External Interface can interface to existing DLLs, sometimes without additional external coding, and is easier to implement.

When writing a primitive, you must take into consideration garbage collection, the two memory spaces (Smalltalk and OS), the appropriate way to access Smalltalk objects, and the way to include in-line execution of Smalltalk code.

Both the Generic External Interface and primitives need to link externally compiled object code into Smalltalk, and under Windows, need to be concerned with 16/32-bit "thunking."

18

SQL Databases

The majority of enterprise information is stored in databases, and whether they be flat files, hierarchical databases, or SQL databases, you need to be able to access this information in Smalltalk. In this chapter, some of the approaches to storage and retrieval of database information are discussed, along with relevant issues and a survey of available options, highlighted by examples of accessing SQL databases from Smalltalk.

Types of Databases

As you develop your Smalltalk applications, you may find that you need to interface to one or more databases that exist on the same or a remote machine. The effort required to do this varies greatly. **Object** databases are by far the easiest to interface to your Smalltalk application. They provide a simple way to store and retrieve information in the format most easily managed in Smalltalk: objects. Smalltalk applications that start out with no database storage are most easily interfaced to an object database after the fact.

The **relational** database on the other hand represents information in a way that is not completely compatible with object-oriented programming. In response, techniques have been developed to interface to this extremely widespread type of database, one of which, the object broker, is an extremely effective method for relational databases.

An **object-relational hybrid** database offers some of the attributes of the object database for object-oriented applications, and provides the legacy relational database compatibility. In fact, it can be thought of as a relational database with a built-in object broker.

Flat file databases, like Btrieve and IMS, can be accessed through specialized interfaces, but since they lack the structure of relational databases, they are even poorer candidates for interfacing to object-oriented systems. The data is there and instances of objects can be created based on the fields in the files, but relationships between objects are very difficult to determine due to the lack of relationships between records.

Other types of databases, such as hierarchical databases, are not common enough to have received enough attention, and suffer from a lack of interfaces to Smalltalk. These databases, if they have a relational front end or an ODBC interface, can be used more easily from Smalltalk.

Object Broker

An **object broker,** or **object request broker** (ORB), provides the mechanism by which nonobject sources of information are turned into objects. The mechanism is becoming very widespread, with the Common Object Request Broker Architecture (CORBA) as a requirement in many projects.

Some examples of Smalltalk object brokers include the Synchronicity Mapping Tool for ObjectStudio, the Object Lens product for VisualWorks, and TopLink for several Smalltalks, made by ObjectPeople.

Techniques

Proxies

In Smalltalk, a `Proxy` class can be created for use with any object that might come from an external source. An instance of `Proxy` can serve as a placeholder for the actual object, when the object does not need to be fully retrieved. This provides the object referencing the `Proxy` with some behavior and an object identity that will be replaced by the complete object when it has been retrieved.

Either a generic `Proxy` or specific versions of `Proxy` can be created for each of the objects that will be retrieved from the database. `Proxies` can also be useful when an asynchronous request for an object is outstanding, but processing continues. When the complete representation of the object becomes available, that new object sends itself the `become:` message with the `Proxy` as an argument. In some cases, that technique is not sufficient, as in VisualWorks, so the `Proxy` must be maintained as a message forwarder to the retrieved object. You could overcome this problem if you were able to change the OOP of an object, so that one might be more easily substituted for another, or if proxies were embedded in the Smalltalk virtual machine, neither of which is likely to happen soon.

Asynchronous Requests

Surprisingly, asynchronous requests to database sources are still not standard in many Smalltalk applications. This is due in part to the lack of preemptive multitasking in the operating system, and the lack of preemptive Smalltalk `Threads` and `Processes`.

The biggest advantage of the asynchronous request is that it gets data while the user is doing something else or the program performs some function. This makes it seem as though lengthy request times are shorter, because while the window draws, it takes up a portion of the response time for the request.

Architectures

There are many possible architectures that involve user interface access to database information. The most common in Smalltalk are the Three-Layer Architecture and the Four-Layer Architecture. Sadly, many people who set out to build one of these systems can end up with a Two-Layer Architecture if they are not diligent about the separation of the layers.

The layers in these architectures consist of Database, Business, Application, and GUI, as defined here:

◆ The Database Layer provides access to the database from Smalltalk. It can be as simple as a SQL interface, or as complex as an object broker.
◆ The Business Layer, or Domain Layer, provides integrity of the data retrieved from and stored to the database. The functionality of this layer is similar to the **relational integrity** (RI) of a relational database.
◆ The Application Layer provides combinations of business classes and information that may be important to this application, but not others. This is where the high-level business rules should be placed,

insulating them from changing object/relational schemas and validity rules.
♦ The Graphical User Interface (GUI) Layer provides presentation and user interaction services. It should provide the best possible functionality for the user and allow the Application and Business Layers to handle the validity and rules for the application.

The following shows the breakdowns of these architectures:

Two-Layer Architecture

Layer 1: Database
Layer 2: GUI

Three-Layer Architecture

Layer 1: Database
Layer 2: Business
Layer 3: GUI

Four-Layer Architecture

Layer 1: Database
Layer 2: Business
Layer 3: Application
Layer 4: GUI

How to Access a SQL Database

The following is a workspace that provides a simple example of access to a SQL Database for VisualSmalltalk. Inspect line by line to observe the process.

```
J := DBIIBMDB2 new.
J connectDataSourceName: 'Digitalk DB2'.
J connectDatabase: 'SAMPLE'.
J connectUserId: 'USERID'.
J connectPassword: 'PASSWORD'.
J connect.

J1 := J currentDatabase.

J2 := J1 executeSQLReadAll: 'SELECT NAME FROM SYSIBM.SYSTABLES'.

J2 := J1 executeSQLReadAll: 'SELECT * FROM SYSIBM.SYSCOLUMNS'.
```

Continued

```
J2 := J1 executeSQLReadAll: 'SELECT NAME FROM SYSIBM.SYSCOLUMNS WHERE
TBNAME = ''SYSCOLUMNS'' '.

J2 := J1 executeSQLReadAll: 'SELECT NAME FROM SYSIBM.SYSCOLUMNS WHERE
TBNAME = ''ORGANIZATION'' '.

J2 := J1 executeSQLReadAll: 'SELECT TBNAME, NAME FROM SYSIBM.SYSCOLUMNS
WHERE TBNAME IN ( SELECT NAME FROM SYSTEM.SYSTABLES )'.

J2 inspect.

J disconnect.

J := nil.
J1 := nil.
J2 := nil.

theDB

theDB := AAMyDatabase new.
theDB connectToDatabase.
(theDB databaseColumnsForTable: 'ADWOBJECT') inspect.
"theDB databaseTablesAndColumns inspect."
theDB disconnectFromDatabase.

AAMyDatabaseView new open

CalculationWindow4 new open

AAMyDatabaseView allInstances inspect

!DBITimeStamp methods !

printSQLOn: aStream
    aStream
        nextPut: $';
        nextPutAll: (self date year printPadZerosTo: 4) ;nextPut: $-;
        nextPutAll: (self date monthIndex printPadZerosTo: 2) ;nextPut: $-;
        nextPutAll: (self date dayOfMonth printPadZerosTo: 2) ;nextPut: $-;
        nextPutAll: (self time hours printPadZerosTo: 2); nextPut: $.;
        nextPutAll: (self time minutes printPadZerosTo: 2); nextPut: $.;
        nextPutAll: (self time seconds printPadZerosTo: 2); nextPut: $.;
        nextPutAll: (self microseconds printPadZerosTo: 6);"nextPut: $.;"
        nextPut: $'
! !
```

LISTING 18.1 An example of connecting to a SQL database from Visual-Smalltalk using the relational database interface.

A more complex example of SQL database access is shown in Listing 18.2. This program reads the contents of a database into memory, converts the data, and writes the data to a different database.

```
"DB2 MVS portion"
myDBM := DBIIBMDB2 new.
myDBM connectDataSourceName: 'Digitalk DB2';
    connectDatabase: 'DB2TEST';
    connectUserId: 'PLETZKE';
    connectPassword: 'JON1';
    connect.

myDatabase := myDBM currentDatabase.
myDatabase setSmalltalkColumnFormat.

myResultA := (myDatabase executeSQL: 'SELECT * FROM USERID.SAMPLE')
asOrderedCollection.
myResult := (myDatabase executeSQL: 'SELECT * FROM USERID.SAMPLE WHERE AGE >
0') asOrderedCollection.

myResult inspect.

myColumnInfoA := myDatabase executeSQLReadAll: 'select tbname, name,
coltype, length, colno from sysibm.syscolumns where tbname =
''USERID.SAMPLE'' order by colno'
myColumnInfo := myDatabase executeSQLReadAll: 'select tbname, name,
coltype, length, colno from sysibm.syscolumns where tbname =
''USERID.SAMPLE'' order by colno'

myDBM disconnect.

"DB2/2"
myDBM := DBIIBMDB2 new.
myDBM connectDataSourceName: 'Digitalk DB2';
    connectDatabase: 'DB22TEST';
    connectUserId: 'USERID';
    connectPassword: 'PASSWORD';
    connect.

myDatabase := myDBM currentDatabase.
myDatabase setSmalltalkColumnFormat.

myResultB := (myDatabase executeSQL: 'SELECT * FROM USERID.SAMPLE')
asOrderedCollection.
myResult2 := (myDatabase executeSQL: 'SELECT * FROM USERID.SAMPLE WHERE AGE
> 0') asOrderedCollection.

myResult2 inspect.
```

Continued

```
myColumnInfoB := myDatabase executeSQLReadAll: 'select tbname, name, coltype,
length, colno from sysibm.syscolumns where tbname = ''USERID.SAMPLE'' order
by colno'
myColumnInfo2 := myDatabase executeSQLReadAll: 'select tbname, name, coltype,
length, colno from sysibm.syscolumns where tbname = ''USERID.SAMPLE'' order
by colno'

myDBM disconnect.
"PARSING"
myResultA do: [ :row |
     myOldRow := row.
     myNewRow := Array new: 15.

     myNewRow
          at:    1 put:  (myOldRow at: 1);
          at:    2 put:  1;
          at:    3 put:  (myOldRow at: 2);
          at:    4 put:  (myOldRow at: 4);
          at:    5 put:  (myOldRow at: 5);
          at:    6 put:  (myOldRow at: 6);
          at:    7 put:  (myOldRow at: 7);
          at:    8 put:  (myOldRow at: 8);
          at:    9 put:  (myOldRow at: 9);
          at:    10 put: (myOldRow at: 10);
          at:    11 put: (myOldRow at: 11);
          at:    12 put: (myOldRow at: 12);
          at:    13 put: (myOldRow at: 13);
          at:    14 put: DBISQLNull;
          at:    15 put: DBISQLNull.

     myString := (myNewRow asSQLDelimitedList: $,).
     myString := myString copyFrom: 1 to: (myString size - 2).

     [myDatabase executeSQL: 'INSERT INTO USERID.SAMPLE ( ', ((myColumnInfo2
collect: [ :each | each at: 2 ]) asSpaceDelimitedList: $,),' ) VALUES (',
myString , ')'.
     ] on: Error do: [ ].
]
myDatabase executeSQLReadAll: 'SELECT * FROM USERID.SAMPLE '.

myResult := myResult copyFrom: 2 to: (myResult size).

myResult size
```

LISTING 18.2 An example of using Smalltalk as a data conversion/migration tool between DB2 on MVS and DB2/2.

Listing 18.3 provides a graphical database viewer that displays the contents of SQL database tables.

```
Object
   subclass: #DatabaseModel
   instanceVariableNames: 'myDBMS myDatabase'
   classVariableNames: ''
   poolDictionaries: ''
   category: 'DatabaseBrowser'!


ViewManager
   subclass: #DatabaseView
   instanceVariableNames:   'aaMyDatabase   columnPane   listPane   statusPane
includeLabelsInWidth'
   classVariableNames: ''
   poolDictionaries: ''
   category: 'DatabaseBrowser'!


Object
   subclass: #TableModel
   instanceVariableNames: 'theTable theRows theColumns theUserID myDatabase'
   classVariableNames: ''
   poolDictionaries: ''
   category: 'DatabaseBrowser'!


ViewManager
   subclass: #TableView
   instanceVariableNames: 'theTableModel'
   classVariableNames: ''
   poolDictionaries: ''
   category: 'DatabaseBrowser'!


!DatabaseModel methodsFor: 'as yet unclassified' !


connectToDatabase
   "Public - connect to My database"

   myDatabase := self getGlobalDatabase.
   myDatabase isNil ifTrue:
      [ myDBMS := DBIIBMDB2 new.
      myDBMS connectDataSourceName: 'Digitalk DB2'.
      myDBMS connectDatabase: 'SAMPLE'.
      myDBMS connectUserId: 'USERID'.
      myDBMS connectPassword: 'PASSWORD'.
      myDBMS connect.
      myDatabase := myDBMS currentDatabase. ]!


database
   ^myDatabase!


databaseColumnLabels
   "Public - answer all column labels for SYSIBM.SYCOLUMNS"
```

Continued

```
      ^(myDatabase executeSQL: 'SELECT NAME, COLNO FROM SYSIBM.SYSCOLUMNS
WHERE' , ' TBNAME = ''SYSCOLUMNS'' ORDER BY COLNO ')
asOrderedCollection
      collect:
          [:eachRow |
          eachRow at: 'NAME'].!


databaseColumnsForTable: aTable
    "Public - answer all column names for aTable"


^myDatabase executeSQLReadAll:
    'SELECT * FROM SYSIBM.SYSCOLUMNS WHERE',
       ' TBNAME = ', aTable printString, ' ORDER BY COLNO '.
!


databaseTables
    "Public - Answer names of all tables in database"


^myDatabase executeSQLReadAll: 'SELECT NAME FROM SYSIBM.SYSTABLES'
!


databaseTablesAndColumns
    "Public - Answer names of all tables and columns"


^myDatabase executeSQLReadAll: 'SELECT TBNAME, NAME FROM
SYSIBM.SYSCOLUMNS WHERE TBNAME IN ( SELECT NAME FROM SYSIBM.SYSTABLES
)'.
!


disconnectFromDatabase
    "Public - Last step, unhooks database connection"


    (myDatabase = self getGlobalDatabase)
    ifFalse:
       [ myDBMS disconnect.
       myDBMS := nil.
       myDatabase := nil.
       ].!


getGlobalDatabase
    "Public - Answer the global database if it exists"


    ^ServiceRegistry globalRegistry serviceNamed: #database!


syscolumnsColumns
    "Public - Answer names of all column parameters in syscolumns"


^myDatabase executeSQLReadAll: 'SELECT NAME FROM SYSIBM.SYSCOLUMNS
WHERE TBNAME = ''SYSCOLUMNS'' '! !
```

Continued

```
!DatabaseView methodsFor: 'as yet unclassified' !

clickedOnTable: aPane
    "Private - Clicked on a Table - update the column display"

    | temp |
    statusPane
        contents: 'connecting...';
        refreshAll.
    aaMyDatabase connectToDatabase.
    statusPane
        contents: 'searching...';
        refreshAll.
    aPane columnLabels: (aaMyDatabase databaseColumnLabels); refresh.
    listPane selectedItem notNil
        ifTrue:
            [temp := (aaMyDatabase databaseColumnsForTable: (listPane
selectedItem contents)).
            self setContentsFor: aPane using: temp.
            aPane refresh.
            ].
    statusPane
        contents: 'disconnecting...';
        refreshAll.
    aaMyDatabase disconnectFromDatabase.
    statusPane
        contents: 'done!!';
        refreshAll.!


contents
    "Private - change the table display to width of contents only"

includeLabelsInWidth := false.
self clickedOnTable: columnPane.!


contentsAndLabels
    "Private - change the table display to width of contents and labels"

includeLabelsInWidth := true.
self clickedOnTable: columnPane.!


createView

    | topPane |

    self
        addView:
            ((topPane := self topPaneClass new)
            owner: self;
            labelWithoutPrefix: 'Database Schema Viewer').          Continued
```

```
        topPane
            addSubpane:
                ((statusPane := TextPane new)
                setName: #statusPane;
                removeVerticalScrollbarStyle;
                removeHorizontalScrollbarStyle;
                framingBlock:
                    [:box |
                    (box leftTop down: 0) extentFromLeftTop: (box width @ (ButtonFont
height + 6))]).
        topPane
            addSubpane:
                ((columnPane := "ListPane" PARTSTablePanePart new)
                setName: #columnPane;
            when: #needsContents
                send: #clickedOnTable:
                to: self
                with: columnPane;
            font: Font fixedSystemFont;
            propertyNumberOfColumns: 16;
            propertyNumberOfRows: 100;
            framingBlock:
                [:box |
                (box leftTop down: (box height // 3) + (ButtonFont height + 6))
extentFromLeftTop: (box width @ (box height - ((box height // 3) + (ButtonFont
height + 6))))]).

        topPane
            addSubpane:
                ((listPane := ListPane new)
                setName: #tablePane;
                when: #needsContents
                    send: #databaseTables:
                    to: self
                    with: listPane;
                when: #changed:
                    send: #update
                    to: columnPane;
                framingBlock:
                    [:box |
                    (box leftTop down: (ButtonFont height + 6))
extentFromLeftTop: (box width @ (box height - (ButtonFont height + 6) //
3))]).

        self menuWindow addMenu:
                ( ( Menu
                    labels: '~Domain Object Generator\Rows' withCrs
                    lines: #()
                    selectors: #( generateDomainObject viewRows) )
                        title: '~View';
                        owner: self;
                        yourself );
```

Continued

```
                        addMenu:
                        ( ( Menu
                            labels: '~Contents\Contents and ~Labels' withCrs
                            lines: #()
                            selectors: #( contents contentsAndLabels ) )
                                title: '~Column Width';
                                owner: self;
                                yourself )

    !

databaseTables: aPane
    "Private - Update aPane contents with database tables"

    statusPane contents: 'connecting...'.
    aaMyDatabase connectToDatabase.
    statusPane contents: 'searching...'.
    aPane contents: aaMyDatabase databaseTables.
    statusPane contents: 'disconnecting...'.
    aaMyDatabase disconnectFromDatabase.
    statusPane contents: 'done!!'.
    !

initialize
    "Private - initialize the object and associate AAMyDatabase instance"

    aaMyDatabase := DatabaseModel new.
    includeLabelsInWidth := true.
    ^super initialize!

open

    self createView. "create a View for this application"
    self openWindow. "open the application window "
    !

selectedTable
    "Public - Answer the currently selected table as a string"

    ^(listPane selectedItem contents) at: 1!

setContentsFor: aPane
using: theContents
    "Private - Set the contents for a pane, using the appropriate method for
the width type"

    includeLabelsInWidth
        ifTrue: [aPane contentsToFitWithLabels: theContents]
        ifFalse: [aPane contentsToFit: theContents]!
```

Continued

```
viewRows
    TableModel new databaseModel: aaMyDatabase; table: (self selectedTable) ;
view.! !


!TableModel methodsFor: 'as yet unclassified' !

columnNames
    "Public - answer all column labels for theTable"


    ^theColumns isNil
       ifTrue:
          [(myDatabase executeSQL: 'SELECT NAME, COLNO FROM SYSIBM.SYSCOLUMNS
WHERE' , ' TBNAME = ' , theTable printString , ' ORDER BY COLNO ')
asOrderedCollection
             collect:
                [:eachRow |
                eachRow at: 'NAME'].
          ]!

databaseModel: aDatabaseModel
    "Public - Answer my database class"


    myDatabase := aDatabaseModel database!

initialize
    "Public - Initialize based on theTable, to retrieve theRows and theColumns
from the database"


    theUserID := (((myDatabase executeSQL: 'SELECT TBCREATOR FROM
SYSIBM.SYSCOLUMNS WHERE' , ' TBNAME = ' , theTable printString)
asOrderedCollection
       collect:
             [:eachRow |
             eachRow at: 'TBCREATOR']) first trimBlanks).
    !


rows
    "Public - answer all rows for theTable"


    ^theRows isNil
       ifTrue:
          [self initialize.
          self rows: ((myDatabase executeSQL: ('SELECT * FROM ' , theUserID ,
'.' , theTable)) asOrderedCollection)]
       ifFalse:
          [theRows]!

rows: myRows
    "Public - Set all rows for theTable"
```

Continued

```
    ^theRows := myRows
!

table: aTableString
    "Public - Set the viewed table to the table represented by aTableString"

    theTable := aTableString.
!

view
    "Public - Open a view on the TableModel"

    TableView new openOn: self.! !

!TableView methodsFor: 'as yet unclassified' !

createView

    | topPane columnPane |
    self
        addView:
            ((topPane := self topPaneClass new)
            owner: self;
            labelWithoutPrefix: 'Table Viewer').
    topPane
        addSubpane:
            ((columnPane := PARTSTablePanePart new)
            setName: #columnPane;
            when: #needsContents
                send: #rowContents:
                to: self
                with: columnPane;
            font: Font fixedSystemFont;
            propertyNumberOfColumns: 1;
            propertyNumberOfRows: 1;
            framingBlock:
                [:box |
                (box leftTop down: 0) extentFromLeftTop: (box width @ (box height
)) ]).
    self menuWindow
        addMenu:
            ((Menu
                labels: '~Save to Database\New Row\Delete Row' withCrs
                lines: #()
                selectors: #(saveToDatabase newRow deleteRow))
            title: '~Data';
            owner: self;
            yourself)!

newRow
```

Continued

```
          "Private - add a new row to the display and the data model"

           | theRows |
          theRows := theTableModel rows.
          theRows notNil
             ifTrue: [ "theTableModel rows:" ((theRows add: (theRows last deepCopy))
        "deepCopy")].
          theTableModel rows inspect.
           !

      openOn: aTableModel
          "Public - Open a TableView on aTableModel"

          theTableModel := aTableModel.
          self createView.
          self openWindow.!

      rowContents: aPane
          "Private - Place the contents of the rows into aPane"

          aPane propertyNumberOfColumns: (theTableModel columnNames size).
          aPane columnLabels: (theTableModel columnNames ); refresh.

          aPane contentsToFitWithLabels: (theTableModel rows).! !
      DatabaseModel comment: '"This provides session level access to some simple
      SQL stuff. I use it to look at the Schema using AAMyDatabaseView. "'!
      DatabaseView comment: '"I use this to view my schema.

      Execute:

      DatabaseView new open.

      To initialize the Framework DB connection and use it, first execute:

      DatabaseView initializeEnvironment.
           "'!
```

LISTING 18.3 A graphical database viewer.

Summary

Database access is important in Smalltalk applications. Most Smalltalk applications will continue to access existing relational, flat file, and hierarchical databases that exist in mainframes, and this process consumes much time and effort during application development. But it can be simplified as remote Smalltalk options from Gemstone and IBM become more mainstream. The Gemstone product provides remote Smalltalk execution on the database server for both object and relational databases, and IBM provides Smalltalk/MVS for use with their series of mainframes. If you do not need a SQL database, you may be able to use object databases to store your objects, the topic of the next chapter titled External Storage and Persistent Objects.

19

External Storage and Persistent Objects

Storing information from the Smalltalk environment can be accomplished in two ways. It can be stored as a textual representation, which is done for much of the development source code and for file-outs. The other way is to store the objects in a binary fashion to disk, a network, or a database. In this chapter, we will explore some of the concepts associated with storing objects outside the image, including:

+ binary storage of objects
+ re-creating objects by storing text
+ object databases

Saving to Files

Often, during development of a program, you want the functionality to save information generated during the execution of the program. It seems simple enough—to store information to a file—and occurs each time you save the image during development. But the user of your application cannot save the image; the image that is delivered to your user (unless he or she is also a Smalltalk developer) remains in the same state as the day you shipped it. The data must be stored in some other way, as a piece of an image in a binary or text format.

Binary Storage

Binary storage has the advantage of providing fast and compact storage of objects. It also comes "out of the box" with many of the Smalltalks, and is able to store any object immediately. The format can store references from one object to another and the complete reference tree of objects, everything down to the simplest pieces, like characters, integers, symbols, or to points that are defined to go no further.

One of the dangers in using this mechanism, though, is that you can inadvertently store the entire image to a secondary file if you are not careful about which objects are referenced in your instances. The mechanism may also appear to be slow if the amount of information stored is excessive. For example, you may wish to only store the information about a Person, but because of the references that aPerson holds, you end up storing their Company, and this company has a thousand other people who must be stored!

Saving the Image

All referenced objects are stored in the image when you save the image; unreferenced objects are garbage collected. The one global, Smalltalk (System in ObjectStudio), contains references to objects that contain references to other objects, and so on. If this object tree does not contain an object, then it will not be stored, but instead will be garbage collected at the next opportunity.

The number of objects stored in SmalltalkAgents when the image is saved approaches 50,000, a large number that represents the entire state of the image in RAM just before saving. This is the fastest way to store binary information because it stores everything, and no time is spent computing the extent of the information saved. Thus, the performance of a binary save will be lower than a complete image save. The different binary object storage mechanisms include BOSS, ObjectFiler, PIPO, and SOM.

BOSS

VisualWorks Smalltalk stores binary objects to a disk file using the Binary Object Streaming Service (BOSS). This subsystem of functionality is included with the basic VisualWorks package, and can be used to store program information, or even programming definitions while you work! These files are not compatible with any other version of Smalltalk, although you can take one from any VisualWorks platform and load it into any other VisualWorks platform.

OBJECTFILER

The ObjectFiler subsystem in VisualSmalltalk also provides binary object storage to disk files and other streams. The format is not portable to any other Smalltalk, nor is it directly portable from a Windows to an OS/2 VisualSmalltalk application.

PIPO

Quasar Knowledge System has a binary storage mechanism called Platform Independent Portable Object (PIPO). This mechanism was modelled after the Apple BENTO (that's a Japanese lunchbox for us gaijin) that was the basis for OpenDoc. PIPO has all the functionality, and any object in the system can be told to archive itself and saved to disk, and likewise can be brought into the system from a file.

SOM/DSOM

You can also use the SOM/DSOM toolkit, available with the IBM Smalltalk/ VisualAge products to store objects to disk files or across servers to other applications. One big benefit of using SOM/DSOM or another standard format is that one version of Smalltalk can share objects with another, or even share objects with a C++ or other enabled application.

Text

The second way to make your objects persistent is to make them *almost* persistent. You do this by creating a textual representation of the object that can be evaluated or filed-in to the image in order to create an *equivalent* object with a different *identity*. The only difference between the objects restored using this method and using a binary or object database method is that the objects are not *identical*, but only *equivalent*. This means that all the information in the object can be the same, but that the *identity* of the object, noted by its object-oriented pointer (OOP), is not the same.

When attempting to follow this approach, you must first identify the parts of the object to be stored, which must be re-created, and determine how this should be done: a string as a string, a symbol as symbol, and references to other objects by querying a manager of instances of that object.

Once the information is identified, a file-out routine must be created. Usually, this is found in a class as the `storeOn:` method. The method takes an instance of a `Stream` as an argument and writes a textual representation of the object on the stream. When evaluated, or filed-in, this text will re-create the object faithful to the code in the `storeOn:` method.

Examples of this abound in Smalltalk. Consider the `Dictionary` class. It has a `storeOn:` method, and using this method (by executing `Smalltalk storeOn: Transcript`), your `Transcript` will be filled with all sorts of wonderful information that exists in the `SystemDictionary` subclass of `Dictionary`. If you were to evaluate this code, you would have an object that is a nearly identical representation of Smalltalk. (Note: This experiment should be performed on a saved image, so that if problems occur, you can recover. The operation is also unlikely to completely succeed because recursive `storeOn:` is not allowed.)

Using an Object Database

We've looked at storing objects in the image, in binary files, and in text files. And in previous chapters, we discussed the storage of objects in relational databases via an object brokering mechanism like TopLink from Object-People or Syncronicity from VMark. Here we will explore the concept of storing objects into an object database.

With object databases, no standard exists for how the objects are stored, what languages can be used to access the objects, the query language for the object database, or the connection mechanism. In short, each object database is significantly different from the next. Standards are emerging, but slowly. For this reason, we will focus on the object databases that are "Smalltalk-friendly."

When using an object database with Smalltalk, the definition of the database's schema is really no different than the model of the application in Smalltalk. If you use instances of a class to store information, then you can store instances of that class in an object database. If you use an `OrderedCollection` or a `Dictionary`, you can store those in the object database. Some OODBs even supply special versions of `Dictionary` and `OrderedCollection` that are more efficient when used with the object database. When classes change in the Smalltalk image, tools exist that can either automatically or manually migrate the existing objects in the OODB to the new version of the class.

Object databases include all the good stuff that you have become accustomed to having in a relational database: concurrent access, record locking, transaction processing including two-phase commit, cursors, security, and so on. They offer more, too. Since there is no mapping between the objects and some other way of storing them, the relationships between the objects can be maintained, and so can the identity of the object. This allows the application to find related objects easily and efficiently, as compared to a relational join.

An object database is also able to garbage collect unused data, as configured by the administrator. This means that unused data (unreferenced, really) will be removed from the database. This can occur during nonpeak periods so that users of the system will not be affected.

Although this all sounds really great, it's not for every application because it cannot drop into place for legacy applications. But object databases can provide a much easier environment in which to program your database application, and more efficient access for those operations that use relationships. In the following sections we'll look at two commercial examples of object databases: Tensegrity, from Polymorphic, and Gemstone from Gemstone.

Tensegrity

Using Tensegrity for object storage is easy. You wrap familiar Smalltalk expressions in a block and use the message `atomic` to ensure a good two-phase commit. You'll notice that all this code looks familiar, and that classes respond to a new message `newPersistent` that is like a `new` but makes the instance OODB-friendly.

```
initialize
    | aDictionary |
    "Wrap the entire block to make it an atomic transaction"
    [
        "Create a container"
        StorageContainer create.
        "Make my Smalltalk class persistent"
        aDictionary := Dictionary newPersistent.
    ] atomic.

createBook
    | newBook |
    newBook := BookDialog new open.
    newBook isNil ifFalse: [
        "Make the book persistent and use two phase commit (atomic)"
        [MyLibrary at: newBook title put: newBook persistent] atomic.
    ].
```

Gemstone

To get a feel for what Gemstone is like, the following is a thumbnail sketch on how to index and use `SelectBlocks` in Gemstone to improve the speed of lookups.

Let's assume we have a domain object `LaptopMemoryPart` with attributes `vendor`, `capacity`, `parity`, and `modelNumber`. Let's also assume that we model our domain objects to hold onto all instances of themselves in a class variable. In Gemstone we would first define our domain object:

```
Object     subclass: 'LaptopMemoryPart'
    instVarNames: #('vendor' 'capacity' 'parity' 'modelNumber')
    classVars: #('AllLaptopMemoryParts')
    classInstVars: #()
    poolDictionaries: []
    inDictionary: SupportDictionary
    constrants:
    isModifiable: false.
```

This creates our domain object, and since the `isModifiable` parameter is `false`, we can now create instances of this class. In Gemstone, only classes that are invariant can be instantiated.

Next we create our collection class as a subclass of a Gemstone `Set`:

```
Set    subclass: 'AllLaptopMemoryPartsSet'
    instVarNames: #()
    classVars: #()
    classInstVars: #()
    poolDictionaries: []
    inDictionary: SupportDictionary
    constrants: (LaptopMemoryPart)
    isModifiable: false.
```

Notice how we constrain this particular subclass of a Gemstone `Set` to hold only instances of the class `LaptopMemoryPart`. This allows Gemstone to do some optimizing under the covers when it comes time for indexing and querying.

In our class initialization methods for `LaptopMemoryPart`, we initialize `AllLaptopMemoryParts` to be an instance of `AllLaptopMemoryParts-Set`. We then proceed to "seed" or fill this set with our `LaptopMemoryPart` instances. Once we have our `AllLaptopMemoryParts` seeded, we can create an index on it. We will use the instance variable `modelNumber` as the index key (assume an accessor for the class variable exists):

```
LaptopMemoryPart allLaptopMemoryParts createIdentityIndexOn: 'modelNumber'.
```

This creates an identity index on the instance variable path for `model-Number`.

Now, let's say that we want to find the laptop memory part whose model number is 19281. Using a regular enumeration block, we might say:

```
LaptopMemoryPart allLaptopMemoryParts detect: [:part | part modelNumber ==
19281].
```

This expression will enumerate through the set to find the correct part. But Gemstone provides a special block called a `SelectBlock` (delimited by { and }) that restricts the statements allowed in the block, but allows for faster queries since `SelectBlocks` will use an index if one exists. So, our example using a `SelectBlock` looks like this:

```
LaptopMemoryPart allLaptopMemoryParts detect: {:part | part.modelNumber ==
19281}.
```

First, notice that the curly braces tip off the fact that we are using a Gemstone `SelectBlock` (try this in the client Smalltalk, and we would get a nasty error message during compilation). The statements inside a `Select-Block` are restricted to conjoined predicates using dot notation. The left side of the predicate must be an instance variable path upon which we are basing our query. In our example, we have only one instance variable in our path (`modelNumber`); however, composite objects with `Collections` can have many more. Since we created an index on this instance variable, Gemstone would execute this `SelectBlock's` query using our index to improve the lookup time. The exact level of improvement depends on several factors, but generally is quite noticeable for large collections.

Summary

You have seen several ways to store your Smalltalk objects: as binary, as text, and as binary in an object database. Perhaps you are even tempted to try out an object database in the near future after seeing how simple it is to write code that interfaces to two very popular object databases. New technology like this is very enabling, and more of it is described in the next chapter on Internet and Web Applications.

20

Internet and Web Applications

When most people talk about the Internet or the World Wide Web, they think of browsers like Mosaic or Netscape connecting to servers all over the world. The Internet contains more than just these browsers, which are primarily HyperText Markup Language (HTML) viewers. Other Internet protocols like Telnet, File Transfer Protocol (FTP), Network News Transfer Protocol (NNTP), Finger, Trivial File Transfer Protocol (TFTP), and Simple Mail Transfer Protocol (SMTP) have been around for years, dating back to the days when the Internet was little more than the National Science Foundation Net (NSFNet) or the U.S. Government's Advanced Research Projects Administration Network (ARPANet). These protocols are primarily for character terminal access and require a true network expert to master. Newer protocols, like Gopher and HyperText Transfer Protocol (HTTP) are the primary constituents of the new generation of Internet applications, and will be discussed, with examples of their use, in this chapter. You will learn about:

- ♦ components of the World Wide Web
- ♦ an implementation of a Gopher client
- ♦ Smalltalk Web servers

- ♦ Smalltalk Web clients
- ♦ commercial implementations of Smalltalk servers
- ♦ an implementation of a simple Smalltalk server
- ♦ an implementation of a simple Smalltalk client

Components of the Web

The Internet and the World Wide Web are simply combinations of some specified protocols. It is helpful to study these protocols in order to understand the transport of information across the Internet using TCP/IP as the base, HTTP and Gopher as the application protocols, and the information that can be transported, like HTML, Java, and Smalltalk source code and objects.

Transport

In order for information to move between one place and another, several layers of transport exist between the two points, the most basic of which is the physical connection that may be wire, telephone, or some combination of both. On top of this is a layer that defines the bits and bytes, the basic component of the digital language of computers. The next layers are composed of the transport of information across the digital wire and the splitting of information into pieces, called packets. TCP/IP is an example of these types of protocols. On top of the TCP/IP layer, application protocols like HTTP and Gopher control the transmission of useful information between two points.

TCP/IP

The Transmission Control Protocol and Internet Protocol together comprise the language of the Internet: TCP/IP. This simple set of protocols provides the necessary communication mechanism between two points on the Internet, and is used by applications that live on the Internet.

HTTP

HyperText Transfer Protocol provides for standard World Wide Web client/server communication. It specifies the states of the server and browser, the method in which the two communicate. The Universal Resource Locator (URL) is an address to a document on the World Wide Web. A few examples of URLs are:

```
http://www.mordor.com/jpletzke
http://www.mordor.com/jpletzke/njsug.html
http://192.192.192.1:80/anydoc.html
```

HTTP commonly uses a standard port number for communications. While any port is acceptable, browsers will generally try to connect to port number 80 on the server machine. This port can be used as the only connection point, or several ports can be used with the port number as part of the URL.

HTTP specifies that a server will listen on this socket, and once a connection has been established, receive a request for an HTML document, respond with that document, and close that connection. Similarly, the client will open a connection to an address, send a request for an HTML document, await the response, wait for the connection to be closed, and then display the document to the user.

Gopher

Gopher "goes for" documents. Gopher became available as a protocol before HTTP/HTML. It seemed as though it might become the standard for Internet communications because it shares in the notion of links to other sites, but it does not provide as slick an interface as the Web browsers, and is falling in popularity. ParcPlace, before the ParcPlace-Digitalk merger, maintained an Internet site called ParcBench that was a Gopher server. It has now been switched to a HTTP server, but the Gopher server can still be used for retrieval.

Some of the fallout from the Gopher standard has to do with the technology and the way the standard was managed. A simple Gopher client application is presented in Listing 20.1, courtesy of IBM, for the IBM Smalltalk/VisualAge product.

```
"    NAME        gopher.st
     AUTHOR        pmuellr@vnet.ibm.com (Patrick Mueller)
     FUNCTION      a simple Gopher client for IBM Smalltalk
     ST-VERSIONS   IBM Smalltalk/VisualAge 2.0
     PREREQUISITES Communications Feature for IBM Smalltalk
     CONFLICTS     nothing I know of
     DISTRIBUTION  world
     VERSION       1.3
     DATE          03/01/95

SUMMARY Gopher

Included is an application for IBM Smalltalk/VisualAge 2.0 that implements a
Gopher client. Requires the Communications feature for IBM Smalltalk/
VisualAge 2.0, for the tcp/ip socket wrappers.           Continued
```

```
Very minimal. Designed to show simple example of Common Widgets and tcp/ip
socket programming.

Patrick Mueller
"!

Application create: #GopherApp with:
        (#( AbtTCPBaseApp CommonWidgets EtBaseTools Kernel)
            collect: [:each | Smalltalk at: each ifAbsent: [
                self error: 'Not all of the prerequisites are loaded']])!


GopherApp becomeDefault!
Object subclass: #Gopher
    instanceVariableNames: 'listWidget textWidget shellWidget data menuStack '
    classVariableNames: ''
    poolDictionaries: 'CwConstants CldtConstants CgConstants '!


GopherApp becomeDefault!
Object subclass: #GopherItem
    instanceVariableNames: 'display selector host port data '
    classVariableNames: ''
    poolDictionaries: 'CwConstants CldtConstants CgConstants '!


GopherApp becomeDefault!
GopherItem subclass: #GopherItemGif
    instanceVariableNames: ''
    classVariableNames: ''
    poolDictionaries: ''!


GopherApp becomeDefault!
GopherItem subclass: #GopherItemMenu
    instanceVariableNames: ''
    classVariableNames: ''
    poolDictionaries: ''!


GopherApp becomeDefault!
GopherItemMenu subclass: #GopherItemMenuReturn
    instanceVariableNames: ''
    classVariableNames: ''
    poolDictionaries: ''!


GopherApp becomeDefault!
GopherItemMenu subclass: #GopherItemSearch
    instanceVariableNames: ''
    classVariableNames: ''
    poolDictionaries: ''!


GopherApp becomeDefault!
GopherItem subclass: #GopherItemText
    instanceVariableNames: ''
```

Continued

```
        classVariableNames: ''
        poolDictionaries: ''!

GopherApp becomeDefault!
GopherItemText subclass: #GopherItemUnknown
    instanceVariableNames: ''
    classVariableNames: ''
    poolDictionaries: ''!

GopherApp becomeDefault!
Application subclass: #GopherApp
    instanceVariableNames: ''
    classVariableNames: ''
    poolDictionaries: ''!

GopherApp becomeDefault!

!Gopher class publicMethods !

defaultServer: aString
    "set the default server"

    Smalltalk at: #DefaultGopherServer put: aString.
    ^aString
!

gifViewer: aString
    "set the default GIF viewer"

    Smalltalk at: #DefaultGopherGifViewer put: aString.
    ^aString!

open
    "Open a gopher menu on default server"
    ^self open: self defaultServer
!

open: hostName
    "Open a gopher menu on the named server (tcp/ip hostname)"
    | gopher |

    gopher := (Gopher new) createWindow.

    (GopherItemMenu fromHost: hostName) view: gopher! !

!Gopher class privateMethods !

defaultServer
    "Answer a String which is the hostname of the default gopher server"
    | server |
```

Continued

```smalltalk
        server := Smalltalk at: #DefaultGopherServer ifAbsent: [''].
        server ~= '' ifTrue: [^server].

        [server = ''] whileTrue: [
           server := CwTextPrompter
              prompt: 'Enter the name of your gopher server'
              answer: 'carvm3'
           ].

        self defaultServer: server.
        ^server!

gifViewer
     "Answer a String which is the name of the program to view GIFs with"
     | viewer |

        viewer := Smalltalk at: #DefaultGopherGifViewer ifAbsent: [''].
        viewer ~= '' ifTrue: [^viewer].

        [viewer = ''] whileTrue: [
           viewer := CwTextPrompter
              prompt: 'Enter the name of your GIF viewer program'
              answer: 'gbmv2'
           ].

        self gifViewer: viewer.
        ^viewer! !

!Gopher publicMethods !

createWindow
     "Create the gopher menu window"

     | shell form text list |

     shell := CwTopLevelShell
        createApplicationShell: 'gopherMenu'
        argBlock: [:w| w
        title: 'Gopher Menu';
        width: (CgScreen default width) // 2
        ].

form := shell
   createForm: 'form'
   argBlock: nil.
form manageChild.

text := form
   createLabel: 'label'
```

Continued

```
    argBlock: [ :w | w
       labelString: ' '
       ].
text manageChild.


list := form
   createScrolledList: 'list'
   argBlock: [ :w | w
      selectionPolicy: XmSINGLESELECT;
      visibleItemCount: 20
      ].
list manageChild.


text setValuesBlock: [:w | w
   topAttachment: XmATTACHFORM;
   topOffset: 2;
   leftAttachment: XmATTACHFORM;
   leftOffset: 2;
   rightAttachment: XmATTACHFORM;
   rightOffset: 2].


list parent setValuesBlock: [:w | w
   topAttachment: XmATTACHWIDGET;
   topWidget: text;
   bottomAttachment: XmATTACHFORM;
   bottomOffset: 2;
   leftAttachment: XmATTACHFORM;
   leftOffset: 2;
   rightAttachment: XmATTACHFORM;
   rightOffset: 2].


list
   addCallback: XmNdefaultActionCallback
   receiver: self
   selector: #selectItem:clientData:callData:
   clientData: nil.


shell realizeWidget.


self listWidget: list.
self textWidget: text.
self shellWidget: shell.
self menuStack: OrderedCollection new.!


data
   ^data!


data: gopherData
   data := gopherData!
```

Continued

```
listWidget
    ^listWidget!

listWidget: aWidget
    listWidget := aWidget!

menuStack
    ^menuStack!

menuStack: aCollection
    menuStack := aCollection!

selectItem: widget clientData: clientData callData: callData
    "Callback sent when an item is selected. Open a viewer
    for the appropriate GopherItem subclass for the item."

    | pos menuItem |
    pos := callData itemPosition.
    menuItem := (self data) at: pos.
    menuItem view: self.!

shellWidget
    ^shellWidget!

shellWidget: aWidget
    shellWidget := aWidget!

textWidget
    ^textWidget!

textWidget: aWidget
    textWidget := aWidget! !

!GopherApp class publicMethods !

addToSystemMenu
    "Add Gopher to the system menu."

    (System systemMenu)
    addLine;
    add: #open label: '~Gopher' enable: [true] for: Gopher.
!


runtimeStartUp
    "Start up the application (for runtime usage)"
    Gopher open
! !

!GopherItem class publicMethods !
```

Continued

```
fromString: aString
    "Answer the appropriate gopher item given the string passed
    from the server"

    | type rest classes |

    type := aString at: 1.
    rest := aString copyFrom: 2 to: aString size.

    classes := self allSubclasses select: [ : class |
    class handlesType = type].

    classes size = 0 ifFalse: [
       ^classes first new parseString: rest
       ].

    ^GopherItemUnknown new parseString: rest!

handlesType
    "Answer a character for gopher item types this class handles"
    ^ nil! !

!GopherItem publicMethods !

data
    ^data!

data: gopherData
    data := gopherData!

display
    ^display!

display: aString
    display := aString!

getData
    "Set lines instance variable to the text for the gopher menu item."

    | abtHost abtPort abtSock rc chunk gData |

    self data: ''.

    self port isNil ifTrue: [self port: 70].

    abtHost := AbtTCPInetHost getHostByName: self host.

    abtHost isCommunicationsError ifTrue: [^nil].
```

Continued

```
        abtPort := AbtTCPPort usingHost: abtHost portNumber: self port.
        abtPort isCommunicationsError ifTrue: [^nil].

        abtSock := AbtSocket newStreamUsingPort: abtPort.

        self selector isNil ifTrue: [self selector: ''].

        abtSock bufferLength: 8192.

        rc := abtSock connect.
        rc isCommunicationsError ifTrue: [^nil].

        rc := abtSock sendData: (self selector, Cr asString, Lf asString).
        rc isCommunicationsError ifTrue: [^nil].

        gData := ''.
        [abtSock isConnected] whileTrue: [
           chunk := abtSock receive.
           chunk isCommunicationsError ifTrue: [^nil].
           gData := gData, chunk contents asString
           ].

        abtSock disconnect.

        self data: gData.!

host
    ^host!

host: aString
    host := aString!

isReturnMenu
    ^false!

menuText
    ^display!

parseString: aString
    "Given a string from a gopher menu, parse into the appropriate pieces."

    | str |

    str := ReadWriteStream on: aString.

    self display: (str upTo: Tab).
    self selector: (str upTo: Tab).
```

Continued

```
        self host: (str upTo: Tab).
        self port: (str upTo: Tab).!
port
    ^port!

port: aString
    aString isString
        ifTrue: [port := aString asNumber]
        ifFalse: [port := 70].!

selector
    ^selector!

selector: aString
    selector := aString!

title
    ^display! !

!GopherItemGif class publicMethods !

handlesType
    "Answer a character for gopher item types this class handles"
    ^ $g! !

!GopherItemGif publicMethods !

prefix
    "Answer the prefix for a gopher menu item for a GIF file"

    ^'@ '!

view: aGopher
    "open a GIF image viewer"
    | platformFn apiName errorBuffer returnCodes rc pgmString stream |

    self getData.

    stream := CfsWriteFileStream openEmpty: 'gopher.gif'.
    stream isCfsError ifTrue: [^nil].

    stream
        nextPutAll: self data;
        close.

    pgmString :=
        'cmd.exe' nullTerminated ,
        '/c start /c "Gopher GIF viewer" "',
```

Continued

```
                    Gopher gifViewer,
                    ' gopher.gif & erase gopher.gif"' nullTerminated nullTerminated.


        apiName := 283. "DosExecPgm"
        platformFn := PlatformFunction
                        callingConvention: 'c'
                        function: apiName
                        library: 'DOSCALLS'
                        parameterTypes: #( pointer uint32 uint32 pointer pointer
pointer pointer)
                        returnType: #uint32.


        errorBuffer := String new: 100.
        returnCodes := ByteArray new: 8.
        rc := platformFn
            callWith: errorBuffer asAddress
            with: 100
            with: 0
            with: pgmString
            with: nil
            with: returnCodes asAddress
            with: 'cmd.exe' nullTerminated.
! !


!GopherItemMenu class publicMethods !

fromHost: hostName
    "Answer a GopherItemMenu for the initial gopher menu from a gopher server"
    ^(self new)
        display: 'Gopher Server at ', hostName;
        host: hostName;
        port: 70;
        selector: '';
        yourself.
!


handlesType
    "Answer a character for gopher item types this class handles"
    ^ $1! !


!GopherItemMenu publicMethods !

asMenu
    ^(GopherItemMenu new)
        display: self display;
        selector: self selector;
        host: self host;
        port: self port;
        data: self data;
        yourself.!
```

Continued

```
asReturnMenu
   ^(GopherItemMenuReturn new)
      display: self display;
      selector: self selector;
      host: self host;
      port: self port;
      data: self data;
      yourself.!


getData
   "Convert text from gopher to menu item lines"

   | stream line col |

   self data isNil ifFalse: [^nil].

   super getData.
   stream := ReadStream on: self data.
   stream lineDelimiter: (Cr asString, Lf asString).

   col := OrderedCollection new.

   [stream atEnd] whileFalse: [
      line := stream nextLine.
      (line = '.') ifFalse: [
        col add: line].
      ].

   self data: col!


prefix
   "Answer the prefix for a gopher menu item which points to another gopher."

   ^'/ '!


view: aGopher
   "Fill the list for the gopher"
   | cursor items returnItem |

   aGopher textWidget labelString: self display.
   aGopher listWidget items: (OrderedCollection with: ' loading ...').

   cursor := CgDisplay default createFontCursor: XCGumby.
   aGopher shellWidget window defineCursor: cursor.

   self getData.
```

Continued

```
        items := (self data collect: [ : line | GopherItem fromString: line]).

        (self isReturnMenu) ifTrue: [
           aGopher menuStack removeLast; removeLast.
           ].

        (aGopher menuStack size = 0) ifFalse: [
           items addFirst: (aGopher menuStack last asReturnMenu)
           ].

        aGopher menuStack addLast: (self asMenu).

        aGopher listWidget items:
           (items collect: [ : i | i prefix , i menuText]).

        aGopher data: items.

        aGopher shellWidget window undefineCursor.
        cursor freeCursor.! !

!GopherItemMenuReturn publicMethods !

isReturnMenu
    ^true!

menuText
    ^'Return to Previous Menu'! !

!GopherItemSearch class publicMethods !

handlesType
    "Answer a character for gopher item types this class handles"
    ^ $7! !

!GopherItemSearch publicMethods !

getData
    "Set the lines for a gopher menu search item. First, get the text to be
    searched for, use this as an additional field in the selector, then get
    the lines just like for a normal gopher menu item which points to a menu."

    | oldSelector searchStr |

    oldSelector := self selector.
    searchStr := CwTextPrompter prompt: 'Enter text to search for'.

    self selector: (oldSelector , Tab asString , searchStr).
    super getData.
    self selector: oldSelector.!
```

Continued

```
prefix
    "Answer the prefix for a gopher menu item for a search"
    ^'?'! !

!GopherItemText class publicMethods !

handlesType
    "Answer a character for gopher item types this class handles"
    ^ $0! !

!GopherItemText publicMethods !

prefix
    "Answer the prefix for a textual gopher menu item"
    ^''!

view: aGopher
    "Open a workspace on a textual gopher menu item"
    | ws cursor |

    ws := EtWorkspace new
        label: self display;
        open.

    cursor := CgDisplay default createFontCursor: XCGumby.
    ws textWidget window defineCursor: cursor.

    ws textWidget setString: ' loading ...'.
    ws resetTextChangeFlag.

    self getData.
    ws textWidget setString: self data.
    ws resetTextChangeFlag.

    ws textWidget window undefineCursor.
    cursor freeCursor.
! !

!GopherItemUnknown publicMethods !

getData
    "Set the lines for an unknown gopher item"
    self data: 'I don''t know how to retrieve this item.'!

prefix
    "Answer the prefix of a menu item for an unknown type of item"

    ^'^'! !
```

LISTING 20.1 A Gopher client for IBM Smalltalk/VisualAge.

Information

The information that travels along the wire of the Internet can be as simple as text or as complex as a small application. Text documents have been enhanced through the HTML standard, and in the future will contain small applications and portable objects.

HTML

The HyperText Markup Language (HTML) is second cousin to the Standard Generic Markup Language (SGML), a text-based language for formatting documents. It provides for formatted text delimiters that enable enhanced character formatting and additional areas for user input to a document. A sample HTML file is shown in Listing 20.2.

```
<HTML>
<HEAD>
    <TITLE>TTEC HomePage</TITLE>
</HEAD>
<BODY>
<H1></H1>
<H1><CENTER>TTEC</CENTER>
</H1>
<H2><CENTER>The Technical Expertise Corporation</CENTER>
</H2>
<HR>The Technical Expertise Corporation provides products and services
for
the technical community. Current activities include a book entitled:
Advanced
Smalltalk Development and development of useful computer applications
for
manipulating electronic information and development of software. <BR>
<BR>
<BR>
Send E-Mail to Jonathan Pletzke of TTEC:
<ADDRESS>jpletzke@mordor.com</ADDRESS>
<BR>
Here's the stuff:
<UL>
<LI><A HREF="advstbk.html">Advanced Smalltalk Development</A> - a
smalltalk
textbook!<BR>
<BR>
<LI>Code Sample Library<BR>
<BR>
<LI>Short Papers on Smalltalk Topics<BR>
<BR>
<LI>Smalltalk Projects<BR>
<BR>
```

Continued

```
<LI><A HREF="consults.html">Smalltalk Consultants Available</A><BR>
<BR>
<LI><A HREF="../NJSUG/njsughome.html">New Jersey Smalltalk Users Group
Home
Page</A>
</UL>
<HR>Contents Copyright 1995, 1996 The Technical Expertise Corporation
</BODY>
</HTML>
```

LISTING 20.2   A sample HTML file from the author's Web site.

A complete description of the HTML format, its syntax, and an explanation of those funky tags can be found in the document entitled *Hypertext Markup Language 2.0* written by Tim Berners-Lee, father of the World Wide Web, and D. Connolly. Reference to this document can be found in the appendices.

Java

Java represents the latest extension to the Internet. It provides the framework for sending Smalltalk-like "applets" (small applications) over the Internet to appropriately enabled Web browsers. The applets are written in a language called Java that is based on Smalltalk and C.

Objects

The potential to send objects across the Internet is becoming more fact than fantasy. With the introduction of Java, the marketplace is embracing this enhancement to the Internet Web concept. With all the work done to store objects in files or databases that are accessible to Smalltalk and other object-oriented languages, and the available standards for these objects like SOM, there should be objects traveling across the Internet with relative ease in the near future. This should really enhance the distributed features of Smalltalk and make Application Partitioning a real industry motivator.

Web Techniques

There are a few basic architectures for using Smalltalk with the World Wide Web. Two of them are for Web server applications, where the clients connect directly to Smalltalk or through a standard Web server. The client strategy is to go directly after the server data and provide customizeable client services.

Web Server

A Web server acts as a repository of World Wide Web documents and information. It waits for Web clients to contact it and request information, dispenses the information, and then closes the client's connection.

Common Gateway Interface

The Common Gateway Interface (CGI) is how most Web servers communicate with external functionality. This interface provides an external calling mechanism to a named script, usually in a subdirectory of the server. The scripts are usually named with a .cgi suffix, and can be in any scripting language supported by the Web server and the host platform. Since many of the Web servers are running under Unix, the scripts are either shell or PERL scripts.

The CGI interface calls a module with an input argument stream. This stream will usually contain a string of information generated by the Web server. The script will then process the information, while the server awaits the response. The output is piped back to the Web server, which in turn passes it to the appropriate client connection. The capacity of the CGI mechanism has not been fully tested, but it is expected to have limitations in bandwidth due to limits in the Unix streaming mechanism.

In this configuration, Smalltalk runs as a separate operating system process, and an interprocess communication mechanism is used to pass the information into Smalltalk from a script. It is not practical for the Smalltalk image to start and stop with each request, as the startup time can be significant.

Advantages of this approach include the ability to use commercially available Web servers in combination with Smalltalk. This frees the Smalltalk programmer to focus more on application issues and less on communications issues. It also removes much of the need to constantly update to the latest specified version of HTML.

Commercial Web servers offer additional features that would be very time-consuming to re-create under Smalltalk. One is the security mechanism add-on to the Netscape server product. The issues and difficulty involved in this security server involve a lengthy development time, and then significant maintenance costs as a Smalltalk security server is brought up to the latest specs with the Netscape security specification.

When integration with existing Web applications and documents on a single server is also important, this approach removes the need to create an entire HTML dispatching mechanism in Smalltalk, and allows other environments besides Smalltalk to execute CGI calls.

Direct TCP/IP—Sockets

A second way to architect a Smalltalk Web server is by directly accepting connections to the Smalltalk image. This means that the Smalltalk image must have a TCP/IP communications feature that will be used extensively. This approach provides greater flexibility for the type of information transmitted to the client. Smalltalk code and objects can be directly shipped to a Smalltalk client as determined by the client's request header.

The limitations of this approach involve the efficiency and capability of Smalltalk to handle concurrent TCP/IP connections. If the Smalltalk environment does not provide lightweight, preemptive threads to manage the incoming connections, performance will be minimal. Features like Security and Java applets must also be manually coded into the server.

Advantages of the approach are its simplicity; another process (the Web Server) is not necessary and there is no need for a CGI mechanism, with its potential bandwidth issues. Plus, there is the ability to send anything that the client and server can both handle, including Smalltalk source code, binary objects, and **SOM/DSOM** objects.

This approach is demonstrated in the upcoming examples because the solution is clearer and does not require any coding outside of the Smalltalk environment.

Web Client

The Web client is the ultimate in fast and small client software. The nature of Web browsers makes them accessible to many more computer configurations than any custom client software. This client/server split puts all of the application logic in the server, and provides the user with only the graphical equivalent of a dumb terminal.

Standard Web Clients

Standard Web clients simply retrieve HTML documents from the source and display them. More sophisticated clients allow the user to save a list of favorite places, cache recent documents, and provide extensions to HTML-like formatted tables. The application functionality is all in the Web server.

Java-Enabled Web Clients

A Java-enabled Web client has the advantage of being able to run small programs sent from the server. Not a dumb terminal, the client has the smarts to run these small applets, which range from simple animations to interactive tools like calculators. The application logic is moved, in very small parcels, from the server to the client, primarily to improve the user experience through limited bandwidth.

Smalltalk Web Client

A Smalltalk web Client, though larger in memory footprint than either the Standard or Java Web clients previously mentioned, allows the Smalltalk programmer to truly partition the application logic between the Web server and the Web client. The advantage of this is that nonenabled browsers can still access a portion of the information, where the Smalltalk client can perform many more functions on the client machine and share objects and Smalltalk source code with the server.

Commercial Solutions

Several commercial products that enable Smalltalk to work on World Wide Web servers have been announced or released recently. These extensions of the Smalltalk environment allow the seasoned Smalltalk programmer and the novice alike to create sophisticated client/server applications that use Standard or Java-enabled clients to retrieve the information. The advantage of these environments is that they provide the same type of data manipulation and retrieval that have made the Smalltalk environment so popular for other types of application development, while providing a whole new market of Smalltalk clients through use of Web clients.

VisualWave

VisualWave is a product from ParcPlace-Digitalk, which uses the same graphical user interface framework as the VisualWorks product to create Web pages (see Figure 20.1). An application is created using the normal VisualWorks procedures. Once the application has been tested, and with the click of a button, the application can now use HTML to render its user interface (see Figures 20.2 and 20.3). This works well in VisualWorks because of the platform-independent GUI layer in the product. This layer has always been a pitfall of the product, as people were unable to get true platform look-and-feel, but were able to switch between the emulated look-and-feel of Macintosh, Windows, OS/2, and Motif with the click of a button. This set of GUIs has now been extended to include the HTML/Web interface. This product uses the CGI interface to work with existing Web servers.

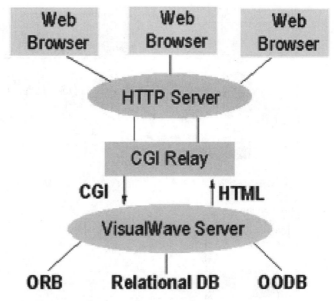

FIGURE 20.1 The VisualWave architecture.

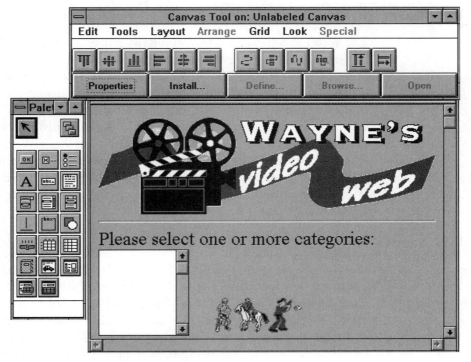

FIGURE 20.2 The VisualWave application editor.

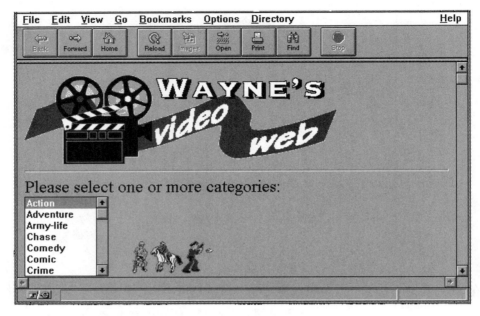

FIGURE 20.3   A live VisualWave application.

Web Parts for VisualAge

The Web Parts for VisualAge/Smalltalk, a product from IBM, provides similar functionality to the VisualWave product, but through a slightly different approach. VisualAge/Smalltalk uses the PARTS Component Software development methodology, and allows many users to graphically build applications using preconstructed parts. IBM has created a new palette of parts that allow interaction with the World Wide Web through the CGI interface of an existing Web server. This is different from VisualWave in that the user interface constructed for the Web can be completely separate from the computer's native platform, so one display can be provided to a manager of the Web system and the content interface can be presented to users of the system (see Figures 20.4 and 20.5).

WebAgents

WebAgents, a product of QKS, for use with SmalltalkAgents, uses a different approach for providing Web service. In this product, the Web clients connect directly with SmalltalkAgents, without going through an existing Web server's CGI interface. QKS claims that this will allow many more users to access the Web server, and improve overall performance. This is due to the SmalltalkAgents' lightweight, preemptive threading architecture among many of this product's technical innovations.

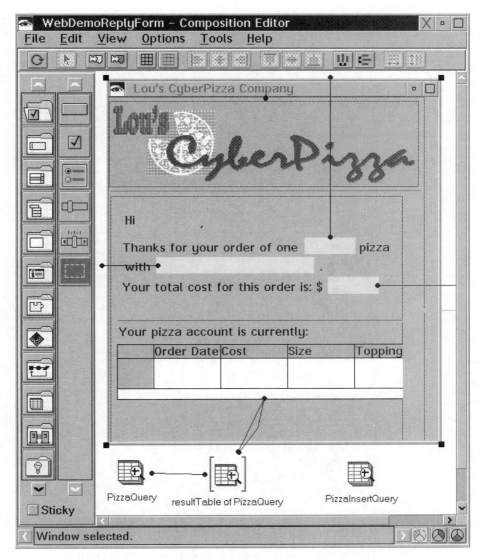

FIGURE 20.4 A Web Parts for VisualAge editing session.

Current Applications of the Technology

So is anyone out there really using this technology? And are they successful with it? Making money with Internet commerce? The answer to these questions is yes. Sites have been deployed with this type of technology since early 1995, before these products were announced. These sites can be found

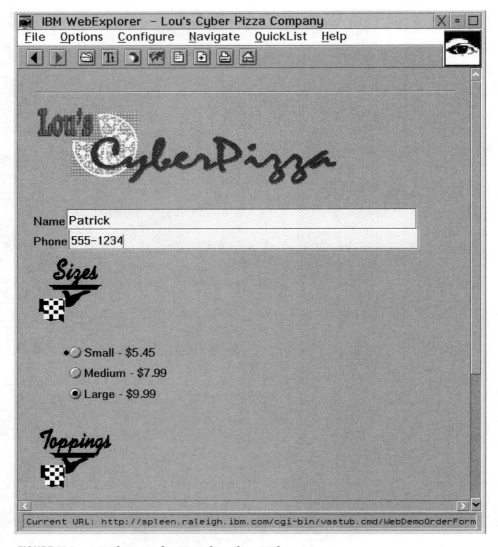

FIGURE 20.5 A Web Parts for VisualAge live Web session.

on the Internet, and don't appear to be any different from any other site to the casual Internet user, but behind the scenes they contain Smalltalk.

Dun & Bradstreet

Dun & Bradstreet's Web site, shown in Figure 20.6, provides access to the Business Background Report, a report ordering and delivery system, shown in Figure 20.7. You can visit this site at http://www.dbisna.com.

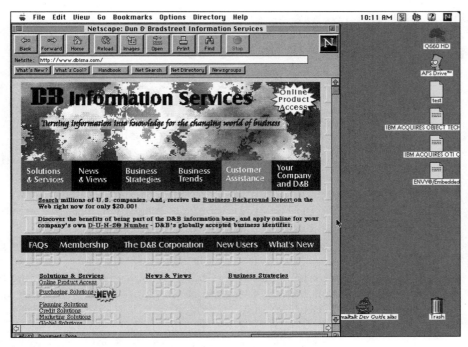

FIGURE 20.6   The Dun & Bradstreet VisualWave Web site.

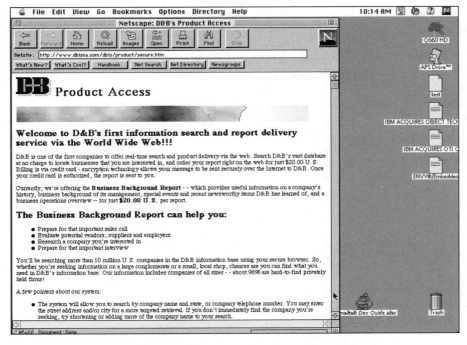

FIGURE 20.7   Accessing the VisualWave application at Dun & Bradstreet.

A Simple Smalltalk Web Server

In order to best understand how Smalltalk Web servers work, a simple Smalltalk Web server is presented here for your use and enhancement. The basic server directly accepts TCP/IP connections, through the use of the sockets libraries available in many Smalltalks.

♦ *Uses direct TCP/IP with sockets:* The basic functionality of the Smalltalk Web server is to listen for a connection on Port 80, receive a request, interpret that request, and generate or answer an HTML document. The flow of control finishes when the server closes the connection and listens for the next connection.

♦ *Needs pre-emptive multitasking for efficiency:* Since this application serves more than one user at a time, some kind of scheduling mechanism is needed. Smalltalk has traditionally been a one-user type of system, with back-end processing applications fewer in number.

♦ *Serves HTML to standard clients:* This server is simple. It serves HTML to standard Web clients, determined by the header information sent with the request. If the client is Java, and you have a Java applet, you can answer that to the client. The client may also be a Smalltalk client, and source code or binary objects may be answered to such a client.

Several versions of this Web server are provided for the different versions of Smalltalk. They have much in common, but the TCP/IP interface is different for each. Listing 20.3 has source code for a simple Web server. This was implemented in VisualSmalltalk. Additional code versions can be found on the CD-ROM.

```
Object
    subclass: #HTMLResponse
    instanceVariableNames: ''
    classVariableNames: ''
    poolDictionaries: ''
    category: 'HTTPServer'!

ReadWriteStream
    subclass: #HTMLStream
    instanceVariableNames: ''
    classVariableNames: ''
    poolDictionaries: ''
    category: 'HTTPServer'!

TCPDaemon
    subclass: #HTTPDaemon
    instanceVariableNames: ''
    classVariableNames: ''
```

Continued

```
        poolDictionaries: ''
        category: 'HTTPServer'!

Object
    subclass: #HTTPRequest
    instanceVariableNames: 'command connection user host accept'
    classVariableNames: ''
    poolDictionaries: ''
    category: 'HTTPServer'!

SocketServer
    subclass: #HTTPServer
    instanceVariableNames: ''
    classVariableNames: ''
    poolDictionaries: ''
    category: 'HTTPServer'!

!HTMLStream methodsFor: 'as yet unclassified' !

address: aString
    "Public - Place aString as bold text"

    ^super nextPutAll: '<ADDRESS>';
    nextPutAll: aString;
    nextPutAll: '</ADDRESS>'!

bold: aString
    "Public - Place aString as bold text"

    ^super nextPutAll: '<B>';
    nextPutAll: aString;
    nextPutAll: '</B>'!

code: aString
    "Public - Place aString as bold text"

    ^super nextPutAll: '<CODE>';
    nextPutAll: aString;
    nextPutAll: '</CODE>'!

cr

    super
        nextPutAll: '<P>';
        cr.!

emphasis: aString
    "Public - Place aString as bold text"
```

Continued

```
      ^super nextPutAll: '<EM>';
      nextPutAll: aString;
      nextPutAll: '</EM>'!


end
   "Public - End the HTML document with the appropriate footer"

   super
      nextPutAll: '</HTML>';
      cr!

endBody
   "Public - End the HTML document body with the appropriate footer"

   super
      nextPutAll: '</BODY>';
      cr!

heading: aString level: anInteger
   "Public - Place aString as bold text"

   ^super nextPutAll: '<H', anInteger asString, '>';
   nextPutAll: aString;
   nextPutAll: '</H', anInteger asString, '>'!


heading1: aString
   "Public - Place aString as bold text"

   ^super nextPutAll: '<H1>';
   nextPutAll: aString;
   nextPutAll: '</H1>'!


heading2: aString
   "Public - Place aString as bold text"

   ^super nextPutAll: '<H2>';
   nextPutAll: aString;
   nextPutAll: '</H2>'!


italic: aString
   "Public - Place aString as bold text"

   ^super nextPutAll: '<I>';
   nextPutAll: aString;
   nextPutAll: '</I>'!


ruler
   "Public - Place aString as bold text"

   ^super nextPutAll: '<HR>'!
```

Continued

```
start
    "Public - Begin the HTML document with the appropriate header"

    super
        nextPutAll: '<HTML>';
        cr!

startBody
    "Public - Begin the HTML document body with the appropriate header"

    super
        nextPutAll: '<BODY>';
        cr!

strong: aString
    "Public - Place aString as bold text"

    ^super nextPutAll: '<STRONG>';
    nextPutAll: aString;
    nextPutAll: '</STRONG>'!

text: aString
    "Public - Place aString as plain text"

    ^super nextPutAll: aString!

title: aString
    "Public - Place the title in the document"

    super
        nextPutAll: '<HEAD>';
        cr;
        nextPutAll: '<TITLE>';
        nextPutAll: aString;
        nextPutAll: '</TITLE>';
        cr;
        nextPutAll: '</HEAD>';
        cr
    !

underline: aString
    "Public - Place aString as bold text"

    ^super nextPutAll: '<U>';
    nextPutAll: aString;
    nextPutAll: '</U>'! !


!HTMLStream class methodsFor: 'as yet unclassified' !
```

Continued

```
on: anIndexedCollection
        "Answer a new instance of the
         receiver on anIndexedCollection."
      ^(self new)
        setCollection: anIndexedCollection;
        setLimits;
        start! !


!HTTPDaemon methodsFor: 'as yet unclassified' !


defaultPort
    ^80
!


serverClass
    ^HTTPServer
! !


!HTTPDaemon class methodsFor: 'as yet unclassified' !


start
    "Public - Start the Server"

(HTTPDaemon openOnPort: 80 serverClass: HTTPServer) start! !


!HTTPRequest methodsFor: 'as yet unclassified' !


accept: aString

    accept := aString!


asHTML
    "Public - Answer a string representing self formatted as HTML"

    ^((HTMLStream on: (String new: 1000))
       title: 'An HTTP Request';
       startBody;
       bold: 'An HTTP Request was received';
       cr;
       cr;
       underline: 'The Document Requested is: ';
       italic: self path;
       cr;
       cr;
       underline: 'The Host ID of the requester is: ';
       italic: self hostID;
       cr;
       endBody;
       end;
       truncate) contents!
```

Continued

```
command: aString

    command := aString!

commandType
    ^command asArrayOfSubstrings at: 1!

connection: aString

    connection := aString!

host: aString

    host := aString!

hostID

    ^host asArrayOfSubstrings at: 2!

httpVersion
    ^command asArrayOfSubstrings at: 3!

path
    ^(command asArrayOfSubstrings at: 2) collect: [ :each | each = $/
ifTrue: [ $\ ] ifFalse: [ each ] ]!

satisfy
    "Public - Satisfy the request, answering an HTML string of the
satisfied result"
    "Document exists in self class default directory, or answer back the
request if absent."

    | result theFile |
    (File exists: (self class defaultDirectory , self path))
       ifTrue:
          [theFile := (File pathName: (self class defaultDirectory ,
self path)).
          result := theFile contents.
          theFile close.
          ]
       ifFalse:
          [result := self asHTML].
    ^result!

user: aString

    user := aString! !
```

Continued

```
!HTTPRequest class methodsFor: 'as yet unclassified' !


defaultDirectory
    ^'D:\VSEW310\HTTP'!


fromStream: aStream
    "Answer a new instance of self based on the contents of aStream"

    ^(self new)
        initialize;
        command: (aStream nextLine);
        connection: (aStream nextLine);
        user: (aStream nextLine);
        host: (aStream nextLine);
        accept: (aStream nextLine)! !


!HTTPServer methodsFor: 'as yet unclassified' !


readOn: aSocket
    | theRequest |

    theRequest := ReadStream on: (aSocket read).
    Transcript show: theRequest contents.
    theRequest := HTTPRequest fromStream: theRequest.
    aSocket write: (theRequest satisfy) .
    aSocket close.
!


writeOn: aSocket

    "Do Nothing"! !


!String methodsFor: 'as yet unclassified' !


asHTML

    ^((HTMLStream on: (String new: (self size + 100)))

        title: '';
        startBody;
        text: self;
        endBody;
        end;
        truncate) contents! !
```

LISTING 20.3 A simple Smalltalk Web server for VisualSmalltalk (the CD-ROM has others).

A Simple Smalltalk Web Client

In order to create a robust Web client, viewers for GIF files, GUI controls, and all the new enhancements must be created. The client presented here (Listing 20.4) is simple, it can understand basic HTML and display the contents; it does not contain features to view and interpret all the types of information and links that can be encountered, as these can be added modularly by the programmer as needed.

The client does contain the capability to receive Smalltalk source code and Smalltalk binary objects. The Smalltalk source code can be executed upon receipt, and the objects can be loaded into the image and executed. This is a unique extension that must be standardized and coordinated between the Smalltalk Web servers and the Smalltalk Web clients.

```
SocketClient
    subclass: #HTTPClient
    instanceVariableNames: 'path'
    classVariableNames: ''
    poolDictionaries: ''
    category: 'HTTPClient'!

!HTTPClient methodsFor: 'as yet unclassified' !

connectedOn: aSocket
    "Public - Connection received on the socket. Make the request"

    self requestPageOn: aSocket
    !

path
    ^path!

path: aPath
    path := aPath!

readOn: aSocket
    "This is where the contents come back as HTML"

    Transcript show: aSocket read.
    self close.!

requestPageOn: aSocket
    "Public - Request the page named in path"

    aSocket write: 'GET ', path, ' HTTP1.0' !

writeOn: aSocket
```

Continued

```
                "Don't do anything here"
    ! !


    !HTTPClient class methodsFor: 'as yet unclassified' !

demo
        "Public - This provides a demonstration of the simple HTTP Client"
        "Now all you need is an HTML parser and a GUI to write on"
        "
        HTTPClient demo
        "


        (HTTPClient openOnHostname: 'localhost' path: '\jon2.htm' ) start
    !


openOnHostname: hostname
        "Defacto standard http port is 80, but can be anything. Use 80 for initial
connect"

        ^self openOnAddress:
            (self socketClass addressClass
                hostname: hostname port: 80)!

openOnHostname: hostname path: thePath
        "Additionally specify the location of the document"

            ^(self openOnHostname: hostname)
            path: thePath! !
```

LISTING 20.4   A simple Smalltalk Web client for Visual Smalltalk (the CD-ROM contains others).

Listing 20.5 shows the workspace used to create and test the Web client on VisualSmalltalk.

```
"Code to start the server"
(HTTPDaemon openOnPort: 80 serverClass: HTTPServer) start

"More general method does the same thing"
HTTPDaemon start

"Code to open a client on the localhost requesting the file named
image1.gif in the default directory which is D:\VSEW310\HTTP"
(HTTPClient openOnHostname: 'localhost' path: '\image1.gif' ) start

"Make sure that any extra instances of client are removed if they fail"
HTTPClient allInstances do: [ :each | each close ]
```

```
"Are there any instances of the client?"
HTTPClient allInstances size

"The whole shootin' match for the Client"
HTTPClient demo
```

LISTING 20.5 A text workspace of test code used for the Visual Smalltalk Web server and client.

Summary

The World Wide Web offers a great opportunity for Smalltalk development. Sophisticated, object-oriented applications can be built rapidly and enhanced more easily in Smalltalk than any other Web development tool. What remains to be seen is whether Smalltalk vendors will reach the market with the tools before others become available.

Another exciting possibility for Smalltalk Web applications is their use within companies in "intranet" applications. These applications would rival those created with Lotus Notes, and probably be much more sophisticated because there are fewer limitations on what can be created. All of this is possible because of the intense efforts being expended on Web technology, and the memory-thin and CPU-thin Web clients, such as Netscape that don't require 16 megs of RAM and a Pentium processor.

21

Neural Networks

In this chapter, you will learn about neural networks, their uses, and their application to Smalltalk applications. A functioning neural network program is included, and the details of its functionality are discussed. The topics covered are:

- neural network concepts
- the mathematical basis for a back-propagation network
- an example Smalltalk neural network back-propagation class
- a real-life application of neural networks
- other Smalltalk neural network resources

Neural Network Basics

A computer neural network models the functionality of a network of neurons in the brain. The ways this is accomplished can be broken into two categories: those models that attempt to mimic the exact functioning of the brain cell from biological research, and those models that attempt to mimic the way the brain learns. The first type of model is often called a **natural neural network,** and the second type is called an **artificial neural network.** Most applications of neural networks are of the second type because artificial neural networks are simpler and attempt to solve the problem of machine learning with a looser correlation to the biology of a brain cell. Therefore, in this chapter, artificial neural networks will be discussed.

A neural network is composed of neurons. There are many similarities between the structure and composition of a neuron in the brain and a neuron in a neural network computer program. Both have three similar components and interconnections that occur in many fashions. In the brain, as shown in Figure 21.1, the three components are: the dendrites, the cell body, and the axons. The dendrites are a web of receptors that serve as an input for stimulus from other neurons. The cell body serves as a processing mechanism that determines how the dendrite stimuli will trigger the neuron. The axon is the output of the neuron and transmits signals to other neurons.

In a neural network computer program, as shown in Figure 21.2, the three components are: the inputs, the node, and the outputs. There is at least one input per neuron, and the inputs are hooked up to the output of other neurons or input data. The node contains storage for the triggering function that determines how the output will be computed based on the input values. There is only one output from a node, but the output may be connected to the input of more than one neuron, or serve as the output for the neural network.

Neurons in the brain are interconnected in many ways, as shown in Figure 21.3. The methods of interconnection, the number of connections, and the operation of these connections are not fully known. Conversely, nodes in a computer neural network are connected in known and predictable ways, as shown in Figure 21.4. Each input can have only one source of data, and each output can go to many inputs. The topology of the network and the number of nodes and the ways they are interconnected is known as the architecture of the neural network.

The architecture of a neural network is the key to obtaining desired results. Variables in architecting a neural network include: number of

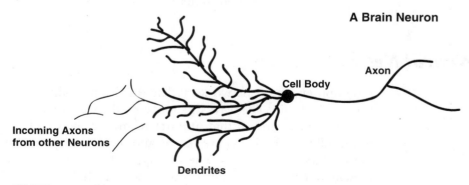

FIGURE 21.1   A brain neuron.

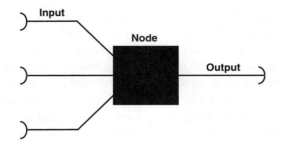

FIGURE 21.2   A computer program neuron.

FIGURE 21.3   A brain neural network.

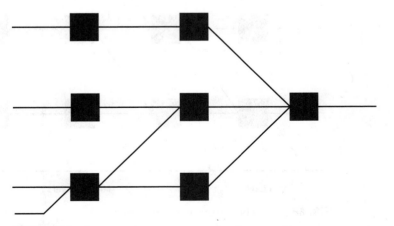

FIGURE 21.4   A computer program neural network.

nodes, number of connections, ways of connecting, node algorithms, types of inputs, number of inputs, number of outputs, and the organization of these items. This multidimensional problem has no set methodology, so a bit of research into other techniques and a creative mind are necessary to create a successful neural network.

Nodes in a neural network can usually be grouped into layers, as shown in Figure 21.5. Layers are useful in that they provide a parallel set of nodes to accomplish a simultaneous set of computations on the inputs of that layer. The outputs of a layer will then feed into another layer. Computation in a neural network usually occurs layer by layer, from the input layer to the output layer. The input layer is the first in the neural network and provides a buffer for input data. The output layer is the last in the system before the data is passed out of the neural network.

Neural networks are used in two phases. The first phase consists of training the neural network with a known set of inputs and an expected set of outputs. The second phase consists of using the neural network to process or recognize inputs to produce outputs that correlate with the training set. The process of training a neural network consists of identifying a set of inputs to the network with the desired outputs. The network is started in training mode, and each set of inputs is presented to the network. The cal-

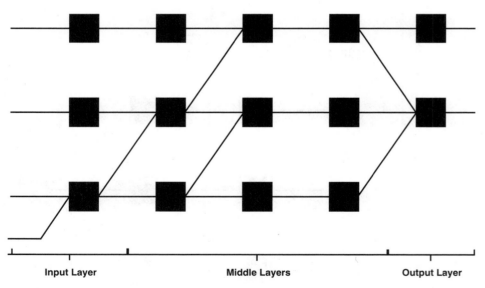

Input Layer   **Middle Layers**   **Output Layer**

FIGURE 21.5 The layers of a neural network.

culated output of the network is compared by the network with the desired output for the input set. The differences between the calculated output and the desired output are used to adjust the weights that are used in the node calculations. All inputs are presented repeatedly to the network until the results stabilize and the total error for the network reaches some predetermined amount. The network may fail to reach a stable point, and more training data may be needed, or a different network architecture may be required. Noise (random numbers) is often introduced in the learning process to ensure that the neural network settles on the appropriate value for the best matching capability.

Once the neural network has been trained, the network can be used with desired input data, and the results of the processing will be the product of the neural network and correlate with the desired functioning of the network. Inputs that match or closely match the input training data should produce the same output results. Inputs that do not resemble any of the trained inputs may not provide meaningful outputs, so a broad training set is desirable. The network is now trained and should be able to distinguish between the various inputs to produce a meaningful output.

There are different algorithms that can be used to simulate neural networks. These algorithms include the back-propagation network, discussed here, and other architectures with names like Hopfield networks and self-organizing feature map networks. The different architectures work well in varying ways and depending on the application, one may serve better than another. Further research into neural networks and algorithms will allow you to implement your own versions of these, and you should check the SmallBrain application in the Smalltalk Archive for implementations of three types of neural networks.

How Neural Networks Work

The details of neural network functionality differ depending on the type of neural network. The following discusses the back-propagation neural network, but this provides a solid foundation for understanding other types of neural networks as well.

All nodes in a homogeneous network are of the same type. A heterogeneous network can consist of nodes of different types. In order to understand the functioning of a neural network, the function of a node within the network must be clear. A schematic depicting a back-propagation node is shown in Figure 21.6.

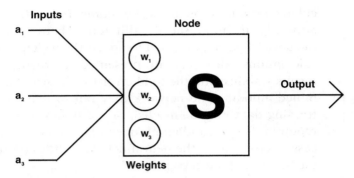

FIGURE 21.6   A back-propagation node.

The inputs are numbered a_1, a_2, and a_3. Each has an associated weight within the node, shown as w_1, w_2, and w_3. These weights allow the network to control the amount of influence that each of the inputs has on the final product of the node. The value computed for the node is S, as shown in Figure 21.7.

The value S can be directly used as the output value of the node, or it can be passed through a threshold function that will determine the triggering (firing of a neuron) of the output. The threshold function can control the range of S to keep it within reasonable bounds, or convert its value to a binary or Boolean value. Each application will dictate the output needed for the nodes.

The neural network "learns" by exposure to a set of inputs and outputs. Figure 21.8 shows three training sets applied to a neural network. Each time a neural network undergoes a training set, the values within the network are automatically adjusted to bring the output closer to what is desired. The training sets are repeatedly used on the network until it achieves a steady state with an acceptable minimum error.

Node Equation

$$S = \Sigma\, a_i w_i$$

$$i = \text{inputs}$$

$$= a_1 \cdot w_1 + a_2 \cdot w_2 + a_3 \cdot w_3$$

FIGURE 21.7   The summation formula for a node.

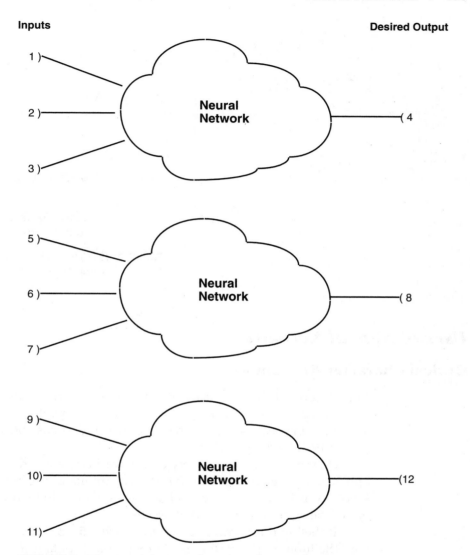

Inputs   **Desired Output**

FIGURE 21.8 Three training sets for a neural network.

The weights inside the network, inside each node, are adjusted by using the result of the total error equation given in Figure 21.9. This figure determines how well the neural network has "learned." Using this number, each weight can be adjusted by the amount given in Figure 21.10.

In the back-propagation network, the process of adjusting weights occurs iteratively in the opposite direction of input processing, and propagates the error back through the network; hence, the name.

$$\sigma = (t_j - a_j) \, f^1(S_j)$$

FIGURE 21.9 Total error for a back-propagation network.

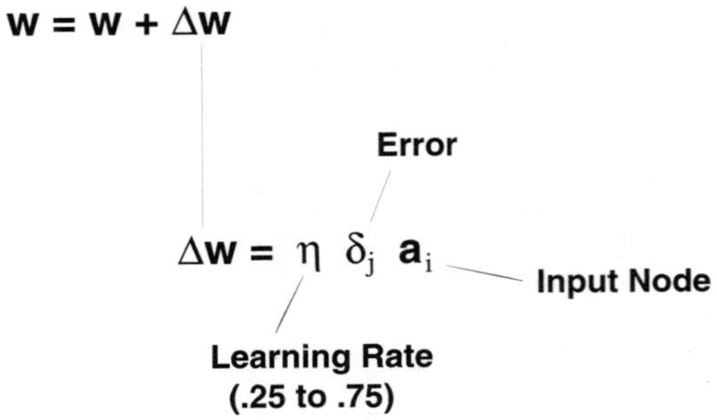

$$w = w + \Delta w$$

$$\Delta w = \eta \; \delta_j \; a_i$$

Error

Input Node

Learning Rate
(.25 to .75)

FIGURE 21.10 The weight adjustment formula for back-propagation.

Uses of Neural Networks

Optical Character Recognition

Neural networks can be used to solve problems that cannot be easily described mathematically. In particular, they are helpful in identifying patterns and, in some cases, may be the only solution possible when the inputs cannot be fully described or known.

One area that neural networks have been applied successfully is in optical character recognition (OCR). The inputs of the system consist of a set of pixels from a scanned-in character, as shown in Figure 21.11. The output of the system is an ASCII character.

If the input is a grid of pixels measuring 5×5 that are either on or off, then the input to the system is binary and 25 inputs is a good first attempt at defining the network. The middle layers are unknown, but depending on the number of characters to be trained, the level of accuracy required, and the speed defined, the middle layers could be numerous with many nodes. Practical experience dictates that more than one middle layer may not help the system.

Training of the system consists of teaching the system a pixel map representation of each character with the expected output of its ASCII character. The system is trained on the pixels associated with the letter A and the ASCII output A. Once the training is complete, the system can then associ-

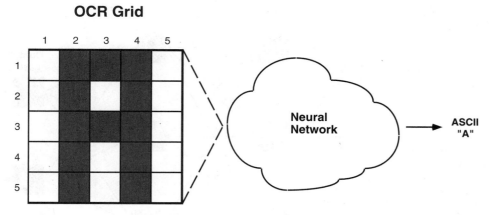

FIGURE 21.11   An optical character recognition neural network.

ate the grid pattern for A with the ASCII character, and proceed to make this conversion repeatedly.

A powerful feature of neural networks enables the network to make the best association if a smudge exists on the original paper. If, for instance, one pixel is turned on because of the smudge, the system will not have been trained with this exact pattern, but may well make the correct association to the correct ASCII character. This means that partial input data sets or slightly incorrect data sets can elicit the correct response. Thus, a slightly different typeface would probably give good results when using a neural network.

Stock Market Forecasting

Another popular use for neural networks is to forecast the stock market. In fact, the technique is used to predict future prices for many streams of data. For example, if you were predicting the price of ParcPlace stock, inputs for the system would consist of prior historical data from standard financial indicators and other Smalltalk and software development statistics. The inputs of the system are time-delayed to predict the future of the system. Let's say the input training data is for 1992 and the expected value set is for 1993. Additional training sets would consist of 1993 inputs for 1994 ParcPlace stock prices. Data from 1994 indicators can then be used to predict the prices of ParcPlace stock during the year of 1995.

While this sounds like a winning solution, keep in mind that not only does the neural network have to be well designed, but the input data choices must be made, the time slices determined, and the network must be con-

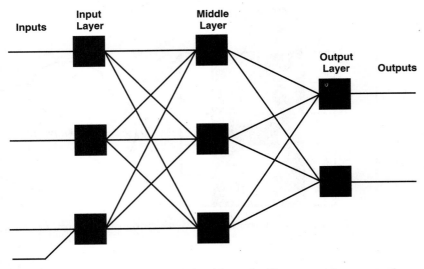

FIGURE 21.12   A fully connected three-layer back-propagation network.

stantly retrained. Nevertheless, people are using neural networks to predict the stock market, some of them successfully!

Back-Propagation Example Code

The following code sample was originally created as a poorly written experimental C program and translated into a rather rough Smalltalk program. The program started as an example of a perceptron (a back-propagation network with no middle layer), and was later modified to handle multiple layers. All layers are fully connected, meaning that the inputs of each node in the second layer are connected to each output in the first layer, as shown in Figure 21.12.

The C source code for the perceptron version of the program is presented in Listing 21.1. The translation from C to Smalltalk is interesting: as the data storage approach changed, memory management became unnecessary (not that there is much in this C code), and the code took on a different light as it was updated to a reasonable level. It also shows that a poor C program becomes even worse when viewed through the eyes of a Smalltalk programmer.

```
#include <stdio.h>
#define jmax 6
#define imax 10
#define categories 6
```

Continued

```
      int i, j, a[imax], x[jmax], t[jmax], input[imax][categories],
       output[jmax][categories], user, jon;
      float w[jmax][imax], s[jmax], c;


 ******************************* main ***/

main()
{
   init();

for (jon = 1; jon < 10; jon++)
   {
   for (user=1; user <6; user++)
      {
      selectset();
      /* printf("!!!!!!!!!! Node Operation !!!!!!!!!!\n"); */
      nodeoperation();
      /* printf("@@@@@ Display @@@@@\n"); */
      display();
      /* printf("###### Weight Adjust ######\n"); */
      weightadjust();
      }
   }
}
init()
{
   for ( j=1; j<jmax; j++ )
      {
      for ( i=1; i<imax; i++ )
        w[j][i] = .0;
      }
   for ( user=1; user<categories; user++ )
      {
      for ( i=1; i<imax; i++ )
        input[i][user]=0;
      for ( j=1; j<jmax; j++ )
        output[j][user]=0;
      }
   input[1][1] = 1;
   input[2][1] = 1;
   input[3][2] = 1;
   input[4][2] = 1;
   input[5][2] = 1;
   input[6][3] = 1;
   input[7][3] = 1;
   input[8][3] = 1;
   input[9][3] = 1;
   input[1][4] = 1;
   input[3][4] = 1;
   input[5][4] = 1;
   input[7][4] = 1;
```

Continued

```
        input[1][5] = 1;
        input[2][5] = 1;
        input[5][5] = 1;
        input[6][5] = 1;
        output[1][1] = 1;
        output[2][2] = 1;
        output[3][3] = 1;
        output[4][4] = 1;
        output[5][5] = 1;
        c = .1;
}

selectset()
{

for ( i=1; i<imax; i++)
    a[i]=input[i][user];
}

set()
{
printf("Please select the input/output set (1-5) \n");
scanf("%d",user);
printf("Your response:\n");
printf("%d",user);
scanf("%d",i);


}

nodeoperation()
{
    for ( j=1; j<jmax; j++)
        {
        s[j]=0;
        for ( i=1; i<imax; i++)
            {
            s[j]=s[j]+a[i]*w[j][i];
            }
        if ( s[j] > 0 )
            x[j] = 1;
            else
                x[j] = 0;
        }
}

weightadjust()
{
    for ( j=1; j<jmax; j++)
        {
        for ( i=1; i<imax; i++ )
```

Continued

```
                {
                w[j][i]=w[j][i] + c*(output[j][user]-x[j])*a[i];
                }
            }
    }

display()
{
    printf("Input: ");

    for ( i=1; i<imax; i++)
        printf("%d",input[i][user]);
    printf("   ");

    printf("Desired Output: ");

    for ( j=1; j<jmax; j++)
        printf("%d",output[j][user]);
    printf("   ");

    printf("Actual Output: ");

    for ( j=1; j<jmax; j++)
        printf("%d",x[j]);
    printf("\n");

}

weightdisplay()
{
    printf("Weights: ");
    for ( j=1; j<jmax; j++)
        {
        for ( i=1; i<imax; i++)
            {
            printf("%f ",w[j][i]);
            }
        }

    printf("*************************************\n");
}
```

LISTING 21.1   A typical (terribly written) C program for back-propagation.

The implementation in Smalltalk is only an example. The program is organized in a single class and does some array memory tricks, but it could be rewritten to exist in several classes with a better encapsulation of related data parts, and could use a different memory management approach. It does serve to provide an example of neural network algorithms and is presented in Listing 21.2.

```
Object subclass: #NeuralDemo
    instanceVariableNames:
        ' a input output w s c user jon imax jmax kmax '
    classVariableNames: ''
    poolDictionaries:
        ' CharacterConstants ' !

!NeuralDemo class methods !

categories
    ^6!

imax
    ^10!

jmax
    ^6!

kmax
    ^4! !

!NeuralDemo methods !

display

    Transcript show: 'Input: ', Cr asString.

    1 to: imax do:
       [ :i |

         Transcript show: (((input at: user) at: i) asString), ' * ' asString.
         ].
    Transcript show: '              ',Cr asString.

    Transcript show: 'Desired Output',Cr asString.

    1 to: jmax do:
       [ :j |
         Transcript show: (((output at: user) at: j) asString),' * ' asString.
         ].
    Transcript show: '              ',Cr asString.

    Transcript show: 'Actual Output',Cr asString.

    1 to: jmax do:
       [ :j |
         Transcript show: (((a at: j) at: kmax) asString),' * ' asString.
         ].
    Transcript show: '              ',Cr asString.
!
```

Continued

```
init
    | categories |

    kmax := self class kmax.
    imax := self class imax.
    jmax := self class jmax.
    categories := self class categories.
    input := Array new: categories.
    output := Array new: categories.
    w := Array new: imax.
    a := Array new: imax .
    s := Array new: jmax.

    1 to: categories do:
        [ :counter |
        input at: counter put: (Array new: imax).
        output at: counter put: (Array new: jmax).
        1 to: imax do:
            [ :i |
            (input at: counter) at: i put: 0.0.
            ].
        1 to: jmax do:
            [ :j |
            (output at: counter) at: j put: 0.0.
            ].
        ].

    1 to: imax do:
        [ :i |
            a at: i put: (Array new: (kmax + 1)).
            1 to: (kmax + 1) do:
            [ :k |
            (a at: i) at: k put: 0.0.
            ].
        w at: i put: (Array new: jmax).
        1 to: jmax do:
            [ :j |
            (w at: i) at: j put: (Array new: (kmax + 1) ).
            1 to: (kmax + 1) do:
                [:k |
                ((w at: i) at: j) at: k put: 0.0.
                ].
            ].
    ].

1 to: jmax do:
    [:j |
    s at: j put: (Array new: (kmax + 1)).
    ].
    (input at: 1) at: 1 put: 1; at: 2 put: 1.
    (input at: 2) at: 3 put: 1; at: 4 put: 1; at: 5 put: 1.
    (input at: 3) at: 6 put: 1; at: 7 put: 1; at: 8 put: 1; at: 9 put:
```

Continued

```
1.
   (input at: 4) at: 1 put: 1; at: 3 put: 1; at: 5 put: 1; at: 7 put:
1.
   (input at: 5) at: 1 put: 1; at: 2 put: 1; at: 5 put: 1; at: 6 put:
1.
   (output at: 1) at: 1 put: 1.
   (output at: 2) at: 2 put: 1.
   (output at: 3) at: 3 put: 1.
   (output at: 4) at: 4 put: 1.
   (output at: 5) at: 5 put: 1.
   c := 0.1.
!

main

   self init.
   1 to: 10 do:
   [ :i |
      jon := i.
      1 to: 6 do:
      [ :j |
      user := j.
      self selectset.
      self nodeoperation.
"      self display."
      self weightAdjust.
      ].
   ].

self inspect.!

nodeoperation
   |temp|

1 to: (kmax) do:
   [ :k |
   1 to: jmax do:
     [ :j |
     (s at: j) at: (k+1) put: 0.0.
     1 to: imax do:
        [ :i |
        (s at: j) at: (k+1) put: (((s at: j) at: (k+1) ) + ((a at: i)
   at: k) * (((w at: i) at: j) at: k)).
           ].
        temp := ((1+ (0.0 - ((s at: j) at: (k + 1)) exp))).
        ( temp = 0 ) ifFalse: [ temp := 1/temp ].
        (a at: j) at: (k+1) put: temp.
        ].
     ].!
```

Continued

```
selectset

    1 to: imax do:
        [ :i |
        (a at: i) at: 1 put: ((input at: user) at: i).
        ].
    1 to: jmax do:
        [ :j |
        (a at: j) at: kmax put: ((output at: user) at: j).
        ].!


weightAdjust

1 to: (kmax) do:
    [ :k |
    1 to: jmax do:
        [ :j |
        1 to: imax do:
            [ :i |
            ((w at: i) at: j) at: k put: (
                (((w at: i) at: j) at: k) +
                c *
                (((a at: i) at: k) *
                (((output at: user ) at: j) - ((a at: j) at: k))) *
                ( 1 / (1 + (0.0- ((s at: j) at: (k + 1)))) - 1 )
                ).
            ].
        ].
    ].!


weightdisplay

    Transcript show: 'Weights'.

1 to: kmax do:
    [ :k |
    1 to: jmax do:
    [ :j |
        1 to: imax do:
        [ :i |
        Transcript show: ((((w at: i) at: j) at: k )asString),' * '.
        ].
    ].
    ].! !
```

LISTING 21.2 Back-propagation neural network code.

The class methods categories, imax, jmax, and kmax, serve simply as sources for the parameters that define the neural network. The categories parameter defines the number of training sets to be used when training the network, imax defines the number of inputs to the network, jmax defines the number of outputs to the network, and kmax defines the number of layers in the network.

The instance variables imax, jmax, and kmax store the values from the class methods and contain the same information. The other instance variables contain the following information:

a—output of each layer

c—learning rate constant

input—training set of inputs

output—training set of outputs

s—summation for each node

w—weights for each node and input

user—counter for all training sets

jon—counter for all passes through training sets

The methods perform the following functions:

display—displays input, output, and expected output

init—initializes variables to beginning state

main—like the C main, main program loop

nodeoperation—computes value for a node

selectset—selects the training set

weightadjust—back-propagates and adjusts weights

weightdisplay—displays the weight values

Possible extensions to the code consist of a graphic interface, saving and loading of training data, saving and loading of weights, support for more neural network topologies and architectures, and a wrapper to provide the code as a functional part for a visual programming tool.

An Application Case Study

A real-world Smalltalk program used neural networks in a full-text search-and-retrieval application. The program enabled a user to view documents of interest by selecting them from a list of documents. The list of documents was ordered to provide the user with the most desired documents first.

One feature of the system used a back-propagation network to provide the user with documents that most closely matched his or her previous document characteristics. This was accomplished by training the network continually as the user worked, using data based on the choices. In this example, the network never truly "learned" the problem, but was continually adjusting based on the user's actions.

The network was used when the user requested more documents. The user could request documents that were "more like" those just viewed, in which case source document parameters were passed through the network, looking for the most positive set. The user could also request documents that were "totally different" from those just viewed. In this case, the parameters passed into the network that gave the least positive response were then displayed for viewing.

In this application, the user was allowed to turn on and off the learning process. The parameters used consisted of document length, document source, and additional summary information. The users of the system liked the idea of the concept, but were not able to discern whether this feature was of any positive benefit.

The neural network algorithm had to be moved to C because of performance requirements. It was implemented in a C generic DLL call, using Digitalk Smalltalk.

Other Neural Network Resources

Other sources for neural network information include some good Smalltalk code from the Smalltalk Archive and textbooks that have been published in the last few years. A very well-architected neural network program was created at University of Illinois Urbana-Champaign by Murali Krishnan. This program works with ParcPlace Smalltalk version 4.1, but loads in VisualWorks as well. A postscript documentation file can be found in the Smalltalk Archive along with the source code and some sample data sets. It includes three types of networks: a back-propagation, a Hopfield net, and a self-organizing feature map network. Each of these algorithms has a graphical interface and is usable within VisualWorks. Other platforms will lack the user interface, but code other than that should be easily ported.

The architecture of the system allows for other types of networks to be implemented because it takes a very generic approach to neural networks, organizing through nodes, layers, and finally the network.

Many volumes have been written on the topic of neural networks. Recently, some have even appeared with object-oriented approaches for C++. The concepts and architectures are worth exploring on your own or through a university class.

Summary

In this chapter, you learned the basics of neural networks, with emphasis on the back-propagation implementation. You should be able to use the code sample and modify it to create your own neural network components. Neural networks can be used in many applications, and you can experiment with networks in your Smalltalk code.

Smalltalk Resources

Online Resources

Usenet

comp.lang.smalltalk
fj.lang.st80
gnu.smalltalk.bug

Internet Archives

```
http:st-www.cs.uiuc.edu
ftp:st.cs.uiuc.edu
ftp:ftp.qks.com
```

CompuServe

Go Smalltalk—QKS Forum
Go PPDT—VisualWorks/VisualSmalltalk

Go VMARK—ObjectStudio/Enfin Smalltalk
Go VISUAL—IBM Smalltalk/VisualAge

Web Pages

http://home.sprynet.com/sprynet/jpletzke
The author's web page—Stop by and say hello!

http://st-www.cs.uiuc.edu/users/smarch/index.html
UIUC Smalltalk Group

http://st-www.cs.uiuc.edu/users/smarch/small.html
Smalltalk Resources

http://www.w3.org/hypertext/WWW
The World Wide Web Initiative: The Project

http://www.amsinc.com/prod/markets/ctg/objtech/hints/index.htm
Smalltalk Hints Index

http://www.gsa.gov/staff/pa/cic/cic.htm
Consumer Information Center—A Public Service Announcement

http://www.tiac.net/users/jsuth
Jeff Sutherland's Object Technology Homepage

http://www.vmark.com/products/objstud/objstud.
ObjectStudio Homepage

http://www.qks.com
QKS—SmalltalkAgents

http://www.yahoo.com/
Yahoo—Search on Smalltalk

http://www.ibm.com/Products
IBM Products—Services and Support

Groups and Conferences

ANSI Standards Group

The Smalltalk ANSI standard development committee is X3J20. Contact the office to order the latest version of the working document. It can be purchased for $30.00 from the X3 Secretariat, Attn: Lynn Barra, 1250 Eye Street NW, Suite 200, Washington, DC, 20005; Ibarra@itic.nw.dc.us or (202)626-5738; (202)638-4922(fax).

User Groups

New Jersey, New York, Washington DC, Massachusetts, and many more. Check out the Web resources for the latest, or look at:

```
http://www.yahoo.com/
```

and search under Computer:Languages:Smalltalk:UsersGroups

Smalltalk Industry Council (STIC)

```
info@stic.org
```

Voice: 919-821-0181
Fax: 919-856-9752

Promotes Smalltalk

Smalltalk Solutions Conference

Two have been held so far in New York City, usually during March.

Contact SIGS
Voice: 212-242-7515
Fax: 212-242-7578

```
http://www.sigs.com/
conferences@sigs.com
```

ParcPlace-Digitalk Users Conference

The first merged conference was a success. Usually held end of summer somewhere in California. Contact ParcPlace-Digitalk for more information.

Smalltalk Vendors

IBM—VisualAge and IBM Smalltalk

IBM Corporation
Dept TA2/002
P.O. Box 12195
Research Triangle Park, NC 27709-9729
Voice: 800-IBM-3333, extension GS059
Fax: 919-254-4820

http://www.software.ibm.com

You can order a 60-day evaluation of VisualAge/Smalltalk, usually at no charge. This is a fully functioning product limited to 100 image saves and 60 days. For OS/2, Windows, or AIX.

Gemstone

15400 N.W. Greenbrier Parkway, Suite 280
Beaverton, OR 97006
Voice: 503-629-8383
Fax: 503-629-8556

Gemstone OODB

OTI (now owned by IBM)

http://www.oti.com

ParcPlace-Digitalk—VisualWorks, VisualSmalltalk

999 East Arques Ave.
Sunnyvale, CA 94086-4593
Voice: 408-481-9090

http://www.parcplace.com

QKS—SmalltalkAgents

Quasar Knowledge Systems
1405 Main Street
Montara, CA 94037-1478
Voice: 415-728-5333
Fax: 415-728-1757

http://www.qks.com

VMARK Software Inc.

50 Washington Street
Westboro, MA 01581-1021
Voice: 800-OBJECTS/508-366-3888
Fax: 508-366-3669

ObjectStudio, Enfin, Synchronicity

Resellers

The Smalltalk Store

405 El Camino Real, #106
Menlo Park, CA 94025-5240
Voice: 800-787-6389/415-854-5535
Fax: 415-854-2557

http://www.smalltalk.com

All things Smalltalk, large and small.

Third Parties

Applied Reasoning Systems Corporation

2840 Plaza Place, Suite 325
Raleigh, NC 27612
Voice: 919-781-7997
Fax: 919-781-4414

info@arscorp.com

Dynamic Diagram Framework, Parcels & Structured Graphics

Ascent Logic Corporation

> 180 Rose Orchard Way, Suite 200
> San Jose, CA 95134
> Voice: 408-943-0630
> Fax: 408-943-0705

> RDD—A case tool developed in VisualWorks and Gemstone.

First Class Software

> P.O. Box 226
> Boulder Creek, CA 95006
> Voice: 408-338-4649
> Fax: 408-338-1115

> `70761.1216@compuserve.com`

> Profiler/V, Object Explorer

O2 Technology

> 3600 West Bayshore Road, Suite 106
> Palo Alto, CA 94303
> Voice: 415-842-7000
> Fax: 415-842-7001

> `o2info@o2tech.com`
> `http://www.o2tech.com`

> O2 Object Database

Object/FX Corporation

> 2515 Wabash Avenue
> St. Paul, MN 55114
> Voice: 612-644-6064
> Fax: 612-644-0366

> `ofx@millcomm.com`

> SpatialWorks

The Object People

885 Meadowlands Drive, Suite #509
Ottawa, Ontario K2C 3N2
Voice: 613-225-8812
Fax: 613-225-5943

`toplink@objectpeople.on.ca`
`http://www.objectpeople.on.ca`

Makers of TOPLink, a great object persistence framework for VA, VS, VW.

Object Resources Software

8912 Oxbridge Court, Suite 300
Raleigh, NC 27613
Voice: 919-847-2221
Fax: 919-676-7501

Class Publisher, Test Manager

ObjectShare Systems

5 Town & Country Village, Suite 735
San Jose, CA 95128-2026
Voice: 408-970-7280
Fax: 408-970-7282

`76436.1063@compuserve.com`

WindowBuilder, WindowBuilder Pro, Subpanes, and more. Great user interface stuff.

ObjectSoft

47 West Division #136
Chicago, IL 60610
Voice: 312-587-9945
Fax: 312-789-7463

TestKit for VisualWorks
VisualKit for VisualWorks

Polymorphic Software

1091 Industrial Road, Suite 220
San Carlos, CA 94070
Voice: 415-592-6301
Fax: 415-592-6302

75010.3075@compuserve.com

Tensegrity Object Database, Graphics Framework/ST (GF/ST)
Excellent products for Smalltalk only.

Rational Software Corporation

2800 San Tomas Expressway
Santa Clara, CA 95051-0951
Voice: 800-728-1212/408-496-3600
Fax: 408-496-3636

product_info@rational.com
http://www.rational.com

Rational Rose/Smalltalk, Objectory

Smalltalk Source Inc.

2360 Briarwood Trail
Cumming, GA 30131
Voice: 770-844-0564
Fax: 770-886-7263

info@smalltalksource.com

ComponentManager for VisualWorks

Smallware Systems

P.O. Box 4258
Rancho Palos Verdes, CA 90275
Voice: 800-431-2226/310-378-8436
Fax: 310-378-9264

smallware@aol.com

EDIT for Visual Smalltalk

Synergistic Software

322 Commons Way
Princeton, NJ 08540
Voice: 609-252-1850
Fax: 609-252-1855

`70233.2017@compuserve.com`

Visual EIS, Reportoire, SQL interfaces

Techgnosis

One Van De Graaff Drive
Burlington, MA 01803
Voice: 800-730-8351/617-229-6100
Fax: 617-229-0557

`newsletter@techg.com`
`http://www.techgnosis.com/techgnosis`

SequelLink ORB

UniSQL

8911 N. Capital of Texas Highway, Suite 2300
Austin, TX 78759-7200
Voice: 800-451-3267/512-343-7297
Fax: 512-343-7383

`info@unisql.com`

UniSQL ORB

Versant

1380 Willow Road
Menlo Park, CA 94025
Voice: 415-329-7500
Fax: 415-325-2380

Versant OODB

Periodicals

Smalltalk Report
Object Magazine
Journal of Object-Oriented Programming

Contact SIGS to subscribe:
Voice: 800-361-1279
Fax: 615-370-4845

subscriptions@sigs.com

Digitalk Newsletter

Contact ParcPlace/Digitalk

ParcPlace Newsletter

Contact ParcPlace/Digitalk

Books

Keys

P   ParcPlace VisualWorks
D   Digitalk VisualSmalltalk
I   IBM VisualAge Smalltalk
V   VMARK ObjectStudio
Q   QKS SmalltalkAgents
Z   Other Smalltalk
1   Novice
2   Beginner
3   Intermediate
4   Advanced
❤   Recommended
†   Needs updating

Z 3

Bertino, Elisa and Martino, Lorenzo. *Object-Oriented Database Systems: Concepts and Architecture,* Addison-Wesley, 1993, ISBN 0-201-62439-7, 264 pages, $27.96

An introduction to object databases better suited for those with object experience. Written in Italian and translated to English.

♥ Z 3

Budd, Timothy. *A Little Smalltalk,* Addison-Wesley, 1987, ISBN 0-201-10698-1, 280 pages, $32.50

A really neat look at the insides of a limited version of Smalltalk called Little Smalltalk. Discusses many advanced topics like stack frames, and more. A must if you want to understand the concepts of the virtual machine.

3

Coad, Peter. *Object Models - Strategies, Patterns, & Applications,* Prentice-Hall, 1995, ISBN 0-13-108614-6, 505 pages, $41.95, diskette

A book on how to do some object models, with lots of examples and a basic object modelling tool that allows you to save and print models.

♥ 3

Gamma, Erich, et al. *Design Patterns - Elements of Reusable Object-Oriented Software,* Addison-Wesley, 1995, ISBN 0-201-63361-2, 395 pages, $36.95

This book, often referred to as the Gang of Four text, includes Ralph Johnson of the University of Illinois in the list of authors. While not written exclusively for Smalltalk, it does include Smalltalk information. It is a good introduction to the concepts of patterns in the first few chapters, and consists of a catalog of patterns for the balance of the book.

♥ † P 2

Goldberg, Adele and Robson, Dave. *Smalltalk-80: The Language,* Addison-Wesley, 1989, ISBN 0-201-13688-0, 585 pages, $31.95

The revised version of the original book entitled *Smalltalk-80: The Language and Its Implementation,* this is the mother of all Smalltalk programming books. (Out of print. I need a copy. Anyone selling?) It contains many of the details of basic Smalltalk programming, but is aging as the state of the art improves. The version of Smalltalk most closely resembling this is the ParcPlace VisualWorks product.

♥ 2

Goldberg, Adele and Rubin, Kenneth S. *Succeeding with Objects*, Addison-Wesley, 1995, ISBN 0-201-62878-3, 542 pages, $45.95

This book is a pleasure to read, and contains much of value to anyone attempting object-oriented development. It deals with many management and team issues and should not be overlooked by nonmanagers because it helps to define roles for object-oriented developers.

P 2

Hopkins, Trevor and Horan, Bernard. *Smalltalk: An Introduction to Application Development Using VisualWorks*, Prentice-Hall, 1995, ISBN 0-13-318387-4, 424 pages

The latest introduction book for the ParcPlace VisualWorks product.

♥ P 4

Howard, Tim. *The Smalltalk Developer's Guide to VisualWorks*, SIGS Books, 1995, ISBN 1-884842-11-9, 624 pages, $39.00, diskette

Two chapters in the middle of the book are highlighted by the author as the most valuable in the book. I agree, as they deal with domain objects and include some nice coding concepts to improve your business modelling and implementation. The other chapters are not to be missed either, if you want details about the VisualWorks GUI.

♥ † I 3

IBM International Technical Support Centers. *Smalltalk Portability: A Common Base*, IBM, 1992, Document Number GG24-3903-00, 63 pages

An oldie but a goodie, as this book serves as the basis for the ANSI standard that IBM proposed. The standard is deviating, and this book is only reference material, but it is interesting.

2

Jacobson, Ivar, et al. *Object-Oriented Software Engineering: A Use Case-Driven Approach*, ACM Press, 1992, ISBN 0-201-54435-0, 528 pages, $48.50

Use cases are defined ad nauseam here, with Objectory software as the solution to all problems. The methodology is sound, and use cases are the most useful description of a software program that I have ever seen.

3

Klimas, Skublics, and Thomas. *Smalltalk with Style*, Prentice-Hall, 1996, ISBN 0-13-165549-3, 127 pages, $15.00

A laundry list of nice ways to write your Smalltalk code. Some of the items are incredibly obvious and simple, but hey, it's only 15 bucks, and there are a few less-than-obvious ones.

❤ 1

Korienek, Gene and Wrensch, Tom. *A Quick Trip to Objectland*, Prentice-Hall, 1993, ISBN 0-13-012550-4, 175 pages, $21.95

My favorite "baby book" for Smalltalk because of the odd, yet readable conversational style and inclusion of Smalltalk code and terms.

D 2

LaLonde, Wilf R. *Discovering Smalltalk*, Benjamin Cummings, 1994, ISBN 0-8053-2720-7, 554 pages, $42.95

A classroom-style textbook for learning how to write applications in Smalltalk. Explanations tend to be long and in detail, so don't expect to move quickly through this one.

† P 3

LaLonde, Wilf R. and Pugh, John R. *Inside Smalltalk*, volume I, Prentice-Hall, 1990, ISBN 0-13-468414-1, 512 pages, $60.00

An early attempt at a Smalltalk book; it contains mostly GUI use of the development environment from an early Smalltalk-80, ParcPlace release.

† P 3

LaLonde, Wilf R. and Pugh, John R. *Inside Smalltalk*, volume II, Prentice-Hall, 1991, ISBN 0-13-465964-3, 553 pages, $61.95

Volume II of the preceding contains many reference items and advanced topics, but is aging quickly.

† D 4

LaLonde, Wilf R. and Pugh, John R. *Smalltalk V: Practice and Experience*, Prentice-Hall, 1994, ISBN 0-13-814039-1, 185 pages, $30.00, diskette

A collection of article reprints and expansions from the periodical *The Smalltalk Report*.

❤ P 2

Lewis, Simon. *The Art and Science of Smalltalk*, Prentice-Hall, 1995, ISBN 0-13-371345-8, 212 pages, $30.00

A nice, brief introduction to Smalltalk, with plenty of useful tips, but lacking in code examples.

D 4

Lorenz, Mark. *Rapid Software Development with Smalltalk,* SIGS Books, 1995, ISBN 1-884842-12-7, 210 pages, $24.00

Reads like it is composed of notes from a Smalltalk developer's scrapbook, but contains many useful bits of information.

[†] 1

Mann, Steve. *The Smalltalk Resource Guide,* Creative Digital Systems, 1994, ISBN 0-9642181-0-0, 226 pages, $40.00

Contains early *Byte* article reprints, and Product technical papers. Also contains some listings for third parties. Needs updating.

[†] D 2

Marchesi, Michele. *Object-Oriented Programming with Smalltalk/V,* $35.80

Yet another book on Smalltalk/V.

[†] V 2

Pinson, Lewis J. and Wiener, Richard S. *An Introduction to Object-Oriented Programming and Smalltalk,* Addison-Wesley, 1988, ISBN 0-201-19127, 502 pages, $37.50

An older introduction.

I 2

Shafer, Dan and Herndon, Scott. *IBM Smalltalk Programming for Windows and OS/2,* Prima, 1995, ISBN 1-55958-749-0, 470 pages, $49.95, diskette

The only introduction book for IBM, the fourth version of Shafer's book (the third version, for SmalltalkAgents, ships with the product).

[†] D 2

Shafer, Dan with Herndon, Scott and Rozier, Laurence. *Smalltalk Programming for Windows,* Prima, 1993, ISBN 1-55958-237-5, 368 pages, $39.95, diskette

A good applications book for Digitalk version 2.0. The code samples will not work as written for version 3.0, and contains several significant typos to the code. Get the corrections list from CompuServe, or use the code on the diskette (it's more up to date than the text).

[†] D 2

Shafer, Dan and Ritz, Dean A. *Practical Smalltalk,* Springer-Verlag, 1991, ISBN 0-387-97394-X, 233 pages

Deals with the DOS version of Digitalk Smalltalk.

❤ 1

Smith, David N. *Concepts of Object-Oriented Programming*, McGraw Hill, 1991, ISBN 0-07-059177-6, 187 pages, $24.95

A close second to *A Quick Trip to ObjectLand*, this takes a more traditional learning approach and contains much valuable information.

❤ I 2-3

Smith, David N. *IBM Smalltalk: The Language*, Benjamin Cummings, 1995, ISBN 0-8053-0908-X, 577 pages, $47.95

A nice book for IBM Smalltalk with an incredible number of code samples. Begins to scratch the surface of some more advanced topics like exception handling.

1

Taylor, David A. *Object-Oriented Technology: A Manager's Guide*, Addison-Wesley, 1990, ISBN 0-201-56358-4, 146 pages

A favorite freebie provided by the object technology vendors, this book gives a manager the lowdown on object-oriented development.

❤ 2

Webster, Bruce F. *Pitfalls of Object-Oriented Development*, M&T Books, 1995, ISBN 1-55851-397-3, 256 pages, $24.95

Helps to overcome many of the objections to object-oriented development, plus helps to show some of the problems that may occur during development. Good insurance against potentially fatal (to the project) problems.

D 2

Wirfs-Brock, Rebecca, et al. *Designing Object-Oriented Software*, Prentice-Hall, 1990, ISBN 0-13-629825-7, 341 pages

Introduces a methodology for creating object-oriented software, called Responsibility-Driven Design. Includes the elusive Class-Responsibilities-Collaborators (CRC) cards, and is the driving methodology for the Digitalk group.

B

Smalltalk Interview Questions

These interview questions are meant to serve as a starting point for qualifying the level of expertise of a Smalltalk programming candidate. They can serve as a springboard for discussion of the various topics, as well as a study guide for potential candidates. These questions cover diverse areas in Smalltalk programming. Additions to this list are welcome; send e-mail to: jpletzke@sprynet.com.

How to Use the Questions

A competent Smalltalk programmer may be able to speak about most of the topics listed here. It is not likely, though, that a competent programmer will be able to answer all of these questions. Perhaps a modest 50 percent should indicate some level of competence, along with relevant programming project experience. This list is not intended to exclude programmers, as Smalltalk programmers of all levels are essential in the programming community. Answers to these questions should serve to identify what areas (and level) a programmer can handle. Beware of trick questions!

433

The Questions

1. What was the original assignment operator in Smalltalk-80?
2. What does the `at:` method of a collection class return?
3. What does the `at:put:` method of a collection class return?
4. What is a "first class object?"
5. Tell me about block variables, arguments, and scope of variables.
6. Explain Smalltalk mathematical notation, including order of operations and the reasons.
7. Why can't you do recursion in Smalltalk?
8. What is the difference between an instance variable, a class variable, and a class instance variable?
9. Describe indexed instance variables versus named instance variables.
10. How do you access indexed instance variables?
11. What is a metaclass, and which objects are instances of a metaclass?
12. What is an abstract class? Can you name an example in Smalltalk?
13. How does Smalltalk support multitasking?
14. Name some examples of how Smalltalk is oriented toward single users. How can these problems be approached or overcome?
15. Suppose you were offered the choice of two tasks with the same tight deadline:

    Write a Smalltalk to C++ cross-compiler.
    Write a C++ to Smalltalk cross-compiler.
    Which task would you choose and why?

16. Explain the difference between: `do:`, `collect:`, `reject:`, `select:`, `detect:`, and (for bonus points) `inject:into:`.
17. Name some of Smalltalk's shortcomings.
18. What is the fundamental difference between an `Array` and an `OrderedCollection`?

Summary

Remember: Many competent Smalltalk programmers may not be able to answer all these questions correctly, and, conversely, someone who can answer these questions is not necessarily the right candidate for your project. Perhaps a quarter of these questions could be answered by a junior-level programmer, and half to three-quarters could be answered by a senior person. Only a true guru Smalltalker who eats, breathes, and sleeps Smalltalk will be able to get 100 percent, and you probably don't want anyone on your project that knows more than you anyway!

C

Class Hierarchy Comparisons

In this appendix the various class hierarchies of each Smalltalk version has been provided for your reference.

 VisualSmalltalk (Digitalk)

```
| recursiveBlock |
  recursiveBlock := [:each :level |
  (1 to: level)
    do:
       [:index |
        Transcript nextPut: $ .
       ].
  Transcript
    nextPutAll: each printString;
    cr.
  (each subclasses asSortedCollection: Class sortBlock)
    do:
    [:item |
    recursiveBlock value: item value: level + 3.
    ].
  ].
```

Continued

```
"Kick the whole thing off"
 (Object subclasses asSortedCollection: Class sortBlock)
   do:
     [:each |
     recursiveBlock value: each value: 0.
     ].
```

```
-Object-
AnnotationManager
ApplicationCoordinator
  DialogCoordinator
    ListChooser
    RichEditParagraphFormatDialog
      RichEditTabStopDialog
    ServiceManagerWindow
  PARTSApplicationCoordinator
  PropertyInterface
  SocketCoordinator
   SocketClient
     BadMathClient
     DaytimeClient
       DaytimeClientUDP
     FortuneClient
     HTTPClient
     MessageClient
   SocketDaemon
     TCPDaemon
       BadMathDaemon
       FortuneDaemon
       HTTPDaemon
   SocketServer
     BadMathServer
     FortuneServer
     HTTPServer
     MessageServer
Behavior
  Class
  MetaClass
BlockClosure
BlockDescription
Boolean
  False
  True
BusinessObjectGenerator
CallBack
  CallBack16
ClassInstaller
ClassReader
ClipboardManager
CodeGenerationPrivateServices
Collection
  Bag
```

Continued

```
HashedCollection
  Dictionary
    EphemeronDictionary
    IdentityDictionary
      MethodDictionary
        PARTSScriptDictionary
      PARTSMirrorCopyDictionary
    PoolDictionary
    PropertyManager
    SystemDictionary
  Set
    IdentitySet
  SymbolSet
  Table
IndexedCollection
  FixedSizeCollection
    Array
      ActionSequence
      CompiledMethod
        CompiledInitializer
        PARTSScript
      HashTable
        BucketHashTable
        LinearHashTable
          WeakLinearHashTable
        LinearInlineHashTable
          LinearIdentityHashTable
          LinearSymbolHashTable
    ByteArray
    Interval
    String
      DoubleByteString
      DoubleByteSymbol
      Symbol
    OrderedCollection
      Process
      SortedCollection
Color
  IndexedColor
  RGBColor
CompilationError
CompilationResult
CompiledMethodDefinition
  PARTSScriptDefinition
CompilerErrorHandler
  NonInteractiveErrorHandler
  SilentErrorHandler
    HaltingErrorHandler
    PARTSSilentErrorHandler
    TraditionalCompilerErrorHandler
  TextPaneErrorHandler
    PARTSTextPaneErrorHandler
```

Continued

```
            WorkspaceErrorHandler
    CompilerInterface
      PARTSScriptCompilerInterface
    CompilerNameScope
      DictionaryScope
        GlobalPoolScope
      MultiplePoolScope
    Context
      HomeContext
      OneArgumentBlock
      TwoArgumentBlock
      ZeroArgumentBlock
    CursorManager
      PARTSCursorManager
    DatabaseModel
    DefinitionGroup
    DefinitionInstaller
    DeletedClass
    Development
    DIB
    DocumentationGenerator
    DragDropObject
      LocalDragDropObject
        PARTSLocalDragDropObject
          PARTSAddPartObject
            PARTSPasteObject
          PARTSEditorMoveObject
    DragDropSession
      LocalDragDropSession
        PARTSLocalDragDropSession
          PARTSAddPartSession
            PARTSCatalogDragSession
            PARTSPasteSession
            PARTSRepeatDropSession
          PARTSDragSession
          PARTSEditorMoveSession
    EmptySlot
    Ephemeron
    EvaluableAction
      CollectionAccessor
        ConstantAccessor
      Message
        LinkMessage
          PARTSAliasMessage
    EventManager
      SessionModel
      SharedValue
        SharedBoolean
      Timer
    Exception
      Error
        APICallError
```

Continued

```
            APICallEntryPointNotFound
            APICallInvalidArgumentType
            APICallUnknownPrimitiveFailure
        ArithmeticError
          ZeroDivide
        BindError
          BindDuplicate
          ClassShapeMismatch
          UnresolvedExternal
        ControlError
          MessageNotUnderstood
            PARTSMessageNotUnderstood
        FileError
          FileAlreadyExists
          FileErrorWriteProtected
        FileSharingViolation
          FileSystemAccessDenied
          TooManyOpenFiles
        PARTSApplicationLoadError
          PARTSCyclicReference
          PARTSEmptyFile
          PARTSFileNotFound
            PARTSNotOnSearchPath
          PARTSIncorrectVersion
        PARTSInvalidApplication
          PARTSNestedPartLoadError
        PARTSInvalidExternalDataItemSize
        SocketError
        UnknownImport
    HostFileSystemError
Notification
  AboutToReplaceFile
    KeyboardInterrupt
    ObsoleteRepositoryConnectionsAllowed
    PessimisticRepositoryOnFirstEditRequest
      PessimisticRepositoryEditAnywayOnFirstEditRequest
      PessimisticRepositoryLockOnFirstEditRequest
    ProcessTermination
    ProgressNotification
  RecompilationNotification
    RepositoryAmbiguousSpecNotification
    RepositoryConfirmation
    RepositoryDescription
    RepositoryInconsistencyAction
    RepositoryInconsistencyDetected
    RepositoryInconsistencyNotification
      PVCSSemaphoreFileNotification
        RepositoryDuplicateEntityInArchiveNotification
        RepositoryLockedForWritingNotification
        RepositoryMissingArchiveNotification
        RepositoryMissingDataDirNotification
        RepositoryUnmappedArchiveNotification
```

Continued

```
                         RepositoryUnmappedRevisionNotification
                     RepositoryReconnectRequest
                     UnregisteredEvent
                 VetoAction
                 Warning
                     LoggedWarning
             PARTSGetExecutionContext
             RecoveryFailure
             RepositoryError
                 RepositoryAccessControlNotSupported
                 RepositoryClientError
                 RepositoryNoLock
                 RepositoryNoWrite
                 RepositoryObjectAlreadyExists
                     EntityRevisionAlreadyExists
                     RepositoryAlreadyExists
                     RepositoryDataAlreadyExistsOnDisk
                     RepositoryEntityAlreadyExists
                 RepositoryObjectDoesNotExist
                     EntityRevisionDoesNotExist
                     RepositoryDataDoesNotExistOnDisk
                     RepositoryDoesNotExist
                     RepositoryEntityDoesNotExist
                 RepositorySystemPathCannotBeResolved
                 RepositoryNoAccessDatabase
                 RepositorySystemError
                 RepositoryAccessDenied
                 RepositoryNoConnection
             TeamVError
                 SemanticError
                 CannotEditModuleError
                 ClassDefinitionError
                 ExistingHandleError
                 ExistingReferencesError
                 InvalidHandleError
                 InvalidNameError
                 MigrationConflictError
                 UndefinedNameError
             TestFailedException
         ExceptionFilter
         ExceptionHandler
         ExceptionSet
         ExpressionEvaluator
             WorkspaceExpressionEvaluator
         ExternalBuffer
             ExternalLong
                 ExternalAddress
                     ExternalGlobalAddress
                     ExternalHeapAddress
                     ExternalSegmentedAddress
             Fd_set
             SelfDefinedStructure
```

Continued

```
SocketStructure
   Hostent
   Linger
   Protoent
   Servent
   Sockaddr_in
   Timeval
   WSAData
VirtualMachineConfiguration
Win32FindData
WinBitmapFileHeader
WinBitmapInfoHeader
   WinBitmapInfo
WinBitmapStruct
WinCharFormat
WinColorref
WinDialogInfo
WinDrawItemStruct
WinEditStream
WinFileTime
WinFormatRange
WinHdItem
WinHdLayout
WinLargeInteger
WinLogBrush
WinLogFont
WinLogPalette
WinLogPen
WinLvColumn
WinLvItem
WinMeasureItemStruct
WinMemorystatus
WinMessage
WinMetafileheader
WinMetafilepict
WinMetaheader
WinMinmaxinfo
WinNmhdr
   WinHdNotify
   WinLvDispinfo
   WinLvKeydown
   WinNmListview
   WinNmTreeview
   WinTbNotify
   WinTooltiptext
   WinTvDispinfo
   WinTvKeydown
WinOfstruct
WinPaintStructure
WinPaletteEntry
WinParaFormat
WinPoint
```

Continued

```
         WinRectangle
         WinStructArray
      WinSystemTime
      WinTbAddBitmap
      WinTbButton
      WinTbSaveParams
      WinTcItem
      WinTextMetrics
      WinToolinfo
      WinTvInsertstruct
      WinTvItem
      WinWindowClass
      WinWindowPlacement
   ExternalHandle
      Atom
      DeviceContext
      DynamicLinkLibrary
         CommonControlsDLL
         CommonDialogDLL
         DynamicLinkLibrary16
            KernelDLL16
            ThunkWin32sDLL
         GDIDLL
         KernelDLL
         MultimediaDLL
         PARTSSpeakerDLL
         RichEdit32DLL
         ShellDLL
         ThunkWin95DLL
         UserDLL
         VirtualMachineDLL
         VirtualMachineExe
         WinsockDLL
         WNetDLL
      ExternalMemoryHandle
         ExternalGlobalHandle
         ExternalHeapHandle
      FileHandle
      WindowHandle
   FileSearchResults
   FileSystemEntity
      FileSystemComponent
         File
      FileSystemContainer
         Directory
            PARTSDosDirectory
               PARTSTeamVDirectory
   FileSystemLocator
      FileSystemPath
         NetworkFilePath
         RepositorySystemPath
      FileVolume
```

Continued

```
Font
GraphicsMedium
  Bitmap
  Printer
  Screen
  StoredPicture
GraphicsTool
  TextTool
  Pen
    RecordingPen
GUIModel
  GUIComplex
  GUIMeasure
  GUIOrganizer
    GUIWidget
      GUIClicker
      GUIDecorator
      GUIPicker
      GUITyper
GUISmalltalkBrand
  GUIENF
  GUISTA
  GUIVA
  GUIVSE
  GUIVW
Handle
  AnnotatedObjectHandle
    ArchivedObjectHandle
      ScopedObjectHandle
        ClusterHandle
        PackageHandle
        SubsystemHandle
      DefinitionHandle
        ClassDefinitionHandle
        PoolDefinitionHandle
        SourceBasedDefinitionHandle
          ClassInitializationDefinitionHandle
          GlobalVariableDefinitionHandle
          InitializationExpressionDefinitionHandle
          MethodDefinitionHandle
          PoolVariableDefinitionHandle
        VariableDefinitionHandle
      SpecificationHandle
    DefinitionVersionHandle
  ToolInterface
HelpManager
  PARTSHelpManager
HTMLResponse
HTTPRequest
Icon
  PARTSIcon
IdentifiedValue
```

Continued

```
ImageList
InitializationFile
InitializationFileSection
InputEvent
KeyboardInputEvent
LayoutUnit
  CompositeLayout
  ComputedLayout
  LayoutFrame
    DialogLayoutFrame
ListItem
  ButtonListBoxItem
  HeaderItem
  ListViewItem
  TreeViewItem
Magnitude
  Association
    PropertyAccessor
      ObjectPropertyAccessor
        GroupPropertyAccessor
      SelectorPropertyAccessor
        LinkPropertyAccessor
      StylePropertyAccessor
        MaskedStylePropertyAccessor
  Character
  Date
  Number
    FixedPoint
    Float
    Fraction
    Integer
      LargeInteger
        LargeNegativeInteger
        LargePositiveInteger
      SmallInteger
    RepositoryRevisionNumber
  Time
  TimeStamp
    PARTSTimeStamp
MciDevice
  MciStream
    CdAudio
    MciFileStream
      AviVideo
      WaveAudio
Menu
  PARTSStandardMenu
    PARTSStandardBracketsMenu
    PARTSStandardEditMenu
      PARTSEditMenu
    PARTSStandardFileMenu
      PARTSFileMenu
```

Continued

```
            PARTSStandardHelpMenu
              PARTSHelpMenu
        MenuItem
        MethodExecutor
        MigrationOptions
        MigrationResult
        NationalLanguageSupport
        NotificationManager
        ObjectChangeMap
        ObjectFiler
        ObjectMutator
        ObjectReference
        ObjectStore
          ObjectStoreWithClient
          SmalltalkLibrary
        ObjectStoreExternal
          ObjectStoreFileExternal
        ObjectStoreFile
          ObjectStoreFileWithVersion
        ObjectStoreObject
        ObjectStoreObjects
          ObjectStoreFileObjects
          SmalltalkLibraryObjects
        ObjectStoreReader
          ObjectLoader
          SmalltalkLibraryBinder
        ObjectStoreRoot
        ObjectStoreSpace
        ObjectStoreSpaceExternals
        ObjectStoreWriter
          ObjectDumper
          SmalltalkLibraryBuilder
            ObjectLibrary
        OperatingSystemInformation
        PARTSApplication
        PARTSApplicationHolder
          PARTSAddObjectDialog
          PARTSWindow
            PARTSChooseFileDialog
              PARTSOpenSaveFileDialog
              PARTSRevisionDialog
                PARTSOpenRevisionDialog
                  PARTSOpenLatestRevisionDialog
                PARTSSaveRevisionDialog
              PARTSPartBrowser
                PARTSNestedPartBrowser
                  PARTSTeamVNestedPartBrowser
              PARTSPartPropertiesEditor
                PARTSPartPropertyDialog
                  PARTSNonvisualPartPropertyDialog
                  PARTSVisualPartPropertyDialog
                    PARTSCommonPropertiesEditor
```

Continued

```
                        PARTSGroupPanePropertiesEditor
                        PARTSOrderedVisualPartPropertyDialog
                   PARTSPartPropertySubdialog
                     PARTSOpenWindowPropertiesEditor
                        PARTSOpenDialogWindowPropertiesEditor
                   PARTSWindowSizeEditor
              PARTSPictureMaskEditor
              PARTSReferenceBrowser
              PARTSScenarioComment
              PARTSScenarioPairs
              PARTSSettingsViewer
                PARTSBackgroundColorSettingsEditor
                PARTSLinkColorSettingsEditor
                PARTSMouseButtonsSettingsEditor
                PARTSSettingsEditor
         PARTSApplicationProperty
         PARTSCatalog
         PARTSCodeGeneratorInterface
           PARTSCodeGeneratorReaderInterface
           PARTSCodeGeneratorWriterInterface
         PARTSDial
         PARTSDragDropSpec
         PARTSDragResult
         PARTSEditor
         PARTSEditorState
         PARTSException
         PARTSFile
         PARTSFileDescriptor
           PARTSDosFileDescriptor
           PARTSTeamVFileDescriptor
         PARTSFileOperationContext
           PARTSLoadContext
           PARTSStoreContext
         PARTSFileProcessor
           PARTSPartFileProcessor
             PARTSExecutablePartFileProcessor
               PARTSExeFileProcessor
           PARTSSmalltalkLibraryFileProcessor
           PARTSSourceFileProcessor
         PARTSFileType
         PARTSFileVersion
         PARTSFormGenerator
         PARTSFormGeneratorItem
         PARTSFramer
         PARTSHostInterface
         PARTSIniFile
         PARTSInterfaceList
         PARTSLink
           PARTSAliasLink
         PARTSLinkEditState
         PARTSLinkReference
           PARTSSublinkReference
```

Continued

```
PARTSLinkSettings
PARTSNonvisualPart
  BusinessObjectGeneratorPart
  BusinessObjectHolderPart
  DatabaseModelPart
  MyPart
  PARTSAddObject
  PARTSClipboardAccessorPart
  PARTSComparisonPart
  PARTSComputationPart
  PARTSConversionPart
  PARTSDiskAccessorPart
  PARTSFileAccessorPart
  PARTSLaunchPadPart
  PARTSLinkJunctionPart
  PARTSPartAccessorPart
  PARTSPrebuiltDialog
    PARTSFileDialogPart
      PARTSAnyFileDialogPart
    PARTSPrebuiltMessageBox
      PARTSConfirmerPart
      PARTSConfirmerWithCancelPart
      PARTSInformationDialogPart
    PARTSPrompterPart
  PARTSPrinterPart
  PARTSSizeWindowPart
  PARTSSpeakerPart
  PARTSStringTemplatePart
  PARTSTimerPart
  PARTSValueHolderPart
    PARTSTypedValueHolder
    PARTSCollectionHolder
        PARTSArrayHolderPart
        PARTSDictionaryHolderPart
      PARTSNumberHolderPart
      PARTSOrderedCollectionHolderPart
      PARTSStringHolderPart
PARTSNotebookPage
  PARTSNotebookPageAttributes
PARTSPropertyStructure
PARTSPropertyUnit
  PARTSPropertyBoolean
    PARTSPropertyPseudoStyle
    PARTSPropertyWindowStyle
      PARTSPropertyBinaryStyle
  PARTSPropertyButton
    PARTSPropertyEditButton
    PARTSPropertyFormGeneratorButton
      PARTSPropertyCreateForm
      PARTSPropertyCreateTable
    PARTSPropertySequenceChildren
  PARTSPropertyButtonGroup
```

Continued

```
                    PARTSPropertyButtonGroupWS
                        PARTSPropertyButtonGroupWSExtended
                PARTSPropertyColorAndFont
                PARTSPropertyDateFormat
                PARTSPropertyDragDrop
                PARTSPropertyFixedList
                PARTSPropertyGraphic
                PARTSPropertyIcon
                PARTSPropertyLineOfButtons
                PARTSPropertyList
                PARTSPropertyMenuAccelerator
                PARTSPropertyStaticText
                PARTSPropertyString
                    PARTSPropertyExpression
                    PARTSPropertyFormattedString
                    PARTSPropertyNumber
                    PARTSPropertyText
        PARTSScenario
        PARTSScenarioEditor
        PARTSScriptContext
        PARTSScriptSource
        PARTSSessionManager
            PARTSDevelopmentSessionManager
            PARTSRuntimeSessionManager
            PARTSWorkbenchSessionManager
        PARTSSettings
        PARTSStringTemplate
        PARTSTeamVInterface
        PARTSTextIcon
        PARTSUpgradeObject
            PARTSUpgradeVisualPart
                PARTSUpgradePanePart
                    PARTSUpgradeTablePane
        PARTSWrapper
        Pattern
            WildPattern
        Point
        Preferences
        ProcessScheduler
        PropertyPage
        ProtectedFrameMarker
        PVCSEntity
            PVCSArchive
            PVCSWorkingDirectory
        Rectangle
        RepositoryAccessPermissions
            RepositoryEntityAccessPermissions
        RepositoryChecker
        RepositoryInconsistency
            RepositoryEntityMapExtraRevision
            RepositoryEntityMapMissingRevision
            RepositoryExtraEntityDir
```

Continued

```
      RepositoryFileInconsistency
        RepositoryExtraArchiveFile
        RepositoryExtraFile
          RepositoryExtraGenerationFile
          RepositoryExtraWriteLockFile
          RepositoryGlobalPVCSTempFile
          RepositoryPVCSemaphore
          RepositoryPVCSTmpFile
          RepositoryWorkingFile
        RepositoryMissingEntityArchive
        RepositoryMissingFile
          RepositoryMissingGenerationFile
          RepositoryMissingReadLockFile
        RepositoryZeroLengthArchive
      RepositoryMissingEntityDir
   RepositoryInconsistencyHandler
   RepositoryObjectSpec
     EntityRevisionSpec
       RepositoryContainerSpec
       RepositoryEntitySpec
       RepositorySpec
         SlavedRepositorySpec
     RepositoryEntityTypeListSpec
   RepositorySanityCheck
   RepositoryServices
   RepositorySystemObject
     RepositorySystemComponent
       EntityRevision
     RepositorySystemContainer
       Repository
       RepositoryEntity
   RepositoryUserOrGroup
     RepositoryGroup
     RepositoryUser
   RepositoryVolume
   ResidueObject
   Semaphore
   Service
   ServiceManager
   ServiceRegistry
   SmalltalkLibraryReporter
   SmalltalkToolInterface
   Socket
     InetSocket
       TCPSocket
       UDPSocket
   SocketChannel
     ArrayChannel
     ArrayOfStringsChannel
     BooleanChannel
     ObjectChannel
       EventChannel
```

Continued

```
        MessageChannel
      SmallPositiveIntegerChannel
      StringChannel
  SocketErrorDescription
  SocketEvent
  SocketRegistration
  SourceManager
    TeamSourceManager
  StatusBox
  StatusField
  Stream
    ReadStream
    WriteStream
      ReadWriteStream
        FileStream
          MixedFileStream
        HTMLStream
        RTFStream
        SocketReadStream
        SocketWriteStream
  StreamReference
      LibrarySourceReference
      SystemStreamReference
  StringDictionaryReader
  StringModel
  StringReference
      SourceChunkReference
  SystemWeakRegistries
  TabControlItem
    TabControlPage
  TableModel
  TeamLibraryInformation
  TeamVInterface
  TeamVToolInterface
  TestCase
    IdentifiedValueTestCase
    SetTestCase
  TestFailure
  TestResult
  TestSuite
  TextSelection
  Tool
  ToolbarItem
    ToolbarButton
      ToolbarToggleButton
    ToolbarSeparator
  TranscriptProxy
  UndefinedObject
  UpgraderForDirectory
  UpgraderForFile
  VariableLocator
```

Continued

```
        VariableLocatorNoSource
    ViewManager
      Browser
        CodeBrowser
          ClassBrowser
          ClassHierarchyBrowser
        Debugger
          PARTSDeveloperDebugger
        MethodBrowser
          SelectorBrowser
      Inspector
        ByteArrayInspector
        DictionaryInspector
        DoubleByteStringInspector
        FieldInspector
        GraphicInspector
        OrderedCollectionInspector
      TextWindow
        PARTSTextWindow
        TranscriptWindow
        WalkbackWindow
      BusinessObjectGeneratorView
      BusinessObjectListView
      DatabaseView
      PARTSBitEditor
        PARTSIconEditor
          PARTSIconEditorWindows
      TableView
      TestMonitor
      WindowDialog
        AboutDialog
        FindReplaceDialog
        ListDialog
          MultiSelectListDialog
          RadioButtonDialog
          SeparatedListDialog
        ObjectLoadDialog
        PARTSDialog
          PARTSContentsEditor
            PARTSArrayEditor
            PARTSDictionaryEditor
            PARTSOrderedCollectionEditor
          PARTSDialEditor
          PARTSPointEditor
            PARTSExtentEditor
          PARTSPropertiesEditor
          PARTSRelativeLayoutDialog
            PARTSFieldOrderDialog
          PARTSSequenceEditor
            S22
            PARTSPathSequenceEditor
```

Continued

```
                  PARTSSimpleTextEditor
                     PARTSSimpleRichTextEditor
                  PARTSTabOrderEditor
               PrintAbortDialog
               ProgressIndicatorDialog
               Prompter
                  PARTSPrompter
               SaveImageAsDialog
               SaveImageDialog
        WeakRegistry
          WeakKeyedRegistry
        Window
          ApplicationWindow
            TopPane
               DialogTopPane
                  DialogWindow
                  PARTSDialogTopPane
                  PARTSPrebuiltDialogTopPane
               MainWindow
               PARTSTopPane
                  PARTSWindowPart
                     PARTSDialogWindowPart
            ControlWindow
              MenuWindow
                 PARTSMenuWindow
                    PARTSMenuBar
                    PARTSPopupWindowOS2
                    PARTSPopupWindowWindows
              ToolTip
            DialogBox
              CommonSystemDialog
                 ColorDialog
              FileDialog
                 PARTSFileDialog
                    PARTSAnyFileDialog
                 FontDialog
                 PrintDialog
              MessageBox
                 PARTSMessageBox
              NewSubclassDialog
            ObjectWindow
              PARTSStarterWindow
                 PARTSStarterWindowWindows
              PARTSTimerWindow
              SocketNotificationManager
              SystemWindow
            SubPane
              ControlPane
                 Button
                    DrawnButton
                       PARTSDrawnButtonPart
```

Continued

```
            PARTSPushButtonPart
        Toggle
          CheckBox
            PARTSCheckBoxPart
            ThreeStateButton
          RadioButton
            PARTSRadioButtonPart
    EntryField
      ComboEntryField
        PARTSComboEntryField
      PARTSEntryFieldPart
        PARTSFormattedEntryField
          PARTSAlphabeticEntryFieldPart
        PARTSDateEntryFieldPart
      PARTSNumericField
        PARTSFixedDecimalEntryFieldPart
          PARTSCurrencyEntryFieldPart
        PARTSFloatEntryFieldPart
        PARTSIntegerEntryFieldPart
      PARTSPhoneNumberEntryFieldPart
      PARTSPictureFieldPart
    PARTSExpressionEntryField
    TextEdit
      SpinButtonEntryField
      TextPaneControl
        PARTSTextPanePart
        RichEdit
    Header
    ListBox
      ButtonListBox
      DropDownList
        ComboBox
          PARTSComboBoxPart
        PARTSDropDownListPart
      ExtendedListBox
      MultipleSelectListBox
        PARTSMultipleChoiceListPart
      PARTSListPanePart
    ListView
    PARTSBaseNotebook
      PARTSNotebook
    RangeControl
      PagedRangerControl
        ScrollBar
        TrackBar
      ProgressBar
      UpDown
    StaticPane
      GroupBox
        PARTSGroupPanePart
      StaticBox
```

Continued

```
              StaticGraphic
                 PARTSStaticGraphicPart
              StaticText
                 PARTSStaticTextPart
           StatusWindow
           TabControl
              PARTSTabControlPart
           Toolbar
           TreeView
        GraphPane
        PARTSGraphPanePart
           PARTSDialPanePart
        PARTSIconPane
     GroupPane
        PARTSMenuPaneWindows
        PARTSNotebookClientAreaPane
        PARTSNotebookPagePane
        PARTSTabControlPagePart
        SpinButton
        ToolPane
           PARTSToolPane
     ListConnectionPane
     ListPane
     PARTSPane
        PARTSGroupPane
           PARTSNestedPart
           PARTSOrderedGroupPane
              PARTSMenuPart
              PARTSToolContainer
           PARTSToolboxPart
        PARTSMenuItemPane
           PARTSMenuBitmapItemPart
              PARTSToolbarItem
                 PARTSToolbarButtonPart
                    PARTSToolbarToggleButtonPart
                 PARTSToolbarSeparatorPart
              PARTSMenuSeparatorPart
            · PARTSMenuTextItemPart
           PARTSMenuLabelPart
        PARTSScrollPane
        StatusPane
        TextPane
        VideoPane
  WindowPolicy
     NoMenusWindowPolicy
     StandardWindowPolicy
     SmalltalkWindowPolicy
  WinLogicalObject
     WinLogicalBrush
     WinLogicalPalette
     WinLogicalPen
  -SelfInitializingObject-
```

VisualWorks (ParcPlace)

```
| recursiveBlock output|
  output := 'classhry.txt' asFilename writeStream.
  recursiveBlock := [:each :level |
    (1 to: level) do: [:index | output nextPut: $ .].
    output nextPutAll: (each printString); cr.
    (each subclasses asSortedCollection: [:x :y | x printString <= y
printString])
    do: [:item | recursiveBlock value: item value: (level + 3)]].
(Object subclasses asSortedCollection: [:x :y | x printString <= y
printString])
  do: [:each | recursiveBlock value: each value: 0.].
output flush.
```

```
Classes that don't inherit from object:
     LensAbsentee class
        LensAbstractProxy class
          LensCollectionProxy class
          LensProxy class
        LensQuerySurrogate class
          LensChildrenSetSurrogate class
          LensExpressionSurrogate class
        LensCommandVariable class
        LensFunctionSurrogate class
          LensArbitraryFunctionSurrogate class
        LensOperationSurrogate class
        LensAggregateSurrogate class
        LensValueSurrogate class
          LensObjectSurrogate class
          LensSubquerySurrogate class
          LensVariableSurrogate class
-Object-
Behavior
  ClassDescription
    Class
      Metaclass
BinaryObjectStorage
  HelpAccessor
BlockClosure
Boolean
  False
  True
Border
  EtchedBorder
BorderDecorationPolicy
  EmulationBorderDecorationPolicy
    CUABorderDecorationPolicy
    MacBorderDecorationPolicy
    MotifBorderDecorationPolicy
```

```
                    Win3BorderDecorationPolicy
                  SmalltalkBorderDecorationPolicy
              BOSSCompiledCodeHolder
              BOSSContents
              BOSSRegisteredObject
              BOSSSpecialObjectLoader
              BOSSTransporter
                BOSSReader
                  BOSSDebugReader
                BOSSWriter
              ByteCodeStream
                CodeStream
                  RecodeStream
              ByteFieldDescriptor
              CDatum
                CArray
                CComposite
                CPointer
                  CCompositePointer
                CProcedurePointer
                  CCallback
              CellProperties
              Change
                ClassRelatedChange
                  ClassChange
                    ClassDefinitionChange
                    ClassOtherChange
                      ClassCommentChange
                  MethodChange
                    MethodDefinitionChange
                    MethodOtherChange
                OtherChange
              CharacterAttributes
                VariableCharacterAttributes
                  PlatformCharacterAttributes
              CharacterComposer
              CharacterEncoder
                ByteCharacterEncoder
                LargeCharacterEncoder
                UnicodeCharacterEncoder
              ClassBuilder
              ClassCategoryReader
              ClassOrganizer
                SystemOrganizer
              CodeLabel
              CodeReader
              Collection
                Bag
                KeyedCollection
                  ColorPreferencesCollection
                    ChainedColorPreferences
                    ColorPreferencesDictionary
```

Continued

```
        LookPreferences
   MethodDictionary
   Palette
      ColorPalette
         FixedPalette
         MappedPalette
            MonoMappedPalette
         CoveragePalette
      StopsDictionary
   LensContainer
      LensBaseContainer
      LensCompositeContainer
   SequenceableCollection
      ArrayedCollection
         Array
            BOSSReaderMap
            DependentsCollection
            ScannerTable
            SegmentedCollection
               LargeArray
               LargeWordArray
            CharacterArray
            String
               ByteEncodedString
                  ByteString
                  ISO8859L1String
                  MacString
                  OS2String
               GapString
               Symbol
                  ByteSymbol
                  TwoByteSymbol
               TwoByteString
            Text
         IntegerArray
         ByteArray
         BinaryStorageBytes
         BOSSBytes
         WordArray
         List
         DependentList
         LensStreamList
      RunArray
      TableAdaptor
      TwoDList
      WeakArray
   Interval
      SlidingInterval
      TextLineInterval
   LinkedList
      HandlerList
      Semaphore
```

Continued

```
            OrderedCollection
              FontDescriptionBundle
              LinkedOrderedCollection
              SortedCollection
                SortedCollectionWithPolicy
                SPActiveLines
                SPSortedLines
          Set
            Dictionary
              CEnvironment
              IdentityDictionary
                PropertyListDictionary
                WeakDictionary
                  HandleRegistry
                    ExternalRegistry
                  WeakAssociationDictionary
                    LinkedWeakAssociationDictionary
                      ExternalDictionary
              LensLinkedDictionary
                LensProtectedLinkedDictionary
              LensRegistry
                LensWeakRegistry
                  LensObjectRegistry
              PoolDictionary
                SystemDictionary
              IdentitySet
                ObjectRegistry
                SignalCollection
      ColumnReorderAgent
      ColumnResizeAgent
      CompiledCode
        CompiledBlock
        CompiledMethod
          AnnotatedMethod
            MarkedMethod
          ExternalMethod
      CompilerErrorHandler
        InteractiveCompilerErrorHandler
        LoggingCompilerErrorHandler
        NonInteractiveCompilerErrorHandler
          QueryCompilerErrorHandler
        SilentCompilerErrorHandler
      ComposedBlock
      CompoundTextEncodingDefinition
      CompoundTextStateNode
      Controller
        ComboBoxButtonController
        ControllerWithMenu
          BitEditor
            ColorBitEditor
          DataSetController
            PaintedDataSetController
```

Continued

```
         LDMCompositeViewController
         LDMElementViewController
         ModalController
           UIPainterController
         ParagraphEditor
           TextEditorController
             InputBoxController
               ComboBoxInputBoxController
         SequenceController
           ComboBoxListController
           EmulatedSequenceController
       DataSetControllerProxy
       LauncherController
       MenuBarButtonController
       MenuButtonController
       MenuController
         MenuAsPopUpController
         MenuAsSubmenuController
         MenuFromMenuBarController
         MenuFromMenuButtonController
       MenuItemController
       NoController
       ScrollbarController
         EmulationScrollBarController
       SelectController
         BasicButtonController
           ToggleButtonController
             RadioButtonController
           TriggerButtonController
         ColoredAreaController
         SliderController
         TabBarController
       StandardSystemController
         ApplicationStandardSystemController
           ApplicationDialogController
             DropDownListController
           UIPainterSystemController
       WidgetController
   ControlManager
   ControlMode
     DrawingMode
       DragMode
         CornerDragMode
         DividerResizingDragMode
         NullDragMode
         OrientationResizeMode
         SelectionDragMode
         SpecDragMode
           PlacementMode
             DragPlacementMode
             SelectPlacementMode
       SelectMode
```

Continued

```
CStructureLayout
CType
  CCompoundType
    CCompositeType
    CEnumerationType
  COopType
  CPointerType
    CArrayType
  CProcedureType
  CQualifiedType
    CTypedefType
  CScalarType
    CIntegerType
    CLimitedPrecisionRealType
  CVoidType
DatabaseCommand
DatabaseTypeMapping
DataSetColumn
DeferredBlock
DefineOpcodePool
Delay
DependencyTransformer
Dialog
DispatchTable
DitherUpTo4
Document
DocumentRenderer
DragDropContext
DragDropData
DragDropManager
DropSource
  ConfigurableDropSource
DropTarget
  ConfigurableDropTarget
DSVDependencyAgent
EncodedStreamConstructor
  ExternalEncodedStreamConstructor
  FileEncodedStreamConstructor
  InternalEncodedStreamConstructor
Exception
ExternalConnection
  FileConnection
ExternalDatabaseBuffer
ExternalDatabaseColumnDescription
ExternalDatabaseError
ExternalDatabaseFramework
  ExternalDatabaseConnection
  ExternalDatabaseSession
  ExternalDatabaseTransaction
ExternalInterface
  InputManager
    NullInputManager
```

Continued

```
        X11InputManager
ExternalLibrary
ExternalLibraryHolder
ExternalObject
  ExternalProcedure
  ExternalVariable
Filename
  MacFilename
  PCFilename
    FATFilename
    HPFSFilename
    NTFSFilename
  UnixFilename
FontDescription
FontPolicy
Geometric
  Bezier
  Circle
  EllipticalArc
  LineSegment
  Polyline
  Rectangle
    CharacterBlock
  Spline
GraphicsAttributes
GraphicsContext
  HostPrinterGraphicsContext
  PostScriptGraphicsContext
  ScreenGraphicsContext
GraphicsDevice
  HostGraphicsDevice
    HostPrinter
    Screen
  PostScriptPrinter
  Printer
GraphicsMedium
  DisplaySurface
    UnmappableSurface
      Mask
      Pixmap
    Window
      ScheduledWindow
        ApplicationWindow
      TransientWindow
  HostPrintJob
  MockMedium
  PostScriptFile
HelpElement
  HelpBook
  HelpChapter
  HelpExample
  HelpLibrary
```

Continued

```
HelpPage
HelpForwarder
HelpSeeAlso
ImageReader
  BMPImageReader
ImageRenderer
  ErrorDiffusion
  PaintRenderer
    NearestPaint
    OrderedDither
ImplementationFont
  CompositeFont
  DeviceFont
    PostScriptPrinterFont
    ScreenFont
      MacFont
      MSWindowsFont
        OS2Font
      XFont
  SyntheticFont
InputSensor
  TranslatingSensor
  WindowSensor
    ApplicationWindowSensor
InputState
InstructionClient
  InstructionPrinter
  InstructionStream
    CodeRegenerator
    Context
      BlockContext
      MethodContext
    Decompiler
InverseColorMap
InverseColorMapInitializer
IOBuffer
  PositionalIOBuffer
KeyboardEvent
KeyboardProcessor
Layout
  LayoutOrigin
    AlignmentOrigin
    LayoutFrame
LDMAbstractVisualBuilder
  LDMGraphBuilder
    LDMProtoMapBuilder
  LDMIndentedListBuilder
LDMArc
LDMElementProxy
  LDMReversingElementProxy
LDMGraph
LDMNodeChild
```

Continued

```
LDMPerspective
LDMRelationsGenerator
LDMRelationship
  LDMFirstOrderRel
    LDMSpecialRel
  LDMHighOrderRel
    LDMDiadicRel
      LDMComposedRel
      LDMOrRel
    LDMMonadicRel
      LDMLimitingRel
      LDMNonReflexiveRel
      LDMTransitiveClosureRel
LDMVariable
  LDMFocusVariable
LensBasicTransporter
  LensSQLTransporter
LensColumnSizeConstraint
LensExceptionInfo
LensGlobalDescriptor
LensMetadata
  LensDatabaseContext
  LensDatabaseIndex
  LensDatabaseTable
  LensDatabaseTableColumn
  LensDataModel
  LensReferenceType
  LensStructureVariable
  LensTableKey
  LensType
    LensDataType
    LensEncodedType
    LensEnumerationType
    LensStructureType
      LensCollectionType
LensPolicy
LensTransactionPolicy
LensTranscoder
LensWeakCollection
LineInformationTable
  OptimizedLineInformationTable
Link
  Process
  SignalHandler
Locale
LocaleSensitiveDataReader
  NumberReader
  TimestampReader
Magnitude
  ArithmeticValue
    Number
      FixedPoint
```

Continued

```
            Fraction
            Integer
              LargeInteger
                LargeNegativeInteger
                LargePositiveInteger
              SmallInteger
            LimitedPrecisionReal
              Double
              Float
            Point
          Character
          Date
          LookupKey
            Association
              LensLinkedAssociation
              WeakKeyAssociation
          VariableBinding
        Time
MC_BTreeNode
MC_FileBTree
MemoryPolicy
Menu
MenuAdornment
MenuBuilder
MenuItem
MenuItemAdornment
Message
  ExternalMessage
  MessageSend
MessageCatalog
  IndexedFileMessageCatalog
MessageChannel
MethodNodeHolder
Model
  ApplicationModel
    AdHocQueryTool
    Browser
      Debugger
      HierarchyBrowser
      MethodListBrowser
      ParcelBrowser
    ChangeList
    CodingAssistant
    ExamplesBrowser
    FileBrowser
    HelpBrowser
    Inspector
      ChangeSetInspector
      CompiledCodeInspector
      ContextInspector
      DictionaryInspector
      SequenceableCollectionInspector
```

Continued

```
            OrderedCollectionInspector
        LabelConstructor
        LensApplicationModel
          LensDataManager
          LensMainApplication
            LensTemporaryMain
        LensApplicationSpecEditor
        LensApplicationStructureView
        LensBrowsingToolModel
          LensGraphView
        LensEditor
        LensMappingEditor
        ParcelList
        QueryEditor
    SimpleDialog
      LensApplicationCreationDialog
      LensDataModelGenerator
      LensKeyEditor
      LensReferenceNameDialog
      LensTablesSelector
      SimpleHelp
    SimpleListEditor
    SpecModel
      IntegratedSpecModel
        ColorToolModel
          DataSetCallbacksSpecModel
          DataSetSpecColumnDetailsModel
          DataSetSpecColumnModel
          PositionToolModel
        LensDFBasicsSliceModel
        LensDFConnectionSliceModel
      UIFinderVW2
      UIPainter
      UIPainterWatcher
        MenuEditor
        UICanvasTool
        UIMaskEditor
        UIMenuEditor
        UIPropertiesTool
      UIPalette
      UISettings
      VisualLauncher
    ChangeSet
    Explainer
    LDMAbstractBody
      LDMRelationsBody
    LDMBrowserModel
    LDMSelectionService
    LensApplicationSpec
    LensSession
    ScrollValueHolder
    SelectionInList
```

Continued

```
                    MultiSelectionInList
              SelectionInTable
              SyntaxError
              TableInterface
              UIDataReference
                LensGraphReference
                  LensContainerReference
                  LensVariableReference
              ValueModel
                ComputedValue
                  BlockValue
                PluggableAdaptor
                  TypeConverter
                ProtocolAdaptor
                  AspectAdaptor
                  IndexedAdaptor
                    SlotAdaptor
                RangeAdaptor
                ValueHolder
                  BufferedValueHolder
                  HelpProxy
                  LensRowHolder
                  Project
                  TextCollector
        NameScope
          LocalScope
            LensScope
          NullScope
          StaticScope
        ObjectMemory
        ObjectTracer
          CodeWriteAnalysisTracer
          CodeWriter
        OSErrorHolder
          OSHandle
            Cursor
            ExternalProcess
              UnixProcess
            IOAccessor
              BlockableIOAccessor
                UnixIOAccessor
                    UnixDiskFileAccessor
                    UnixPipeAccessor
                MacIOAccessor
                  MacDiskFileAccessor
                PCIOAccessor
                  PCDiskFileAccessor
        Paint
          DevicePaint
          Pattern
          SimplePaint
            ColorValue
```

Continued

```
      CoverageValue
    SymbolicPaint
      HierarchicalSymbolicPaint
  PaintPolicy
    LuminanceBasedColorPolicy
  Parcel
  PostScriptFontBody
  PrintConverter
  PrintPolicy
    NumberPrintPolicy
    StringPrintPolicy
    TimestampPrintPolicy
  ProcessHandle
  ProcessorScheduler
  ProgramNode
    MethodNode
    ParameterNode
    StatementNode
      ReturnNode
      ValueNode
        ArithmeticLoopNode
        AssignmentNode
        CascadeNode
        ConditionalNode
        LeafNode
          BlockNode
          LiteralNode
          VariableNode
        LoopNode
        SequenceNode
        SimpleMessageNode
          MessageNode
  ProgramNodeBuilder
    LensMethodGenerator
  ProgramNodeEnumerator
    ReadBeforeWrittenTester
  Promise
  QueryOperation
    LensQuery
  QueryOperationAccessor
  RangeMap
  RasterOp
  RecursionLock
  RemoteString
  ResourceRetriever
  RowAdaptor
  Scanner
    ChangeScanner
    MessageFileParser
    Parser
  SequenceableCollectionSorter
  SharedQueue
```

Continued

```
Signal
SimpleBorder
  BeveledBorder
  Win3Border
SmalltalkCompiler
  Compiler
    LensCompiler
    QueryCompiler
SourceFileManager
  SourceCodeStream
SPFillLine
Stream
  ExternalDatabaseAnswerStream
    LensAnswerStream
      QueryStream
  PeekableStream
    EncodedStream
    PositionableStream
      ExternalStream
        BufferedExternalStream
          ExternalReadStream
            CodeReaderStream
            ExternalReadAppendStream
            ExternalReadWriteStream
          ExternalWriteStream
            CodeWriterStream
      InternalStream
        ReadStream
        WriteStream
          ReadWriteStream
            ByteCodeReadWriteStream
        TextStream
  Random
StreamEncoder
  ByteStreamEncoder
  CompoundTextStreamEncoder
  UnicodeStreamEncoder
  UTF8StreamEncoder
StreamPolicy
StringCollationPolicy
StringParameterSubstitution
SystemError
SystemUtils
Test1
TextAttributes
  VariableSizeTextAttributes
TextMeasurer
  CharacterScanner
    CharacterBlockScanner
    CompositionScanner
    DisplayScanner
Timestamp
```

Continued

```
TimeZone
UIAspectPath
  LensAspectPath
UIBuilder
UIDefiner
UIDispatcher
UILookPolicy
  CUALookPolicy
  DefaultLookPolicy
  MacLookPolicy
  MotifLookPolicy
  Win3LookPolicy
UISpecEnumerator
  AspectEnumerator
  FilteredSpecEnumerator
  LensSpecReplicator
UISpecification
  ComponentSpec
    NamedSpec
      ArbitraryComponentSpec
      CompositeSpec
      DividerSpec
      GroupBoxSpec
      LabelSpec
      RegionSpec
      SubCanvasSpec
        EmbeddedDetailSpec
      WidgetSpec
        ButtonSpec
          ActionButtonSpec
          LinkedDetailSpec
        CheckBoxSpec
        MenuButtonSpec
        RadioButtonSpec
      DataSetColumnSpec
      MenuComponentSpec
        DataSetSpec
        LDMBrowserSpec
        SequenceViewSpec
          ComboBoxListSpec
        TableViewSpec
        TextEditorSpec
          InputFieldSpec
            ComboBoxSpec
      MultiSpec
      NoteBookSpec
      SliderSpec
  FullSpec
  SpecCollection
    CompositeSpecCollection
  SubSpec
    UIEventCallbackSubSpec
```

Continued

```
        WindowSpec
    UndefinedObject
    UninterpretedBytes
      GraphicsHandle
    UserMessage
    VariableDefinition
      InstanceVariable
        LensInstanceVariable
      LocalVariable
        ArgumentVariable
        TemporaryVariable
      PseudoVariable
      ReceiverVariable
      RemoteVariable
      StaticVariable
        UndeclaredVariable
    VisualComponent
      DragHandle
      Icon
      Label
        AlignmentLabel
        LabelAndIcon
      LDMVisualTreeConnection
        LDMBroomConnection
      OpaqueImage
        OpaqueImageWithEnablement
      PixelArray
        CachedImage
        Image
          Depth16Image
          Depth1Image
          Depth24Image
          Depth2Image
          Depth32Image
          Depth4Image
          Depth8Image
      RowVisual
        RowLabelVisual
      TextLines
        ComposedText
          InputFieldComposedText
        TextList
      VisualBlock
      VisualPart
        CompositePart
          BorderDecorator
            TableDecorator
          ComboBoxView
          ComposingComposite
            MenuBar
              CUAMenuBar
              MacMenuBar
```

Continued

```
            MotifMenuBar
            Win3MenuBar
         CUAScrollBar
DependentComposite
   CompositeView
      LDMBrowserBodyView
      LDMCompositeView
         LDMGraphCompositeView
      LDMElementView
      MenuView
         CUAMenuView
         MacMenuView
         MotifMenuView
         Win3MenuView
      UIPainterView
   NoteBookComposite
   ReComposingComposite
   SubCanvas
DependentPart
   View
      AutoScrollingView
         ComposedTextView
            TextCollectorView
            TextEditorView
               InputFieldView
                  ComboBoxInputFieldView
      TableView
         GeneralSelectionTableView
      BitView
         ColorBitView
      BooleanWidgetView
         ActionButton
         LabeledBooleanView
            LDMArrowView
      ColoredArea
      DirectBitView
      LauncherView
      MenuItemView
         CUAMenuItemView
         MacMenuItemView
         MotifMenuItemView
         Win3MenuItemView
      NotifierView
      Scrollbar
         EmulationScrollBar
            CUAScrollBarSlider
            EmulationFixedThumbScrollBar
               MacScrollBar
               Win3ScrollBar
            MotifScrollBar
   SimpleView
      BasicButtonView
```

Continued

```
            ComboBoxButtonView
              CUAComboBoxButtonView
              MacComboBoxButtonView
              MotifComboBoxButtonView
              Win3ComboBoxButtonView
            LabeledButtonView
              CheckButtonView
                CUACheckButtonView
                DefaultLookCheckButtonView
        MacCheckButtonView
        MotifCheckButtonView
        Win3CheckButtonView
      PushButtonView
        ActionButtonView
            CUAActionButtonView
            MacActionButtonView
            MotifActionButtonView
            UndecoratedActionButtonView
            Win3ActionButtonView
        MenuBarButtonView
            CUAMenuBarButtonView
            MacMenuBarButtonView
            MotifMenuBarButtonView
            Win3MenuBarButtonView
        MenuButtonView
            CUAMenuButtonView
            MacMenuButtonView
            MotifMenuButtonView
            UndecoratedMenuButtonView
            Win3MenuButtonView
        RadioButtonView
            CUARadioButtonView
            DefaultLookRadioButtonView
            MacRadioButtonView
            MotifRadioButtonView
            Win3RadioButtonView
      ScrollerButtonView
        CUAScrollerButtonView
        MotifScrollerButton
        VisualPairButton
  ScrollingView
    SelectionView
      DataSetView
        PaintedDataSetView
      SequenceView
        ComboBoxListView
        MultiSelectionSequenceView
      TabBarView
        HorizontalTabBarView
        VerticalTabBarView
    SliderView
      MacSliderView
```

Continued

```
                Win3SliderView
        MotifMenuItemSeparatorComponent
    SimpleComponent
      GroupBox
      PassiveLabel
      VisualBinderComponent
      VisualDivider
      VisualRegion
    Wrapper
      GeometricWrapper
        FillingWrapper
          StrokingWrapper
        GraphicsAttributesWrapper
        GridWrapper
        PassivityWrapper
        ReversingWrapper
          StrikeOutWrapper
        ScalingWrapper
        TranslatingWrapper
          LayoutWrapper
            BoundedWrapper
              BorderedWrapper
                MenuBarWrapper
              BoundingWrapper
            LDMAbstractElementWrapper
              LDMGraphElementWrapper
              LDMListElementWrapper
          ScrollWrapper
            DataSetScrollWrapper
            SlaveScrollWrapper
        WidgetStateWrapper
        WidgetWrapper
          SpecWrapper
    WidgetDragDropCallbacks
    WidgetPolicy
      CUAWidgetPolicy
      MacWidgetPolicy
      MotifWidgetPolicy
      SmalltalkWidgetPolicy
      Win3WidgetPolicy
    WidgetState
    WindowDisplayPolicy
      DoubleBufferingWindowDisplayPolicy
```

 VisualAge/IBM Smalltalk (IBM)

```
| recursiveBlock |
recursiveBlock := [:each :level |
(1 to: level)
  do:
```

Continued

```
        [:index |
          Transcript nextPut: $ .
        ].
    Transcript
      nextPutAll: each printString;
      cr.
    (each subclasses asSortedCollection: Class sortBlock)
      do:
        [:item |
          recursiveBlock value: item value: level + 3.
        ].
    ].
    "Kick the whole thing off"
    (Object subclasses asSortedCollection: Class sortBlock)
      do:
        [:each |
          recursiveBlock value: each value: 0.
        ].
```

```
-Object-
AbtAlignmentObject
AbtAppBldrRecord
AbtAttributeDefaultViewMaker
AbtAttributeToAttributeConnection
AbtAttributeToCodeHookConnection
AbtBasicObjectCodeGenerator
  AbtConnectionCodeGenerator
    AbtAttributeToAttributeConnectionCodeGenerator
    AbtAttributeToCodeHookCodeGenerator
    AbtEventToActionConnectionCodeGenerator
    AbtEventToCodeHookCodeGenerator
  AbtPartBuilderCodeGenerator
    AbtSubpartBuilderCodeGenerator
      AbtInstanceBuilderCodeGenerator
        AbtInternalSubpartBuilderCodeGenerator
      AbtTopLevelPartBuilderCodeGenerator
        AbtAppBldrPartBuilderCodeGenerator
        AbtVisualLayoutPartBuilderCodeGenerator
AbtBeginUndoBlock
AbtCharacterTranslator
AbtCodeGeneratorContext
  AbtBuilderCodeGeneratorContext
AbtColorPaletteChoice
AbtCommonFeature
  AbtFeature
AbtCommonFeatureInstaller
  AbtFeatureInstaller
AbtConnectionObject
  AbtConnectionMaker
  AbtConnectionModifier
AbtCwValueSetItem
AbtDistributeSpaceObject
```

Continued

```
AbtDragDropSpec
AbtDragStatusObject
  AbtHandleDragStatusObject
  AbtPartDragStatusObject
    AbtAddNewPartStatusObject
  AbtTabbingTagDragStatusObject
AbtEndUndoBlock
AbtError
  AbtConverterError
AbtFeatureSpec
  AbtAbstractAttributeSpec
    AbtAttributeSpec
    AbtDictionaryAttributeSpec
    AbtSubpartAttributeSpec
    AbtVariableAttributeSpec
  AbtActionSpec
    AbtSubpartActionSpec
  AbtEventSpec
    AbtSubpartEventSpec
AbtFeedbackObject
  AbtXorGraphicsFeedbackObject
    AbtLineEndPointFeedbackObject
    AbtLineMidPointFeedbackObject
    AbtMultiRectangleOutlineFeedbackObject
    AbtRectangleOutlineFeedbackObject
      AbtArcOutlineFeedbackObject
AbtFileSpec
AbtFormatAndVerificationHelper
AbtGenericPartBuilderGenerator
AbtGraphicalObject
  AbtArrowLine
    AbtArrowPolyLine
  AbtEditOutline
  AbtHandle
  AbtHotSpot
  AbtOutline
  AbtTabbingTag
AbtGraphicsDescriptor
  AbtBitmapDescriptor
  AbtIconDescriptor
  AbtImageDescriptor
AbtGridSnapObject
AbtHeadlessAppContext
AbtHelpAccessor
AbtHelpSpec
AbtHoverHelpDescriptor
AbtIconArray
AbtIconCache
AbtIconGadget
AbtInputPolicy
  AbtEditPartInputPolicy
    AbtContainerDetailsColumnEditPartInputPolicy
```

Continued

Continued

```
          AbtAttributeToCodeHookConnectionBuilder
          AbtEventToActionConnectionBuilder
          AbtEventToCodeHookConnectionBuilder
        AbtFeatureBuilder
          AbtAbstractAttributeFeatureBuilder
          AbtBasicAttributeFeatureBuilder
        AbtInterfaceSpecBuilder
        AbtPartBuilder
          AbtSubpartBuilder
            AbtInstanceBuilder
              AbtExternalSubpartBuilder
              AbtInternalSubpartBuilder
            AbtVariableBuilder
          AbtTopLevelPartBuilder
          AbtAppBldrPartBuilder
  AbtBuildPartsObjectSpace
  AbtCompoundType
    AbtNonContiguousCompoundType
  AbtConnectionParametersSpec
  AbtDependencySpec
  AbtEdgeConstant
  AbtEdgeConstraint
    AbtEdgeAttachment
      AbtEditEdgeAttachmentSpec
    AbtEdgeAttachmentConstraint
      AbtRunEdgeAttachmentConstraint
  AbtEventConnection
    AbtEventToActionConnection
    AbtEventToCodeHookConnection
  AbtInterfaceSpec
  AbtLanguageElement
  AbtLanguageElementCategory
  AbtOperation
    AbtUpdateOperation
      AbtClassUpdate
        AbtAppBldrPartClassUpdate
          AbtAppBldrViewClassUpdate
      AbtCollectionOperation
        AbtCollectionAdd
          AbtCollectionAddAll
        AbtCollectionAddAfterIndex
          AbtCollectionAddAllAfterIndex
        AbtCollectionAddBeforeIndex
          AbtCollectionAddAllBeforeIndex
        AbtCollectionAtPut
        AbtCollectionNonUpdateOp
        AbtCollectionRemove
          AbtCollectionRemoveAll
        AbtDictionaryRemoveKey
    AbtUndoableOperation
      AbtAddInterfaceFeature
        AbtUpdateInterfaceFeature
```

Continued

```
        AbtCatalogAddCategory
        AbtCatalogAddPart
        AbtCatalogRemoveCategory
        AbtCatalogRemovePart
        AbtChangeSubpartVariableAssignment
        AbtCollectionDeferredUpdateOperation
          AbtDictionaryDeferredUpdateOperation
          AbtIndxCollectionDeferredUpdateOperation
        AbtConnectionOperation
          AbtAddCodeHookOperation
            AbtUpdateCodeHookOperation
          AbtAddConnectionOperation
            AbtUpdateConnectionOperation
        AbtDeleteInterfaceComponent
        AbtGenericDeferredUpdateOperation
          AbtDeferredUpdateOperation
            AbtBuilderDeferredUpdateOperation
              AbtConverterBuilderDeferredUpdateOperation
              AbtSubpartDeferredUpdateOperation
                AbtAppBldrViewDeferredUpdateOperation
                AbtFormViewUpdateOperation
              AbtDragDropSpecDeferredUpdateOperation
              AbtFramingSpecDeferredUpdateOperation
            AbtPartBuilderAddSubparts
            AbtPartBuilderAddSubpartsRelativeToIndex
              AbtPartBuilderAddSubpartsAfterIndex
              AbtPartBuilderAddSubpartsBeforeIndex
            AbtPartBuilderChangeName
            AbtPartBuilderChangePartClass
              AbtPartBuilderChangeSecondaryPartType
            AbtPartBuilderRemoveSubparts
            AbtPartBuilderReparentSubparts
            AbtPartBuilderReparentSubpartsRelativeToIndex
              AbtPartBuilderReparentSubpartsAfterIndex
              AbtPartBuilderReparentSubpartsBeforeIndex
            AbtRemoveConnectionsOperation
            AbtReorderConnectionBuilders
            AbtReorderSubpartBuilders
            AbtReorderSubpartBuildersToIndexes
AbtParameterSpec
AbtPart
  AbtCompositePart
    AbtAppBldrPart
      AbtAppBldrView
        AbtAbstractSettingsView
AbtBasicGraphicsDescriptorSettingsView
  AbtGraphicsDescriptorSettingsView
AbtBasicSettingsView
  AbtAppBldrViewSettingsView
    AbtGenericAttributesBrowser
    AbtTableSettingsView
  AbtComboBoxViewAttributesPage
```

Continued

```
        AbtConstantFramingSpecView
AbtDetailedFramingEdgeView
  AbtFramingSpecView
  AbtLabelViewAttributesPage
    AbtCascadeMenuItemAttributesPage
      AbtButtonLabelAttributesPage
        AbtLabelMenuItemAttributesPage
AbtActionDefinitionView
  AbtAddPaletteCategoryView
  AbtAddPartView
  AbtApplicationPrerequisitesView
  AbtApplicationsOrganizerView
    AbtArchiveAppChooser
    AbtAttribCodeHookDependencyView
    AbtAttributeCodeHookSettingsView
  AbtAttributeDefinitionView
    AbtAttributeToAttributeConnectionView
    AbtBasicDatatypeSettingsView
    AbtBasicDragDropSettings
        AbtDropDownListComboBoxDragDropSettings
      AbtDropFilterableDragDropSettings
      AbtSpinButtonDragDropSettings
  AbtBasicEditMaskSettingsView
  AbtBasicGraphicsTypeSettingsView
    AbtGraphicsTypeSettingsView
  AbtBasicHelpAttributesPage
  AbtBasicViewAttributesPage
    AbtBasicMenuItemAttributesPage
    AbtBasicShellViewAttributesPage
  AbtColorChooserView
  AbtConnectionDebugger
  AbtConnectionFeaturesDialog
  AbtContainerDetailsColumnAlignmentPage
  AbtContainerDetailsColumnAttributesPage
  AbtContainerDetailsViewAttributesPage
  AbtContainerIconAreaAttributesPage
  AbtContainerIconListAttributesPage
  AbtContainerPreview
  AbtContainerTreeChildrenAttributesPage
  AbtContainerTreeHierarchyPolicyAttributesPage
  AbtCUASettings
    AbtContainerSettings
      AbtContainerGeneralPage
      AbtIconGadgetPages
        AbtIconGadgetPage
    AbtNoteBookSettingPages
      AbtNoteBookJustification
      AbtNoteBookLayout
  AbtDatatypeChooserView
  AbtDatatypeSettingsView
    AbtBooleanDatatypeSettingsView
  AbtCharacterDatatypeSettingsView
```

Continued

```
            AbtDateDatatypeSettingsView
            AbtDbcsDatatypeSettingsView
            AbtEditMaskSettingsView
              AbtIntegerEditMaskSettingsView
                AbtFloatEditMaskSettingsView
              AbtStringEditMaskSettingsView
            AbtIntegerDatatypeSettingsView
            AbtMonetaryAmountDatatypeSettingsView
            AbtNumberDatatypeSettingsView
              AbtDecimalDatatypeSettingsView
              AbtFloatDatatypeSettingsView
            AbtSSNDatatypeSettingsView
            AbtStringDatatypeSettingsView
              AbtSymbolDatatypeSettingsView
            AbtTimeDatatypeSettingsView
            AbtUSAStateDatatypeSettingsView
            AbtZipCodeDatatypeSettingsView
        AbtDebugSelectBreakView
        AbtDebugSelectTraceBreakView
        AbtDebugSelectTraceView
        AbtDebugTraceBreakView
        AbtDragableListItemsView
          AbtReorderConnectionsView
        AbtDragDropSourceOperationSettings
          AbtDragDropSpinButtonSourceOperationSettings
        AbtDragDropTargetOperationSettings
          AbtDragDropSpinButtonTargetOperationSettings
          AbtDragDropTargetDropFilterableOperationSettings
        AbtDrawnButtonViewAttributesPage
        AbtDrawnListViewAttributesPage
          AbtDropDownListAttributesPage
          AbtDropDownListComboBoxAttributesPage
          AbtEditMaskChooserView
          AbtEditPartsListView
          AbtEventCodeHookSettingsView
        AbtEventDefinitionView
          AbtEventToActionConnectionView
          AbtFileSelectionPrompterAttributesPage
        AbtFindView
          AbtFormattedTextViewAttributesPage
          AbtFormViewAttributesPage
          AbtFormWallpaperAttributesPage
          AbtFrameViewAttributesPage
          AbtGenericAttributesView
          AbtGroupBoxViewAttributesPage
          AbtGroupMembersView
          AbtHotSpotViewAttributesPage
          AbtIconGadgetPreview
          AbtIconViewAttributesPage
        AbtImbeddablePaletteView
          AbtInterfaceUpdateButtons
          AbtLabelMarginAttributesPage
```

Continued

```
    AbtLanguageStatementsSelectorView
    AbtLimitedClassBrowserView
    AbtListViewAttributesPage
    AbtManageUsersView
    AbtMessagePrompterAttributesPage
  AbtMultiLineEditViewAttributesPage
  AbtMultipleSelectListViewAttributesPage
  AbtMultiViewSwitcher
    AbtDebuggerViewSwitcher
    AbtPartClassViewSwitcher
      AbtAppBldrViewSwitcher
  AbtNewApplicationRequestView
    AbtNewPartRequestView
  AbtNIsEditorView
    AbtNoteBookButtonDimensionsPage
  AbtNoteBookPageTabPage
  AbtNoteBookPreview
    AbtObjectFactoryAttributesPage
  AbtPackageApplicationView
  AbtParameterTableView
  AbtPartClassView
    AbtCompositionEditorView
    AbtInterfaceDefinitionView
      AbtFeaturesInterfaceDefinitionView
  AbtPMNotebookPageAttributesPage
  AbtPMProgramStarterAttributesPage
  AbtPortablePMNotebookViewAttributesPage
  AbtPortableWINNotebookViewAttributesPage
    AbtPreferencesBrowsersView
  AbtPreferencesCEView
  AbtPreferencesStartupView
  AbtPreferencesView
  AbtPreviewFrame
  AbtProductInfoView
    AbtProgramStarterAttributesPage
  AbtPromoteFeatureDefinitionView
  AbtPromoteFeaturesView
  AbtPromotePartView
    AbtPrompterCommonAttributesPage
    AbtPushButtonViewAttributesPage
      AbtPushButtonMenuItemAttributesPage
  AbtQuickStartView
    AbtRadioButtonSetAttributesPage
    AbtRadioButtonSetSupplementalAttributesPage
    AbtRowColumnViewAttributesPage
    AbtScaleViewAttributesPage
    AbtScriptDebuggerView
    AbtScriptEditorView
    AbtScrollableInfoView
    AbtScrolledStripView
    AbtScrolledWindowViewAttributesPage
    AbtSelectorChooserView
```

Continued

```
            AbtSeparatorViewAttributesPage
            AbtSetGridSpacingView
            AbtShellViewAttributesPage
            AbtSliderDetentSettingsPage
              AbtSliderTickSettingsPage
            AbtSliderScaleSettingsPage
            AbtSliderViewAttributesPage
            AbtSpinButtonListSettings
            AbtSpinButtonNumericSettings
            AbtSpinButtonViewAttributesPage
            AbtSubAppCodeView
              AbtSubpartAttributeSelectorView
              AbtTableColumnSettingsPage
              AbtTableViewAttributesPage
              AbtTextPrompterAttributesPage
              AbtTextViewAttributesPage
              AbtTextViewSupplementalAttributesPage
              AbtToggleButtonViewAttributesPage
                AbtToggleButtonMenuItemAttributesPage
              AbtUndoListView
              AbtWINNotebookPageAttributesPage
          AbtApplicationPart
          AbtClassPart
          AbtContainerTreeChildrenAccessor
          AbtDebugConnectionSelector
          AbtFileSelectionPrompter
          AbtMessagePrompter
          AbtPreferencesBrowsersObject
          AbtPreferencesCEObject
          AbtPreferencesStartupObject
          AbtTextPrompter
          AbtUserPart
      AbtBasicView
        AbtBasicScriptDebuggerView
        AbtCompositeView
          AbtContainerView
          AbtDrawingAreaView
            AbtObjectGraphicsView
              AbtFreeFormSurfaceView
          AbtIconGadgetView
          AbtManagerView
            AbtFormView
              AbtChildManagerView
               AbtFrameView
                  AbtGroupBoxView
                AbtShellView
              AbtNoteBookPageView
              AbtSwitcherView
            AbtRowColumnView
              AbtCwMenuView
          AbtNoteBookView
            AbtNoteBookViewWithForm
```

Continued

```
      AbtPortableNotebook
        AbtPortablePMNotebookView
        AbtPortableWINNotebookView
      AbtPortableNotebookPageView
      AbtScrolledWindowView
      AbtTableView
        AbtNIsTableView
      AbtValueSetView
AbtGadget
  AbtContainerDetailsColumn
AbtPrimitiveView
  AbtAbstractTextView
    AbtFormattedTextView
    AbtTextView
      AbtMultiLineEditView
        AbtListInputView
    AbtArrowButtonView
  AbtColorPaletteView
  AbtDropDownListComboBox
    AbtComboBoxView
  AbtExtendedScrollable
    AbtExtendedList
      AbtContainerIconAreaView
      AbtExtendedLinearList
        AbtContainerList
          AbtContainerDetailsView
            AbtContainerDetailsTreeView
          AbtContainerIconListView
            AbtContainerFlowedIconListView
            AbtContainerIconTreeView
        AbtDrawnListView
  AbtHotSpotView
  AbtIconView
    AbtDeletedClassView
    AbtSuperimposedIconView
      AbtVariableIconView
  AbtLabelView
    AbtCascadeButtonView
    AbtDrawnButtonView
    AbtPushButtonView
    AbtRowColumnItemVisualPart
      AbtMenuItemCascadeVisualPart
      AbtMenuItemToggleVisualPart
      AbtRowColumnItemHeaderVisualPart
    AbtToggleButtonView
  AbtListView
  AbtMultipleSelectListView
  AbtRadioButtonSet
  AbtScaleView
  AbtSeparatorView
    AbtMenuSeparatorVisualPart
  AbtSliderView
```

Continued

```
            AbtSpinButtonView
            AbtTableColumnView
          AbtScriptBrowserView
    AbtConverter
      AbtBooleanConverter
      AbtCharacterConverter
      AbtClassConverter
        AbtClassAsisConverter
      AbtDateConverter
      AbtDbStringOnlyConverter
      AbtIntegerConverter
        AbtNumberConverter
          AbtDecimalConverter
          AbtFloatingPointRepresentationConverter
          AbtMonetaryAmountConverter
      AbtPrimitiveStringConverter
      AbtSSNConverter
      AbtStringConverter
        AbtNIsEditGroupPoolConstConverter
        AbtNIsEditorConverter
          AbtNIsEditorFilenameConverter
          AbtNIsEditorGroupNameConverter
          AbtNIsEditorMRIClassNameConverter
          AbtNIsEditorPrefixConverter
        AbtSymbolConverter
      AbtTimeConverter
      AbtTimeStampConverter
      AbtUSAStateConverter
      AbtZipCodeConverter
    AbtCwConnectionView
      AbtCwEventConnectionView
        AbtCwActionConnectionView
        AbtCwCodeHookConnectionView
    AbtCwEditPart
      AbtCompositeEditPart
        AbtContainerEditPart
        AbtFreeFormEditPart
        AbtIconGadgetEditPart
        AbtNoteBookEditPart
        AbtNoteBookPageEditPart
        AbtPortableNotebookEditPart
        AbtPortableNotebookPageEditPart
        AbtRowColumnEditPart
          AbtContainerDetailsViewEditPart
          AbtMenuBarEditPart
          AbtMenuEditPart
          AbtReorderConnectionsEditPart
        AbtScrolledWindowEditPart
        AbtShellEditPart
        AbtTableEditPart
      AbtDeferredUpdateEditPart
      AbtEditConnection
```

Continued

```
              AbtEditEventToActionConnection
          AbtMenuBarEntryEditPart
          AbtPrimitiveEditPart
            AbtContainerDetailsColumnEditPart
            AbtHotSpotEditPart
          AbtRowColumnEntryEditPart
            AbtMenuItemEditPart
            AbtReorderableConnectionEditPart
          AbtTableColumnEditPart
          AbtWrapperEditPart
            AbtAppBldrViewWrapperEditPart
            AbtVariableEditPart
              AbtTearOffAttributeEditPart
    AbtFormInputChecker
    AbtHierarchyPolicy
      AbtIconHierarchyPolicy
    AbtNewPartInfo
    AbtNIsEditGroup
    AbtNIsEditItem
    AbtObjectFactory
    AbtProgramStarter
    AbtSubAppCode
    AbtTableColumn
    AbtVariable
        AbtAppBldrViewWrapper
        AbtDeferredUpdateManager
      AbtViewObjectConversionManager
        AbtViewFormatManager
          AbtTextViewFormatManager
      AbtWidgetConverterManager
        AbtCollectionConverterManager
          AbtListConverterManager
            AbtButtonSetConverterManager
              AbtDropDownListComboBoxConverterManager
                AbtComboBoxViewConverterManager
              AbtMultipleSelectListConverterManager
            AbtSpinButtonConverterManager
          AbtLabelConverterManager
          AbtUserModifiableObjectConverterManager
            AbtTextConverterManager
              AbtListInputConverterManager
            AbtMLEConverterManager
    AbtPartsCatalog
        AbtPartsCategory
        AbtPreferencesCatalog
        AbtRecord
        AbtForeignRecord
        AbtSelectedSet
        AbtStack
        AbtUndoStack
        AbtTypeField
        AbtArrayField
```

Continued

```
                    AbtCByteArrayField
                    AbtCCharArrayField
                    AbtCByteField
                    AbtCCharField
              AbtCDoubleField
              AbtCFloatField
              AbtCHandleField
              AbtCLongField
                AbtCIntField
              AbtCOBOLField
                AbtCOBOLBinaryField
                  AbtCOBOLCOMPXField
                    AbtCOBOLCOMP5Field
                AbtCOBOLCOMP1Field
                AbtCOBOLDisplayField
                  AbtCOBOLNumericDisplayField
                    AbtCOBOLHostNumericDisplayField
                AbtCOBOLDoubleField
                AbtCOBOLPackedDecimalField
                AbtCOBOLPointerField
              AbtCompoundField
              AbtCPointerField
                AbtC16ThunkedPointerField
              AbtCShortField
                AbtCInt16Field
              AbtCULongField
                AbtCUIntField
                AbtCVoidField
              AbtCUShortField
                AbtCUInt16Field
              AbtViewConstraint
                AbtViewAttachmentConstraint
                AbtViewAttachmentSpec
          AbtOperationError
          AbtOSIconGadget
          AbtOSNoteBookPage
          AbtPackedStringFormatterVerifier
          AbtPartTypeRef
            AbtPartInstanceRef
          AbtPOMObjectExtractor
          AbtPOMObjectPersistor
          AbtProcessSynchronization
            AbtThreadSynchronization
          AbtPseudoNIsEditGroup
          AbtPseudoNIsEditItem
          AbtQuantity
            AbtMonetaryAmount
          AbtSelectorValidator
          AbtSimpleParser
            AbtDateParser
            AbtMiscSmalltalkParser
            AbtTimeParser
```

Continued

```
AbtSliderDetent
  AbtSliderTick
AbtStreamLineReader
AbtTableCell
AbtTableCellManager
AbtTableColumnManager
AbtTableColumnSizer
AbtTableGeometry
AbtTableGridDrawer
AbtTableLabel
  AbtTableColumnLabel
  AbtTableCornerLabel
  AbtTableRowLabel
    AbtNIsTableRowLabel
AbtTableLabelManager
AbtTableMinimalConverterAdapter
  AbtTableToTextConverterAdapter
AbtTableScrollManager
AbtTableSelectionPolicy
  AbtTableSingleSelectionPolicy
AbtTearOffAttributeMaker
AbtTearOffAttributeSpec
AbtThreadManager
AbtTimedWait
  AbtConditionalWait
AbtTrace
AbtUnit
  AbtMoney
AbtUSAState
AbtVariableAttribute
AbtVariableEvent
AbtVariableExecutableFeature
AbtViewApplicationAbtPackage
AbtVisualPolicy
  AbtCreateNewEditVisualPolicy
    AbtConnectionEditVisualPolicy
    AbtFreeFormSurfaceVisualPolicy
    AbtIconEditVisualPolicy
      AbtSuperimposedIconEditVisualPolicy
    AbtMenuItemEditVisualPolicy
    AbtReorderConnectionItemEditVisualPolicy
    AbtRowColumnVisualPolicy
      AbtMenuEditVisualPolicy
      AbtReorderConnectionsVisualPolicy
  AbtUsePartAsVisualPolicy
    AbtAppBldrViewVisualPolicy
    AbtHotSpotVisualPolicy
    AbtTableColumnVisualPolicy
    AbtUseCompositePartAsVisualPolicy
      AbtFormVisualPolicy
      AbtMenuBarVisualPolicy
      AbtPortableNotebookPageVisualPolicy
```

Continued

```
                    AbtTableUseCompositePartAsVisualPolicy
                    AbtUseNonsizeableCompositePartAsVisualPolicy
        AbtWidgetFormatter
          AbtTextWidgetFormatter
        AbtWorkQueue
        AbtWrapperExecutableFeature
        AbtZipCode
        ApplicationSwapper
          ApplicationDumper
          ApplicationLoader
        Behavior
          ClassDescription
            Class
            Metaclass
              EmShadowMetaclass
        Block
          AbtHashBasicBlock
          BlockContextTemplate
          EsOptimizedBlock
            EsEmptyBlock
        Boolean
          False
          True
        CfsDirectoryDescriptor
        CfsFileDescriptor
        CfsFileStream
          CfsReadFileStream
            CfsReadWriteFileStream
          CfsWriteFileStream
        CfsLeadEncodedFileStream
          CfsLeadEncodedReadFileStream
            CfsLeadEncodedReadWriteFileStream
          CfsLeadEncodedWriteFileStream
        CfsStat
          CfsDirectoryEntry
        CfsVolumeInfo
        CgArc
        CgBitmapFile
        CgByteStream
          CgByteArrayByteStream
          CgFileByteStream
          CgNullByteStream
        CgCharStruct
        CgColorDatabase
        CgDeviceIndependentImage
        CgDisplay
        CgFileFormat
        CgIconFileFormat
          CgPMICOFileFormat
          CgWinICOFileFormat
        CgImageFileformat
          CgPCXFileFormat
```

Continued

```
      CgPMBMPFileFormat
      CgTIFFFileFormat
      CgWinBMPFileFormat
    CgFontDirectory
    CgFontEntry
      CgFontAliasEntry
      CgFontBitmapEntry
      CgFontScalableEntry
    CgFontInformation
    CgFontName
    CgFontPath
    CgFontProp
    CgFontResolution
    CgFontScalable
    CgFontScaled
    CgFontServer
      CgPMFontServer
    CgFontStruct
    CgFontTable
    CgGC
    CgGCValues
    CgIcon
    CgID
      CgCursor
      CgDrawable
        CgPixmap
        CgPrinterWindow
        CgWindow
      CgFont
    CgLogicalFontDescription
    CgPalette
      CgDirectPalette
      CgIndexedPalette
    CgPaletteEntry
    CgPixmapFormatValues
    CgPresentationSpaceCache
    CgPrinterScreenInfo
    CgPrintJobAttributes
    CgRegion
    CgRGBColor
    CgScreen
      CgPrinterScreen
    CgSegment
    CgServer
      CgPMServer
        CgPMPrinterServer
    CgServerResource
      CgFontResource
        CgPMFontResource
    CgTextItem
    CgVisual
    CgWildMatch
```

Continued

```
ClassObjectEntry
Collection
  Bag
  EpHashDictionary
    EpNonBasicHashDictionary
  EpLargeDictionary
    EpLargeHashedDictionary
  EpLargeIdentitySet
  EsLargeSymbolSet
  EsWeakSet
    EsWeakIdentitySet
  KeyedCollection
    Dictionary
      EsPoolDictionary
      EsSmalltalkDictionary
    EsWeakDictionary
      EsWeakIdentityDictionary
    LookupTable
      AbtIndexedDictionary
        AbtIndexedIdentityDictionary
        AbtOrderedDictionary
          AbtOrderedIdentityDictionary
      AbtWeakKeyLookupTable
        AbtWeakKeyIdentityDictionary
      AbtWeakValueLookupTable
      EsAtomDictionary
      IdentityDictionary
  SequenceableCollection
    AdditiveSequenceableCollection
      OrderedCollection
        AbtBufferedCollection
      SortedCollection
    ArrayedCollection
      Array
        AbtPersistencyGroup
        EsWeakArray
      ByteArray
        EsLeadEncodedBytes
      EsLongArray
    EsString
      DBString
      String
        Symbol
    Interval
  Set
    AbtIdentitySet
    EsIdentitySet
    EsSymbolSet
CompiledMethod
  EaCompositeCompiledMethod
  EmShadowCompiledMethod
Context
```

Continued

```
      BlockContext
      MethodContext
   CwAccelerator
   CwAnyCallbackData
      AbtCwContainerOutlineCallback
      AbtCwContainerSelectCallback
      AbtCwNbPageChangedCallbackData
      AbtEwHoverHelpCallbackData
      AbtTableSelectionCallbackData
      AbtTableValueCallbackData
      CwComboBoxCallbackData
      CwConfirmationCallbackData
         AbtGridPacketRequestCallbackData
         CwPageChangeCallbackData
         CwTextVerifyCallbackData
      CwDrawingCallbackData
         AbtGraphicalObjectCallbackData
         CwPrinterDrawingCallbackData
      CwListCallbackData
      CwRowColumnCallbackData
      CwToggleButtonCallbackData
      CwValueCallbackData
      EwColumnHeadingSelectionCallbackData
      EwDragChangeCallbackData
      EwDragLeaveCallbackData
      EwDragOverCallbackData
      EwDragStartCallbackData
      EwDrawBackgroundCallbackData
         EwIconListDrawBackgroundCallbackData
         EwTableListDrawBackgroundCallbackData
      EwDrawnListDrawCallbackData
      EwDropCallbackData
      EwListCallbackData
         EwCellValueCallbackData
         EwChildrenCallbackData
         EwEditCallbackData
            EwBeginEditCallbackData
               EwBeginEditCellCallbackData
            EwEndEditCallbackData
               EwEndEditCellCallbackData
         EwListSelectionCallbackData
            EwIconListSelectionCallbackData
            EwTableListSelectionCallbackData
         EwVisualInfoCallbackData
            EwIconVisualInfoCallbackData
               EwIconTreeVisualInfoCallbackData
            EwTreeVisualInfoCallbackData
      EwSliderValuesCallbackData
      EwSourceCancelCallbackData
      EwTargetCancelCallbackData
   CwAppContext
   CwCallbackRec
```

Continued

```
CwClipboardPendingRec
CwEvent
  CwExposeEvent
  CwInputEvent
    CwButtonEvent
    CwKeyEvent
    CwMotionEvent
CwExtendedDialog
  CwMessageBoxDialog
    CwWorkingDialog
      CwProgressDialog
  CwTextSearchDialog
CwExtendedPrompter
  AbtExtendedMessagePrompter
    AbtNamedButtonExtendedMessagePrompter
  CwFontPrompter
    AbtFontPrompter
  CwTwoButtonPrompter
    CwExtendedTextPrompter
      CwPasswordPrompter
    CwListPrompter
      CwDoubleListPrompter
    CwListSelectionPrompter
      CwDoubleListSelectionPrompter
    EpPackagingSpecificationPrompter
    EtUserCreationDialog
CwFontList
CwFormConstraint
CwFormEquation
CwMenu
CwMenuBar
CwMenuEntry
  CwMenuPushButton
    CwMenuCascadeButton
    CwMenuToggleButton
  CwMenuSeparator
CwPrinterShell
CwPrompter
  CwFileSelectionPrompter
  CwMessagePrompter
  CwPrinterPrompter
  CwTextPrompter
CwResourceSnapshot
CwRowColumnConstraint
CwTextManager
  CwTextPrintingManager
  CwTextSelectionManager
    CwSmalltalkTextSelectionManager
  CwTextUndoManager
CwWidget
  CwBasicWidget
    CwComposite
```

Continued

```
        AbtCwContainer
        AbtCwNoteBook
        AbtCwValueSet
        CwBulletinBoard
          CwCompositeBox
            CwMessageBox
            CwSelectionBox
          CwForm
            CwEmbeddedShellDecorations
        CwDrawingArea
        CwEmbeddedShell
        CwFrame
        CwRowColumn
        CwScale
        CwScrolledWindow
          CwMainWindow
    CwPrimitive
      CwArrowButton
      CwComboBox
      CwLabel
        CwCascadeButton
        CwDrawnButton
        CwPushButton
        CwToggleButton
      CwList
      CwScrollBar
      CwSeparator
      CwText
    CwShell
      CwOverrideShell
      CwWMShell
        CwTopLevelShell
        CwTransientShell
          CwDialogShell
    CwExtendedWidget
      AbtBrowserWidget
        AbtScriptBrowserWidget
      AbtEwHoverHelp
      AbtScriptDebuggerWidget
      CwExtendedComposite
        AbtObjectGraphicsWidget
          AbtFreeFormSurfaceWidget
        AbtRadioButtonSetWidget
        EwBasePage
        EwNotebook
          EwPMNotebook
          EwWINNotebook
        EwPage
      CwExtendedPrimitive
        AbtDirectEditWidget
        CwDrawingAreaBasedExtendedWidget
          AbtCwColorPalette
```

Continued

```
                AbtIconWidget
                   AbtSuperimposedIconWidget
                AbtTableWidget
                   AbtNIsTableWidget
             CwObjectList
                CwHierarchyList
             EwScrollable
                EwList
                   EwIconArea
                   EwLinearList
                      EwContainerList
                         EwIconList
                            EwFlowedIconList
                            EwIconTree
                         EwTableList
                            EwTableTree
                      EwDrawnList
                EwSlider
                EwSpinButton
       CwWidgetGeometry
       CwWidgetHierarchySnapshot
       CwWidgetSnapshot
       DdeCallbackData
       DdeCallbackRec
       DdeClass
          DdeClient
          DdeServer
       DdeFormat
       DdeItem
       DdeServerManager
       DdeTopicDatabase
       Delay
       DsDistributedSystemConfiguration
       DsObjectSpace
          DsLocalObjectSpace
       EmBuilderClass
       EmBuilderSubApplication
          EmBuilderApplication
       EmClassCallbackData
          EmClassChangeCallbackData
          EmMethodChangeCallbackData
       EmClassCreator
       EmCompressor
       EmConfigurationMap
       EmErrorReporter
          AbtErrorReporter
       EmFileOutInterface
       EmImageBuilder
       EmInterface
       EmLibrary
       EmLibraryObject
          EmLibraryHeader
```

Continued

```
    EmLibraryPointer
  EmLibraryPrimitives
  EmMethodDecoder
  EmMethodLinker
  EmRecord
    EmArrayOfTimeStamps
    EmClassDefinition
    EmConfigurationMapPrivilegesRecord
    EmModifiableRecord
      EmExtendableRecord
        EmClassEditions
        EmConfigurationMapLineups
        EmDiskDictionary
          EmDictionaryOfValues
            EmDictionaryOfStrings
            EmDictionaryOfTimeStamps
          EmEditionsDictionary
          EmFixedDiskDictionary
        EmSubApplicationEdition
          EmApplicationEdition
      EmMethodEdition
      EmRecordEntry
        EmAssociationEntry
          EmEditionEntry
          EmStringEntry
          EmTimeStampEntry
        EmClassEditionEntry
        EmClassEntry
        EmConfigurationMapLineupEntry
      EmRootTypeRecord
        EmConfigurationMapRecord
        EmSubApplicationParts
          EmApplicationParts
        EmUserRecord
    EmSwappedObjectRecord
    EmUserFieldRecord
  EmSelectorInformation
    EmExtendedClassInformation
  EmSortedHierarchy
  EmSystemConfiguration
  EmSystemConfigurationDumper
  EmTextCompatibilityFilter
  EmUser
  EpApplicationProtocolManager
    EpCrossApplicationProtocolManager
  EpCalculateMinimumComponentsPolicy
    EpBaseImageComponentMinimumComponentsPolicy
    EpStandardMinimumComponentsPolicy
  EpDialogExpressionPrompter
  EpDumper
    EsDumper
      EsRomerImageDumper
```

Continued

```
                    EsImageDumper
        EpImage
        EpImageComponent
        EpImageComponentConfiguration
          EpDefaultImageComponentConfiguration
        EpImageComponentRule
          EpDefaultImageComponentRule
        EpMethod
        EpNewPackagingSpecificationRepresentation
        EpOrderedCollection
        EpOutputStream
        EpPackagedImage
          AbtEpPackagedImage
        EpPackagedImageHandler
        EpPackagingConfiguration
        EpPackagingOption
          EpAllStatistics
            EpCompressCode
            EpCorrectManagerStructures
          EpMakeCatalogsResident
          EpOptimizeAssociations
          EpRemoveCategories
          EpRemoveSourcePointers
          EpRemoveUnusedApplicationClasses
          EpRemoveUnusedMetaclasses
          EpSaveOutputDirectory
          EpShowIncludedComponents
          EpUniqueEmptyMethodDictionary
        EpPackagingOptions
        EpPackagingProblem
          EpInvalidClassReference
          EpInvalidGlobalReference
          EpNoImplementor
            EpImplementorInUnusedClass
            EpSymbolReferenceToClassOrGlobal
        EpPackagingProblems
        EpPackagingRule
          EpExplicitRule
            EpChangeRule
              EpInitializeRule
                EpInitializeClassVariableRule
                EpInitializeGlobalRule
                EpInitializePoolVariableRule
              EpReplaceRule
                EpReplaceClassRule
                  EpReplacingClassRule
                EpReplaceClassVariableRule
                EpReplaceGlobalRule
                EpReplaceMethodRule
                  EpReplacingMethodRule
                EpReplacePoolVariableRule
            EpCollapseClassRule
```

Continued

```
      EpExcludeRule
        EpExcludeClassRule
        EpExcludeGlobalRule
        EpExcludeInstancesClassRule
        EpExcludeMethodRule
        EpExcludePoolVariableRule
        EpExcludeVariableRule
          EpExcludeClassInstanceVariableRule
          EpExcludeClassVariableRule
          EpExcludeInstanceVariableRule
        EpRemoveVariableRule
          EpRemoveClassInstanceVariableRule
          EpRemoveInstanceVariableRule
      EpIncludeRule
        EpIncludeClassRule
        EpIncludeGlobalRule
        EpIncludeMethodRule
        EpIncludePoolVariableRule
        EpIncludeVariableRule
          EpIncludeClassInstanceVariableRule
          EpIncludeClassVariableRule
          EpIncludeInstanceVariableRule
      EpMakeConstantRule
        EpMakePoolDictionaryConstantRule
        EpMakePoolVariableConstantRule
      EpReducePoolDictionaryRule
      EpUnmarkRule
        EpUnmarkClassInstanceVariableRule
        EpUnmarkClassRule
        EpUnmarkClassVariableRule
        EpUnmarkGlobalVariableRule
        EpUnmarkMethodRule
        EpUnmarkPoolVariableRule
        EpUnmarkVariableRule
    EpIgnoredPackagingRule
    EpImplicitRule
      EpImplicitExcludeRule
        EpAutomaticExcludeRule
        EpDefaultExcludeRule
        EpUnavailableRule
        EpUnusedRule
      EpImplicitIncludeRule
        EpAutomaticIncludeRule
        EpDefaultIncludeRule
        EpGivenRule
        EpImplicitlyReducePoolDictionaryRule
EpPackagingSpecification
  EaRuntimeSpecification
    AbtBaseEaRuntimeSpecification
      AbtEaRuntimeSpecification
  EpStandardRunTimeSpecification
    AbtBaseEpStandardRunTimeSpecification
```

Continued

```
                AbtEpStandardRunTimeSpecification
      EpPaddedTextItem
      EpPoolVariable
      EpProgress
      EpReference
        EpSelectorReference
          EpSelectorFilterReference
      EpRulePolicy
        EpApplyRulePolicy
          EpNonApplyUnassignedRulePolicy
        EpQueryRulePolicy
        EpSystemRulePolicy
      EpRuleSet
      EpStatistics
      EpVariable
      EsAsyncMessageQueue
      EsAtom
      EsByteCodeArray
      EsCallbackBallot
      EsCallbackInterface
      EsCallbackRecord
      EsCommentCache
      EsCompiler
      EsDebuggerLocal
      EsDebugInfo
      EsDeferredCallback
      EsError
        CfsError
        CompilerError
      EsImageStartUp
        EsNIsImageStartUp
          EsWindowSystemStartUp
            EaRuntimeStartUp
            EpRuntimeStartUp
            EtWindowSystemStartUp
              AbtBaseWindowSystemStartUp
                AbtWindowSystemStartUp
      EsLabel
      EsParseNode
        EsAPIType
          EsAssignmentExpression
        EsBlankLine
        EsBlock
          EsCascadedExpression
        EsComment
          EsCommentText
        EsLocalReference
          EsMessageExpression
        EsNot
        EsOptimizedBooleanReceiver
          EsIdentical
          EsIsNil
```

Continued

```
            EsNotIdentical
            EsNotNil
          EsOptimizedMessages
            EsOptimizedWith0ArgBlocks
              EsAnd
              EsIfFalse
              EsIfTrue
              EsIfTrueIfFalse
                EsIfFalseIfTrue
              EsOr
              EsTimesRepeat
            EsToByDo
              EsToDo
            EsWhileStatement
              EsWhileFalse
              EsWhileTrue
    EsMessagePattern
      EsBinaryPattern
      EsKeywordPattern
      EsUnaryPattern
    EsMethod
    EsPrimary
      EsBrackettedExpression
      EsLiteral
        EsArrayLiteral
          EsByteArrayLiteral
        EsCharacterLiteral
        EsIdentifier
        EsNumberLiteral
        EsStringLiteral
        EsSymbolLiteral
          EsAtomLiteral
      EsVariable
        EsGlobal
        EsInstance
        EsLocal
          EsArgument
        EsMagicVariable
          EsMagicFalse
          EsMagicNil
          EsMagicSelf
          EsMagicSuper
          EsMagicTrue
      EsPrimitiveExpression
        EsPrimitiveWithFunction
          EsAPIPrimitiveExpression
          EsUserPrimitiveExpression
      EsScannerToken
    EsSelector
      EsBinarySelector
      EsKeywordSelector
      EsUnarySelector
```

Continued

```
EsStatement
EsTemporaries
EsParser
EsQueue
EsScanner
  EsCommentScanner
EsScope
EsWeakList
EtFileNamePrompter
EtPrerequisiteCollectingPrompter
EtProgressReporter
EtStringComparer
EtTextHighlighter
EtWindow
  EsDebugger
    EtDebugger
      AbtScriptDebugger
  EtBrowser
    EpPackagedImagesBrowser
    EpPackagedPoolDictionaryBrowser
      EpPackagedGlobalsBrowser
    EpPackagingOptionsBrowser
    EpRulesBrowser
    EpSymbolArgumentsBrowser
    EtAbstractMethodsBrowser
      EtClassBrowser
        AbtScriptBrowser
        EtApplicationBrowser
          EtAbstractApplicationsBrowser
            EpAbstractPackagedApplicationsBrowser
              EpPackagedApplicationsBrowser
              EpPackagedClassesBrowser
          EtApplicationsBrowser
            EtApplicationManager
                AbtApplicationsOrganizer
                EtApplicationEditionsBrowser
                  EtApplicationConfigBrowser
          EtChangesBrowser
            EtApplicationsChangesBrowser
          EtClassesBrowser
        EtClassEditionBrowser
        EtShadowApplicationBrowser
      EtMethodsBrowser
        EtHighlightingMethodsBrowser
          EpPackagedMethodsBrowser
            EpKnownSymbolsBrowser
            EpPackagingProblemsBrowser
              EpResumablePackagingProblemsBrowser
        EtMethodEditionBrowser
      EtConfigurationMapsBrowser
      EtTextComparisonBrowser
    EtInspector
```

Continued

```
        EtDictionaryInspector
          AbtIndexedDictionaryInspector
        EtIndexedCollectionInspector
      EtWorkspace
        EpPackagerWorkspace
        EtTranscript
  EwDragAndDropAdapter
    EwSourceAdapter
      EwBlockSourceAdapter
      EwContainerListSourceAdapter
        EwIconAreaSourceAdapter
      EwTargetAdapter
      EwContainerListTargetAdapter
        EwIconAreaTargetAdapter
  EwDragAndDropManager
  EwDragAndDropSession
  EwEditPolicy
    EwComboBoxEditPolicy
    EwTextEditPolicy
    EwToggleButtonEditPolicy
  EwHierarchy
  EwHierarchyPolicy
    EwIconHierarchyPolicy
  EwImageDragger
    EwFarImagesDragger
    EwNearImagesDragger
    EwSingleImageDragger
  EwListInputMapper
    EwSelectionMapper
      EwBrowseSelectionMapper
      EwCellBlockSelectionMapper
      EwCellSingleSelectionMapper
      EwExtendedSelectionMapper
        EwExtendedRangeSelectionMapper
      EwMarqueeSelectionMapper
      EwMultipleSelectionMapper
      EwReadOnlySelectionMapper
      EwSingleSelectionMapper
      EwTableColumnMapper
  EwListVisibleNode
    EwContainerListNode
      EwIconListNode
        EwIconTreeNode
      EwTableListNode
        EwTableTreeNode
    EwIconAreaNode
  EwNotebookRow
  EwNotebookTab
    EwPMTab
    EwWINTab
  EwRegion
  EwRenderContext
```

Continued

```
EwSliderScale
EwSliderTickMark
  EwSliderDetent
EwSystemColors
EwSystemPortability
EwTableColumn
EwTabScroller
EwuFilePath
ExceptionalEvent
ExceptionalEventCollection
LCCollate
LCCType
LCMessages
LCMonetary
  LCNumeric
  LCTime
  Locale
  Magnitude
    AbtTimestamp
    Association
      EsPoolAssociation
    Character
    Date
    EmTimeStamp
    Number
      Decimal
      Float
      Fraction
      Integer
        LargeInteger
        SmallInteger
    Time
  MappingRule
    ChangeRule
      InitializeRule
      ReplaceRule
    CollapseRule
    ExcludeRule
      RemoveRule
      UnavailableRule
      UnusedRule
    GivenRule
    IncludeRule
  Message
    DirectedMessage
  MethodDictionary
  NIsMessageCatalog
  NIsMessageCatalogHeader
  NIsPlatformResourceConverter
    RCConverter
  ObjectSwapper
    ObjectDumper
```

Continued

```
      ObjectLoader
OSCall
OSClipboard
OSDialogBox
  OSFileDialog
    OSMessageBox
OSEvent
  AbtOSPageChanged
  OSExpose
  OSInput
  OSUpdate
OSEventManager
OSObject
  AbtHeapObject
    AbtThreadRequest
  AbtPointer
  AbtThreadState
  CfsOSStruct
    CfsOSFdate
    CfsOSFilefindbuf3
  CfsOSFilelock
  CfsOSFtime
  CfsOSHdir
  CfsOSHfile
CgFontCursor
CgPCXInfoHeader
CgPMBMPCoreHeader
CgTIFFInfoHeader
CgTIFFTag
CgWinBMPInfoHeader
  CgPMBMPInfoHeader
OSBaseType
  OSAddress
  OSImmediateType
  OSStringZ
OSObjectPointer
OSStorage
  OSStruct
    OSAccel
    OSAcceltable
    OSAcvp
    OSAdditionalmetrics
    OSArcparams
    OSAreabundle
    OSAvaildata
    OSBandrect
    OSBitmaparrayfileheader
    OSBitmaparrayfileheader2
    OSBitmapfileheader
    OSBitmapfileheader2
    OSBitmapinfoheader
      OSBitmapinfo
```

Continued

OSBitmapinfoheader2
  OSBitmapinfo2
OSBooktext
OSBtncdata
·OSByteArray
OSCdate
OSCharbundle
OSChrmsg
OSClassinfo
OSCmdmsg
OSCnrdraginfo
OSCnrdraginit
OSCnrdrawiteminfo
OSCnreditdata
OSCnrinfo
OSContextrecord
OSConvcontext
OSCountrycode
OSCountryinfo
OSCptext
OSCreatestruct
OSCtime
OSCursorinfo
OSDatetime
OSDdeinit
OSDdestruct
OSDeletenotify
OSDena1
OSDesktop
OSDevopenstruc
OSDIgtemplate
OSDIgtitem
OSDragimage
OSDraginfo
OSDragitem
OSDragtransfer
OSDrivdata
OSEaop
OSEaop2
OSEasizebuf
OSEntryfdata
OSErrinfo
OSEscmode
  OSExceptionregistrationrecord
  OSExceptionreportrecord
OSFacenamedesc
OSFattrs
  OSFattrsExt
OSFdate
OSFea
OSFea2
  OSDena2

Continued

```
OSFea2list
OSFealist
OSFfdescs2
OSFieldinfo
OSFieldinfoinsert
OSFiledlg
OSFilefindbuf
OSFilefindbuf2
OSFilefindbuf3
OSFilefindbuf4
OSFilelock
OSFilestatus
OSFilestatus2
OSFilestatus3
OSFilestatus4
OSFocafont
OSFocametrics
OSFontdefinitionheader
OSFontdlg
OSFontfilemetrics
OSFontmetrics
OSFontsignature
OSFpreg
OSFramecdata
OSFsallocate
OSFsinfo
OSFsqbuffer
OSFsqbuffer2
OSFtime
OSGea
OSGea2
OSGea2list
OSGealist
OSGradientl
OSHcinfo
OSHelpinit
OSHelptable
OSHprogarray
OSIconinfo
OSIconpos
OSImagebundle
OSKerningpairs
OSLinebundle
OSLorder
OSMarkerbundle
OSMatrixlf
OSMenuitem
OSMfp
OSMinirecordcore
OSMIectIdata
OSMIeformatrect
OSMIemargstruct
```

Continued

```
OSMIeoverflow
OSMIeSearchdata
OSMqinfo
OSMsemsg
OSNotifydelta
OSNotifyrecordemphasis
OSNotifyrecordenter
OSNotifyscroll
OSObjclass
OSObjectimage
OSOdpoint
OSOrder
OSOrderGbel
OSOrderGbpth
OSOrderGcalls
OSOrderGcbimg
OSOrderGeescp
OSOrderGescp
OSOrderGfpth
OSOrderGmpth
OSOrderGopth
OSOrderGpscbe
OSOrderGsbicol
OSOrderGscpth
OSOrderGsgch
OSOrderGsia
OSOrderIGbblt
OSOrderIGcarc
OSOrderIGcbox
OSOrderIGcchste
OSOrderIGcparc
OSOrderIGcsflt
OSOrderIGebb
OSOrderIGedb
OSOrderIGeff
OSOrderIGsap
OSOrderIGscc
OSOrderIGsmc
OSOrderIGsprp
OSOrderIGssb
OSOrderIGsslw
OSOrderIGstm
OSOrdersGbblt
OSOrdersGcarc
OSOrdersGcbox
OSOrdersGcchste
OSOrdersGcparc
OSOrdersGcsflt
OSOrdersGsap
OSOrdersGscc
OSOrdersGsmc
OSOrdersGsprp
```

Continued

OSOrdersGssb
OSOrdersGsslw
OSOrdersGstm
OSOwnerbackground
OSOwneritem
OSPageinfo
OSPageselectnotify
OSPanose
OSParam
OSPib
OSPipeinfo
OSPipesemstate
OSPointerinfo
OSPointl
OSPoints
OSPolygon
OSPolyset
OSPresparams
OSPrfprofile
OSPrintdest
OSProgdetails
OSProgtitle
OSProgtype
OSPrquinfo3
OSQmsg
OSQueryrecfromrect
OSQueryrecordrect
OSQversdata
OSQword
OSRecordcore
OSRecordinsert
OSRect1s
OSRectl
OSRenderfile
OSRequestdata
OSResultcodes
OSRgb
OSRgb2
OSRgnrect
OSSbcdata
OSSearchstring
OSSemrecord
OSSfactors
OSSizef
OSSizeI
OSSizes
OSSIdcdata
OSSmhstruct
OSSpoolattach
OSSqpopendata
OSStartdata
OSStatusdata

Continued

OSStylechange
OSSwblock
OSSwcntrl
OSSwentry
OSSwp
OSSwpushort
OSTib
OSTib2
OSTrackinfo
OSTreeitemdesc
OSUserbutton
OSViofontcellsize
OSViosizecount
OSVoid
OSVolumelabel
OSVorder
OSVscdata
OSVsdraginfo
OSVsdraginit
OSVstext
OSWndparams
OSType
OSLhandle
OSHab
OSHaccel
OSHapp
OSHatomtbl
OSHbitmap
OSHdc
OSHdir
OSHenum
OSHfile
OSHini
OSHmf
OSHmodule
OSHlib
OSHmq
OSHobject
OSHpal
OSHpipe
OSHpointer
OSHproc
OSHprogram
OSHps
OSHqueue
OSHrgn
OSHsavewp
OSHspl
OSHstd
OSHstr
OSHswitch
OSHtimer

Continued

```
          OSHvdd
          OSHwnd
          OSPid
          OSTid
        OSPointer
          AbtHeapPointer
OSWidget
  AbtOSValueSet
  OSButton
  OSComboBox
  OSMenu
  OSMenuItem
  OSScale
  OSScrollable
    OSComposite
      AbtOSContainer
      AbtOSContainerParent
      AbtOSNoteBook
      OSEmbeddedShell
      OSEmbeddedShellDecorations
      OSGroupBox
      OSShell
    OSListBox
    OSTextEdit
  OSScrollBar
  OSStatic
PlatformFunction
PlatformLibrary
Point
Pointer
Process
  UIProcess
ProcessorScheduler
Rectangle
ReturnParameter
  NullReturnParameter
Semaphore
Signal
SimpleTextOutput
StackInfo
Stream
  EsRandom
  PositionableStream
    ReadStream
    WriteStream
      CodeStream
      ReadWriteStream
SubApplication
  AbtBaseSwapperCrossloading
  AbtConverterBaseApp
  AbtConverterUISubApp
  AbtCwEmbeddedShellApp
```

Continued

```
AbtEditBuildersSubApp
AbtEditCodeGenerationSubApp
AbtEditCompositionViewsSubApp
AbtEditConnectionsSubApp
AbtEditConverterSettingsViews
AbtEditDebugSubApp
AbtEditInterfacesSubApp
AbtEditMenusSubApp
AbtEditPartsCatalogSubApp
AbtEditPartsSubApp
AbtEditPMProgramStarterSubApp
AbtEditPreAndPostCodeExprSubApp
AbtEditScriptEditorSubApp
AbtEditStartupSubApp
AbtEditStringSeparation
AbtEditViewsSubApp
AbtForeignRecordPMApp
AbtFormInputCheckerSubApp
AbtNLSAdditionsSubApp
AbtNLSSubApp
AbtOS2FileSpecApp
AbtPMEditBuildersSubApp
AbtPMEditCompositonViewsSubApp
AbtPMEditViewsSubApp
AbtPMHelpApp
AbtPMPrimitiveBaseSubApp
AbtPMPromptersAppWithUI
AbtPMRunPlatformInterfaceSubApp
AbtPMRunViewsSubApp
AbtPMRunWidgetsSubApp
AbtPromptersAppWithUI
AbtRunProgramStarterOs2PlatformSubApp
AbtThreadsAppESPM
AbtWaitPMSubApp
AbtWinPMCWAdditionsSubApp
AbtWinPMEditBuildersSubApp
AbtWinPMEditResourceSavingSubApp
AbtWinPMEditStartupSubApp
AbtWinPMEditViewsSubApp
AbtWinPMRunPlatformInterfaceSubApp
AbtWinPMRunViewsSubApp
AbtWinPMRunWidgetsSubApp
Application
  AbtBaseApp
  AbtBaseResourceSavingApp
  AbtBaseRuntimePackaging
  AbtBaseRuntimeReplacementMethods
  AbtBaseToolsAdditionsApp
  AbtBuildInterfacesApp
  AbtBuildPartsApp
  AbtBuildViewsApp
  AbtCFSAdditionsApp
```

Continued

AbtCLDTAdditions
AbtCodeGenerationBaseApp
AbtCommonProductInstallerApp
AbtConverterExamplesApp
AbtConverterExamplesSettingsViewApp
AbtCWAdditionsApp
AbtCwBaseAdditionsApp
AbtEditBaseApp
AbtEditBuildersApp
AbtEditNLSApp
AbtEditProgramStarterApp
AbtEditRecordStructureApp
AbtEditRepositoryApp
AbtEditRepositoryBaseApp
AbtEditResourceSavingApp
AbtExternalObjectsApp
AbtForeignRecordStructureApp
AbtHelpApp
AbtNLSCreationApp
AbtNIsFinalizationApp
AbtObjectGraphicsApp
AbtOperationsApp
AbtPartPackagerApp
AbtPersistencyBaseApp
AbtPrimitiveBaseApp
AbtProductInstallerApp
AbtPromptersApp
AbtRecordStructureApp
AbtRecordStructureBaseApp
AbtRunInterfacesApp
AbtRunPartsApp
AbtRunPlatformInterfaceApp
AbtRunProgramStarterApp
AbtRuntimePackaging
AbtRuntimeReplacementMethods
AbtRunViewsApp
AbtRunWidgetsApp
AbtTableWidgetApp
AbtThreadsApp
AbtTraceApp
AbtViewApplication
AbtWaitApp
CommonExtendedWidgets
CommonFileSystem
CommonGraphics
CommonPrinting
CommonWidgets
CwEmbeddedShellSupport
CwResourceSaving
DecimalMath
DsConfigurationApp
DynamicDataExchange

Continued

```
            EaDumper
            EaLoader
            EaRuntimePackaging
            EaRuntimeReplacementMethods
            EaRuntimeStatusWindow
            EaSupport
            EmClassDevelopment
            EmImageSupport
            EmLibraryInterface
            EmMethodDecoding
            EmMethodLinking
            EmShadowApplication
            EpPackager
            EpRuntimeSupport
            EpStandardSpecificationSupport
            EpTextPadding
            EsCodeGeneration
            EsDebuggerSupport
            EsParsing
            EsSourceDebuggerSupport
            EsWindowSystem
            EtBaseTools
            EtTools
            EwBase
            EwContainerDragAndDropSupport
            EwContainerSupport
            EwDragAndDropSupport
            EwDrawnListSupport
            EwListSupport
            EwNotebookSupport
            EwSliderSupport
            EwSpinButtonDragAndDropSupport
            EwSpinButtonSupport
            EwSupport
            Kernel
            LibraryObjects
            NIsExternalizationRuntime
            NIsExternalizationTools
            NIsImageSupport
            PlatformEvents
            PlatformFramework
            PlatformInterface
            PlatformWidgets
            Swapper
      CfsImplementationPM
      CfsImplementationPMWin
      CfsStreams
      CgFontSupport
      CgImageSupport
      CgImplementationSupport
      CgPMImageSupport
      CgPMImplementationSupport
```

Continued

CgWinAndPMImageSupport
CLDT
CLIM
CommonPrintingEmulatedPlatforms
CommonPrintingPM
Core
CPM
CwEmbeddedShellSupportPM
CwEmbeddedShellSupportPMWIN
CwEmulatedEmbeddedShellSupport
CwExtendedWidgetFramework
CwImplementationSupport
CwPrompters
DdeImplementationSupport
DdePMImplementationSupport
EaDumperES
EaLoaderES
EaRuntimeStatusWindowPMWin
EmApplicationSupport
EmClassDevelopmentES
EmImageSupportES
EmLibraryAccess
EmLibraryAccessES
EmLibraryInterfaceES
EmLibrarySchema
EmLibrarySchemaES
EmMethodDecodingES
EmMethodLinkingES
EmShadowSubApplication
EpApplicationProtocol
EpBaseInterface
EpBrowsers
EpConversion
EpImageComponentFE
EpImageDumping
EpPackagerES
EpPackagerFE
EpSpecificationSupport
EsBytecodeGeneration
EsTTYTools
EtConfigurationManagement
EtConfigurationManagementES
EtDevelopment
EtDevelopmentES
EtToolsES
EwPMSupport
LibraryObjectsES
NIsExternalizationToolsDLL
NIsExternalizationToolsPM
ObsoletePlatformFramework
PMPlatformAccessors
PMPlatformEvents

Continued

```
      PMPlatformExtensions
      PMPlatformFramework
      PMPlatformFunctions
      PMPlatformWidgets
      SwapperCrossloadingToES
      SwapperES
      WindowsAndPMPlatformEvents
      WindowsAndPMPlatformFramework
      WindowsAndPMPlatformWidgets
TranscriptTTY
UndefinedObject
VariableReference
  ClassVariable
    UnknownVariable
  GlobalVariable
  SharedVariable
```

SmalltalkAgents (QKS)

```
Object
  AEDescriptor
    AEDescriptorList
      AERecord
        AppleEvent
  AEObject
  APMLayer
    ComponentLayer
    ModuleLayer
    WindowLayer
      FloatingWindowLayer
      ModalWindowLayer
      StandardWindowLayer
  AppleEventHandler
    WorkbenchAppleEventHandler
  ArchivedObject
  Behavior
    MessageDictionary
      Instantiator
        Class
        MetaClass
  BehaviorCloner
  BlockClosure
  Callback
    ControlAction
    NMIListDefinition
    WindowDefinition
      APMWindowDefinition
      MenuWindowDefinition
      PaletteWindowDefinition
  Canvas
```

Continued

```
        GraphicPort
          DesktopPort
          OffscreenPort
          PrinterPort
          SystemGraphicPort
          WindowPort
            SystemWindowPort
    ClassReader
    ClipboardObject
    CodeMgr
    Collection
      Bag
      FontFamily
      KeyedCollection
        Set
          AssociationDictionary
            IdentityAssociationDictionary
              SymbolDictionary
                PVDictionary
                  ExternalMethodDictionary
                  Namespace
                    Pool
                    ScopedExecutionSpace
                  StructureDictionary
        Cache
        Dictionary
          EquivalenceDictionary
          IdentityDictionary
            MessageSuite
            SemanticMessageDictionary
        EquivalenceSet
        IdentitySet
      List
        Interval
          TimeSpan
        SortedList
        String
          StyledString
          Symbol
          Text
        Switch
        Token
      Menu
        MIList
        NMIList
          MethodListMenu
          ModuleMenuList
      Queue
        LinkedList
          TimerTaskList
      Stream
        ADSPStream
```

Continued

```
                    FileStream
                    PrintStream
                    RandomStream
                    TCPStream
                    TelnetStream
                    UDPStream
CompiledMethod
Compiler
Component
  APMComponent
    APMWindow
      MSWindow
  APMFramer
    APMWindowFramer
      MSWindowFramer
  GestaltObject
  HTree
  InformationModel
    PreferenceObject
      PreferenceObjectWithBlock
  MenuBarObject
  MI
  Module
    WorkbenchModule
  NMI
    NMIColor
  UIComponent
    Button
      ButtonWithState
        CheckBox
          CheckBox3D
          NewLookCheck
        RadioButton
          NewLookRadio
          PictureRadioButton
          RadioButton3D
        MenuButton
          LabeledMenuButton
        MUIButton
          Button3D
          MUIDefaultButton
          NewLookButton
            NewLookDefaultButton
          TDButton
        PictureButton
        ViewLinkOutput
          ViewLinkInput
      CellMatrix
        ScrollableList
      EditableTextField
        TEField
          CodeTEField
```

Continued

```
                    TDTEField
                Indicator
                  Slider
                    Scroller
                      MUIScroller
                MenuList
                MovieController
                StaticTextField
                TreeView
                UIComponentCollection
                  CBPane
                  CEToolbar
                  Pane
                    ECLTProject
                      ECLTMPWProject
                      ECLTThinkCProject
                    PreferencePane
                      PreferenceColorPane
                      PreferenceFontPane
                      PreferenceStringPane
                        PreferenceIntegerPane
                    ScrollablePane
                  PaneWindow
                    CBHierarchyView
                  UIComponentMatrix
                      RadioButtonMatrix
                  UIWindow
                    BrowserWindow
                      CodeEditor
                        CodeBrowser
                      DescriptionBrowser
                      ProjectBrowser
                      WindowEditor
                    ChooserWindow
                      ListChooser
                      LiteralChooser
                      MethodChooser
                      NBPChooser
                      SelectorChooser
                      VariableChooser
                    ClipboardWindow
                      ComponentPropertyWindow
                    ConsoleListener
                    ECLTWindow
                    EHelpWindow
          InfoWindow
          MessageWindow
          ModalWindow
            AboutBoxWindow
            AboutSmalltalkAgents
            ExceptionNotifier
            NewProjectWindow
```

Continued

```
            Notifier
                ChangeNotifier
                ProgressWindow
                QuitNotifier
            PrintingNotifier
            Prompter
            StartupDialog
            TEResponder
        ObjectInspector
        SetInspector
            DictionaryInspector
                AssociationDictionaryInspector
                    ExternalMethodDictionaryInspector
                    LibraryInspector
                StructureDictionaryInspector
                SymbolDictionaryInspector
            StructureInspector
            ThreadDebugger
        PaletteWindow
            CEBookmarkView
            CECategoryView
            CEHierarchyView
                PBTreeView
            ClassDetailView
            ColorPaletteWindow
            MethodDetailView
            SearchReplacePalette
            TearOffMenuWindow
            TextTool
            WEInfoPalette
            WEToolPalette
        PreferencesWindow
        StatusWindow
        TDB
        TextEditor
        XW
    WEComponent
DeletedClass
Device
  AudioInputDevice
  AudioOutputDevice
  ClockDevice
    ContextFreeClock
  CursorDevice
  DeviceControlBlock
    ADSPDevice
    AppleTalkDevice
    ASPDevice
    ATPDevice
    EthernetDevice
    FileControlBlock
        MovieFileControlBlock
```

Continued

```
            ResourceFileControlBlock
        IPDevice
    DeviceControlEntry
    DisplayDevice
        GraphicDevice
        TTY
    KeyboardDevice
    LogDevice
    Network
        ADSPCCB
        ADSPListener
        AppleTalkAddress
        AppleTalkGlobalInfo
        ICMPReport
        NBPEntity
        TCPGlobalInfo
    PrintJob
    SharedMemory
    Specifier
        DeviceSpecifier
        FDSpecifier
            DirectorySpecifier
        FileSpecifier
        VolumeSpecifier
DialogItem
Document
ECLTMethodTable
EntryPoint
ExceptionHandler
    DefaultExceptionHandler
ExternalCode
ExternalCodeModule
    ECLTLibrary
    VMCodeModule
ExternalMethodDescriptor
FontInfo
    FontMetricInfo
Framer
FSSpec
GeographicalRegion
GraphicCell
    GFrameCell
    GMethodCell
    GMethodCell2
    GVariableCell
    PreferenceListCell
    StructureInspectorCell
GraphicPrimitive
    Bitmap
        PixelMap
    Color
    ColorPalette
```

Continued

```
            ColorTable
            Cursor
              ColorCursor
              CursorList
                CursorCList
            Icon
              ColorIcon
              SmallIcon
            MenuColor
              MenuBarColor
            Pattern
              ColorPattern
            PenState
            Picture
            Point
            Polygon
            Rectangle
              Arc
              LineSegment
              Oval
              RoundRectangle
            Region
            ScrapStyle
            TextStyle
        HFSSpec
        HyperCardCallback
        IconSuite
        MacintoshStructures
          ATEntityName
          IconList
          PatternList
          PPCLocationNameRecord
          PPCPortInfoRecord
          PPCPortRecord
          PPCTargetID
          ProcessInfoRec
          ProcessNumber
        Magnitude
          Association
          PublicVariable
            ExternalMethod
            PublicVariableAlias
            StructureElement
          Coordinate
          Matrix
            FloatMatrix
          NaN
          Number
            Complex
            Integer
              Boolean
                False
```

Continued

```
              True
           LargeInteger
           SmallInteger
             Character
           UndefinedObject
        Rational
          Float
             Infinity
          Fraction
        Time
    ModuleEntryPoint
    Movie
    NativeCode
    ObjectFile
    ObjectModule
    PatternMatcher
      WildPatternMatcher
    Positioner
      WindowPositioner
    QueueElement
      LinkedListElement
         Message
            Event
               UIEvent
                  UICursorEvent
                     UIButtonPressEvent
                     UIButtonReleaseEvent
                     UIMotionEvent
                  UIDiskEvent
                  UIKeyEvent
                  UISwitcherEvent
            Exception
            RecordableMessage
               SemanticMessage
               Transaction
         Thread
            UIScheduler
    Resource
    Script
      Language
         Dialect
         LanguageRegion
    SemanticLayer
    Semaphore
    SharedFrame
    SmalltalkParser
    Sound
    SoundCommand
    Stack
    TranscriptObject
    Unit
      Currency
```

Continued

```
        Distance
        Volume
        Weight
    Util
    WETool
      ButtonTool
    CheckBoxTool
      PaneTool
      RadioButtonTool
      ScrollableListTool
      SelectionTool
      StaticTextFieldTool
      TEFieldTool
    WindowType
```

 ObjectStudio (VMARK)

```
Object
  Behavior
    ClassDescription
        Class
        MetaClass
  BlockContext
  Boolean
    False
    True
  ClassCodeReader
  Collection
    Bag
    ByteCodeDecoder
    IdentityBag
    IndexedCollection
      Array
        ActionSequence
        ActiveFormsArray
        EventParticipants
      ByteArray
      DateInterval
      Interval
      OrderedCollection
        SortedCollection
        TreeViewNode
      String
        FileNameString
        Message
        Symbol
      Vector
    LookupTable
    Set
      Dictionary
```

Continued

```
            IdentityDictionary
               AcceleratorTable
               GlobalDictionary
               JoinDictionary
               LoadableApplicationDictionary
            IdentitySet
            SymbolDictionary
CompiledBlock
CompiledMethod
   QuickMethod
ControllerInfo
   ICComponentInfo
ControllerItem
   ButtonCtrl
   CheckBoxCtrl
   LineCtrl
   ListCtrl
      ComboCtrl
      DropDownListCtrl
      MSListCtrl
         MSMutexListCtrl
         MSSubMenuCtrl
      RadioButtonCtrl
      SliderCtrl
      SubMenuCtrl
         HelpMenuCtrl
         WindowsMenuCtrl
      SyncListCtrl
      TabListCtrl
         LinkedTabListCtrl
         MSTabListCtrl
            LinkedMSTabListCtrl
         TreeViewCtrl
         WorkplaceTabularListCtrl
            NewItemTabularListCtrl
            WorkplaceJoinListCtrl
            WorkplaceLinkedTabularListCtrl
      ValueSetCtrl
   NoEntryFieldCtrl
      MIEntryFieldCtrl
         TextEditorCtrl
            ReferenceHyperTextCtrl
         SmalltalkEditorCtrl
            ClassFileEditorCtrl
               ClassFileEditorNoMenuCtrl
      TextCollectorCtrl
   NoteBookCtrl
      LinkedNoteBookCtrl
   ObjectHandlerCtrl
      ListHandlerCtrl
      WorkplaceTemplateCtrl
         WorkplaceEditTemplateCtrl
```

Continued

```
        PictureCtrl
          DrawPadCtrl
             BitmapCtrl
          ToolbarCtrl
          TwoDGraphCtrl
             BarChartCtrl
        RectCtrl
          TableCtrl
        StatusLineCtrl
          QuickHelpStatusLineCtrl
        StringCtrl
          DateCtrl
          MaskFieldCtrl
          MLStringCtrl
          NumberCtrl
          SpinButtonCtrl
             NumericSpinButtonCtrl
          TopicBoxCtrl
      ControllerProxy
      Cursor
        LocalCursor
      CutJoin
      Database
        LocalDatabase
           InternalDatabase
      DDEClientSession
      DDEServerSession
      DesignerAlignmentManager
      DesktopWPObjects
        DesktopWPDataObjects
          DesktopWPBatchQuery
          DesktopWPClass
          DesktopWPInterface
             DesktopWPInterfaceComponent
          DesktopWPModel
          DesktopWPProgGen
          DesktopWPQuery
          DesktopWPReport
        DesktopWPFolders
          DesktopWPInterfaces
             DesktopWPNewInterface
          DesktopWPModels
             DesktopWPNewModel
          DesktopWPQueries
          DesktopWPReports
             DesktopWPNewReport
        DesktopWPOperators
          DesktopWPDelete
          DesktopWPDisplay
          DesktopWPEdit
          DesktopWPPrinter
        DesktopWPSystem
```

Continued

```
Differential
DiffOp
Directory
DrawPort
  Bitmap
    TransparentBitmap
  MetaFile
  PrintPort
EditorFile
EditorFileList
EditorWindowList
EventParticipation
  EPControllerItem
  EPForm
  EPInterfacePart
  EPTable
File
Font
Form
  DialogBox
    MessageBox
      ModalMessageBox
    ModalDialogBox
  Page
  SubForm
    ContainerForm
      AdjustableForm
      WorkAreaContainer
  SystemTranscriptForm
  WorkplaceWindow
    WorkplaceHandlerWindow
      WorkplaceListHandlerWindow
    WPENFINWorkplaceWindow
FormItem
  FormButton
  FormCheckBox
  FormLine
  FormList
    FormCombo
    FormDropList
      FormDropCombo
    FormMSList
      FormCheckList
      FormMutexCheckList
    FormRadioButton
    FormSubMenu
      FormHelpMenu
      FormMSSubMenu
      FormWindowsMenu
    FormSyncList
    FormTabList
      FormFormattedList
```

Continued

```
                    FormLinkedTablist
                    FormMSTabList
                      FormLinkedMSTabList
                    FormTreeView
                    FormWorkplaceTabularList
                      FormNewItemTabularList
                      FormWorkplaceJoinList
                      FormWorkplaceLinkedTabularList
        FormNoEntryField
          FormMIEntryField
            FormTextEditor
             . FormClassFileEditor
                  FormClassFileEditorNoMenu
                FormReferenceHyperText
              FormSmalltalkEditor
            FormTextCollector
        FormNoteBook
          FormLinkedNoteBook
        FormObjectHandler
          FormListHandler
          FormWorkplaceTemplate
            FormWorkplaceEditTemplate
        FormPicture
          Form2DGraph
            FormBarChart
            FormGraphicsLegend
            FormLineGraph
            FormPieChart
            FormScatterGraph
          FormDrawPad
            FormBitmap
            FormToolbar
        FormRect
          FormTable
        FormSlider
        FormStatic
        FormStatusLine
          FormQuickHelpStatusLine
        FormString
          FormDate
          FormMaskField
          FormMLString
          FormNumber
          FormPassword
          FormSpinButton
            FormNumericSpinButton
        FormTopicBox
        FormValueSet
GraphicsStream
  FormattedGraphicsStream
Help
Icon
```

Continued

```
InterfacePart
  Controller
    DataManagerController
    DesktopTutorialView
    ENFINController
      ApplicationDefinitionController
      CIGController
      ClassBrowserController
      ConfigurationNotebookController
      CreateDatabaseController
      CreateReportController
      DatabasesController
      DatabaseSelectionController
      DebugInterfaceController
      DesignerOptionsController
        ControllerOptionsDialogController
        EventEditorController
        ExternalDatabaseController
        FItemOptionsController
          ChangeItemClassController
          EntryFieldOptionsController
          FMultiItemOptionsController
          FormButtonOptionsController
          FormGraphicsLegendOptionsController
          FormGraphicsOptionsController
          FormHandlerOptionsController
            FormListHandlerOptionsController
            FormObjectHandlerOptionsController
          FormItemStandardOptionsController
          FormLineOptionsController
          FormListOptionsController
          FormRectOptionsController
          FormSliderOptionsController
          FormSpinButtonOptionsController
          FormStatusLineOptionsController
          FormTabularListOptionsController
          FormToolbarOptionsController
          FormTreeViewOptionsController
          FormValueSetOptionsController
          NoteBookOptionsController
        FormItemLinksController
        FormItemOptionsController
        FormOptionsToolDialogController
        GridAndSnapToolController
        ICOptionsDialogController
          InterfaceComponentOptionsController
        MenuToolDialogController
          MethodAndEventHookupsDialogController
          MethodEditorController
          NewItemToolController
          SyncGroupsController
        DisplayMethodController
```

Continued

```
        DropDatabaseController
        DropTableController
    EditView
    FileDialogController
      OpenDialogController
        LoadClassDialogController
        MSOpenDialogController
          TextEditorOpenController
      SaveAsDialogController
        SaveAsNameDialogController
        SQLSaveAsDialogController
    FolderEditController
    FormatController
      DateFormatController
      NumericFormatController
      StatusLineFormatController
      StringFormatController
    FormatGraphView
    FormBackgroundOptionsController
    GlobalBrowserController
    InspectorController
      DictionaryInspectorController
      DisplayStackController
      SetInspectorController
    LoadableApplicationBrowserController
    LoadingAppController
    ModelEditorController
      ModelEditorGraphController
    MultiLineOptionsView
    NameSessionController
    PageSetupView
    ProgramGeneratorController
    ReportEditorController
    ReportOptionsView
      ReportBitmapController
      ReportBoxOptionsView
      ReportGraphOptionsView
      ReportItemOptionsView
      ReportLegendView
      ReportLineOptionsView
    ReportOutputController
    ReportPreviewController
    ReportTimeView
    ResultDisplayController
    SQLBrowserController
    SQLDynamicController
      SQLAliasController
      SQLCalculatedColumnController
      SQLCopyListController
        SQLGroupController
        SQLOrderController
-     SQLEditor
```

Continued

```
            SQLJoinController
            SQLParametersController
            SQLSearchConditionController
            SQLSelectionController
            SQLValueController
         SQLWindowController
         TableDefinitionController
         TableListController
         TableNameController
         TextEditorMDIController
         WindowListController
         WorkspaceController
         WPENFINController
      ENFINVCSAgent
      FixedItemsController
      HierarchyBrowserController
      MDIController
         FormEditorController
      TableEditDataController
      TextEditorController
         TextEditorBookmarksController
         TextEditorBufferListController
         TextEditorFindController
            SearchPatternController
            TextEditorReplaceController
         TextEditorGotoController
         TextEditorMacroController
         TextEditorOptionsController
         TextEditorTemplateController
      TutorialDisplayView
      TutorialEditorView
      WorkplaceListHandlerController
         DesktopWPInterfacesHandlerController
            DesktopWPFolder
            DesktopWPModelsHandlerController
         TutorialListHandlerView
   InterfaceComponent
      ICBitmapSelector
      ICBrowserExplanationEditorController
      ICEditorStatusLine
      ICFloatingToolbar
JoinField
JoinInformation
LayoutDescription
Magnitude
   Association
   Character
   Date
   Number
      Decimal
      Float
      Fraction
```

Continued

```
                        Integer
                            LongInteger
                            SmallInteger
                    Time
                    TimeStamp
                MethodContext
                Model
                    ENFINModel
                Module
                    ENFINModule
                ObjectLink
                    ClassLink
                        RunTimeClassLink
                    LinkCtrl
                    ModelLink
                    SQLLink
                    TableLink
                OutputDevice
                Picture
                    DisplayBitmap
                    Graph2D
                        BarChart
                        GraphicsLegend
                        LineGraph
                        PieChart
                        ScatterGraph
                PMHandle
                Point
                Primitive
                Query
                    SqlBatch
                    SqlDirect
                    SqlParse
                        SqlDelete
                        SqlInsert
                    SqlSelect
                        SqlSubSelect
                    SqlUpdate
                Rectangle
                Report
                ReportEditorItem
                ReportItem
                    ReportBitmap
                    ReportBox
                    ReportGraph
                        ReportBarChart
                        ReportLegend
                        ReportLineGraph
                        ReportPieChart
                        ReportScatterGraph
                    ReportLine
```

Continued

```
      ReportString
        ReportMLString
        ReportNumber
        ReportStatic
    ReportPart
      LevelBreak
    SelectItem
    SelectList
    Setup
    SmalltalkMessage
      Action
        LinkedAction
    SqlArray
    SqlExpression
      SqlCurrent
        SqlCurrentOf
      SqlLengthFunction
      SqlScalar
        SqlScalarFunction
        SqlScalarOuter
    SqlOrder
    SqlPredicate
      SqlBetweenPredicate
      SqlComparePredicate
      SqlCondition
      SqlExistPredicate
      SqlInPredicate
      SqlLikePredicate
      SqlNullPredicate
    SqlSelectedField
    SqlSet
    StateNode
    Stream
      ClassSourceStream
      EditorSourceStream
      FileStream
      PrintStream
    Structure
    Table
      VectorTable
    Text
      DateText
      NumericText
    TextColor
    TextEditorMacro
      TextEditorReplaceMacro
    TextStyle
    Timer
    Token
      STToken
    TokenList
```

Continued

```
        STTokenList
ToolbarItem
   ToolbarBitmap
   ToolbarButton
   ToolbarLabel
   ToolbarSpace
TrackingAnimator
TutorialDelete
TutorialModel
UndefinedObject
WorkplaceObject
WPTableRow
```

D

ANSI Smalltalk Standard

The ANSI Smalltalk standard development committee, X3J20, is nearing completion of the first published working paper of the standard, available in the summer of 1996. This draft covers most of the functionality that is not platform-dependent and does not handle the GUI. Although this draft addresses only a small portion of the Smalltalk environment, it is probably more thorough a standard than for other languages, in that it covers a portion of the class library and not just the coding syntax, which is nearly identical in all versions of Smalltalk.

A summary of the various classes and methods defined by this ANSI draft is presented here for your reference. Sticking to these classes and methods should provide your code with ANSI portability from one version of Smalltalk to another.

Standard Globals: Classes and Objects

Classes

Global Name	Protocols	Grouping
Array	<array class>	Collections
	<sequenceableCollection class>	

Bag	<bag class>	Collections
	<collection class>	
Collection	<collection class>	Collections
	<instantiable class>	
Date	<date class>	Date and Time
Float	<float class>	Numerics
	<variableByteClass>	
Fraction	<Fraction class>	Numerics
Interval	<interval class>	Collections
OrderedCollection	<orderedCollection class>	Collections
	<sequenceableCollection class>	
ReadStream	<readStreamFactory>	Streams
ReadWriteStream	<readWriteStreamFactory>	Streams
Set	<set class>	Collections
	<variable class>	
	<collection class>	
	<instantiable class>	
Sorted Collection	<sortedCollection class>	Collections
	<variableClass>	
	<collection class>	
	<instantiable class>	
Time	<time class>	Date and Time
	<magnitude>	
TimeStamp	<timestamp class>	Date and Time
	<number>	
	<date>	
	<time>	
WriteStream	<WriteStreamFactory>	Streams

Smalltalk Objects for System-Oriented Services

Selector	*Function*
systemMessageLog: aStream	Assign aStream for logging system-generated messages.
errorMessageLog: aStream	Assign aStream for logging error messages; other messages, for example, warnings and informational mes-

sages, will be logged to the stream specified in #systemMessageLog:

garbageCollect	Perform garbage collection and free up unused memory.
garbageCollectFor: aTimeInterval	Perform garbage collection for the duration aTimeInterval.
availableMemory	Return the amount of free memory in the system.
timeToRun: aBlock	Time taken to evaluate aBlock.
invocationParms	Return external parameters in a collection of strings, for instance, all parameters on the command line when the Smalltalk program is invoked.
startup	Allows user to specify actions to be taken after the system starts up.
shutdown	Allows user to specify actions to be taken before the system shuts down.
exit	Exit program (termination).
exitTo: aString	Exit to execute the code defined in program file represented in aString.
exitWithReturn: aString	Exit to execute the code defined in program file represented in aString, and then return.
checkpoint	Save execution state.
checkpoint: aSymbol	Save execution state using aSymbol as the checkpoint identifier.
restart	Restart from the default checkpoint.
restartFromCheckpoint: aSymbol	Restart from checkpoint identified by aSymbol.
traceOn: aStream	Generate a trace of the message flow to aStream. Note: Other parameters can be defined to control what to trace besides the message flow; for example, specific instance variables.
traceOff	Turn trace off.

Fundamental Protocols

Object

Instance Methods:

= comparand

= = comparand

~= comparand

~~ comparand

class

copy

hash

identityHash

iskindOf: candidateClass

isMemberOf: candidateClass

isNil

notNil

perform: selector

perform: selector with: argument1

perform: selector with: argument1 with: argument2

perform: selector with: argument1 with: argument2 with: argument3

perform: selector withArguments: arguments

printOn: target

printString

respondsTo: selector

yourself

Class Methods

new

Instantiator

Instance Methods

new

Boolean

Instance Methods

& operand

| operand

and: operand
eqv: operand
ifFalse: operand
ifFalse: falseOperand ifTrue: trueOperand
ifTrue: operand
ifTrue: trueOperand ifFalse: falseOperand
not
or: operand
xor: operand

nil

Instance Methods

= comparand
== comparand
~= comparand
~~ comparand
class
copy
iskindOf: candidateClass
isMemberOf: candidateClass
isNil
notNil
printOn: target
printString

Collections

Collection

Instance Methods

asArray
asBag
asByteArray
asOrderedCollection
asSet
asSortedCollection

asSortedCollection: discriminator

collect: transformer

conform: transformer

detect: discriminator

detect: discriminator ifNone: exceptionHandler

do: operation

includes: target

inject: initialValue into: operation

isEmpty

notEmpty

occurrencesOf: target

reject: discriminator

select: discriminator

size

Class Methods

new: count

with: firstElement

with: firstElement with: secondElement

with: firstElement with: secondElement with: thirdElement

with: firstElement with: secondElement with: thirdElement with:
  fourthElement

abstractDictionary

Class Methods

new: count

array

Class Methods

new: count

bag

Instance Methods

add: newElement

add: newElement withOccurrences: count

addAll: newElements
collect: transformer

Class Methods
new: count

contractibleCollection

Instance Methods
remove: oldElement
remove: oldElement ifAbsent: exceptionHandler
removeAll: oldElements

dBString

Instance Methods
asDBString

dequeue

Instance Methods
add: newElement
addAllFirst: newElements
addAllLast: newElements
addFirst: newElement
addLast: newElement

dictionary

extensibleCollection

Instance Methods
add: newElement
addAll: newElements

hashAccessibleCollection

Instance Methods
rehash

identityDictionary

Instance Methods
at: key

interval

Instance Methods
, operand
collect: transformer
copyFrom: start to: stop
copyReplaceAll: targetElements with: replacementElements
copyReplaceFrom: start to: stop with: replacementElements
copyReplaceFrom: start to: stop withObject: replacementElement
copyReplacing: targetElement withObject: replacementElement
copyWith: newElement
copyWithout: oldElement
increment
reject: discriminator
reverse
select: dscriminator
size

Class Methods
from: start to: stop
from: start to: stop by: step

orderedCollection

Class Methods
new: count

readableString

, operand
< operand
<= operand
> operand

>= operand

asClassPoolKey

asGlobalKey

asLowercase

asNumber

asPoolKey

asString

asUppercase

byteAt: index

copyReplaceAll: targetElements with: replacementElements

copyReplaceFrom: start to: stop with: replacementElements

copyReplaceFrom: start to: stop withObject: replacementElement

copyReplacing: targetElement withObject: replacementElement

copyWith: newElement

indexOf: pattern matchCase: flag startingAt: start

match: target

nullTerminated

sameAs: operand

subStrings

subStrings: parameter

sequenceableCollection

sequenceContractibleCollection

Instance Methods

removeAtIndex: index

removeFirst

removeLast

sequenceExtensibleCollection

Instance Methods

add: newElement after: target

add: newElement afterIndex: index

add: newElement before: target

add: newElement beforeIndex: index

addAll: newElements after: target
addAll: newElements afterIndex: index
addAll: newElements before: target
addAll: newElements beforeIndex: index

sequenceReadableCollection

Instance Methods

, operand
= operand
after: target
at: index
basicAt: index
before: target
copyFrom: start to: stop
copyReplaceAll: targetElements with: replacementElements
copyReplaceFrom: start to: stop with: replacementElements
copyReplaceFrom: start to: stop withObject: replacementElement
copyReplacing: targetElement withObject: replacementElement
copyWith: newElement
copyWithout: oldElement
do: operation
doWithIndex: operation
findFirst: discriminator
findLast: discriminator
first
from: start to: stop do: operation
from: start to: stop doWithIndex: operation
indexOf: target
indexOf: targetifAbsent: exceptionHandler
indexOfSubCollection: target startingAt: start
indexOfSubCollection: target startingAt: start ifAbsent:
    exceptionHandler
last
reverse
reverseDo:
with: otherCollection do: operation

sequenceWriteableCollection

Instance Methods

at: index put: newElement

atAll: indices put: newElement

atAllPut: newElement

basicAt: indexput: newElement

replaceFrom: start to: stop with: replacementElements

replaceFrom: start to: stop with: replacementElements startingAt:
    replacementStart

replaceFrom: start to: stop withObject: replacementElement

set

Instance Methods

add: newElement

addAll: newElements

collect: transformer

Class Methods

new: count

sortedCollection

Instance Methods

, operand

add: newElement

asSortedCollection

collect: transformer

reverse

sortBlock

sortBlock: discriminator

Class Methods

new

new: count

sortBlock: discriminator

with: firstElement

with: firstElement with: secondElement

with: firstElement with: secondElement: with: thirdElement

with: firstElement with: secondElement: with: thirdElement with: fourthElement

string

Instance Methods

asSBString

asSymbol

at: index put: newElement

atAll: indices put: newElement

atAllPut: newElement

byteAt: index put: newElement

copyReplaceAll: targetElements with: replacementElements

copyReplaceFrom: start to: stop with: replacementElements

copyReplaceFrom: start to: stop withObject: Message: replacementElement

copyReplacing: targetElement withObject: replacementElement

copyWith: newElement

replaceFrom: start to: stop with: replacementElements

replaceFrom: start to: stop with: replacementElements startingAt: replacementStart

replaceFrom: start to: stop withObject: replacementElement

symbol

Instance Methods

, operand

argumentCount

asString

asSymbol

collect: transformer

copy

copyFrom: start to: stop

copyReplaceAll: targetElements with: replacementElements

copyReplaceFrom: start to: stop with: replacementElements

copyReplaceFrom: start to: stop withObject: Message: replacementElement

copyReplacing: targetElement withObject: replacementElement

copyWith: newElement

copyWithout: oldElement

reject: discriminator

reverse

select: discriminator

universalString

Instance Methods

addLineDelimiters

asByteArray

asDBString

asSBString

asString

at: index put: newElement

atAll: indices put: newElement

atAllPut: newElement

bindWith: parameter1

bindWith: parameter1 with: parameter2

bindWith: parameter1 with: parameter2 with: parameter3

bindWith: parameter1 with: parameter2 with: parameter3 with:
parameter4

bindWithArguments: arguments

byteAt: index put: newElement

replaceFrom: start to: stop with: replacementElements

replaceFrom: start to: stop with: replacementElements startingAt:
replacementStart

replaceFrom: start to: stop withObject: replacementElement

trimBlanks

trimSeparators

Exceptions

error

Instance Methods

defaultAction

isResumable

exception

Class Methods
handles: exception
new
signal

exceptionBuilder

Instance Methods
key: keyValue
messageText: signalerText

exceptionDescription

Instance Methods
defaultAction
description
isResumable
key
messageText

exceptionInstantiator

Instance Methods
new
signal

exceptionSelector

Instance Methods
, anotherException
handles: exception

ExceptionSet

Instance Methods
, anotherException
handles: exception

exceptionSignaler

Instance Methods
signal
signal: signalerText

valuable

extensions to **valuable** to support exceptions

Instance Methods
ensure: terminationBlock
ifCurtailed: terminationBlock
on: selector do: action

signaledException

Instance Methods
exit: exitValue
isNested
outer
pass
resignalAs: replacementException
resume
resume: resumptionValue
retry
retryUsing: alternativeBlock
return
return: returnValue

Notification

Instance Methods
defaultAction
isResumable

Warning

Instance Methods
defaultAction

Numerics

number

Instance Methods

* operand

\+ operand

– operand

/ operand

// operand

< operand

= operand

> operand

@ operand

\ operand

~= operand

abs

arcCos

arcSin

arctan

asFloat

asFraction

asInteger

ceiling

copy

cos

degreesToRadians

exp

floor

floorLog: operand

lessGeneralThan: operand

ln

log: operand

moreGeneralThan: operand

negated

negative

positive
printOn: output
printString
quo: operand
radiansToDegree
raisedTo: operand
raisedToInteger: operand
reciprocal
rem: operand
rounded
roundTo: factor
sign
sin
sqrt
squared
strictlyPositive
tan
to: stop
to: stop by: step
to: stop by: step do: operation
to: stop do: operation
truncated
truncateTo: factor

magnitude

Instance Methods
< operand
<= operand
> operand
>= operand
between: min and: max
max: operand
min: operand

float

Instance Methods
= operand
fractionPart
integerPart
lessGeneralThan: operand
moreGeneralThan: operand

Class Methods
pi

fraction

Instance Methods
= operand
denominator
lessGeneralThan: operand
moreGeneralThan: operand
numerator

integer

Instance Methods
= operand
allMask: mask
anyMask: mask
asCharacter
bitAnd: operand
bitAt: index
bitInvert
bitOr: operand
bitShift: shift
bitXor: operand
clearBit: index
even
factorial
gcd: operand
highBit

isBitSet: index
lcm: operand
lessGeneralThan: operand
moreGeneralThan: operand
noMask: mask
odd
printOn: output base: base
printOn: output base: base showRadix: flag
printStringRadix: base
printStringRadix: base padTo: count
printStringRadix: base showRadix: flag
setBit: index
timesRepeat: operation

File I/O

fileStream

Instance Methods
dataType
position
close

Class Methods
named: nameString dataType: dataType accessMode: accessMode
named: nameString dataType: dataType
named: nameString accessMode: accessMode
named: nameString

readFileStream

Instance Methods
position: index

writeableFileStream

Instance Methods
flush

Streams

gettableStream

Instance Methods
atEnd
do: argument
next
next: amount
nextMatchFor: anObject
skip: amount
skipThrough: anObject
upTo: anObject

puttableStream

Instance Methods
cr
nextPut: anObject
nextPutAll: aCollection
space
tab

ReadStream

Instance Methods
peek
peekFor: anObject

Class Methods
on: aCollection

ReadWriteStream

Class Methods
on: aCollection

sequencedStream

Instance Methods
contents
isEmpty
position
position: amount
reset
setToEnd

WriteStream

Class Methods
on: aCollection

Valuables

abstract-valuables

Instance Methods
argumentCount
valueWithArguments: @argumentArray
valueWithArguments: @argumentArray ensure: ensuredValuable
value: @argument ifTruncated: @cleanupValuable

niladic-valuable

Instance Methods
argumentCount
ensure: @ensuredValuable
ifTruncated: @cleanupValuable
value

iterating-valuable

Instance Methods
whileFalse
whileFalse: @iterationBlock

whileTrue
whileTrue: @iterationBlock

monadic-valuable

Instance Methods
argumentCount
value: @argument
value: @argument ensure: @ensuredValuable
value: @argument ifTruncated: @cleanupValuable

dyadic-valuable

Instance Methods
argumentCount
value: @argument1 value: @argument2
value: @argument1 value: @argument2 ensure: @ensuredValuable
value: @argument1 value: @argument2 ifTruncated: @cleanupValuable

E

On the CD-ROM

The CD-ROM contains many freeware, shareware, and demonstration items, including four versions of Smalltalk, one of which is a demonstration-only copy, the contents of several Internet public domain and shareware archives, code samples from the book, and product demonstration and information from vendors.

Versions of Smalltalk

Public Domain

Little Smalltalk—for Unix, Mac
GNU Smalltalk—for Unix, DOS, Windows NT

Demonstration/Pre-Release

Smalltalk MT for Windows NT
Smalltalk X—for Unix

Archives

Manchester Archives (under University of Illinois)

University of Illinois Archives

Code Samples from the Book

AutoDocumentor

HTTP Server

HTTP Client

Personal Information Manager Framework

Development Tools

Sample Primitives and External Methods

Sample Database Code

Neural Network program

What Is Freeware/Shareware?

Freeware is software that is distributed by disk free of charge, through bulletin board systems and the Internet. It can be distributed freely as long as its use follows the license agreement included with it.

Shareware (also known as user-supported software) is a revolutionary means of distributing software created by individuals or companies too small to make inroads into the more conventional retail distribution networks. The authors of shareware retain all rights to their software under the copyright laws, while enabling free distribution. This gives users the chance to freely obtain and try out software to see if it fits their needs. Shareware should not be confused with Public Domain software, even though they are often obtained from the same sources. If you continue to use shareware after trying it out, you are expected to register with the author and pay a registration fee. What you get in return depends on the author, but may include a printed manual, free updates, telephone support, and more.

Hardware Requirements

The software listed here should run on any Microsoft Windows-equipped PC version 3.1 or later. Macintosh and Unix users can access the source code by browsing the CD-ROM.

User Assistance and Information

The software accompanying this book is being provided as-is, without warranty or support of any kind. Should you require basic installation assistance, or if your media is defective, call our product support number at 212-850-6194 weekdays between 9 A.M. and 4 P.M. ESTime. Or we can be reached via e-mail at: **wprtusw@wiley.com.** To place additional orders or to request information about other Wiley products, call 800-879-4539.

I N D E X

D

WILEY
Publishers Since 1807